A History of Socialist Thought

A History of Socialist Thought

From the Precursors to the Present

Subrata Mukherjee
Sushila Ramaswamy

Sage Publications
New Delhi ❖ Thousand Oaks ❖ London

Copy ~~right © Subrata Mukherjee and Sushila Ramaswamy~~ *2000*

First published in 2000 by

Sage Publications India Pvt. Ltd.
M-32 Market, Greater Kailash, Part 1
New Delhi 110 048

Sage Publications Inc
2455 Teller Road
Thousand Oaks, California 91320

Sage Publications Ltd.
6 Bonhill Street
London EC2A 4PU

Published by Tejeshwar Singh for Sage Publications India Pvt. Ltd., typeset by Deo Gratis Systems, Chennai in 10/12 Palatino and printed at Chaman Enterprises, Delhi.

Library of Congress Cataloging-in-Publication Data
Mukherjee, Subrata, 1944–
    A history of socialist thought : from the precursors to the present/ by Subrata Mukherjee, Sushila Ramaswamy.
        p.   cm.   (cloth)   (pbk.)
    Includes bibliographical references and index.
    1. Socialism—History. 2. Socialism—Philosophy. I. Ramaswamy, Sushila. II. Title.
HX36 .M834 355—dc21   2000   00-033272

ISBN: 0-7619-9437-8 (US-Hb)   81-7036-929-0 (India-Hb)
         0-7619-9465-3 (US-Pb)   81-7036-938-X (India-Pb)

Sage Production Team: Jagdish Dewan, Parul Nayyar, Mathew P.J. and Santosh Rawat

For Eduard Bernstein

❖ Contents

❖ *Preface and Acknowledgments*

The concept of socialism is as old as civilization itself. As with other modern ideologies, it is difficult to define socialism since there are many variations within it, but common to all strands of socialism is a commitment to equality, fraternity, absence of exploitative relationships and socialized humanity. Plato and Aristotle were the earliest to direct our attention to the consequences of inequality in society, and they emphasized on the equitable distribution of wealth, rewards and honours to ensure stability and justice. More's *Utopia* though republican in orientation was hailed as the earliest of the socialist tracts for it offered an indictment of the emerging commercial society. Since the nineteenth century, socialism emerged as a coherent doctrine providing both a critique and an alternative to liberal democratic capitalism.

This book provides a detailed and a critical account of the dominant schools and theorists of socialism. It analyzes the varied controversies within socialism, namely, the tensions between egalitarianism and efficiency, role of the market and importance of planning, and reform versus revolution. In the light of feminist interpretations, the views of the socialists in espousing and furthering the cause of women has been critically dissected. It also explains the multiple reasons for the collapse of communism, the disarray of democratic socialism and the future of socialism.

Socialism essentially arose as a moral and humanitarian critique of early liberalism. In its critique it focussed on the wastefulness, injustice, exploitation and inequality within capitalism. It promised a humane, democratic, free and an equal society. However, in trying to provide an alternative, except for social democracy, all the other variants and, in particular, Marxism-Leninism fell short of its libertarian ideals. Marxism, by shying away from theorizing about rights, freedom, political power and the role of authority in socialist society, did not offer any scope for a constitutional government and political democracy; nor did it ensure efficiency and commodious living for its citizens. Instead, it led to a repressive and totalitarian state, and the subjugation of civil society logically followed only such a denial. The Leninist experiment had its critics. All of them pointed to the lack of democracy and freedom within the former Soviet Union. Leninism was not an aberration from Marx's original vision, for it could not have been conceived without Marx. The latter's major intellectual deficiency was disregarding the different possibilities that could emerge from his theory. For the collapse of communism the originators themselves are responsible because they remained ambivalent about what they understood as the best order.

Lichtheim once wrote that the choice is between socialism and democracy. The collapse of communism proves that it is important to combine the two. If socialism has to remain relevant, it must retain its moral and libertarian ideals which would involve a commitment to democracy, human rights, equity, social justice and non-violence. The one person who espoused such a vision was Eduard Bernstein. Exactly one hundred years ago he announced the obsolence of Marxism to advanced industrialized countries and emphasized the need to simultaneously realize democracy and socialism without being dogmatic.

With the universalization of democracy, which is the true basis of proportionate equality, social democracy would have to work towards strengthening and guaranteeing access to resources, education and justice to all the people. Its contract is not with any country, religion, or group but with the people of the world. Its agenda in the post-communist world would have to aim for radical action aiming at human liberation within an overall commitment to constitutional and democratic institutions and culture. Any change would have to be non-violent, gradual, majoritarian and with protection of minority rights.

In writing this book, we have incurred many debts. We would like to extend our sincere thanks to Mr. H.C. Jain, Librarian and staff of the South Campus Library, University of Delhi and Ms. Madhu Maini, Librarian and staff of Jesus and Mary College. We would also like to thank the staff of the following libraries: American Centre, New Delhi, American Studies Research Centre, Hyderabad, British Council, New Delhi, Central Library of the University of

Delhi, Indian Institute of Public Administration, New Delhi, Indian Council of World Affairs, New Delhi, and the Max Mueller Bhavan, New Delhi for their assistance. We would like to express our gratitude to our students and colleagues, friends Professor M.P. Singh and Mr. Alan Chong for their help and encouragement. Finally, we would like to express our gratitude to the editorial and production teams of Sage Publications, for bringing out this book. We alone are, however, responsible for all the errors and shortcomings.

The book is dedicated to the memory of Eduard Bernstein (1850–1932) the finest and the best exponent of social democracy.

1

❖ *Introduction*

Socialism is a product of the modern world. It has no precedent in the ancient or the medieval worlds but they do contain preconditions. From the
beginning of written records we find evidence of revolts of the poor against
the rich, of oppressed peoples against ruling elites, and of dreams of a perfectly just and usually egalitarian human order. Sometimes these are pic-
tured as acts of human will and reason, sometimes as part of the wrath of
God against worshippers of false gods or the ungodly wicked and the unfolding of his rewards to the righteous, or even to the humble (Crick 1998:
1).

One can have democracy without socialism, and vice versa. Whether the
two can be effectively combined is the prime question of our age (Lichtheim
1975: 302).

The crucial difference between capitalist and socialist society is the relative
importance of politics and economics in the distribution of rewards. In capitalism it is primarily the market mechanism which accounts for the inequality
of income, prestige and employment, whereas in socialist society it is the
political dimension which explains social differences (Turner 1986: 109).

Socialism has an older ancestral origin than democracy in the sense
that the debate about equality and inequality is as old as civilization
itself. Ever since Plato lamented that every city is a city of two—one
of the rich and the other of the poor, and Aristotle's caution that
inequality everywhere is the cause of revolution—the question of
creating a just, equal stable and efficient society has been the core
of political speculation. Ideas, central to socialism—like equitable
distribution of wealth, reward and honour as a prerequisite to a
just society, and concern for the poor, oppressed and the deprived—
have always been a part of intellectual thinking. However, socialism, like democracy as we understand it, is essentially a modern

concept. To trace the origins of socialist ideas to Classical Antiquity, like Gray did, creates an ambiguity for it overlooks its modern concerns, viz., that it arose first out of commercialization and then became a reaction to the Industrial Revolution which decisively shaped human societies and lives. For the first time in human history there was a tremendous sense of optimism that it was possible to create a prosperous, abundant, free, equal and rational society for all with the aid of technology and science. This optimism was taken note of by Liebknecht who observed Marx's enthusiasm for a Great Exhibition in London in 1851 when he spoke about the revolutionary potential of electricity replacing steam. Socialists accepted industrialization but not capitalism, and instead proposed a society based on equality, cooperation and sociability.

As with most modern ideologies it is difficult to define socialism since there are many variations within it. Dr. Angelo Rappaport listed 39 definitions of socialism in his *Dictionary of Socialism* (1924) and he was still not clear in his own mind as to what it meant. Berki (1975) identified four basic tendencies in socialist ideology: egalitarianism, moralism, rationalism and libertarianism. Caute (1966) observed that popular sovereignty was central to the Left. Crick (1998) identified socialism with a special form of democracy and a set of values first espoused during the French Revolution: liberty, equality and fraternity. It would be a mistake to treat socialism, Marxism and communism as though they were identical. In doing so one would overlook their theoretical diversity and the debates within. Like all other major ideologies, socialism too has become an umbrella ideology. 'Socialism is in fact the theoretical genus of which Marxism is a species and anarchism another; communism is best viewed as political practice, rather than as an ideology' (Goodwin 1992: 105). However, common to all strands of socialism is a commitment to equality, human solidarity, non-exploitative relationships and socialized humanity.

Beyond this general agreement, socialists differed. Not all of them favoured common ownership of property and the means of production. Some wanted to achieve socialism through violent revolutions, while others stressed on peaceful and gradual change. Some claimed that they had discovered the laws of historical development and projected socialism as the inevitable destiny, while others remained content in just projecting what they considered to be a perfect society. For some socialism was a universal human ideal while others saw it as the goal and aspiration of the working class. Some socialists wanted to abolish the state altogether, while others perceived it as an instrument of freedom and cultural elevation. While for some socialism was international, others confined it within their own national boundaries.

Cole pointed out that the term 'socialism' was used in 1827 in an *Owenite Co-operative Magazine* to describe generally Owenism. It symbolized anything that was opposite to individualism—'social' in contrast to 'individual'. Pierre Leroux (1797–1871), a follower of Saint Simon, used the term in *Le Globe* in 1832 to describe Saint Simonism. After 1840 it was increasingly used across Europe to mean common ownership of means of production. The term then travelled widely to all the corners of the world and within a century one heard of different doctrines like Arab socialism, African socialism, Asian socialism and Gandhian socialism. It is because of such a variety that socialism was described as a hat which had lost its original shape after being worn by many heads.

The Beginnings

In the aftermath of the French Revolution the first indication of socialism was in the writings of Francois Noel 'Gracchus' Babeuf (1760–97) and Fillippo Michel Buonarroti (1761–1837) who were inspired by the writings of Jean Jacques Rousseau (1712–78), and the utopians of the Enlightenment. The link that joined the older utopian visions with the post-industrial socialist doctrines was Rousseau who was trenchant in his criticism of the modern unequal society. In *Discourses on the Origins of Inequality* (1755), he distinguished between natural and social inequality. He considered both capitalism and socialism to be unequal. In the former, wealth was the basis to secure benefits and, in the latter, power conferred privileges. He was against egalitarianism, for it led to levelling, and preferred a society that would take into account natural endowments (Fried and Sanders 1964).

Motivated by a passion for equality, the early socialists argued that all individuals had an equal right to the wealth of the earth. They identified private property as a source of inequality and hence demanded its abolition in the hope that this would lead to human sociability. Most socialists unequivocally repeated Rousseau's belief that the individual was essentially good but was corrupted by society. The Babouvists were not only critical of the existing society but also suggested conspiracy by the oppressed and exploited to organize the new society. They also recommended that, with universal education, people would be able to govern themselves through elected bodies. This in itself was a significant demand, considering Paine castigated modern society for keeping the majority of people illiterate.

Babouvism was important because it focused on the contradictions within the revolutionary slogans of liberty and equality, articulated in 1789. Babuef advocated socialization of industry and land, universal right to work, equal natural right to earth and its goods, and ensuring rough parity for human happiness. He contended that freedom meant not only legal and civil liberties but also the unhindered pursuit of economic activities; not just physical protection against arbitrary power but abolition of slavery, exploitation, misery and inequality. This was only possible with the destruction of capitalism. He interpreted socialism to mean class war whereby the exploited could secure their emancipation, freedom and equal status.

> . . . the Babouvist movement marks the point at which liberal democracy and communism began to part company, as it came to be seen that equality was not a completion of liberty but a limitation of it (Kolakowski 1981a: 186).

After 1830s a further distinction arose between socialism and communism, and between libertarian and authoritarian socialism, a distinction that still confronts socialists today. The communists demanded abolition of private property, absolute equality of consumption through the use of force by the oppressed and exploited. 'Communism' was associated with the theories of Etienne Cabet (1788–1856)[1] and came into use in France after the Revolution of 1830. The French word was *communaute* — meaning common ownership. In Britain the word was imported from France by John Goodwyn Barmby, an Owenite. In the 1840s communism had a distinct militant connotation and differed from socialism. Marx and Engels deliberately chose the word 'communist' for their manifesto to convey the idea of revolutionary class struggle along with the notion of common ownership and enjoyment, distancing themselves from utopianism (Cole 1953: 7–8). While the conservatives

attacked the notion of individualism politically and held it responsible for the disintegration of society, the socialists assailed *laissez
faireism*.[2]

Doctrine of Anarchism

Anarchism differed from Marxism both in the methods of struggle
and the theory of the state. It arose within the socialist movement
mainly as an extreme left-wing philosophy, combining the greatest
individual development with the greatest communal unity. In a
full-fledged anarchy the individual and the community mutually
reinforced and coalesced one another. It placed supreme value on
individual freedom, inspired by Rousseau's idea of autonomy, and
abhorred authority that was not self-regulatory. Anarchism originated with Gerrard Winstanley (1609–60) and William Godwin
(1756–1836) but developed as a coherent doctrine in the writings
of Pierre Joseph Proudhon (1809–65), Michael Bakunin (1815–76)
and Prince Peter Kropotkin (1842–1921). Kropotkin, unlike his fellow anarchists, was inherently a pacifist. He realised the absurdity
of violent revolutions, for human beings were inherently good,
sympathetic and cooperative. Unlike Mahatma Gandhi (1869–1948)
who described himself as a philosophical anarchist, Kropotkin did
not develop an elaborate mechanism of non-violent mass action.

Anarchism rejected the state for it had just one purpose: to limit,
control and subordinate the individual. In fact, anarchy did not
mean chaos, as popularly understood, but an absence of authority
since government was considered an absolute evil. Once the legal-
bureaucratic state with its economic inequalities was abolished,
society would acquire a new moral basis. Unlike liberalism, anarchism rejected a constitutional law-governed state for it only provided formal protection and safeguards, and normally served the
ruling classes. It rejected the contractual basis to government since
most states arose by conquest and with help of force. The rejection
of the state and government meant repudiation of all political systems and political methods because politics itself was corrupting.
Two themes — distrust of state and rejection of authoritarian
socialism — interlaced one another and, in a nutshell, constituted
the anarchist critique of and challenge to Marxism.

Anarchism and Marxism grew as critical schools within the
industrialized capitalist society and highlighted its evils like

dehumanization, alienation, inequality, oppression and exploitation. Both desired the overthrow of capitalism and its state along
with representative parliamentary institutions. While Anarchism
considered the state to be the basic source of social injustice, Marxism characterized it as belonging to the superstructure, conditioned
and determined by the economic base. For Anarchism the abolition
of the state was the immediate goal, whereas for Marxism it was
the ultimate goal.

The notion of the transitional proletarian state was the most vital
difference between them. For Marxism the proletarian revolution
led to the destruction of the capitalist state and the institution of
the dictatorship of the proletariat. Anarchism feared that the dictatorship of the proletariat would lead to the dictatorship on the
proletariat. It stressed that all revolutions, including the Marxist,
perpetuated and extended tyranny. Instead of the proletarian
dictatorship, it proposed voluntary, self-regulating, spontaneous
socio-economic relations which people created and sustained for
themselves.

> The Anarchists, with their plurality of views, opposed the
> dogmatism of the Marxists; they were also against the capture
> and use of the state as advocated by the German Social Demo-
> cratic Party. The Anarchists had a less rigid notion of class
> than Marx or Lenin and did not believe in the inevitability of
> class war — an idea which Proudhon considered merely waste-
> ful! . . . To the Anarchists, the dictatorship of the proletariat
> signified the substitution of a new class of oppressors. As Sorel
> said, proletarian dictatorship meant merely a change of mas-
> ters. Furthermore, the Anarchists rightly doubted the state's
> capacity to wither away (Goodwin 1992: 133).

Reform vs Revolution

In the formative period of evolution of the socialist doctrine there
was a difference regarding the methods employed for its realization.
From Babeuf came the stress on insurrection and revolution which
was kept alive by Louis Auguste Blanqui (1805–81)[3] 'thus providing
a link between the Jacobin Left and the nineteenth century radicals'
(Kolakowski 1981a: 214). Blanqui scorned parliamentarism and

majority rule principle, and defended the need for a small organized disciplined party to foment a revolution. He even rejected the role of trade unions. His belief in insurrection was total and unflinching. He did not think it was possible to outline the ideal society before it materialized.

As opposed to Blanquism, Jean J.C. Louis Blanc (1811–82), inspired by Saint Simon, stressed on gradual reform by the state to mitigate inequality, exploitation, economic crises and unemployment. His *L' Organization du travail* (1849) pleaded for radical social reform like free compulsory education, universal right to work, technical progress, combination of private and socialized industries without mass exploitation and violence. He wanted a key role for the state in economic planning and development of self-governing welfare services to enable the workers to conduct themselves. He looked upon universal suffrage as a way to transform the state and make it attuned to the needs and welfare of the multitude. He opposed the doctrine of class war and wanted to supersede capitalism peacefully. Blanc, unlike Marx, believed that ideas shaped history and, like Condorcet, hoped that with gradual enlightenment and dissemination of knowledge the desired social changes would materialize. His ideal was a 'social republic' based on the solidarity of all classes, nationally and internationally.

Blanc could be termed as the first 'social democrat' (Cole 1953: 169). His ideas were followed up by Lassalle and the German social democrats while Blanqui's successors were Tkachev and Lenin. Both these traditions developed, matured and survived through the nineteenth into the twentieth century. It was Lenin who 'made communism a potent global force' (Remnick 1998: 42). The Bolsheviks thought it was possible to restructure society on the basis of a master plan, disregarding accumulated wisdom of generations. However, its rejection within seven decades cast serious aspersions about its relevance, both as a method and a goal. Popper and Berlin pointed to the limitations of the Utopianism.[4] Havel denounced 'violence' as not being 'revolutionary enough'.

The First World War was a watershed for European socialism for it brought about a schism between communism and social democracy. Having broken away from communism, the social democratic parties began to identify with liberal democracy. Though they were antagonistic to capitalism, they did not have a clear-cut alternative to offer. Moreover, social democracy was caught in the inter-war crisis of liberal democratic capitalism. The Second World War renewed hopes for social democracy. Laissez-faire capitalism was discredited by the Great Depression. It was difficult to visualize a market-led recovery to overcome the devastation of industries and economy caused by the war. State intervention and regulation of the economy was imperative under the circumstances. Keynes prepared the ideological basis by contending that widening the base of consumption and diffusion of incomes and wealth was the key to a vibrant economy. It was not difficult for social democracy to identify with Keynesianism and participate in the reconstruction of the war-torn economies of Europe.

The central themes of the post-war ideology of social democracy were socialization of the means of production, planning, social citizenship and equality. Socialization of the means of production was seen as a third way between communism and capitalism because the community would have economic power without the rigid centralization characteristic of the former Soviet model. The overall coordination and planning by the state would be complemented with decentralized planning initiatives which meant worker participation and private enterprise. The social democrats, with the exception of Cole, never 'engaged in constitutional speculation . . . (they) gave much more thought to what the state should do than to what it should be' (Marquand 1997: 3).

Planning was the second key element. In case of the British Labour Party, planned economic development meant guarantee of full employment and high standards of living with the state directing the policies of main industries, services and financial institutions. The Socialist Party of Austria understood it to mean a crisis-free expanding economy. It did not advocate socialization of the means of production nor planning but accepted the necessity of economic security by increasing national productivity. In Norway there was a shift towards accommodating market forces and liberalization following large scale planning and regulation in the 1940s. The Socialist Labour Party in Sweden undertook a grand plan of transforming the economic organization of the bourgeois society by giving the people the control over production.

Third was the idea of social citizenship state which meant extending the liberal principles of political equality into the social and economic spheres. In Britain[5] the chief architect of the welfare state Sir William H. Beveridge (1879–1963) considered the state as necessary to abolish social evils and guarantee full employment, social security from cradle to grave, a national health service, public housing, old-age pension and a war against ignorance and squalor. It was made possible by the new economics of Keynesianism. Tawney, a brother-in-law and friend of Beveridge, was appreciative of the great advancement made by the welfare states in Western Europe in alleviating human misery. Freedom was possible only when individuals led a decent and dignified life. He was, however, critical of soullessness of the welfare state. In Scandinavia, Western Europe and New Zealand there were provisions for comprehensive universal coverage and equal benefits to all the individuals giving them the right to basic security and welfare.

A number of developments interlaced with one another to produce a new version of socialism in the post-Second World War era that led to actualization of the welfare state. First, the relative decline of the manual working class meant that the parties became more heterogeneous in terms of class composition. This meant that, in order to succeed electorally, they needed to mobilize people from wider social and economic backgrounds. Second, in the 1950s Western European countries experienced unprecedented growth rate guaranteeing full employment, economic prosperity and social security to all, including the working class, confirming Macmillan's oft-quoted statement that one never had it so good. Mass miseries were mitigated and poverty became a minority concern and, in many parts of the world, invisible. Heilbroner paraphrasing Habermas pointed out that:

> capitalism organizes the material life of humankind more satisfactorily than socialism . . . . capitalism had successfully created the seventy five percent society. The majority are comfortable. The rest are not. But the economic minority does not constitute enough of an economic or political threat to get the political will of the mainstream in motion to find a solution (Heilbroner 1989: 4, 6).

Third, there were structural changes in the economy, for instance ownership was separated from control of capital leading to the extinction of the overbearing owner-boss and the emergence of a new species of salaried managers. The managerial revolution that Burnham (1941) spoke of transformed capitalism, bringing to the forefront a technocratic style of control which many called post-industrial society[6] (Bell 1974; Brezezinski 1979; Dahrendorf 1959; Drucker 1989; Lichtheim 1963; Tofler 1979). Fourth, with the institutionalization of Keynesianism, governments controlled the mixed economy indirectly. Economic power gravitated from private to social hands without a large-scale transfer of ownership or introduction of direct controls. Keynesianism guaranteed private ownership of the means of production with democratic control over the economy. It defended equality through greater diffusion of incomes and wealth, broad consumption base and economic expansion. It laid the foundations of welfare capitalism, which meant profits and social security schemes. Finally, the conflicts between capital and labour became muted because trade unions gained better bargaining strength to get concessions without confrontations. These developments inaugurated an era of 'end of ideology' (Bell 1966). The marriage between liberal democratic capitalism and social democracy in the 1950s and 1960s was outlined in Anthony Crosland's *The Future of Socialism*. He pointed out that twentieth-century capitalism qualitatively differed from its earlier phases for it is less individualistic, more egalitarian and democratic. 'In my view Marx has little or nothing to offer the contemporary socialist, either in respect of practical, policy, or of the correct analysis of our society, or even of the right conceptual tools or framework' (Crosland 1956: 2).

Crosland's thesis at convergence was agreed to by liberals like Galbraith and Schumpeter. However, Wright Mills furnished a severe indictment of contemporary capitalism. His analysis of the power elite composed of those who controlled the means of production, political power and death reinforced Eisenhower's conception of the military industrial complex. This elite, highly organized, controlled and dominated the rest of the unorganized mass. Dahl criticized the analysis on the ground that the data was insufficient. Parsons found it full of generalizations on the basis of a very short-term experience. Sweezy felt that Mills had blurred inter-class relationships and did not suggest a way out.

End of Ideology to Eurocommunism

In the aftermath of the Second World War, along with attempts for a more precise, scientific and value-free social science came the assertion that the present age had achieved in the advanced industrialized countries a pluralist-democratic structure. Any effort to dissect this contemporary phenomenon with some critical perception was held to be absolutely irrelevant. This was the major plank of the 'End of Ideology' theorists who took it for granted that no further innovation was either possible or necessary in the realm of social and political ideas.[7] Two major developments, first in the 1960s in the activities of the New Left and subsequently in the 1970s in Eurocommunism, nullified this basic assumption. While the New Left was too critical to be constructive, the Eurocommunists, in spite of their wide differences, opened up new avenues for fundamental innovations in the comtemporary theory and practice of Marxism.

Eurocommunism demonstrated in theory and practice that communism in Western Europe was dedicated to the preservation, respect and further advancement of traditional human rights and freedom, subordination of the state to the interests and welfare of the people and a European common market to advance the condition of the working class throughout the member-states. Eurocommunism was significantly a new political reality of European politics and of East–West relations in 1970s for it responded to the 1956 XXth Congress of the Communist Party of Soviet Union (CPSU) and events like the Hungarian and Czech revolts, the Sino-Soviet split, the rise of *d'etente* in international politics and the long-term structural changes within advanced capitalism. It was a combination of ideological and political tendencies displayed by several non-ruling communist parties in Western Europe, Japan and Australia.

Eurocommunism espoused the idea that, in the context of advanced capitalism, it was possible to conceive of socialism with a humane face within a democratic polity and a pluralistic society. It rejected insurrectionism and desired changes within the framework of constitutionalism. Interestingly, Eurocommunists, like the end of ideology proponents, were careful to emphasize that their prescriptions were not universally valid as certain countries like Vietnam or Laos did not have a pluralist society and a parliamentary system.

Eurocommunists observed that advanced capitalism had its shortcomings, peculiarities and exploitative mechanisms which democratic socialism and the welfare state had failed to rectify. They distinguished themselves from social democracy for their aim was to transcend and not administer, the capitalist system, and work out a socialist alternative without a dictatorship of the proletariat. They understood exploitation not merely in the economic sense, for they focussed on the ideological apparatus of the state like the Church, educational institutions and the media. In this context, they pointed to the continuing inequalities within the socialist societies and what they hoped for was the establishment of a 'real working people's democracy'.

Eurocommunism questioned and opposed the 'general line' of the International Communist Movement as defined by Moscow. It rejected the Marxist-Leninist orthodoxy in ideology, politics, economics and culture, and denied its universal applicability. It refused to subordinate national interests to those of the erstwhile USSR or to that of international communism. Eurocommunism asserted the right of each communist party to interpret, update and, if necessary, revise the teachings of Marx, Engels and Lenin. It was inspired by Togliatti's concept of 'progressive democracy' outlined in 1944–46 which rejected the Leninist conception of a Vanguard Party. It insisted on mass organizations and multi-party system that represented the working class and allied forces within the conditions of pluralist competition.

Togliatti was the first within international communism to point out that Stalinism represented a systematic phenomenon and could not be seen as a temporary aberration or the personal machinations of a single leader. Inspired by Gramsci, Togliatti and the Italian communists spoke of a gradual transformation of the civil society as a prelude to the conquest of power, thereby rejecting the concept of the dictatorship of the proletariat. Since the memory of Mussolini's rule was still fresh, the Italians did not want any kind of dictatorship, including that of the proletariat. Togliatti claimed that 'any proposal to create once again a centralized international organization was unacceptable' since the whole communist movement had become poly-central in which Moscow no longer held a unique place.

We always start from the idea that socialism is the regime in which there is the widest freedom for the workers, that they in fact participate in an organized manner in the direction of the entire social life. Therefore, we greet all positions of principle and all facts showing us that this is the reality in all the socialist countries and not only in the Soviet Union. On the other hand events that sometimes disclose the contrary to us damage the entire movement (Togliatti, cited in McLellan 1979: 149).

The Spanish and subsequently the French Communist Parties followed the Italian example. In 1976 the Communist Party of France (PCF) declared that the concept of the dictatorship of the proletariat was obsolete. Hadded proposed a new version of *paragraph 9 of the Preamble of the PCF Statues*, suggesting erasure of all references to the dictatorship of the proletariat. The deletion would be compensated by the addition of another word in paragraph 11, that perceived the working class as the 'directing force of the struggle for the transformation of society'. To support his proposals, Haddad argued that the dictatorship of the proletariat, although still had historic value, applied only to 'certain circumstances of the class struggle'; that the various forms of Fascism had given dictatorship an ugly connotation; and that dictatorship was incompatible with democracy.

Santiago Carrillo (1922), the Secretary General of the Communist Party of Spain, published *Eurocommunism and the State* (1977) in which he rejected the concept of the dictatorship of the proletariat because it suggested bureaucratization, one-party dominance and uncontrolled political power. He observed that revolution was impossible in highly industrialized countries and stressed the need to realize socialism and democracy with multi parties, parliamentary and representative institutions, universal suffrage, trade unions, freedom of opposition, human rights and popular participation. He denied the charge that he was proposing a new or a third path as an alternative to both orthodox Marxism and social democracy.

Carrillo pointed out that the dictatorship of the proletariat was necessary in Russia for the proletariat was a minority in comparison to the peasants. In Western Europe, due to large numbers in working class salaried professionals and comprehensive welfare measures, there was no need to smash the state machinery. He specifically emphasized the need to preserve the productive forces and social services that were created in these societies. He recognized the role of private enterprise in creating these though he emphasized the utmost need to socialize the means of production. Though advanced capitalism was ripe for revolutionary changes yet neither mechanical nor automatic transformation was desirable or feasible. In any such change power need not be the monopoly of one single party. It would be a new political formation that would consist of different groups acting on a consensual basis, respecting one another's individuality and independence. He ruled out the need for a super party. Carrillo insisted that Eurocommunism was not a mere tactical manoeuvre but a new interpretation of Marxism. He hoped that the progress of socialist movement in advanced capitalism would help Soviet communism to develop beyond the one-party state. The Eurocommunists' posture was akin to Bernstein's revisionism which claimed to revise the doctrine without renouncing the commitment to socialism.

The striking originality of East European Marxism was two-fold. One was the firm conviction that the existing Marxist regimes were far from perfect and that there was a need to rectify these distortions. The reversal to capitalism was ruled out even though it questioned the validity of Marxist presumptions. It desired to reshape Marxism in the light of experiences in contemporary socialist societies. Second, these writings were full of optimism, in sharp contrast to the tone of pessimism in non-socialist countries.

Many East European humanists (Korac, Markovic and Schaff) and dissidents (Bahro, Djilas and Medvedev), like the Eurocommunists, rejected Leninism but emphasized the democratic and humanistic outlook of Marxism. State socialism, according to them, was dehumanized, exploitative, oppressive and in no way different from capitalism. They demanded fundamental human freedoms, advocated workers' control of industries as a way of decentralizing economic power and reducing the influence and control of the state and party bureaucracies.

Mikaly Vajda, a pupil of Luk'acs, called 1970s the 'decade of the crisis of Marxism'. He tried to solve the many severe conflicts in the erstwhile communist societies of East Europe. Freedom was his central concern, for the pointed to its denial in these societies. The worker was not free under state socialism any more than under capitalism. He was not involved in the production process nor did he have access to free trade unions. The interdependence among socialist nations also circumscribed freedom. Vajda did not think property relations to be the only arena of conflict, for even in the absence of class politics, society was hierarchical with oppressed sections being vulnerable. It was erroneous to presume that a classless society would lead to homogeneity and equality. He rejected Marx's perception that political power could be deduced exclusively from economic power.

For Vajda, the primary question was a political one involving issues of decision making and political power. He did not perceive socialism to be superior or even equal to democracy. A democratic power structure ensured the satisfaction of the needs of all social groups, including minorities. Since Marxism as a doctrine of redemption did not and could not redeem its promises it was futile to speak of replacing capitalism with socialism. Instead the urgent task was a movement towards democracy. The imperative need for democracy in all spheres of life, both political and economic, was stressed by Medvedev also. Though Vajda never spelt out the methods by which democracy would be attained, he could realize like Carrillo and Miliband the need for a total reassessment of the Marxist conception of the state and an acceptance of human freedoms, most succinctly expressed by Miliband:

> Regimes which do either by necessity or by choice depend on the suppression of all opposition and the shifling of all civic freedoms must be taken to represent a disastrous regression in political terms, from bourgeois democracy, whatever the economic and social achievements of which they may be capable . . . . the civic freedoms which, however inadequately and precariously, form part of bourgeois democracy are a product of centuries of unremitting popular struggle. The task of Marxist politics is to defend these freedoms; and to make possible their extension and enlargement by the removal of their class boundaries (Miliband 1977: 189–90).

Alexander Dubcek, who promised socialism with a humane face in Czechoslovakia (1968) demanded rights for the non-communists and voluntary associations, freedom of speech, association, constitution-based personal freedoms, including right to property and a system of just reward for efficient workers without sacrificing their essential faith in Marxism-Leninism. He argued that socialism could not mean merely the liberation of the working class alone but making it possible for a fuller development of human personality than bourgeois democracy. He also underlined that there could be many roads to socialism. Dubcek stressed the need for change and did not harbour any counter revolutionary sentiments as alleged by Moscow while justifying armed intervention in Czechoslovakiai in August 1968. In fact, his proposals were nipped in the bud without even a trial. History proved Dubcek right for the ossified, alienated totalitarian Soviet model collapsed because of its inability to reform from within. The Prague Spring was the beginning of the end of a dream to create a socialist man in a socialist society. It was significant that the Brezhnev era which witnessed not only an intervention in Czechoslovakia but a more expansionist policy in the Third World was characterized by Gorbachev as a period of stagnation in which attempts were made to improve without changing anything. Dubcek's personal hardships and sacrifices did not go waste for they paved way for the Velvet Revolution of 1989 which brought to an end the entire communist system in Europe and the disintegration of the Soviet Union. The myopic vision of the doctrine of limited sovereignty incapacitated the one party Communist states to reform and become democratic and pluralistic like the multi-party systems of the West.

Third World Developments and Dependency Theory

A distinctive brand of socialism was articulated by African leaders like Nkrumah, Nyerere and Senghor. They dismissed social democracy and marxism as unsuited for the African temperament and conditions. They argued that African society was naturally socialistic, community-based and classless. Unlike European socialism which spoke of redistribution of wealth, African socialism focussed on the joint creation of wealth. Nyerere's *Ujamaa* spoke of traditional family ties, communal ownership and commitment to work which were compatible with the solidarist philosophy of one party democracy. Senghor attacked the alienation and spiritual poverty of Western civilization and identified economic democracy and spiritual freedom as components of African socialism. However, the *Ujamaa* movement had its own difficulties, namely low productivity and limited output. The dual strategy of a public and private sector created tension in implementing the socialistic principles. Nyerere in the late 1980s moved away from the solidarist model to a multi-party system accepting that one-party state was an exception in a specific situation in Africa and not the general rule. Like the Leninist one-party model the solidarist model could not become a viable and functional alternative to the pluralist multi-party democracy.

In India as early as the 1830s, socialist ideas in general and Owenism in particular were discernible. Rammohun Roy (1776–1833) met Owen in 1832–33 and held a long discussion on the subject of religion under socialism. Bankim Chandra Chatterjee (1838–94) was the first to use the terms 'socialism' and 'communism'. In *Samya*, meaning equality (1871),[8] he acknowledged the influence of the early socialists and Rousseau. Bankim considered inequality as the single factor that retarded progress and discussed at length Rousseau's views regarding him, along with Buddha and Jesus, as contributing to man's quest for equality. He endorsed Rousseau's distinction between natural and socio-economic inequalities. The reasons for misery in India was due to the discord between the landlord and the peasants, and the social distance between man and woman. Like the early socialists, Bankim championed the cause of gender equality and praised J.S. Mill's *The Subjection of Women* (1869) for deftly handling the subject of women's oppression and subjugation. He wholeheartedly endorsed Mill's views and only pointed out that Indian women were more oppressed than their European sisters. Swami Vivekananda (1863–1902) in 1896 predicted that the next upheaval which would usher in another era would come from Russia or China and prophesied that the ultimate will would be that of the proletariat. Vivekananda is often described as the first Indian socialist. Alongwith sister Nivedita he met Kropotkin.

There were no references to Marx except in an article published in *Amrit Bazar Patrika* in 1903. It was the Russian Revolution of 1917 which generated interest in socialism. Many nationalists hoped that the British rule might end one day as Tsarism did in Russia. M.N. Roy (1887–1954) also moved away from radical nationalism to revolutionary Marxism. Acharya Narendra Deva (1889–1956) was critical of the narrow social base of the capitalist democracy which could be corrected through major involvement of the people. He identified social revolution, active participation in socialist programmes and fight against imperialism as the core ideas of the Left. Though he followed a Marxist analysis, he was not dogmatic for he cherished personal freedom and democratic institutions. Ram

Manohar Lohia (1910–67) denounced Marxism and liberalism. As a democratic socialist, he firmly believed in democracy, individual freedom, equality and pluralism. He dismissed all concentration of authority and power as evil. Jaiprakash Narayan (1902–79) denounced communism since it alienated and exploited the common man. He gave up Marxism and became a socialist and finally a liberal Gandhian.

About two decades ago, Daniel P. Moynihan argued that the majority of the Third World leadership was neither Marxist nor liberal but Fabians, with the enormous influence exerted over them by Harold J. Laski (1893–1951). Though such claims were grossly exaggerated, yet the fact was that Fabians did have influence, both in India and elsewhere.[9] In this context it would be appropriate to mention Joseph Baptista (1864–1930), a Goan Christian who was educated at Cambridge. He was the oldest member of the Fabian Society, a great trade union leader and later on the President of the All India Trade Union Congress (AITUC) in 1922. Baptista vigorously compaigned for an eight-hour legislation, increase in wages and improved conditions of labour. He exerted considerable influence on Bal Gangadhar Tilak (1856–1920), an ardent nationalist, during 1914–20, whose awareness of the Left increased by this association.

In the late 1930s Subhas Chandra Bose (1897–1945) was critical of the Congress Socialist Party for following Fabian precepts. Sibnarayan Ray pointed out that since the twenties of this century two different streams of socialist thought crystallized in India, one emanating from the Fabians and the other from the Comintern. In this context he correctly observed that

a sizeable section of Indian intellectuals is inclined towards a peaceful and constitutional variety of socialism, thanks partly from the indigenous tradition but scarcely less to the influence of people like Bernard Shaw, Sydney and Beatrice Webb, R.H. Tawney, H.J. Laski, G.D.H. Cole and Lord Beveridge (Ray 1962: 378).

An attempt was made to understand the causes of economic development and underdevelopment, and in particular the problem of Third World poverty which was acute and in sharp contrast to the affluence and prosperity of Western Europe, United States and Japan. With achievement of political independence, acquisition of economic power and self reliance became the key issues. In this context many questioned the assumption that the growth in world trading would eliminate poverty and backwardness. Raúl Prebisch argued that the theory of interdependence and free trade worked well in the nineteenth century but was unsuited in the twentieth century. This was because in the nineteenth century division of labour based on exchange of agricultural and industrial goods was mutually beneficial whereas in the twentieth century this system benefitted the manufactured goods exporting countries. 'Reality is undermining the outdated scheme of the international division of labour' (Prebisch 1950: 1).

Prebisch proposed national and international solutions. In the international sector he insisted that the developed countries give special treatment to raw material exporting countries and help Third World economies to reform domestic industry to a point where the nation consumed its own locally produced manufactured goods whatever may be the cost. This would increase domestic employment and income leading to expansion of market and industrialization.

Unlike Prebisch, the Dependency theorists analyzed the problem of underdevelopment in terms of international structures and processes countering the Ricardian theory of comparative advantage. They also criticized the Modernization theory of the 1950s which regarded modernity to include, among others, factors like value system, individual motivation and capital accumulation. Dependency theory was described differently by various authors. However, common to all these versions were certain basic elements. The important departure in this theory was its rejection of modernization theories of Rostow, Pye and Apter. It followed the Leninist heritage of Marxism for it linked the continued impoverishment and underdevelopment to the sustained unequal exchange with the developed West. Whereas for Lenin, imperialism was the last stage of capitalism, for the Dependency theorists the link was still gloomier as it was the very basis for the perpetuation of inequality and dependency. A dependency was a 'reflex of the expansion of the dominant nations and is geared towards the needs of the dominant economies; e.g. foreign rather than national needs' (Bodenheimer 1974: 158).

However, the essential presumption of the dependency theory that the peripheries would always remain raw materials exporting countries was negated by the fact that the entire Third World put together exports more manufactured goods than raw materials. Another important contention that was disproved was that the Third World countries would always remain peripheral and dependent. This is shown by the spectacular performance of the Asian newly industrialized countries (NICs) (Harris 1986; Mukherjee 1992).

Immanuel Wallerstein rejected the teleology of the Modernization theory and the theoretical positivism of the dependency theory. As an alternative to both, he conceived the world system theory which stated that the national societies could be analyzed properly on the basis of their links with international networks of exchanges. The capitalist world economy is a global system of 'commodity chains' of two categories of producers and consumers consisting of the core (Britain, Germany, Japan and the United States); the semi peripheries (Mediterranean countries) and the peripheries which are primarily agricultural (Africa, Asia and Latin America). Like the Dependency theorists he pointed to the asymmetry between the core and the peripheries. He too overlooked the radical transformation within the system and the sea changes in the peripheries.

Socialism in Post-Communist Phase

The collapse of communism in the former Soviet Union and its Eastern Europe satellites has led to the realization that the choice today is not between shades of capitalism and that of socialism but between constitutionalism, rule of law, independence of judiciary and democracy, on the one hand, and authoritarianism, on the other hand. The experience of last four decades has demonstrated that democracy is a necessity for economics as it is for politics. This is true of both the developed and the developing countries. The reasons for this shift mainly lie in the track record of revolutionary regimes both with regard to economic growth and protection of basis human rights. In both these spheres their performance was dismal. The excesses during the cultural revolution in China, the pathetic economic situation of Cuba, the horrors in Kampuchea and the famine in Ethiopia have made it clear that such regimes were unable to deal with the basic problems and requirements of their people.

The communist systems led to centralized planning, collectivization, bureaucratization, one party dominance, monolithic state and a command economy resulting in shortages, stagnation, ecological destruction, low productivity, non-competitiveness and a declining Gross National Product (GNP). Not only was the rigid and bureaucratic planning slow and cumbersome, it also led to lack of motivation and self esteem. In order to succeed it needed force and compulsion. When these were partially dismantled its inner contradictions surfaced. The problems faced by the former Soviet society and economy were enormous. The death rate which was 6.9 per 1,000 in 1964 rose to 10.3 in 1980. Life expectancy in case of men and women declined from 67 to 62 years and from 76 to 73 years, respectively. The Soviet Union was the only industrialized country to experience such a decline. There was a steep rise in infant mortality rate. The Gross Domestic Product (GDP) which was 4.9 per cent in 1966–70 decreased to 2.2 per cent in 1981–85. There was stagnation in coal and steel production. Agricultural production was below the plan level. Officially statistics were not available since 1980 regarding grain production but it was estimated to be a mere 1.8 per cent in the period 1981–85. Rationing in important food items were introduced in some Soviet cities in the late 1970s and early 1980s. 'By the early 1980s it was obvious that the Soviet Union was failing to make the transition from a fairly primitive stage of economic development based on exports of primary products into a modern Western-based economic system' (Elliott 1991).

The isolationist economic policies that these communist states pursued with the aim of self sufficiency and independence led to a GNP which was less than 25 per cent and their share of exports was merely 14 per cent. This meant that they were out of the prevailing trends towards internationalization of the production process. It also meant that the three important components of modern business organization — increased efficiency, product quality and consumer choice — did not become a part of socialist culture and remained an exclusive preserve of capitalism. The inconvertibility of their currencies aggravated their lack of competitiveness. Galbraith pointed to this lack of competitiveness and adaptability in meeting new requirements and challenges. 'Capitalism in its original or pristine form could not have survived. But under pressure it did adapt. Socialism in its original form and for its first tasks did succeed. But it failed to adapt' (Galbraith, cited in R. Hague et al. 1992: 417).

This, coupled with the success stories of the East Asian Tigers made the communist model unattractive. The spectacular success of the Asian NICs proved that economic liberalism allowed late modernizers to catch up with the others within a shorter span of less than two generations. Their hardships and privations seem less bearable to the large scale social terror unleashed by the former communist regimes. (Fukuyama 1992: 41–42). The promise of Khurshchev that USSR would overtake the West remained an empty one. In a comparative perspective the communist regimes as opposed to liberal democracy lacked resilience, adaptability and the capacity to respond and absorb societal and technological changes thus becoming in the process a dinosaur. Moreover with the emergence of a commercial world the military alliances and adventures look both illegitimate and unprofitable. The former Soviet Union attained rough armaments parity with the United States but was way behind in terms of economic power. Japan occupied the second position. It lagged behind in technology a fact taken note by Andrei Sakharov, who commented that all the important innovations and discoveries originated in the West since the Second World War. 'Socialism was incapable of moving fully into, let alone generating, the new hi-tech economy, and was therefore destined to fall even further behind . . . it failed to achieve the mass production of consumer goods' (Hobsbawm 1991: 121).

The world-wide failure of Marxist-Leninist communism was also due to a fallacious and erroneous conception of the market. The mistakes were broadly two: anthropological and economic (Ross 1990: 6). The anthropological mistake was to presume, as Marx did, that 'law of history' dictated fundamental antagonism between capital and labour. 'The dream of socialism with a human face will always be a dream: it is based on a mistaken view of man' (Ibid.: 16). Democratic institutions and culture, extensive social security measures, trade unions activities and labour welfare laws have improved the position and working conditions of the proletariat. The economic mistake was compounded by continuing to view capitalism as it existed in its early phase of development ignoring the structural changes that took place as enumerated above. Moreover the idea of a free market solely governed by the principle of profit which the Marxists attacked was a myth for there never was one. Even Adam Smith, the guru of *laissez-faire* and market, granted to the state three duties, namely: (*a*) defence, (*b*) administration of justice and protection of every member of the society, and (*c*) maintenance of public works and public institutions which meant universal public education, public health and labour laws. Thus within the ambit of last two functions he 'offered an intellectual framework for a generous and compassionate government consistent with a competitive market economy' (Meyerson 1989: 67).

Che, an advocate of planning, could lucidly comprehend the problems of stagnation within the Soviet economy as early as 1964. He advocated a combination of economic planning with market or what he called 'law of value'. This suggested the need to accept complexity if economic regulations were to be effective and also indicated a willingness to check results against what was happening elsewhere (Blackburn 1991: 216).

> The starting point is to calculate the socially necessary labour required to produce a given article, but what has been overlooked is the fact that socially necessary labour is an economic and historical concept. Therefore, it changes not only on the local (or national) level but in world terms as well. Continued technological advances, a result of competition in the capitalist world, reduces the expenditure of necessary labour and therefore lowers the value of the product. A closed society can ignore such changes for a certain time, but it would always have to come back to these international relations in order to compare product values. If a given society ignores such changes for a long time without developing new and accurate formulas to replace the old ones, it will create internal interrelationships that will shape its own value structure in a way that may be internally consistent but would be in contradiction with the tendencies of more highly developed technology (for example in steel and plastics). This would result in relative reverses of some importance, and, in any case, would produce distortions in the law of value on an international scale and making it impossible to compare economies (Che, cited in Blackburn 1991: 215–16).

Nove contended that the bureaucracy's dominant role within the communist societies could be reduced by relying on markets and commodity production for that would encourage participation and self management (Nove 1983: 227–28). The Yugoslavian leader Ante Markovic admitted that contemporary socialism was unable to solve the problems of either efficiency or political democracy.

Economic failure undermined the legitimacy of an already unpopular political system in the former Soviet Union. Even seventy years after communism was established, the majority of the citizens did not, as Tucker (1987) pointed out, believe in the myth of communism. Not more than 2 per cent of the members of the Communist Party believed in its programmes and policies. There was an universal indifference to official pronouncements. This was in spite of the fact that socialist societies were insulated from information. Alcoholism and the desire to emigrate was widespread. Solzhenitsyn pointed out that the Gulag, the concentration camp system, originated during Lenin's time. The terror and cruelty increased during Stalin's time. Many people who suffered during Stalin's time were innocent. The anger was compounded by the fact that the regime did not own responsibility for the heinous crimes perpetrated against its own citizens. There was total lack of political democracy, along with suspension of liberties and abrogation of civil society.

From the moment the Bolsheviks seized power in 1917, the Soviet state systematically attacked all potential competing sources of authority in Russian society, including the opposition political parties, the press, trade unions, private enterprises, and the Church. While institutions remained at the end of the 1930's bearing some of those names, all were ghostly shadows of their former selves organized and completely controlled by the regimes. What was left was a society whose members were reduced to "atoms" unconnected to any "mediating institutions" short of an all-powerful government . . . . the human relations that make up the society's fabric — the family, religion, historical memory, language — became targets, as society is systematically and methodically atomized, and the individual's close relationships are supplanted by others chosen for him, and approved by the state . . . . the ultimate goal of totalitarianism: not simply to deprive the new

Soviet man of his freedom, but to make him fear freedom in favour of security, and to affirm the goodness of his chains even in the absence of coercion (Fukuyama 1992: 24).

The presence of a self serving, corrupt and privileged elite which Djilas characterized as the 'new class' did more to alienate the masses from the system which prided in being equal and just. Morally, the communist systems did not respect the self worth and esteem of the ordinary citizen. Havel condemned the communist societies for undermining and humiliating the ordinary person's moral character and dignity, and their belief in their own capacity to act as moral agents. It was no small credit that Rabindranath Tagore (1861–1941) could as early as 1930 see Bolshevism as transitory and that it was a medical treatment for a sick society. He commented 'indeed the day on which the doctor's regime comes to an end must be hailed as a red letter day for the patient' (Tagore 1960: 111).

In the 1970s social democracy failed to cope with the crises that resulted from international recession. Within the social democratic parties there was internal tensions over new issues like women's rights, environmental protection, disarmament, peace, NATO, defence of the West and the membership of European Community. It is rather ironical that in recent years 'the more fundamental critique of the successful forms of production comes from the Greens rather than the socialists' (Ash 1990: 21). Since 1980 social democracy lost both its intellectual and political ascendancy which it had exercised since the Second World War. In the face of international recession, an interventionist state became more a cause than a cure to the problem. Too much state meant greater bureaucratization which entailed waste, red tapism, inefficiency, inertia — in short, a nanny state. Most communist parties in western Europe declined electorally.[10] The reason for it was long period of economic crises in the Soviet Union which alienated their traditional voters. Most of them had disassociated themselves with the Soviet political model and, with the crises on the economic front, the disillusionment was total. The new Right demanded rolling back of the state, deregulation and liberalization of economy, greater role for the market. Social democracy has made a come back in all the West European countries in the 1990s primarily because the electorate felt unequivocally that capitalism and democracy ought to be combined w:th governments satisfying the minimum expectations of social welfare of the people and, in particular, the least advantaged.

As Amartya Sen has rightly demonstrated that a mere rise in GNP and production was not enough as true development meant enrichment of the life of an average person. He categorically asserted that liberalization without a concern for the poor and underprivileged was not acceptable. Crucial to this whole process was democracy which is foundational and cited the Chinese example to emphasize that dismantling of health service and radical marketization of rural China was possible only in the absence of democracy.

Conclusion

The twentieth-century critiques and foes of liberal democracy, mainly fascism and communism, just could not match the promise and fulfillment of the former. While fascism was relegated to history after its defeat in the Second World War, communism collapsed due to its own internal contradictions and its failure to evolve mechanisms of self correction. The unpredicted but inevitable collapse of Marxist regimes is as significant as the fall of the Roman Empire. 'Nothing in our past thinking, or in anyone else's prepared us for the remarkable turn of events in the Soviet Union. So much the worse for theory, so much the better for life' (Howe 1990a: 133).

The communist regimes lost sight of the fact that socialism did not merely mean scientific planning, efficient administration nor public welfarism but, as Tawney emphasized, a moral quest, a philosophy of individual fulfillment with emphasis on compassion, fellowship and participation are important components of socialist theorizing and practice. 'True Socialism' according to Laski 'is libertarian and not authoritarian' (Laski 1925: 12). The biggest ideological inadequacy of Marxism-Leninism was in ignoring this libertarian aspect of socialism while projecting itself as an alternative to liberal democracy. In this attempt it overlooked the important historical fact that socialism arose because of the inadequacy of early liberalism to fulfil its promise of economic well being (Watkins 1976: 43). It ignored the protection afforded by liberal constitutionalism against harm 'by the coercive instruments of politics without due process and in violation of *habeas corpus'* (Sartori 1995: 103). In fact, the common point between communism and fascism, in spite of their differences, was their willingness to dispense with democracy and the labour movement (Lichtheim 1975: 286).

Socialism with its equalitarian and libertarian impulse will always play the role of a critic. It brought issues like social justice and equity into the agenda of political theorizing in general and liberal democratic theory in particular. The lessons that emerge from the entire evolution of the socialist doctrine in the twentieth century is the total rejection of what Cole called the deadening determinism of Marxism. It would no longer mean state owner-ship and control of the economy, centralized planning, distrust of market mechanisms and outright opposition to private ownership of the means of production and exchange. The meaning of social-ism is to be found in the struggle of the underprivileged and the deprived, to widen as far as possible equality of opportunity and justice for all within a civilized order of democracy and rule of law. A socialist society might not be attainable but socialism defi-nitely taught us the importance of egalitarianism, social justice and fraternity — values that no civilized human society could afford to ignore. One hundred years ago Bernstein emphasized that socialism and democracy were synonymous. He pointed out that socialism stood for a higher culture and did not symbolize merely the miseries of the working class. He categorically insisted that socialism had nothing to do with dictatorship which belonged to a lower civili-zation. He stressed that political and economic activity was an on-going one which the socialist movement had to undertake within and on behalf of the democratic system. It was not merely an end, as Lenin insisted, but both a means and an end. The challenge for contemporary socialist theory is to evolve a mechanism of general welfare and safety nets without compromising with merit, com-petitiveness, adaptability and growth in a world of quick, unprec-edented and unexpected changes and rising expectations. The political challenge is to reduce the gulf between the rulers and the ruled by accepting the foundational concept of democracy and fight against inequality be it in the name of class, gender, ethnicity or what Samir Amin called the unequal exchange between the de-veloped and the underdeveloped.

Endnotes

1. Cabet gave an idealistic description of the communist society, 'Icaria' in *Voyage en Icarie* published in 1840 under a pseudionym. He attributed inequality as the cause of social evils which could be remedied only by common ownership. He ruled out private property and monetary transactions in the ideal society. All would be obliged to work, would eat the same food, wear the same clothes and live in the same kind of dwelling. He believed in God and regarded Christianity as essential to the Christians to go back to the ideals of early Christianity in *Le Vrai Christianisme* (1846), namely the concern for the poor.

2. Among the early socialists it was Jean-Charles-Léonard Sismonde de Sismondi (1773–1842) who first launched a frontal attack on the theories of classical economists and in particular Ricardo in his *New Principles of Political Economy* (1819), *The Agriculture of Tuscany* (1802) and *Wealth* (1803). Sismondi advocated freedom of international trade and opposed monopolies and large landed estates. He favoured state intervention to guarantee the worker a minimum standard of living and social security. He demanded strict control over population growth. He defended agriculture against machine-based industrialism, attacked primogeniture and tenant farming and demanded improvements in agricultural methods. In *Studies on the Constitutions of Free Peoples* (1836) he rejected universal suffrage and complete democracy since the workers were not ready for it. He defended the rights of minorities especially that of the intellectuals and urban middle class. Sismondi was a prolific writer for he wrote *History of the Italian Republics* in 16 volumes. *History of the French* in 31 volumes, *History of the Literature of Southern Europe* in 4 volumes and *Studies in the Social Sciences* in 3 volumes. He understood socialism to mean state guarantee of fair wages, material security and human welfare.

3. Blanqui regarded communism as the final goal towards which all societies were moving. Capitalism was continually getting depleted thereby affected production and profits. He described 'capital as labour stolen and suppressed', i.e., abstracted from the producers' incomes. He also feared that the bigger capitalists would crush the smaller ones.

4. See the section on Marx in this book.

5. Social insurance was introduced in Germany in 1880s and in Britain in 1914 but a comprehensive scheme was adopted by the British Labour Government between 1945–50.

6. Its indicators were (*a*) importance to authority rather than ownership; (*b*) spread of public ownership creating a new balance between public and private sectors transcending the bourgeois characteristics of capitalism; (*c*) a significant role for science; (*d*) a change in the composition of the ruling class as consisting of heads of bureaucratic hierarchies, cabinet ministers, administrative staff and judges. The new society, economically was a service economy rather than a good producing one, reflecting a change in the occupational structure. In comparison to the total population, the low skilled workers are less than 10 per cent. The demand for those with greater education and qualifications is on the increase. The pyramidical shape of occupational distribu-

tion of the working population has given way to a diamond shaped one because of rapid expansion in educational opportunities allowing persons from the poor and deprived families to avail of higher university degrees, end of family capitalism, growth of large scale bureaucracies and increase in government (Lipset 1979: 9).

7. See the section on Marcuse in this book, for an analysis of the democratic-pluralistic view of advanced capitalism.

8. Bankim's interest in socialism did not endure long for there was a complete transformation in his views. He withdrew the book from circulation, in spite of doing well in the market, and became absorbed in the religious revivalist movement.

9. The former Prime Minister and Senior Minister of Singapore, Lee Kuan Yew also mentions in his memoirs *The Singapore Story* (1998) about the tremendous influence the Fabians in general and Laski in particular wielded. He pointed out that Laski's Marxist socialist theories profoundly influenced colonial students including himself. However, contrary to Laski's assertion that it was natural resources which held the key to a nation's prosperity. Lee pointed out that it was development of human resources and technology which played a crucial role in alleviating inequalities and eliminating absolute mass poverty.

10. The vote of the French Communist Party (PCF) declined from 20.5 per cent in 1978 to 9.8 per cent in 1986. In Finland the party registered a fall from 18.7 per cent in 1979 to 13.8 per cent in 1983. In Netherlands the decline was from 4.4 per cent in 1972 to 1.7 per cent in 1977. In Italy its share fell from 29.9 per cent in 1983 to 26 per cent in 1987. Similar trends were indicated in Austria. Belgium, Luxemburg, Denmark, Portugal, Spain and Switzerland.

2

❖ *The Precursors*

Thomas More

Thomas More's *Utopia* is often considered to be a reflection on the conflict between the ancient (or medieval) and the modern worlds. If there is general consensus on *Utopia's* central theme, noteworthy is the range of opinions concerning More's position in the controversy. Was he an 'ancient' or conservative? A modern or socialist? Or was he joyously playing with both deficient and hence absurd positions (Engeman 1982: 131).

. . . the *Utopia* remained comparatively an isolated and unimportant episode in the political philosophy of its time. It illustrated rather the dying utterance of an old ideal than an authentic voice of the age that was coming into being (Sabine 1973: 406).

More's vision of human progress was modelled on Plato's *Republic* and conceived in terms of imagining a perfect society as the best means of achieving at least its partial realization in an imperfect materialist world (Guy 1980: 11).

Human beings, even in the savage stage, dreamt of a paradise much beyond their actual and realizable existence. A tribe in Brazil, Ghirani , wandered all around Brazil in the quest of a 'land without evil'. All the ancient civilizations and religions produced wide varieties of utopias; and the Chinese, the Hindus, the Japanese and the Arabs, all portrayed ideal states and imaginary heavens. Similiarly Taoism, Theravada Buddhism and medieval Muslim treatises abound with great variety of utopian elements. However, it was equally a fact that the number and variety of utopian visions that came out of Western civilization is much more than what we find in other civilizations. As in range and variety of political theorizing Western civilization has given the lead, it is the same with regard to utopias too.

In fact, the moment the word utopia is mentioned it is Sir Thomas More's (1478–1535) classic by the same title that comes to mind. It was a two-part document written in Latin under the title *A Pamphlet truly Golden no less beneficial than enjoyable concerning the republic's best state and concerning the new Island Utopia* (1516). The word 'utopia' itself originated with More and his equally famous friend, the humanist Desiderius Erasmus (1466–1536). Before the publication of the work they referred to it as 'Nusquama' which in Latin meant nowhere. However, More's dissatisfaction led to a formation of the new word utopia combining the Greek word *ou*, which had a negative connotation with the Latin *U* and Greek noun *topos* meaning region or place. The utopian formation was called *Eutopia* which meant ideal, prosperous and perfect.

Apart from his fame of a martyr's end, More's permanent place in the history of humankind rests on this little work which he wrote when he was 38-years-old. The first English translation of the *Utopia* was by Ralph Robinson in 1551. In 1557 a collected edition of More's English works was published and in 1565–66 a collection of his Latin works was published. Besides being a successful lawyer, businessman, humanist, grammarian, poet, a man of religion, More was also a moral philosopher.

More was born in a place where the teaching of the Greek philosophers like the Stoics, the Epicureans, the Cynics, Plato (428–347 B.C.) and Aristotle (384–322 B.C.) was debated amongst a small circle of dedicated scholars. In this intellectual setting, More developed a passionate liking for Greek philosophy. What was unique in his effort was his attention to the utopian novels of the Greeks which came to him in fragments preserved in Diodorus, Siculus and in the Greek biographies recorded by Plutarch. Many scholars have drawn a parallel between Lambulus and Euhemerus and even there were suggestions that the *Utopia* was largely influenced by the revolutionary Spartan King Agis IV. However, though the Greek utopias influenced More to a very large extent yet there is no doubt about the originality and novelty of his enterprise.

More wrote at a time when the great explorations had begun and these exerted tremendous influence on his writings and perceptions. This enabled him to contrast the state of nature from the state of innocence, a point of view that one discerned in all of his writings. He was influenced by the rising spirit of rationalism and felt that learning would instill in the youth the values of piety towards God, benevolence towards men, modesty of heart and Christian humility. He gave the fear of God a more prominent place than reason and philosophy.

During More's time England was in a transition, emerging from a feudal set-up and becoming a nation of merchants. The rural economy was yielding to a money economy and state regulations of labour and industrial activities was being replaced by private enterprises. His *Utopia* captured these momentous changes. Unlike the church fathers, he felt communism was the remedy to the ills of an industrial society. The tract attacked the social evils of its times, especially in England — the misrule by the rich, oppression of the poor, diplomatic intrigue, ruinous war, excessive taxation and the cruel legal system. The latter part of the tract described an imaginary communist society on the island of utopia. It recommended a programme of democratic reform in which a republican principle of city federation dominated the aristrocratic and monarchical principles. While More echoed many of the ideas of Plato, St. Augustine of Hippo (354–430) and St. Thomas Aquinas (1224–74), he was also a precursor to Denis Diderot (1713–84), Thomas Jefferson (1743–1826) and the early socialists. The tract contained socialist ideas in its embryonic form though the major orientation is republican, democratic and bourgeois. It formed a part of More's humanistic reform and was the outcome of his experiences as a man of business, diplomat, politician and an Erasmian reformer.

Biographical Sketch

More was born in London on 7 February, 1478. His maternal grandfather, Thomas Granger became the Sheriff of London in 1503. From his paternal side most of his relatives were men of law. His father, John More, became Sergeant of Law, Judge of the Common Pleas, and Judge of the King's Bench. More attended the London School of St. Anthony. At the age of 12 his father put him into domestic service with Lord Chancellor John Morton who later became a cardinal and a leading supporter of Henry Tudor. More learnt a great deal about the world of politics from Morton and acquired under his tutelage the latter's anti-aristrocratic and humanitarian ideals. This enabled him to champion clerical reforms in the later part of his life. All these had a profound impact that was evident in his *Utopia*.

More studied Greek and other classical languages and literature at Oxford. This prepared him not only to join Erasmus and Colet in religion and reform but also enabled him to become a lawyer, a businessman and a politician. When he turned 16 he was sent to Lincoln's Inn. Here he studied law, lived with the Carthusian monks and shared their devotional life. In 1499 he completed his first business deal when he was 21. Two years later he joined the bar and practised law reluctantly.

More was elected as a member of parliament in 1504 and played a crucial part in the rejection of unreasonable sums of money demanded by Henry VII. He used his talents as a grammarian and as a lawyer to defend the interests of the middle class of merchants and landed gentry — his class. After his parliament debut, he did a lot of legal work for the most influential English capitalists, the Company of London Mercers. By this time it became clear that his interests were secular rather than spiritual.

In 1505 More married Jane Colt, daughter of an Essex country gentleman. He settled down to family life and legal business. He closed the door to priesthood and monasticism. He fathered four children. Jane died in 1511 after which More married again, this time a middle-aged widow Alice Middleton. After his first marriage, More rose rapidly in the legal profession. He represented the City of London in 1510. In the same year he began to act as a City Judge, having been appointed an Under-Sheriff of London. His literary and rhetorical skills also developed. In 1517 he entered the Council of Henry VIII, and headed a trade mission to Calais as his first assignment.

More pursued his independent scholarship and writing besides his professional life. As a grammarian, he translated Greek poems and four short plays by the Greek ironist Lucian. As a rhetorician, he wrote a declamation in reply to Lucian's *Tyrannicide*. As a poet, he wrote a few poems in English. As a historian, he was the author of an unfinished historical biography *History of King Richard III* (1513–18). This was written in both Latin and English. He also translated the biography of the fifteenth-century Italian philosopher Pico della Mirandola. As a moral and a political philosopher, he wrote the *Utopia* in 1516. In 1523 he wrote a defence of Henry VIII against Martin Luther (1483–1546).

After 1518 More became the Commissioner of Peace for Kent to make inquisition concerning matters as murders, felonies and trespasses. In 1521 he became Under-Treasurer of the Exchequer and was knighted. His daughter Margaret married William Roper. He became the Speaker of the British House of Commons in 1523. In 1524 he became the High Steward of the University of Oxford and in 1525 he was appointed the Chancellor of the Duchy of Lancaster. In 1526 he was made one of the four Counsellors — with the Bishop of Bath, the Secretary, and the Dean of the Chapel — to attend the King constantly. He was valued at court for his wit, learning and eloquence, as well as for his legal acumen and standing with the merchants of the city. In 1529 he was appointed as the Chancellor of England and was the first layman to occupy that office.

When More resigned as the Chancellor on 16 May 1532, the feeling was that there was none who was better suited for the office than him. He resigned over the 'Submission of the Clergy' which ceded veto power over ecclesiastical legislation to Henry VIII. By 1531 his career had nearly ended. In 1533 Henry VIII married Anne Bolyen and was excommunicated. On 13 April 1534, More refused to swear support to the Act of Succession and was subsequently imprisoned on 17 April. During his imprisonment in the Tower of London, he wrote *A Dialogue of Comfort against Tribulation*. On 1 July he was tried and convicted of treason. The English parliament passed the act to sentence him to death. However, the passage was not smooth for it met with stiff opposition. He was executed on 6 July 1535. He was canonized in 1935.

Philosophical Influences

The *Utopia* resembles Plato's *Republic* (380 B.C.) in many respects. Plato exerted considerable influence and the first edition contained many statements about the relationship of the island of utopia with Plato's *Republic*. The criticism of Plato's abstract philosophy was also apparent when More asserted that King Utopus had built a 'philosophical city' without taking recourse to abstract philosophy. For More virtue was moral, unlike Plato for whom it was metaphysical. Though Plato spoke of abolition of private property and private households, his views were more ascetic. His society was hierarchical and non-egalitarian.

Utopia, which originally, became an island, and the Poet Laureate of this new secluded ideal state, Auemolius declared 'I am a rival of Plato's *Republic*, perhaps even a victor over it'. A close friend of More, Peter Giles, also declared the superiority of the *Utopia* over the *Republic*. The argument in support of this assertion was that Plato's basic theoretical framework was pure abstraction whereas More, by his skillful portrayal of the actual situation of the utopia detailing its laws and resources, created an atmosphere for the reader in which the reader felt that he was in the utopia itself.

The incompleteness of Plato's *Critias* with the absence of the ideal city promised to Socrates (470–399 B.C.) gave More an opportunity, after a gap of two thousand years to think that his own work completed the Platonic dialogue. More read the *Republic* in Greek under the influence of the English humanists and throughout the rest of his life, and in crucial moments like the one before his execution, he always looked to Socrates for solace, courage and guidance. 'In the Platonic tradition, More's *Utopia* marvelously interwove rational argument, moving scenes, and history, creating an artistic balance not often achieved by latter day utopians' (Manuel and Manuel 1979: 121).

The *Utopia* was divided into two parts. The first was in the form of a dialogue between More and an imaginary traveller criticizing the prevailing social conditions in England, the enclosure movement, the penal code and the existing pattern of international relations. The second part described in detail the social, political, economic and religious conditions that would be found in the utopia. More asked his readers to imagine a fictitious world through the eyes of an imaginary sailor and Portuguese scholar, Raphael Hythloday well-versed in Greek. Hythloday left his possessions and family to join Amerigo Vespucci in search of high adventure. During their adventure they came across an island of *Utopia*, meaning nowhere. More described the tremendous advances the people of *Utopia* had achieved and contrasted it with the English way of life.

More condemned the rulers who through fair and foul means sought to enlarge their kingdoms rather than rule peacefully. He was critical of the cruel punishments meted out to the petty thieves and other poor victims of circumstances who were denied an opportunity to earn an honest living but were forced to steal. He denounced spendthrifts who performed no useful work and were served by idle and loitering servingmen. He was also against a large army and the institution of private property, and the latter in particular prevented a commonwealth from being governed justly. This was because the rich lived prosperously while the poor were miserable and forced to perform daily labour. The only solution to this unequal situation was to ensure an equal and just distribution of property and the elimination of private possessions. He also advocated equitable laws that would lessen the powers of monarchy and restrict men's excessive wealth and pride.

Description of the Utopia

The *Utopia* was 2 miles broad and shaped like a crescent. It consisted of 54 cities, some of which within 24 miles of one another and some were separated by more than a day's walk. The chief city Amaurot was in the centre. Agriculture was the mainstay of the economy of the city state. Every citizen had to spend part of his time in one of the great farm houses. The latter consisted of about 40 men and women. Most of the work would be divided between the town and country so that everyone acquired the skills in trades and farming. During harvesting time many from the city would come to help in gathering grain and other produce of the soil. The amount of agricultural products needed by the city were calculated in advance and the citizens would be allocated to farm work in proportion to these needs. No trade or work was held in high esteem.

Everyone would work for six hours and rest for eight hours. The remaining time was left to the citizen's discretion. Six hours were enough for everyone to perform useful work so that none was idle. Surplus labour would be directed towards repairing highways. There would be a monthly exchange of goods between the city and the country. Distribution of goods would be on communistic lines. Every month or so a representative of each family took the goods that his family had manufactured to one of the four great public markets situated in different parts of the city. These goods were in turn carried to warehouses. Everyone got according to his requirements. There was no need for monetary transactions. Hoarding of silver and gold was forbidden. All used common utensils. More even advocated national health, state education, religious toleration and the ordination of women.

The streets of the *Utopia* were commodious and handsome' with fair houses and gorgeous buildings which never needed to be locked and bolted. Every tenth year the houses could be changed by lots. A lot of importance was given to gardens with vineyards, fruits, flowers and herbs. Each block competed with the other for being adjudged the best garden. Though families lived in private houses, they had common dinning halls with each hall used by 30 families of 10–16 persons. These halls were presided over by the magistrates.

During meal time a trumpeter called all families to their respective halls which were provided with nurseries so that mothers could feed their infants. The provisions were ordered by block stewards from the common market at specified hours during the day. Women helped in the preparation of the meals. Every meal was preceded by an essay on good manners and virtues. Midday meals were informal. Evening meals were accompanied by music and perfumes to create an atmosphere of cheerfulness. Though all were permitted to eat in their homes, none would do it willingly for common dinning was more pleasurable than eating alone. More, refining Aristotle's dictum that man was a social animal, argued that conducive social arrangements were an essential requirement for a happy social existence.

Each citizen had a voice in the government. Every 30 families in the city elected a magistrate or *philarch*. These 10 magistrates chose an *archphilarch* and the latter would elect a prince for life. Matters of great importance were sent to the *philarch* who after consultations with the families placed it before the city. The method of choosing officials was controlled and the important ones were chosen from a very limited group. All ambassadors, priests and even the prince were chosen from a group of scholars. In the *Utopia* only a select few ruled — based on the fact that they were naturally superior — but their rule was based on the consent of the governed. Elections were through secret ballot to prevent the possibility of development of factions. Foreign travel was permitted provided one had a passport. None could leave the city without permission otherwise one was treated as a fugitive. Those who had committed serious crimes were given severe punishments like doing dirty work. Discussion of public policy outside strictly official channels was prohibited to prevent the subversion of the constitution, and if attempted, was punishable by death.

The primary goal of the *Utopia* was discipline and not liberty. None wasted time. They played and worked according to government regulations. It was an egalitarian society with none going hungry or being homeless. There was no private property for that led to inequality. An unequal society undermined the stability and prosperity of the commonwealth. Houses were open to all. There was no privacy and a citizen distinguished himself through virtuous action in service of the community. Unlike Plato's ideal state, the institution of family was retained for the desire for family was a natural instinct. Marriages were by individual choice. Unlike Plato, More did not advocate equality of sexes. The family was headed by the male and the women were confined to the private sphere. Premarital sex and adultery were punished with death. Divorce was not forbidden but it was difficult to obtain one for it required the consent of the political authorities. The aim of the *Utopia* was the maximization of happiness of the largest number of people. The contemplation of truth, the study of art and literature, the enjoyment of good health, rest, moderate eating and drinking were regarded as worthy legitimate pleasures.

> The moral purpose of a community, as More idealized it, was to produce good citizens and men of intellectual and moral freedom, to do away with idleness, to supply the physical needs of all without excessive labour, to abolish luxury and waste, to mitigate both poverty and wealth, and to minimize greed and extortion; in short, to reach its consummation in "free liberty of mind and the garnishing of the same" (Sabine 1973: 405).

All children received practical education in crafts and liberal education offered by the priests. The priests were also entrusted with enforcing manners and virtues. Good opinions that were useful for the preservation of the republic were instilled. Education was of practical nature. It involved the study of sciences, arithmetic, geometry and agriculture. Each student selected his own trade. Children with marked abilities were exempt from labour so that they could devote their time for studies. All were encouraged to spend time in profitable learning.

Conclusion

Kautsky interpreted More as a socialist living ahead of his times. Proponents of socialism found in More's writings ideals with which they empathized, namely abolition of private property, the universal obligation to work, equal rights, right to equal wealth, state management and control of production, and the removal of poverty and exploitation. The utopias written from the sixteenth to eighteenth century were propelled by the idea that inequality, oppression and injustice was contrary to God's or Nature's plan.

Though More espoused the cause of the rising middle class in England, he was extremely critical of the contemporary English society. His *Utopia* was a conception of a perfect society. The general tone of the *Utopia* was one of discipline and strict order. Though it imitated Plato's *Republic*, it contained egalitarian and republican ideals and was against monarchical and aristocratic principles. Like Plato, More also did not tell us the method of attaining his *Utopia*. It suffered from the same drawback that plagued Plato's *Republic*, namely what was desirable may not be feasible.

Toynbee (1934) compared the social structure of the imaginary human societies with the 'arrested civilizations' of Spartans, Eskimos and Nomads and also with that of social insects. The ant heap or beehive epitomized the same two striking features: the phenomena of caste and specialization, and the perfect adaptation of the society to its particular environment. He conceded that these features were true of all utopias with the singular exception of More which explained its uniqueness. Unlike Plato's ideal, there was little static social rigidity. In fact, More decided to wait for a while before publishing it for he felt the need to revise his views on peace, war, morality, marriage and clergy. He was torn between his clearcut idealistic aspirations and the practicality of achieving these good reforms.

John Milton (1608–74) rejected the utopias of More, Campanella[1] and Bacon[2] as unrealistic though More's efforts was noble and sublime. It was Erasmus who paid him the greatest tribute by calling him gentle, happy and sweet natured person. Morris regarded him as instinctively sympathetic to the communism of the medieval society and an opponent of absolute monarchy, for it robbed the peasants and helped the new men of agrarian capitalism. He was also impressed by its egalitarian abundance, abolition of parasitism and idleness, and the general obligation of all to work. More retained humane values in order to combat the twin attacks of mercantile individualism and aggressive nationalism.

If one used Popper's (1945) framework that utopian attempts like More's was dangerous, pernicious and self defeating it was because such attempts did not permit competition and opposition. A more realistic attempt would be to make life less intolerable and unjust for each generation. Such an approach would be tolerant and reasonable. An utopia was a critical reflection that emerged usually during a period of uncertainty and rapid change. While it promised reform it also projected an ideal. More's tract belonged to this utopian tradition which incidentally formed an important component of socialism. Utopianism remained alive even after the onset of the Industrial Revolution as exemplified in the works of Morris.

James Harrington

. . . James Harrington is a 17th century figure of some considerable intrinsic interest. Not only was he the only avowed Machiavellian of the time but the controversies in which he engaged, particularly with Hobbes are of enduring importance as they touch upon the nature of both power and law (Shklar 1959: 662).

The central significance of *The Commonwealth of Oceana,* and the central reason for regarding its author as a creative genius, is not that it is utopian or republican, but that it confronts the problem of defacto authority by offering, for the first time in intellectual history, an explanation of the English Civil Wars as a revolution, produced by the erosion of one political structure and the substitution of another through processes of long-term social change (Pocock 1992: xix).

He seems to have missed greatness of thought, just as he missed vigour of action; . . . beauty of character, just as he missed that many-splendoured tongue, the English prose of the seventeenth century; to have missed power while he sought wisdom. He is dull — not only because he cannot write save in shrewd pedestrian fashion, but also because he does not really understand his fellow-men . . . (The book had) details checked by considerable lack of originality, or perhaps lack of any desire to get away from the traditional institutions of England (Hearnshaw 1952: 174, 182).

Sir James Harrington (1611–77) has been called by the British as the 'greatest of our commonwealthmen' (Maitland 1911: 21). He belonged to seventeenth-century England when political theorizing was rich and diverse (Sabine 1939: 3). In *The Commonwealth of Oceana* (1656) and other political writings written in the backdrop of the English Civil War he articulated the civic humanist tradition of English republicanism that had a decisive influence on the Anglo-American political thought. An essential principle of civic humanism was that the full development of the virtuous and public spirited individual was possible only within the public realm. Harrington adapted the Machiavellian perspective and projected the *Oceana* to be the embodiment of such a realm. He was a convinced and outspoken republican though he was an aristocrat by birth and an intimate friend of Kind Charles I.

Harrington believed that in a well-governed state human beings did not trust others but instead relied on good laws and order. Since the government was the key institution of the body politic its formal establishment was central to his discussion of politics. He was prepared to offer a clean slate and start afresh with Cromwell as the sole legislator. His *Oceana* was a practical utopia planned in a manner that it could be realized. His work was partly philosophic and speculative but predominantly historical.

Harrington acknowledged that a multiple of factors was responsible for the bloody conflicts that characterized the last years of the reign of Charles I but the main cause was the uneven distribution of land ownership. He explored the relationship between political and economic power. He was unhappy with conventional explanations that the civil war was due to factional politics and the rejection of the divine rights theory. He was the only political philosopher who laid threadbare the social causes of the Puritan Revolution. (Sabine 1973: 459).

Like John Locke (1632–1704) Harrington was influenced by the discovery of America—the written constitution, unlimited extension of the elective principle, separation of the three functions of government, equal division of property among children, principle of indirect election, short tenure of power, multiplication of officers, system of checks and balances, rotation, ballot, use of petitions, popular ratification of constitutional legislation, special machinery for guarding the constitution, religious liberty, popular education—all these features are an integral part of the American constitution and political process. In fact, Jefferson and Theodore Roosevelt studied Harrington's theories and were influenced by it. The *Oceana* was an imaginary historical construct similar to Plato's allegory of the cave. It did not portray a no-place or *outopia* but, instead, was a fictionalized and instantly recognizable England in its immediate present and not too distant future. Harrington hoped to realize his ideal commonwealth in the British Isles. *Oceana* was England, Marpesia Scotland and Panopaea Ireland. 'Oceana combines the two aspects of Western utopias: the speaking picture of how the perfect commonwealth is achieved, and the argument-proofs historical, psychological, scriptural, economic, as to why the new society is best' (Manuel and Manuel 1979: 363).

Biographical Sketch

Harrington was born on 3 January 1611. His father, Sir Sapcote Harrington of Upton, Northamptonshire, and Rand, Lincolnshire, was an aristocrat. He was the eldest son and married late in life. He studied at Trinity College, Oxford in 1629 and was admitted in 1631 to Middle Temple. He did not play any significant role in the country or national politics before or after the First Civil War.

Harrington went on an extensive tour of the Continent and in particular to Netherlands and Italy in 1631, served in an English regiment in the low countries and observed at first hand the functioning of the Venetian political system. In 1639 he accompanied Charles I to Scotland. In 1647 at the suggestion of his politically active cousin and namesake Sir James Harrington he became a Gentlemen of the Bedchamber to the captive Charles I and remained with the King till his execution on 30 January 1649.

Harrington returned to a life of study and published his *The Commonwealth of Oceana* in 1656. From 1656 to 1660 he published a number of short political works to explain and elaborate on the ideas of *Oceana*. *The Prerogative of Popular Government* (1657) and *The Art of Lawgiving* (1659) was published. In *Rota: The Principles of Government* (1660) he called for a balanced democracy evolving from a popular assembly. On 28 December 1661 he was arrested on unsubstantiated charges of conspiracy. He suffered a mental and a physical collapse while in prison in Plymouth. On his release, he resumed his life in Westminster. He did not publish anything on politics but wrote an essay *The Mechanics of Nature* on his medical and philosophical implications of his condition. He died on 11 September 1677 in Westminster, London.

Institutional Arrangement

Harrington proposed that England would be divided equally into 20,000 parishes by a 1,000 surveyors. People would be taught the use of ballot. Above the parishes came the 100s, 1,000 in number, which would be grouped into 50 tribes. The deputies from the parishes would be known as overseers, constables and churchwardens. People would be classified as freemen or servants, youth and elders, horse and foot.

The constitution would be made by the Lord Archon with a council of 50 legislators with the council of Prytans below it. The latter would meet in public and keep in constant contact with popular demands and pass them on to the legislators. The constituent body would have the leisure to make decisions. The central government would consist of the senate composed of elected knights and 'the people' or the prerogative tribe composed of elected deputies and together would constitute the parliament of *Oceana*. It would be sovereign. The elected representatives would hold office for a fixed periods by rotation. The senate alone would debate while the people would decide on the broad questions that were put to them after preparation by the senate or the councils. Harrington laid tremendous stress on separation of powers. The executive power in the *Oceana* was with the four councils and these would be a council of state, a council of war, a council of trade and a council of religion. The council of state would fulfill the functions of a committee on foreign affairs, supervise provincial councils and prepare business for the senate. The council of war also would conduct the business of a foreign office but in great secrecy without communicating its proceedings to the senate. It was with the consent of the people and senate that a war could be proclaimed. The council of war would function like the supreme court. It could enforce death penalty without appeal. The council of trade would advise and instruct the senate. All councillors would receive liberal salaries. The council of religion would look after the universities and would encourage learning. All benefices would be improved up to a value of £100 a year. A directory of public worship would be prepared by separate appeals to the two universities to consult all their divines above the age of 40 and to return answers to the council.

Harrington proposed a national church without coercive powers. Its teachers or divines and their audiences would be purely voluntary. Freedom would be permitted to any congregation that was not Popish, Jewish or idolatrous. It was noteworthy that he shared the common prejudice against, and had a poor opinion of, the Jews and felt that Israel was an appropriate place for them. The officers of any congregation could appeal to the council, and the council to the senate, but none would have any coercive power.

Harrington looked to the universities as instruments of religious truth. Ministers would not meddle with politics. The parson or vicar of a parish would be carefully selected. On the death of such a parson, the congregation would send one or two elders, duly provided with a certificate from the overseers, to the vice-chancellor of one of the universities, notifying him of the vacant benefice and of its value. He would call a congregation which would choose a fit person. The latter's duties would be to pray, preach and administer the sacraments according to the directory. If unacceptable to a majority through a ballot vote at the end of the year, he would return to the university and the process of choice would start again. It was not clear as to what constituted a 'fit person' but subsequently he explained it as an order that 'restores the power of ordination to the people'. He was hopeful that his 'national religion' would satisfy the great majority of the people. He also provided for independent congregations and denied the state any coercive power in dealing with them. However, he did not attempt to define their place within the state. He was convinced that peace and tranquillity was possible only when religious controversies died down and when God was removed from the ambit of politics.

Harrington also gave a detailed idea about education which would depend on the type of government it had to support. There would be free endowed schools for the whole population controlled by the 'censors of the tribe' but staffed by the clergy. If a man had only one son, then the parents could decide on the choice of education their son would receive. If he had more than one, then the state would decide on the school and his way of life till the age of 15. Education would not stretch beyond the age of 15 except for those who have chosen one of the learned professions. Harrington also encouraged foreign travel by granting unlimited passes and recommendations for young people who wished to make the 'grand tour'. After their return they would hand in a written report on the countries they had visited and these reports, if good, were to be published at government expense. The school would aim at fostering wisdom and courage in the young.

Harrington defined government as an art whereby a civil society of men instituted and preserved upon the foundation of common right or interest. Like Plato he contended that the principles of government were two-fold—internal, or the goods of the mind, and external, or the goods of fortune. The first consisted of such virtues as wisdom, prudence, courage, and the second included wealth. He ignored the goods of the body for they were conducive to victory or empire. A legislator who could unite both the goods of the mind and the goods of fortune in one government came closest to God. He proposed a bicameral legislature which would be elected justly from the middle class and thus sought to end despotism.

Harrington distinguished between authority and power, and his focus was on the latter. Empire was based on dominion, and dominion was based upon property, real and personal. He spoke of sovereignty as the integration of power and authority. While power rested on riches, and the most important form of riches was land, authority rested on the goods of fortune, namely wisdom, prudence of courage. He asserted that political power was based on property, and the government was the upholder of law. Liberty for the state comprised of the rule of law while liberty for the human person was in the rule of reason. The distinguishing trait of a commonwealth was that it was a government by law and not by men.

Harrington, through his agrarian law, proposed equal division of land among a man's children or limiting bequest to not more than £2,000 in land. The idea that the eldest son would inherit property violated every principle of justice and was detrimental to political equality. No woman would receive more than £1,500 either by bequest or as a marriage portion. This provision was to ensure that there would be no mercenary marriages and that the physique of the race would be improved. Equal division of property was prescribed to provide stability to political power. According to Bernstein, Harrington had accurately diagnosed the class relationships prevailing in the seventeenth-century England. Tawney considered Harrington as the first English writer to find the causes of the political upheaval in social and economic changes. '*Oceana* was partly social history, partly a programme based on it' (Tawney 1941: 18).

As early as 1646 the Army demanded an agrarian law that would set an upper limit of one hundred marks a year to the property which was in the possession of any landowner. In 1647 the soldiers demanded that no duke, marquis or earl would have more than £2,000 a year, and that the income of other classes would also be proportionately limited. Harrington made this agrarian law by advocating what was already being discussed and debated. In an anonymous pamphlet published in 1649 the English Commonwealth was criticized for the uneven share that people had of land and its goods. Reiterating More, the author desired that the property of the rich be given to the poor. During the Putney debates of 1647 adult suffrage was demanded and in 1648 a group of Levellers, before Winstanley demanded communism and pleaded for equality of property.[3] While Harrington was the first to establish the link between political change and economic factors Winstanley could comprehend that political freedom without economic equality would be empty and that economic equality was possible only with the abolition of private property and wage labour. The Levellers in general accepted the sanctity of private property but they desired the extension of democracy within the boundaries of capitalist system.[4] Harrington's emphasis on property owning middle class was an advancement on the existing narrow base of franchise as evident from the fact that till the Reform Act of 1832 only 41 per cent of the British population had the right to franchise.

Harrington was convinced that property would always be used to support the army for no one would be secure of his possessions unless he had some defence. There were two ways of protecting property: by violence and by rule of law. The latter was possible only when possessions and military power were evenly divided so that none could encroach successfully upon anyone else. This would be the economic basis of the rule of law. Harrington was one of the earliest propounders of the balance of power thesis. It would be effective for once there existed a common interest in maintaining the existing property arrangement it could be defended by the pooled strength of a citizen militia. His concern was property and not economic life. 'He never spoke of rents, sales or profits, only of property. Changes in ownership of property, not economic development were his sole concern' (Shklar 1959: 670).

Both Harrington and Winstanley gave a lot of political import-ance to landed property. Though the latter advocated communal cultivation as a remedy for the ills of England he could understand the other important dimensions of economic life. He criticized the way in which tolls in market towns violently robbed the country people who used them and felt this would end with the abolition of buying and selling. He felt the need for state monopoly for for-eign trade, one of the first things the former Soviet government established after assuming power in 1917. He felt that apprentice-ship would be preserved if the wage system was abolished. He also advocated annual elections of officials in companies, univer-sal and equal education for men and women for ensuring good and orderly government (Hill 1975: 136-8). Both Harrington and Winstanley influenced Defoe's thought about property. Defoe spoke of equal rights to property and pointed to the distortions inherit-ance entailed. Property was accumulated through force and de-ception. He also believed that it was for the protection of property that the government existed and latter, with the help of religion, protected the proprietors and the rich.

Contrary to Thomas Hobbes (1588–1679) who observed that convenants were useless without the sword, Harrington argued that the hand which wielded the sword would be the militia. Since the latter was a beast with 'a great belly' which had to be con-stantly fed; and that it could not be fed without 'pastures', this ultimately involved distribution of land. Without the pasture the 'public sword' would be 'a name or mere spitfrog'. Since land was the basic form of property, its widespread distribution would en-sure a stable government. Any person controlling acres of land would, by sheer economic necessity, control the government also. Using examples from history he pointed out that popular govern-ments were less susceptible to sedition. The 'superstructure' or the government would ensure a law that ensured the widespread distribution of land. Within the superstructure none would be able to develop vested interests in any given office. Harrington along with many others like the Fifth Monarchists opposed primogeni-ture. Consequently the English Civil War was caused by the tendency to concentrate land ownership through the law of pri-mogeniture.

Harrington partly derived his observations from Aristotle that revolutions were caused by inequalities of property and partly from Niccolo Machiavelli (1469–1527) that popular governments and a powerful nobility were incompatible. Land widely distributed among the commoners would be a countervailing force against the nobility. An equal commonwealth could be achieved through the agrarian law, rotation in office, the ballot and the separation of powers.

Conclusion

Harrington's republicanism was more akin to Machiavelli's than to Plato's. He was concerned with the *de facto* sources of potential power. His focus was on the cause of collapse of the English parliamentary monarchy for which he explored the alternatives that would replace it. He accepted the Polybian argument that government had to balance the claims of one, few and many. He accepted that historic monarchy was not good and became worse in course of its existence. He accepted many of the premises of Hobbes but while the latter argued a case for absolute monarchy, Harrington defended republicanism. Implicit in the latter's scheme of government were constitutional ideas that were already familiar in the seventeenth century, namely the need for a written constitution, a legislature with powers of constitution-making and the need to distinguish between statutory and constitutional law.

Making extensive use of history, Harrington's *Oceana* was an imaginary theoretical construct. He admired ancient prudence but his theory offered a rigorous analysis of issues never dealt with before, namely the role of property, the military power of the state and the link between the two. He compared himself with William Harvey for he pointed out that he had stated the political anatomy of past constitutions that were durable in the same manner that Harvey had discovered blood circulation. His historical analysis was more profound than any English writer who preceded him (Pocock 1992: xxi). This was a utopia which had a solid historical base. Interestingly the book was dedicated to Oliver Cromwell who was seen as a mythical law-giver. It is noteworthy that a contemporary of Harrington, Winstanley too dedicated *The Law of Freedom* (1652) to Cromwell appealing to him for positive action that would eliminate wage labour and restore common property.

Harrington proposed to show it was the dissolution of the government that led to the civil war, and not vice versa.

Harrington looked at property as the foundation of the state and its distribution paralleled the forms of government of one, a few or many. In a monarchy, property was monopolized by the monarch and the rule of governance was sustained by mercenaries. In a mixed monarchy, land ownership was held by the great magnates and their retainers bore arms. In a commonwealth, property was widespread and supported by a citizen army. While earlier historians looked to Harrington as a spokesman of the gentry, recent historians like Pocock have emphasized his assimilation of civic humanism and classical republicanism associated with Machiavelli. For Harrington, a citizen militia with sufficient land would ensure its independence and not remain beholden to its superiors.

Like Plato's ideal, More's *Utopia* along with Harrington's *Oceana* influenced subsequent discourse on the subject. For instance, Immanuel Kant (1724–1804) defended the dreams of Plato, More and Harrington though he distanced himself from their futurist projections by distinguishing Millennium from Utopia. Kant supported the optimism and conscious expectations of the future but he cautioned against any scheme of a paradise on earth. For Kant, a universal civil order had to be based on greatest freedom.

Harrington's ideal was human perfection. He looked to God as pure intelligence and human beings as instruments of that intelligence's presence in the material and organic world. Freedom could be realized if the intelligence of all citizens were combined and it was for this reason that he desired a government which would be exercised by both the industrious and the leisured class. He certainly claimed that political balance resulted from the balance of property. He was the first to use the term 'superstructure', a term that become the key word in Marxist political theory.

Endnotes

1. Fra Tomaso Campanella (1568–1639) was a neo Platonist philosopher, pragmatic humanist, lyrical poet and a renaissance scholar. His *City of the Sun* (1623) inspired by Plato's *Republic* conceived of a society free of property and family. He set aside Aristotle's criticisms as irrelevant and pointed out that the manifest benefits of community far outweighed its disadvantages. The community of women was needed not only for enlisting women's services but also for the

improvement of the human race since sexual intercourse would be regulated by the state.

2. Francis Bacon's (1561–1626) *The New Atlantis* (1627) described an utopian society founded on a scientific principle based on equity and humanism, namely that man was the measure of all things.

3. Winstanley outlined his vision of an ideal in *The Law of Freedom in a Platform: or True Magistracy Restored* (1652). He believed that the great social change would not be brought about by the property-less with the spirit of God but that a rational appeal had to be made to the government of property owners. He was convinced that unless all the three institutions of the clergy, lawyers and law were destroyed, England's miseries would not end. He felt the need to alter the existing property arrangements. He also advocated the right of every person to have unrestrained access to use the earth for subsistence. True freedom was only possible if productive land was restored to its original status of a common treasury. He did not mind if unproductive property was privately owned. Bernstein regarded Winstanley as the precursor of Marx.

4. During the Puritan Revolution in England, the Leveller movement consisting of people who were economically the lower middle class and religiously the Independents and the Sects espoused limited government, freedom of conscience, religion, speech and press, the right of every person to a jury trial and to the compulsory process for obtaining witnesses, abolition of death penalty except for murder and treason, protection against self incrimination, equal protection and application of law, separation of powers and biennial parliamentary elections based on universal manhood suffrage. The Diggers, on the contrary, linked social reforms and justice with religious freedom, abolition of private property since it was the root cause of all social evils like greed, covetousness and reducing many to the position to wage earners. Its most outstanding leader was Winstanley.

3

❖ Early Socialists

Saint Simon

Thus Saint-Simon's great contribution to socialist theory lay in his insistence on the duty of society, thought of a transformed state controlled by *les producters*, to plan and organize the uses of the means of production so as to keep continually abreast of scientific discovery . . . For Saint-Simon what mattered to humanity was not politics but the production of wealth, in a sense wide enough to include the products of the arts and of science as well as of industry and agriculture (Cole 1953: 49–50).

In Saint-Simon the age of organization found its philosopher and, in his writings, its manifesto (Wolin 1960: 376).

Revolutionary, anti-Jacobin, anarchist, socialist, positivist, technocratic, proto-totalitarian, Christian-radical these are only the principal ways in which disciples and critics have tried again and again, in different context, to identify him, . . . Yet his work has continued to smile as inscrutably as Mona Lisa (Ionescu 1976: 5).

Claude-Henri de Rouvroy de Saint Simon (1760–1825) was the first socialist thinker to grasp the logic and dynamics of the new industrial system that emerged in Western Europe in the early years of the nineteenth century. He was also a pioneer in espousing a naturalistic science of society that would rationally guide in the reconstruction of society. He was the founder of an evolutionary organicist theory which found ramifications in the works of Herbert Spencer (1820–1903) and Marx. As a product of the French Enlightenment, he looked to England as the seat of comparatively free institutions and liberty, and hoped that France would emulate these.

Unlike Rousseau, he was optimistic about the benefits of technology and human progress. As a rationalist, he believed in science and knowledge and disliked the clergy. He accepted the enlightenment faith that, with help of knowledge, one could transform society. He, however, distanced himself from its critical and revolutionary perceptions for his intention was to be inventive and constructive. Saint Simon was a towering intellect whose genius was acknowledged by J.S. Mill and Durkheim. Engels praised his 'breath of view' describing him as the 'most erudite and all round mind of his time' and the second most encyclopedic mind after Hegel. He played an influential role in positivism, sociology, political economy and philosophy of history, besides socialist thought.

Saint Simon's idealistic humanitarianism, perception of social history as a progressive phenomenon and his scheme for a scientifically planned industrial economy attracted the attention of Marx and Engels. He hoped to transform nation states into great productive corporations led by scientists and technicians, anticipating Burnham's thesis of a managerial revolution. It was a socialism that bestowed immense faith in technocracy. Like Jeremy Bentham (1748–1832) and Smith, he professed a cult of efficiency and control as techniques for social improvement, but differed from them in articulating a collectivist and organic view of society. Like some of the conservatives, he emphasized on social beliefs, ceremonies and traditions but differed from them for he was enthused about material progress under the industrial society (Bowle 1954: 104). He emphasized on the general well-being, happiness and cooperation within the community. Being inherently sceptical of politics and politicians, he desired a social order that was organized by and in the interest of the producers on the principle of 'from each according to his ability to each according to his needs', a phrase that Marx borrowed.

Saint Simon was concerned with the elimination of poverty and material and cultural elevation of the proletariat. Though he believed that the proletariat suffered in the industrial society, he did not look upon them as a viable political force capable of fomenting a revolution. He never spoke of class struggle because of his inherent faith in cooperation and goodwill. He believed in a world governed by a scientific elite and was the first to identify the main features of the emergent industrial society. He also defended, like More, the right as well as the universal obligation to work. He was enthused about the potential of industrialization to create abundance, fellow feeling and harmony.

> Saint Simon was original in combining the two characteristic strains in early nineteenth century thought. On the one hand, like Kant and Hegel, he faced the problem of contemporary religion, and evolved a cult of Humanity which was further elaborated by Comte. On the other, like the Utilitarians, he faced, . . . the crisis of Industrial Revolution (Bowle 1954: 102).

Saint Simon and his disciples emphasized the importance of a harmonious order. Saint Simon, and subsequently Fourier, were attracted towards the Newtonian view of an orderly and perfectly integrated universe for both drew analogies between the laws of social attraction and the laws of universal gravitation. They emphasized on the physiological harmony of the human body and believed that this arrangement could be reproduced in society, a belief which was reiterated subsequently by Cabet.

Saint Simon, Fourier and Owen were excited about the future and wrote extensively about it. They were labelled as 'utopian socialists' by Jerome Blanqui in his *History of Political Economy* (1839), a term which Marx and Engels adopted subsequently, to grossly underplay their pioneering efforts to propogate the socialist theory. Their works were revered by their followers and decisively influenced Marx. They coined words that became part and parcel of the socialist lexicon.

There were broadly four stages in Saint Simon's works and activities. The first, between 1814–15, was the formative period when he was influenced by the developments in science and abstract humanism. During the second stage, he refused to see capitalism as a permanent and natural system and worked towards its replacement. The third stage began when his followers and disciples, on his death, elaborated and developed Saint Simonism as a socialist doctrine. It included abolition of private ownership of the means of production, distribution of goods according to labour and ability, and planned production patterned after the capitalist credit banking system. It established a nexus between exploitation and the institution of private property responsible for the crisis and anarchy within capitalism. Significantly, they saw socialism as developing within capitalism. During this period Saint Armand

Bazard (1791–1832) and Barthelemy Prosper Enfantin (1796–1864) published the *Doctrine de Saint Simon: Exposition* (1828–30). The fourth stage from 1831 represented the decline of Saint Simonism.

Biographical Sketch

Saint Simon was born on 17 October 1760 in Paris in a family of noble descent. As a boy he was bitten by a mad dog. He was known to be stubborn and self willed. In 1779 he sailed to America and fought with Lafayette in the American War of Independence. He was taken prisoner and interned by the British in Jamaica. On his release, he went to Mexico where he presented to the Spanish Viceroy his first great engineering project, a scheme for a trans-oceanic canal through Lake Nicaragua. In 1786 while in Holland he got involved in an abortive plan along with the Dutch and French to drive the British out of India. He then went to Spain with the intention of linking Madrid to the sea. During the French Revolution he renounced his title, presided at revolutionary meetings, took charge of the National Guard in his locality and invested in real estate. He was arrested in 1793 on a mistaken identity. The government was looking for Belgian bankers by the name of Simon bankers. In prison Saint Simon claimed his innocence by drafting a long memoir to the Committee of Public Safety. He survived the terror and was saved from execution.

Saint Simon made enormous wealth and used it to encourage scientists and artists, who in turn introduced him to the latest intellectual fashions. His brief marriage of 7 August 1801 to Alexandrine-Sophie Goury de Champgrand ended in a disaster for they were divorced on 24 June 1802. While touring Switzerland in 1802 he met Madame de Stael (1766–1817), the most celebrated woman of his time. He believed that their union held historical significance. He took to philosophy when Charlemagne, from whom his family claimed descent, appeared in a dream and told him that he would be a well known philosopher. Equally convinced of a special destiny and greatness, he instructed his valet of long years of service to wake him up every morning with the sentence 'Remember, Monsieur le Comte, you have great things to do'.

In *Letters from an Inhabitant of Geneva* (1803) Saint Simon proposed governance by a scientific elite, a theme that continued in his subsequent writings. He sent a copy of this book to Bonaparte who was then the First Consul. Initially he took interest in natural rather than social sciences and was enamoured, like Bentham, of technological schemes like building a canal through the Isthmus of Suez. In 1813 he wrote *Report on the Science of Man* followed by *On the Industrial System* (1821), *Industrial Catechism* (1823–4) and *The New Christianity* (1825).

Saint Simon spent his later years in poverty and distress and in 1814 he was sent to a mental asylum. In 1815 he obtained an official employment which he lost with the Restoration of the Bourbons. He died in 1825.

Science, Organization and New Religion

Saint Simon occupied a midway position between liberalism and socialism. (Lichtheim 1969: 46). His more radical followers claimed him to be a socialist but his position remained quite ambiguous for he did not regard the interests between the entrepreneurs and the working class as hostile. He was also silent on the issue of private property. He regarded producers, scientists and artists as the three useful classes and organizers of the new society. Artists meant more than the practitioners of the fine arts. They included all the *litterateurs* and *savants* in every field except that of natural science.

Saint Simon admired and was fascinated by the emerging captains of industry and regarded them as pre-eminent and independent within society and with other classes depending on them for work. The *industriel* (entrepreneurs, producers and scientists) would be entrusted with the task of directing public fortune, ensuring economy of public expenditure, restricting arbitrary power and promoting public good. They had the greatest capacity for positive administration though he was ambiguous about how they would gain political power.

> The producers are not interested in whether they are pillaged by one class or another. It is clear that the struggle must in the end become one between the whole mass of the parasites and the whole mass of the producers . . . This question must be decided as soon as it is put directly and plainly, considering the immense superiority in power of the producers over the non-producers (Saint Simon, cited in Lichtheim 1969: 48).

Unlike the other early socialists for whom association meant small groups organized in a particular occupation or place of work, Saint Simon planned for an universal association which would, unite the entire society, the European continent and ultimately the whole world. He tried to create a science of humanity and a universal philosophy of history for the purpose of advancing the lives of human beings. He understood history, like Machiavelli did, as alternating between destruction and construction. However, his approach was eurocentric for he regarded non-European societies as still in the childhood stage and hence not meriting any serious introspection. On the contrary, within Europe there were two great constructive epochs — the first was the world of classical antiquity represented by Graeco-Roman civilization and the second, the medieval world of Christendom. He also praised the period from the Reformation to the Enlightenment for the progress that Europe had made, and had the historical sense to gauge its importance.

Saint Simon had a passion for both 'universal law' and 'law and order'. He disliked chaos that entailed revolutions and wars. In this context, he was severely critical of the French Revolution for it destroyed institutions — outmoded and archaic — without creating an alternative for the want of an unifying principle. He desired a peaceful world order based on common law but he did not formulate it in a precise manner. He wanted a society organized for the welfare of the poor but distrusted democracy which he equated with the rule of the ignorant and the majority. In his anti-democratic convictions he accepted the prevailing prejudice of the educated and the propertied, something that he could not transcend in spite of being a towering intellect and a gifted individual. He wanted persons of knowledge to rule by which he meant the great industrialists. 'The industrial order, by providing a new structure for society, a new principle of authority, a new form of integration, was to be the counter-revolutionary antidote to the agitation of the masses, the de-revolutionizing remedy for the present social agony' (Saint Simon, cited in Wolin 1960: 378).

Saint Simon's ideal was a cooperative commonwealth ruled bureaucratically by an aristocracy of science. Though not a man of science he gave scientists a place of pride in the modern society. He looked to them as a floating elite with no natural class affiliation. Along with the moralists and administrative directors they averted the present moral crisis and could create a good society for the future. He was confident that if scientists occupied the top slots in social organizations conflicts, would cease and reason would prevail. He opposed violence and revolution and was confident that feudal rulers would relinquish their power and position peacefully after being convinced that their days were over. The scientists possessed unified knowledge to infuse spirit of solidarity. They could act as trustees of the poor for they had the knowledge to increase productivity, diffuse purchasing power and raise general well being. He also included the bankers as part of the great industrialists for as natural leaders of the industrious poor they provided credit and played a crucial role in industry and economic planning.

He differed from Marx in viewing bourgeoisie, scientists and proletariat alike as members of the productive working class: all are natural allies in the struggle against feudalism and cobeneficiaries of the future industrial system. In fact he saw bankers, engineers and manufacturers (under science advisement) as the best qualified revolutionary leaders of the working class coalition and hoped that, through their managerial effectiveness and wisdom, destructive class struggles would disappear (Martel 1968: 593).

Saint Simon emphasized order which was crucial to a scientific social organization with an aim to guarantee good work for all. Creativeness was the goal of a good social organization. Besides economic development, arts and moral sciences would also play a pivotal role. In the process, he stressed on the importance of education. He desired to provide universal primary schooling for all. He never spoke of rights and freedom, which was a serious omission in his political theory. Saint Simon looked to the nineteenth century as the epoch of applied natural science and believed in perfectibility of human society and progress made possible by scientific knowledge. He visualized the possibilities of creating enormous wealth through scientific use of technology unhindered by private property and its laws of inheritance. This arrangement could be transferred to the state when it became an association of workers. He desired a system in which merit alone would be recognized and rewarded, and that meant abolition of privileges that birth and inheritance gave. He also insisted that every one perform labour which would be the basis of respect within the community. He dismissed the privileges of the old world based on idleness. Each had right to property according to the services rendered. Production would be planned and organized with a gradation of authority and ranks. The directing authorities would decide the value of services rendered by each to society and the rewards they would receive. This was the best possible and desirable principle of equality. He never spoke about fundamental antagonisms between the employers and employees, for he looked upon them as a single class with common interest as against those who did not do useful work. There was no room for class and power conflicts, since the natural elite of an industrial scientific society was based on talent, intelligence and capacity which were instantly recognizable. Since organizational society was based on rule of law rather than men, slowly political rule would disappear. Administration, rather than government, would be important. 'Government would be reduced to nothing, or almost nothing. Political action would be reduced to what is necessary for establishing a hierarchy of functions in the general action of man on nature and to clearing away obstacles to useful work' (Saint-Simon, cited in Wolin 1960: 378).

The good society would be a harmonious association of individuals embodying the total needs of humankind, namely, rational-scientific, manual-administrative, and sensory-religious. Saint Simon like the Enlightenment *philosophes* believed that despite human inequality all individuals had an equal capacity for governance and holding of public office. However, he insisted that individuals were drawn by a passion for equality with others for higher status or greater wealth but also expected a satisfaction of their true social nature and immutable psychological aptitudes.

In the Saint Simonian world outlook, organic inequality among men, inequality in the social hierarchy, and difference of social function were natural and beneficent, wholly superior to the *egalite turgque* of the Jacobin revolutionaries, which was an equality of slavery beneath an omnipotent state authority. Born unequal in their faculties, men required a society in which each was allotted a function. If a man operated in a social class to which he did not naturally belong, performing functions for which he was not naturally equipped, he would be wasting his own talents and reducing the total creative potential of humanity. Among Saint Simon's last words to his favorite disciple was a definition of the quintessential goal of his doctrine and his life's work: to afford all members of society the greatest possible opportunity for the development of their faculties (Manuel and Manuel 1979: 602).

Saint Simon emphasized the maximization of production through optimum development and utilization of individual capacities for production and creation rather than consumption and distribution. He did not see the human person as all reason but a combination of rational, active and religious devoted to moral, intellectual and physical ends. These three qualities manifested themselves in artists, scientists and industrialists. Saint Simon was convinced that once individual capacities were freely exercised and utilized to the maximum, there would be no room for the exercise of power. He was also confident that men would be so charmed by the pleasures of peace of the industrial civilization that they would willingly renounce the desire for absolute power and domination. He castigated the French Revolutionaries for merely attempting to improve the governmental machinery without any effort to subordinate government to administration.

> Saint Simon was emphasizing the distinction between the exercise of power based on physical force and of direction founded on a recognition of superior capacity in the elite, between the command function and the organization of an association for the common welfare . . . . Saint Simon laid down the principle that a government was best when it governed least and most cheaply (Manuel 1997: 322–23, 324).

Saint Simon derived inspiration from Marie Jean Marquis de Condercet (1743–94) who conceived of a hegemonic role for science and supported Napoleon. He, however, went beyond Condercet, for he explicitly advised all classes to establish a scientific priesthood of the Religion of Newton as a new universal spiritual power. In that he was prophetic as the modern society subordinates technology, military and civilian activities to science. He differed from Condercet for he did not recognize equality as an ideal. He stressed the hierarchic nature of the industrial scientific society. He never made class divergences the motive force of change or conflict accepting differences as natural and desirable. While he looked to scientists and industrialists as men of special excellence, he denigrated manual labourers. He was against levelling and accepted differentiation in terms of distribution of material rewards as a feature of the new society (Giddens 1974: 25; Ionescu 1976: 28) and anticipated the contemporary arguments in favour of a just meritocracy. Saint Simon was the originator of the idea of European integration. He believed that every nation state would merge within a European confederative association for a prosperous economy needed larger territorial units. Within the nation state the central government would diminish for it would not be able to provide order amidst the new demands of the corporate world which would demand a decentralized administrative state. There would be two central institutions — European, and deliberative and administrative. The advent of the industrial-technological society with its distinctive functional specialization would accelerate internationalization which would eventually lead to the disappearance of the nation state. Political parties would eventually be subordinated to corporate organizations. Central to the industrial technological society was a plan which would embrace all the activities of the society with the aim of ensuring justice and happiness. It would epitomize scientific rationality. The national legislative assemblies were subordinated to an European Parliament which would be multi-cameral. The first chamber was one of invention, consisting of technicians and artists with the responsibility to prepare yearly plans of public works. The second was one of examination or scrutiny consisting of 300 members, scientists and experts. It would examine the projects of the other chamber and prepared a programme of general public education. The third was the executive chamber formed by other two chambers.

Saint Simon hoped to formulate a new religion compatible with Baconian science. He emphasized on the brotherhood of man, the need to adapt religion to new conditions and, above all, to mitigate the problems of people. He criticized the Catholics and Protestants and insisted that moral and spiritual progress could be achieved only with improvement in material conditions. He impressed upon the need for new Christianity to abolish both poverty and war. He castigated the Catholics for being heretics obsessed with theology and oblivious of technological progress. Regarding Protestants he attacked Luther for neglecting men's happiness on earth. Since modern society had the means to abolish poverty, religion no longer had to acquiesce with it. All along, Saint Simon was passionately committed to improving people's lives even though he was not a democrat or a levelling socialist (Bowle 1954: 113). He was confident that technological progress would transform Christendom.

Saint Simonism

After Saint Simon's death in 1825, Saint Simonism flourished as a coherently organized school till 1833 when it was declared illegal. Under the Restoration Monarchy (1830) it was not successful, but after the July Revolution of 1830 with its identification with the republican cause, its influence grew and its following was estimated around 40,000. Its support can be gauged by the fact that even after it was banned in 1833, it continued to have widespread influence till 1848, the year of revolutions in Europe.

The Saint Simonian movement was efficiently organized in colleges, churches and missions both in France and abroad. It was primarily a movement of the intellectuals with very little or no participation of the working class. Its target was the educated which in the nineteenth century meant people who did not belong to the working class. The terminologies they used were not only novel but difficult to understand. Even many of their ideals looked queer and eccentric. Saint Simon himself was regarded as a bizarre and an eccentric thinker.

With their commitment to Saint Simon's concept of the industrial class of the productive and not the parasitic rich, the movement attempted to unite all the productive people in society. With their emphasis on industrial development and government-sponsored public works, their appeal was restricted to the middle class. By espousing the idea of the liberating role of technology, the Saint Simonians attracted engineers, scientists, technical and businessmen to their movement. The expansion of industry in that period vindicated Saint Simon's ideas.

Saint Simonians appealed to the young and, after 1830, to the working class. The increase in the numbers of the working class made them appreciate their aspirations and understand the process of revolutionary changes. But this was not enough to perpetuate the movement on religion and moral questions. Saint Simonians' rejection of Christianity and call for a new religion of humanity called 'New Christianity' with a new moral code aimed at public service was extremely liberal and radical, alienating them from the mass of people. Their support and defence of authoritarianism ignoring basic human liberties repelled many as well.

Saint Simonians were responsible for the economic expansion of the Second Empire, particularly with regard to development of banks and railways. Enfantin conceived of a society for planning the Suez Canal. Both Bazard and Enfantin called for the establishment of a new Church and, in keeping with their idea of sexual equality, stressed the need for a 'mother' as well as a 'father' to symbolize the union of intellect and feeling, spirit and body. In 1858 Enfantin published *La Science de l' homme* giving a detailed exposition of Saint Simon's science and in 1861 *La Vive eternelle* outlining Saint Simonian religion. The brothers, Emile and Issac Pereire, promoted the first French railway from Paris to Saint-Germain, established the first industrial investment bank in France, the credit mobilizer, and named the first ships of the *Compagnie generale Transatlantique* after Saint Simon and his disciples.

> In the hands of some of his more zealous followers, Saint Simon's doctrines were made to seem ludicrous. Yet his own insight was considerable, and it was the Saint-Simonians' more diffuse (but no less intense) belief in Marxism which gave that doctrine its command over so large a part of the world (Bell 1968: 507).

Saint Simonians were believers in technocracy and order which meant scientific, industrial and economic organization devoid of military and police power. They rejected parliamentary democracy and the ballot box. They believed that France would lead the whole word towards the new order. Though they admired England for being a first rate industrial power, they rejected *laissez faireism* and were anguished by the plight of the English workers. Saint Simonians, like their master, contributed to the history of socialism the idea of planned economy to ensure full employment, wide dispersal of purchasing power and rewards commensurate with the services rendered.

Women and Family

Saint Simon did not say much about women and the gender question but his followers regarded the nuclear family as the breeding ground of selfishness leading to social dissensions. Instead of small families, they proposed large happy ones that would love and share. Their views on sexual equality and women's suffrage inspired J.S. Mill, and the latter acknowledged that it was under their influence that he began to think in terms of stages of progress. The first stage was when women were held as slaves. During the second stage, women secured a more permanent hold over their masters through legal marriage but that represented another kind of slavery. It was only when men and women became equal partners that a society was truly civilized.

Enfantin called women to define appropriately the relationship between the sexes in the new social order. He envisioned an equal but different role for each sex and, at a first glance, it seemed that he imbibed the prejudices of his times. However, since he and other Saint Simonians cherished emotion over reason, the new society would be one where love and sentiments would triumph and, in that sense, women could also be become priests and artists. They supported and justified women's full participation in all public functions.

Enfantin also stressed the need for a new sexual morality in the new society though he assured his followers that he was not endorsing unregulated licence. However, Bazard and Leroux remained unconvinced of these assurances. Enfantin also spoke of the need to destroy the existing social hierarchy in which women were considered and treated as slaves.

Saint Simonians contributed to women's cause in three ways which helped in the crystallization of an independent women's movement. They instilled greater confidence in them, educated them for political experience and provided a theoretical justification for their activism (Moses 1982: 265). As early as 1832 Saint Simonian women pleaded for women's education, employment and reform of family laws in civil matters and this in itself was a momentous development considering they were pioneers. It was 16 years later that the Seneca Falls Declaration of Women's Rights was announced in 1848 in the United States and 37 years that Mill's *The Subjection* was published.

Marx and the Early Socialists

Marx and the other Marxists were critical of early socialists though they showered lavish praise on them at the same time. Engels acknowledged the indebtedness of German theoretical socialism to the works of Saint Simon, Owen and Fourier for, despite their utopianism and fantasies, they indicated trends and highlighted matters which made it easy for later socialists to prove the same scientifically. In the *Communist Manifesto* (1848) Marx and Engels praised the early socialists for attacking every single basis of the existing order, and by doing so they provided the raw materials for the upliftment and education of the working class. The early socialists anticipated the emerging new social order. While Saint Simon laid threadbare the dynamics of the industrial society, Owen realized that industrialization was here to stay and there was no question of returning to the pre-industrial past. Within the existing industrial society they tried to mitigate mass miseries, redress exploitation and alleviate poverty. Saint Simon's contributions were the following: (*a*) realization of the possibility of boundless expansion of science and technology, (*b*) understanding that the inexhaustible natural resources of the globe could be tapped and utilized and (*c*) acceptance that the full flowering of human capacities leading to perfection and elimination of conflict was possible in the industrial society. Saint Simon looked to antagonism as the primary evil of society and love. For Owen, it was charity and for Fourier it was the fulfillment of passions. Marx was indebted to Saint Simon for his theory of the separation of civil society from the state and, later on, of government from administration (Ionescu 1976: 24). Marx praised Owen for his emphasis on virtues of cooperation based on social organization of labour within the factory system. Fourier was complimented for his emphasis on the diverse needs of the community and for stressing the importance of reciprocity within the community.

There were four differences between Marx and Saint Simon. First, while Saint Simon analyzed industrial society, Marx dissected capitalist society. Second, the former was concerned with the post-revolutionary society while the latter was concerned with the historical inevitability of the socialist revolution. Third, Saint Simon, unlike Proudhon, believed that political organization was necessary in a society but that organization could not be centralized. On this point he differed from Marx's transitional state, the dictatorship of the proletariat. He considered class struggle as necessary but he did not foresee the conflict between the workers and the capitalists as inevitable. He rejected the idea of a classless society as meaningless, for society would always need an educated elite, and considered the industrialists and the scientists as the natural leaders of the workers. He held that society would always consist of the poor, rich and the *industriel*. On this issue Saint Simon seemed more realistic than Marx who, in comparison, was utopian and romantic. Both believed in transformation of human nature as being a prerequisite for a transformation in society but Marx tried to achieve in through reason whereas Saint Simon sought to achieve it through faith (Ionescu 1976: 26–7).

In spite of the lavish praise for the early socialists, Marx and Engels were critical of them for being anti-scientific and anti-revolutionary. Their greatest failure was their inability to recognize the revolutionary potential of the working class. Unlike the classical economists, Saint Simon approached the economic system from the perspective of the producer rather than the consumer since he regarded production as a means to ensure well being, an idea revived by Sorel subsequently[1]. The industrial society would be a planned one since his conception of society was organic and hierarchical.

Conclusion

Saint Simon comprehended the new social forces that were unleashed by the political revolution and scientific advancements and insisted on the need for a planned organization and control of production for common interest. In his understanding:

> ... organization connoted far more than a simple condition of social harmony and political stability. Organization promised the creation of a new structure of power, a functioning whole superior to the sum of the tiny physical, intellectual and moral contributions of the parts (Wolin 1960: 377).

Saint Simon taught the importance of organization as having a decisive power and importance over all things, a lesson that both

socialists and capitalists learnt. He was the first to see the importance of economic organization in the affairs of the modern society
and affirmed the crucial role economics played in social evolution.
He was also the first to contemplate a new encyclopedia which
assembled together all the new advancements in science. He admired the medieval separation of temporal and spiritual powers
because that led to the establishment of an independent, international and pre-eminent body of the educational elite.

Saint Simon opposed vague and abstract principles and thought
it appropriate that society ought to be guided by scientific knowledge and reason. Social issues would be understood by the method
of positive or natural science. His disciples, the Saint Simonians,
consisting of some of the most well known personalities of contemporary France, testified his tremendous attraction to those who
followed his scientific method.

Saint Simon along with Marx was credited by Durkheim for realizing that the contemporary reality was distinctly different from
the earlier traditional social orders though their prescriptions of a
new order were grossly different. Saint Simon did not look at the
ugly side of industrial capitalism, though his analysis foresaw four
developments that are clearly visible today. First is the role of corporate bodies to make and impose their decisions on society. The
second is the hierarchy based on science and exercise of knowledge. Third is the conception of partnership among the different
European states. Fourth is the inadequacy of nation state to cope
with forces of internationalism unleashed by industrial and technocratic forces (Ionescu 1976: 53–55).

Saint Simon was important for comprehending both early socialism and positivism. 'His is the first technocratic theory related
to the new industrialism' (Curtis 1962b: 129). However, his socialism was authoritarian and hierarchical because of his emphasis on
order and regulation. He desired a new social order that recognized and rewarded talent, expertise, competence and scientific
knowledge. It would be a just meritocracy in which scientists, artists, bankers and industrialists occupied a pride of place. Since they
made unparalleled contributions to the progress and development
of the modern industrial society, their loss was tantamount to an
irrevocable loss for the nation. In comparison, the aristocrats, bureaucrats and civil servants who controlled and dominated were
harmful because they spent their wealth in a way which was of no

direct use to science, fine arts and professions. Apart from leading a very adventurous life, Saint Simon's prophecies and proposals of building a Panama Canal, like Bentham, and European integration proved his extraordinary capacity to grasp the momentous changes that were possible due to technological revolution. He could clearly see that technology would drastically change society and looked to skilled people as the key to the glory, civilizational advancement and prosperity of a nation for without them 'the nation would become a lifeless corpse' (Curtis 1992b: 138).

Saint Simon also emphasized on solving social problems with the help of positive or natural science. Positivism dismissed the search for final causes and believed that, through scientific observation and testing, knowledge could be obtained. Based on this information laws of science and laws of social sciences could be formulated and order established. Action could be taken on the basis of accuracy in prediction through an understanding of regular laws. Positivism was elaborate and refined by Auguste Comte (1798–1857) the most famous disciple of Saint Simon and at one time his secretary.

Saint Simon would remain a reference point in not only comprehending the nature of early socialism and the part his theories played in encouraging scientific explorations, inventions and discoveries, but also in understanding the entire course of subsequent French political theorizing, mainly that of Comte and Durkheim. He was brilliant to comprehend the revolutionary role of technology but his projects looked mechanical for he failed to dissect the process of politics and its relative autonomy, a necessity even in a highly organized technocratic society. He overlooked the importance of politics for, as Lasswell rightly observed, it was politics that decided 'who gets what, when and how'. A technological society needed more popular control and, in failing to do so, his theory, just like Burke's theory of representation, is obsolete today.

Robert Owen

Owen was one of the "new men" who transformed Britain in the age of industrial revolution. That, unlike most of his fellow employers, he was an instinctive humanist doubtless accounts for his gradual conversion to a form of socialism. In other respects he represented the industrial middle class of his age, not least in his boundless optimism, his faith in science and his conviction that machinery, from being a curse, could be turned into a blessing for mankind (Lichtheim 1969: 114–15).

His (Owen) life of untiring devotion and sacrifice proved one of the great sources of inspiration to those who followed later in the socialist, cooperative and trade union movements, as well as those who worked in behalf of child training, or labour legislations, of prison reforms and of similar causes (Laidler 1927: 122).

Owen has been the founder of British socialism, and of British Co-operation. He shares with the elder Sir Robert Peel the credit of having started the movement for factory reform. He holds an assured place in the history of educational experiment. He was the founder of the "Rationalist" movement, and occupies an important position in the chain of ethical and secularist activities. And with all this he combined the not easily reconcilable roles of a great, self-made employer and an outstanding leader and inspirer of the Trade Union movement. To be sure, he did not do quite all these things at one and the same time; but to have crowded them all into one lifetime, however long, is remarkable enough (Cole 1953: 86).

Robert Owen (1771–1858) was justifiability hailed as the father of British socialism. His sympathies and commitment to socialism stemmed from his experiences as an industrialist who had direct contact with the workers. He lived in England that was the most industrialized and mechanized country at that time, which was why he criticized and assessed the consequences from an ethical point of view, a perspective that Fourier subsequently adopted. The ethical perspective was rooted in religious humanitarianism. 'The real originality that gives value to Owen's work is that he begins from an acceptance of the vastly increased power which the Industrial Revolution had brought, and sees in just this increase of power the opportunity for the new moral world' (Williams 1961: 43). It was this remarkable insight that was the starting point of Marx's dialectical assessment of capitalism, the immense possibilities amidst squalor and hunger.

There was an awareness arising out of the impact of industrialization, a sense of misuse, human degradation and waste. For redressing this imbalance the need and the right of the community to interfere and change the existing situation drastically to bring about a better and more humane world was emphasized. The very low opinion of traders and manufacturers was reflected in the writings of Charles Dickens (1812–70). In the nineteenth century, this rejection of existing commercial society led to the idealization and glorification of the pre-industrial period as epitomized in the writings of Cabet, Fourier and Morris. Life had to be spent in enjoyable work which was not possible in the prevalent industrial society since labour turned men into machines, destroying their individuality. It enslaved man to 'profit-grinding masters'. It was only Owen who accepted the contemporary industrialized society and tried to alleviate its consequences. He realized that there was no going back nor was it possible to recreate the past.

Owen's concept was outlined in A *New View of Society* (1813). Its original title was *Essays on the Principle of the Formation of the Human Character* (1813–15). Its gist was that social problem was a moral one for it depended on those in authority to decide what kind of world they intended to make for the others to live in. His disappointment with existing government led him to explore unconventional arrangements and worker's emancipation. He was also an educational reformer who had immense faith in moulding and shaping human lives beyond the localism of its existence.

Owen's goal was 'enhancement of life — a sober, practical, humanism. The basis will be physical well being; sobriety, order, recreation, good sense. The ideal is thoroughly civilian' (Bowle 1954: 145). He disliked militarism and change desired to achieve through non-revolutionary constitutional mechanism, an aspect that characterized the dominant strand of British socialist thought. Like Bentham, he believed that all segments of society — rich, poor, rulers and ruled ought to have one interest, i.e., the rationality of all humankind. He hoped that correct knowledge would destroy anger and hatred and reconstruct society without violence. Owen dismissed the past and was confident that the future would be one of rationality. He was optimistic that through right knowledge and policies governments would be able to abolish poverty, misery and unemployment for enough could be produced for everyone's subsistence and enjoyment. He also believed that forces of religious hatred and nationalism would go into oblivion. Like Saint Simon he held that industrialization offered a choice to the governments: either to neglect the poor and deprived, keep them in ignorance, squalor and brutality and face the consequences of unemployment and revolution, or create a society through education and wider purchasing power for all to secure their well being and happiness. He was convinced that both the goals could be attained. Education would make people benevolent and charitable. Through a communitarian plan, scientific production would increase unprecedented productivity, wealth and prosperity. Owen stated two propositions which have retained their relevance even today. First, that change in the mode of production affected relationships among producers and second, that the Industrial Revolution was an important change which created a new kind of human being (Williams 1961: 44). He objected to change because the relationship between the employer and the employee centred around the gains they could secure from one another. He offered a choice between his new moral world and anarchy. The key thing was social engineering, by which he meant moulding people and society with proper means to the right extent by men in important responsible positions.

Owen was a successful self-made industrialist, philanthropist and a versatile untiring social reformer. From philanthropy he moved to communitarian ideas and played a pivotal role in cooperative movements and trade unionism in England. His philosophical outlook was materialistic for he believed that the individual's character could be improved by external circumstances, namely, by the way he lived and worked. To that effect he favoured communal ownership of the means of production and the development of a classless and efficient society based on cooperation, social justice, equality and universal civic education rather than competition and elitism. The Marxists, and in particular Engels, were attracted by Owen's philanthropic work and pioneering reforms though they were critical of his rejection of class struggle and revolutionary method of transforming society. They regarded Owenism as too slow and unworkable.

Biographical Sketch

Owen was born in 1771 in Newton, Montgomeryshire in Central Wales. He was the son of a Welsh saddler and ironmonger with very little formal education. He left school and went to work at the age of nine. However, he became one of the best public speakers and writers in English. Among the early socialists, his thoughts truly represented a continuation of the themes of enlightenment, namely belief in progress and rationality.

When Owen was eighteen, after being an apprentice in a drapers' shop, he borrowed some money and set up a small cotton spinning

mill of his own in Manchester. The following year he was appointed
the manager of a large mill employing some 500 workers. In 1800,
already a wealthy person with a widespread reputation, he became manager and part-owner of the famous Lanark Cotton Mills,
the largest in Scotland. He married the daughter of David Dale,
the man from whom the mills were bought. Here he tried out his
ideas on management and claimed them to be practical vindication of his theory. From 1815 to 1820 it was referred to as the Mecca
of reformers. He proposed the creation of communities to end unemployment. He also went to the US and established a model community called New Harmony in Indiana. This was started in 1821
and ended in 1829.

Owen returned to England in 1829 and got involved in the nascent trade union and co-operative movement. He also committed
himself to a strong ethical sectarianism and espoused the cause of
socialism. He was the main organizer of the National Equitable
Labour Exchange, which was founded in 1832, and the Grand
National Consolidated Trades Union founded in 1834. His disciples
founded the Rochdale Pioneers' Co-operative Society in 1844. His
last experiment in community-making, Queenswood, ended in
1845.

Among Owen's other writings were *Essays on the Formation of
Character, Social System* (1821), *The Book of the New Moral World* (1836–
44) and *The Future of the Human Race* (1853). Pamphlets written by
him between 1815–20 included *Observations on the Effect of the Manufacturing System, Report on the Poor, Memorial to the Allied Power,
Address to the Workmen and Report to the County of Lanark*.

Owen was militantly opposed to the clergy but he was not an
atheist nor a materialist. He believed, like Rammohun Roy, in the
principles and practices of rational religion for he acknowledged
the existence of a single creative force. His faith in the moral goodness of all human beings was affirmed because he looked to them
as God's creatures with a divine element in them. He died in 1858.

Human Nature: Owen's View

Owen had an optimistic view of human nature, regarding it as tremendously malleable and capable of infinite changes and improvements. He looked to happiness as the primary object of human
existence and an ideal social organization, but this would not be

individualistic. It would be collective for everyone to enjoy. As a rationalist, he believed unhappiness was due to error.

Owen believed in one master idea that human character was determined by circumstances and environment and had nothing to do with the individual. Evil conditions led to evil persons while good conditions produced good people. The existing society was full of selfishness, ignorance, vice, hypocrisy, hatred and enmity. A new world proceeded on the assumption that an individual's character was made for him and not by him. An acceptance of this cardinal truth would lay the foundations for change in environment that made good characters.

> . . . any general character, from the best to the worst, from the most ignorant to the most enlightened, may be given to any community, even to the world at large, by the application of proper means; which means are to a large extent at the command and under the control of those who have influence in the affairs of men (Owen, cited in Laidler 1927: 110).

Owen believed that education enabled human beings to lead a better life. Education had to be universal, compulsory and moral, inculcating values of brotherhood, hard work, tolerance and goodwill. Good environment was ensured through good education and by abundant supply of wealth with none living in abject poverty.

Labour Welfare Measures

Owen was categorical that an ideal society could be attained if it guaranteed full employment. For this purpose a labour bureau would be provided to ensure perpetual employment of real national utility in which all who applied would be immediately employed. Through continuous employment some of the bad habits that circumstances instilled could be eliminated. On this point Owen's ideas coincided with that of Voltaire who supported gainful employment on the grounds that it took care of boredom, poverty and need. But Owen's novelty was his plea for full employment, which was later to be advocated by Keynes.

Owen also believed that the basis of labour was land which must be individually cultivated, for that would keep most labourers adequately employed. Every agrarian community would have 800–1,200 persons occupying a village with 600–800 acres of land. Each worker would have access to food and the whole population would be agriculture-based with manufacturing industries as appendages. Food, clothing and education would be provided and the community would reside in one large square. Each would be well-dressed, well-trained, well-educated and well-informed with the most benevolent attitudes and values. Good hygienic environment would change human mentality.

Owen desired changes in property relations. He wanted to eradicate evils like ignorance and enmity, which he hoped could be achieved through legislative policies, education and private action. In 1813–14 he drew attention of his fellow manufactures to the greater productivity of clean, well-kept and well-oiled machinery. He then added that: 'If, then, due care as to the state of your inanimate machines can produce such beneficial results, what may not be expected if you devote equal attention to your vital machines, which are far more wonderfully constructed?' (Owen, cited in Laidler 1927: 111).

From 1815 to 1818 Owen campaigned and concentrated his energies to alleviate the worst and miserable consequences of the factory system. In 1815 he organized a conference of employers in Glasgow to protest against the heavy import duties on cotton and to explore the possibilities of improving the conditions of labour. He regarded cotton trade as more injurious than slavery in the American colonies but his plea for ending cotton trade was unsuccessful.

Owen also pleaded by writing extensively and placing before the British Parliament petitions for lowering the working hours in the factories to twelve in a day, which would include a lunch break for one-and-half hour. He also demanded prohibition of employing children below 10 and to limit the workday of those less than 12-years-old to 6 hours a day. He proposed the establishment of schools for reading, writing and arithmetic. Many of these demands were incorporated by Sir Robert Peel in a bill which was eventually passed in 1819.[2] However the legislation watered down many of his demands and had meagre effect on labour conditions. Owen dismissed it as useless for it did not provide for a mechanism of inspection to ensure that its provisions were implemented.

Cooperative Ideal

Owen proposed common ownership and cooperatives for managing the crises resulting from over production. He agreed that mechanization led to an increase in production but unless consumption kept pace, unemployment and industrial crises could not be averted. This meant that social welfare rather than private profit had to be the goal of industry. He was convinced that the alternative to capitalism and private enterprises was common ownership. A beginning could be made by uniting the unemployed in villages spread over 1,000 to 1,500 acres of land. It could accommodate 500 to 2,000 who combined farming with manufacturing. They would live in large buildings (quadrangles) built in form of a square situated in the centre of each community. It would contain common dormitories, dining rooms, libraries, reading rooms, schools, gardens, recreation centres and playgrounds. Each family would have a separate apartment. It would take care of children up to 3-years-old, after which they would be handed over to the community to be educated. The parents would be able to see their children only during lunch time and other intervals.

Owen desired that all except children would be engaged in productive work and each community would be supervised by a qualified technician. The communities would be established by individuals, parishes, counties or the state. These would be self-contained, independent economic units having the advantages of both the city and the country. They would be technically efficient, economical in living, educative and distributive, and superior to the then existing industrial communities. Though they would be independent they would not be isolated. Both poverty and unemployment would be eliminated and all would work in a spirit of cooperation and brotherhood.

In 1819 Owen campaigned in London to raise money for his experiments but did not succeed much. He appealed to the labourers to put an end to their ignorance and poverty, and offered his assistance, but the workers were more keen on parliamentary reforms and ignored his appeal. He ran for parliament twice but was defeated. In 1820 the county of Lanark asked for his recommendations on remedying unemployment. In his report he reiterated his views on communes and cooperatives. The remedy was in labour currency which meant adopting human labour as the standard of value. A certain quantity of labour constituted a unit of value and those performing labour would obtain a paper note signifying the units of value they had produced. With this they could buy other goods costing similar amounts of labour.

Owen in the *Social System* took up a complete communist position eliminating the institution of private property altogether for that would promote overall happiness of all individuals. Anxious to realize his ideals in practice, he purchased the Rappist community at Harmony, Indiana in the United States, consisting of 30,000 acres of land for £30,000 and called it 'New Harmony'. The experiment failed after three years, impoverishing Owen. Another similar experiment was started in Orbiston in Glasgow in 1825 but that too failed.

Owen returned to England and resumed his fight for a system of labour exchange as a means of alleviating the intolerable conditions in England in the 1830s. The producers would take their goods to these exchanges and would receive in return vouchers or labour notes stating the amount of labour time in the form of commodities that they had left on deposit. In return for these vouchers, they could obtain at any time goods valued at a like amount of labour time. The labour bureau would ask a small commission for overhead expenses but there would be no exploiting middlemen. He also demanded the establishment of labour exchange banks in connection with these exchanges.

Owen also conceived of the idea of combining trade unions and cooperative societies into one single organization with the aim of transforming them in a communistic sense so as to place the whole country on a cooperative basis. He envisaged cooperative societies consisting of trade unions which exchanged their goods through labour exchanges. A general congress would replace the parliament and would sit in London to conduct the business of the country. Such a plan would be accomplished without violence and choas.

Women and Family

Owen's *On Marriages of the Priesthood of the Old Immoral World* (1835), though not a feminist tract, was singularly critical of the injustice, cruelty and misery of the women within the contemporary state of marriage. He felt that such a system harmed not only women in particular but also men and children, society and human nature in general. Pleading for justice to women's cause, he demanded the elimination of all forms of oppression that made cooperative life impossible. He viewed marriage as an artificial institution buttressed by religion imposing bondage, self-denial, self-restraint, delusion and mutual ignorance on the couple. It nurtured all kinds of evils and miseries. These vices were not merely confined to the private sphere but also percolated into the public realm. All these worked against the exercise of reason.

To the early socialists, liberalism was inadequate in relieving the daily miseries of women and the working class for it secured and guaranteed only formal legal rights without coalescing it with social and economic rights. They were critical of capitalism because of its competitive ethic which encouraged selfishness. It undermined voluntarism, benevolence and cooperation, virtues that they desired in a socialist system. The early socialists stressed on the need to restructure the whole social and economic order and looked to emancipation of women as crucial to the realization of a free and an equal society.

It was the group of individuals collectively and pejoratively described by Marx and Engels as the "utopian socialists" who did most to seal the bond between socialism and feminism. Their treatment of the problem continued to be influential throughout the century. All Marxist writing on the family and the position of women, including work by Engels as well as Bebel, reveals a substantial debt to the early socialists, especially Fourier (Donald 1988: v).

The early socialists attacked marriage because it denied civil rights to women and was a source of self-degradation. They contended that women were treated as commodities in the marriage market, reducing their position to that of a prostitute. This naked truth was concealed in terms of affection, compassion and love glorified as purely womanly qualities. Hence the problem was not economic but moral, for the values, marriage and nuclear family inculcated had its effects in the public sphere.

The early socialists desired replacement of the competitive and contractual basis to relationships — both societal and marital — with one based on mutual love, solidarity and compassion, the basis of a truly honest and enlightened rational society. They dismissed marriage as an artificial institution supported by the Church and the state. Misery, boredom, deception, cruelty and adultery were due to love being confined in rigid structures and norms which eventually permeated and corrupted society as a whole. They defended voluntary, open and reciprocal relationships which could be realized if the family, like capitalism and religion, was abolished. Here they differed from both Mary Wollstonecraft (1759–97) and J.S. Mill (1806–73) who advocated a reform of family life basing it on equality, individuality, independence, freedom, reason and self worth of the partners.

Like Plato, they criticized the family on both moral and economic grounds. They dismissed household work as inefficient and monotonous, and recommended collectivization of domestic work and public responsibility for child-rearing. This change, they hoped, would elevate domestic work to a higher status undermining the sexual division of labour and its unpleasant consequences like drudgery, repetitiveness and boredom. They suggested collective responsibility for domestic chores and child-rearing. They were confident that private families would cease to exist with the abolition of private property and inheritance. However, the family would continue for the fulfillment of emotional and biological needs of the individuals. They recommended training of children by specialists rather than parents, for the latter made bad teachers. Women would have the choice of pursuing their traditional responsibilities or take up productive work, but in both the cases they would be economically and emotionally independent of their husbands. They would enjoy greater freedom for self-development and a constructive role in public life.

Owen regarded the nuclear family as wasteful because it was labour-intensive. It was anti-social and harmful because parents passed off their ignorance, prejudices and selfishness to their children without any introspection or scrutiny of their own beliefs. Families competed with one another and fettered their interests, thereby injecting into the social stream values like ego, meanness, hostility and self centredness. A child remained ignorant of the skills and qualities which were needed to sustain community life, which was why he demanded common rearing and education of children. He preferred the 'great family of mankind' to kinship values or private families. Nuclear families encouraged and promoted inequality which was detrimental to the larger interests of society, for wealth married wealth and poor families were further pushed towards poverty, reinforcing class stratification.

Owen was confident that general promiscuity within the socialist society because of the abolition of marriage and private families would automatically lead to the development and reinforcement of the bond of natural affection and chastity. It would lead to spontaneity and harmony. Such relationships would not be based on lust. Both adultery and prostitution would become unattractive, making room for permanent and monogamous unions. In some occasions he even regarded marriage as the cause of fundamental social decay. In many places, Owen saw marriage along with religion and private property as the irrational trinity contributing to the oppression and exploitation of the individuals. He was hopeful that if one was destroyed, the others would cease to exist. He looked to the emancipation of women as a part of the holistic societal change. Common to all the three aforesaid institutions of oppression was the fact that they generated vice, antagonism and ignorance. Each reinforced the other. Religion supported a single family unity, which in turn taught selfishness that sustained competitive spirit.

Owen influenced and was influenced by William Thompson (1785–1833).[3] The former's idea of egalitarian communities and equal distribution of wealth found its place in Thompson's conception of an ideal society. In turn, Thompson made Owen understand the discrimination women faced in the 'old world'. Owen, like Thompson, defended sexual equality on the grounds that women were morally superior for they were inherently compassionate and loving. They were degraded under the present economic and marital arrangement. Owen was confident that with the emancipation of women, society and humanity would be regenerated. Interestingly, Owen like Gandhi perceived women to be inherently peaceful, tolerant and non-violent, which was why they according to Gandhi made the best soldiers in a non-violent *satyagraha*.

Together, the ideas of Owen and Thompson formed the basis for the London Cooperative Society which was founded in 1824 with the idea of advocating a 'new social science'. It opened up a trading store and, with the help of Thompson, drafted the articles for an 'Association of Mutual Cooperation, Community of Property and Equal Means of Enjoyment' in 1825, 25 miles off London. The articles reflected Owen's theories on the need to provide good and sound education for the youth, the rationale to combine agriculture and manufacture, communal rearing of children, sharing of public space and alleviating the chores that women do. It also promised complete freedom to women from domestic work. Cooking, washing heating of apartments were done on a large scale by scientific principles. All necessary but menial and unpleasant tasks were performed on rotation by adult members, if not by the youth. 'By combining Owen's communal plan with Thompson's emphasis on the importance of affording women equal respect with men, the London Cooperative Society created on paper, at least, a blueprint for women's liberation' (Kolmerten 1990: 27). In practical terms Owenites proposed communities of 2000 that would perform common educational recreational, productive and domestic activities. Cooking, child rearing and caring, and dining would be shared. Scientific gadgets would be used for helping with daily chores. These tasks would be performed by women which would take about 4–5 hours per day. They would have leisure time for creative pursuits. Women over the age of 25 would instruct others in lessons of equality so that men and women could live as equals. This equality would be made possible by education, economic prosperity and mechanical innovations.

Orbinston (1825–27) was the first British Owenite community to admit women to the committee of management and offer freedom from 'domestic slavery'. Cooking, cleaning and washing was communal and was done by machines. The experiment did not succeed for lack of cooperation from the men. Furthermore, women's political equality was undercut economically by the constitution. According to the articles of agreement, the profits were divided equally among the members but their daily needs would be met by their own labour, requiring that each individual prepared an estimate of the hourly value of his labour and present it to the 'general store' for reimbursement. The wage rates were judged according to the standards prevailing outside the community with the hope of attracting skilled labourers. Women's communal work was counted excluding their domestic work.

Ralahine (1831–33) combined political equality with economic inequality. Women had the right to vote for the nine-member governing committee. However, their wages were permanently fixed at a lower rate than those of the lowest paid in the community.

Domestic labour was limited to women but women were not restricted to household work. The Community of Equality planned at New Harmony conceived of a new world without private property and religion. Women were not confined to domestic chores and had equal educational and sufficient leisure time for mental improvement and rational enjoyment.

None of these experimental communities survived with much success. Ironically women did not relish the idea of common life having been accustomed to their notion of privacy and individual comfort. They also realized that they had to work harder by way of taking care of the needs of the whole community and not just of their individual family and that became strenuous. By the 1830s the idea of private domestic households once again gained popularity among the working class. Women with children were keen to get their husbands to shoulder greater responsibilities and obligations. The communities also failed for the promised technological innovations that would alleviate the drudgery of domestic work did not take place, making collective household work all the more stressful.

Furthermore, competition for jobs and wages was another source of tension between men and women. Men, by and large, were keen to keep women out of the labour market. In many of these communities there was hardly any kind of sexual equality. As far as supporting suffrage was concerned, women participated in the struggle for demanding male enfranchisement. By the 1850s when women suffragettes fought for female enfranchisement, it was usually regarded as an upper-class movement. Owenism also lost its appeal by this time. The socialists did not attempt to realize socialism with feminism. Instead, they focused more on labour versus capital and in the process took up the cause of women.[4]

Both Owen and Fourier inspired the small community movements in the early nineteenth century and it differed from the earlier self-sufficient communes for it was not sustained by a religious law. Though they used the name of God to identify a life giving principle but that was not a personal God with powers to intervene in these newly founded secular communities. Using their personal experiences with industries they had complete confidence in the gradual spread of community systems as being better. They rejected violent revolutionary methods of social change and had faith in childhood education and the principle of human motivation which would be the basis of change. They believed that systematic training would inculcate moral conduct, leading to habit formation and making human beings receptive to the power of reason and persuaded by argument. They hoped that these new communities would develop within the existing system but independent of it.

Between the late 1850s and the early 1880s there was no socialist movement, either Marxist or Owenite, in Britain. The Christian socialists who were active in the late sixties and the early seventies ceased to call themselves by that name. The closest to a socialist body was the Land and Labour League about which Marx wrote with tremendous enthusiasm in the late 1860s. It demanded land nationalization and, along with it, home colonization, national, secular, gratuitous and compulsory education, suppression of private banks of issue, a direct and progressive property tax in lieu of other taxes, liquidation of national debt, abolition of the standing army, reduction in the hours of labour and equal electoral rights with payment of members. The programme incorporated both Owenism and Chartism. To take care of the immediate problem of unemployment, it proposed to settle the unemployed on the nationalized land and army, before its final disbandment, as a 'pioneer force to weed, drain and level the wastes of cultivation'. It was not popular because it was too radical as compared to the Land Tenure Reform Association founded in 1870 under the influence of J.S. Mill.

Conclusion

Many of Owen's proposals seemed unrealistic and grounded on the assumption that the time for change had come. His cooperative socialism was based on his conviction that human character could be moulded by circumstances and environment, which was why he attempted to bring about reforms. He was regarded as a benevolent man by Malthus. His most important practical experiments were related to the labour conditions in the New Lanark Mills. His colonies, communist society and labour exchanges did not do well. There were not many takers. Besides, the conditions within communal living were regarded as too restrictive and paternalistic. He regarded industrial slavery to be worse than black slavery, an aspect fully explored and developed by Cole in his conception of industrial democracy. Owen, like Bentham, wanted to combine justice with efficiency and considered a government to be good if it produced the greatest happiness for the greatest number, but this could not be realized in an individualistic society. He emphasized social means to realize general welfare.

Owen remained oblivious of the realities of economic and social injustice and merely condemned the church and its doctrines for the ills in the world. He also endorsed uncritically Bentham's best known premise that the ultimate end of a government was the greatest happiness of the greatest number. He did not bother to enquire whether the government was capable of attaining that end, and this despite the fact that he wrote at a time of widespread political and social discontent and when there was a precedent in William Godwin's *The Enquiry Concerning Political Justice* (1793). Godwin had argued that the reform of the government had to be the starting point for it encouraged violence and injustice and an ideal society would be one where free and independent persons led collective lives with the help of reason without authority, government and agencies of law.

In spite of these failures and shortcomings, Owen exerted strong influence on the social thinking in England. His critique of capitalism and advocacy of cooperative living influenced nineteenth century conservatism and socialism. His critique of wastage, injustices and unemployment within the present society formed an integral part of socialist lexicon. He exerted enormous influence over the trade union and cooperative movements in Britain and was not only their 'champion and theoretician but also their first large scale organizer' (Kolakowski 1981a: 194). He worked relentlessly for improvements in working conditions and better labour measures. He emphasized on the importance of social happiness and self reliance. He fought relentlessly against poverty, unemployment, exploitation, crime, inequality and degradation. He realized that machines degraded labour into a dispensable commodity, encouraged competition for wealth and divided men, making them selfish. However, he was one of the earliest to realize how the benefits of machine technology could be put to the positive and definite improvement of the human society by cultivating a communitarian ethic where machines were subordinated to human existence. Besides technology, he had tremendous faith in education and labour reforms as leading to a humane and a happy society.

Charles Fourier

Francois-Marie-Charles Fourier shares with Cabet and Saint Simon the distinction of having pioneered the early French socialist movement. There the resemblance ends (Lichtheim 1969: 31).

No two persons could well be more different in their approach to the social question than Saint-Simon and Fourier, though they were both precursors of socialism (Cole 1953: 62).

The most sustained effort at combining productive power, desire and community was made by Charles Fourier (Wolin 1960: 395).

Francois-Marie-Charles Fourier (1772–1837) was not the first socialist since he was preceded by Saint Simon but he was the first to criticize the bourgeois civilization from a materialist perception of human nature. He was also a visionary, one who imagined a detailed socialist paradise in a grand manner. He was ridiculed for his elaborate schemes and before he could perfect them he died. Like his predecessors, Fourier believed that the bourgeoisie benefitted primarily from the great political turmoil and that its social dominance was concealed by the liberal theorists. He, like Rousseau, rejected large scale industrialization and distrusted technical progress. Socialism meant maximizing individual freedom and minimizing public regulations. An ideal socialist organization would be based on a proper understanding of the desires and capacities of the human individual.

Engels praised Fourier for his dialectical analysis of social problems. His writings, noticeably the emphasis on spontaneity and personal development, played a significant role in the 1968 student revolution in France. He was regarded as a 'forerunner of Anarchy' by Kropotkin. He was amongst the earliest to champion women's liberation and equality. He also influenced Proudhon, the surrealists and the champions of counter culture in the 1960s and 1970s.

Biographical Sketch

Fourier was born on 7 April, 1772 at Beasancon in a middle-class merchant family which sold linen. He studied at a local academy. Whatever he became or achieved, he owed to his reading and to his reflections on what he read. The family lost most of its posses-sions and wealth during the French Revolution. He buried the hopes of his father by joining Lyons as a petty bureaucrat and began earn-ing his living as a clerk and a commercial traveller. He inherited a modest sum from his mother. He wrote books during leisure time. For most part of his life he lived in Paris. During the Revolution Fourier observed and condemned the unscrupulous practices of the merchants hoarding grain at will. He was imprisoned and was nearly guillotined. He lost his patrimony. After that he led an un-eventful solitary life. He remained a bachelor. His passions were for cats and good food. His habits were meticulous. The moment he conceived of the *phalanstery* he looked for details and develop-ed a complex system of living and working arrangements. He con-stantly collected, counted, catalogued and analyzed. If during a walk something attracted him he incorporated it in his design for the ideal.

Fourier authored *Theory of Four Movements* (1808), *Association of Domestic Agriculture* (1822) and *New Industrial Communal World* (1829). Though he wrote a lot there was no grand treatise that out-lined his whole system in detail. He analyzed 144 evils of civilized society which included commerce, deception and cuckoldry. He pointed out that the earth responded to eight-stage cycles of 40,000 years of good times and corresponding bad times. He sought to establish a harmony between the cosmic order and social order and believed that Newton's laws of gravity applied to both. Newton inspired Fourier the same way that Darwin influenced Marx. How-ever, while Fourier discovered passionate code from Newton's theory of attraction, Marx inferred from Darwin a process of strug-gle. Unlike Godwin and Owen, Fourier believed in the benevolent Creator who had aspirations for men to lead a good life in circum-stances far better than the existing ones. Hence all human impulses were good.

Fourier noted that periods of confusion, savagery, patriarchy and barbarity had been relegated to history. The peak was harmony and the contemporary period was civilization. Harmony would be characterized by free governance, mature and free human beings and orderly organization. He evolved a complex system of 810 personality types that would have to be fulfilled to reach civiliza-tion. His ideal was harmonism or *phalanstery* which he regarded as the highest social form for it satisfied and developed everyone's needs and passions. It would one where animals and humanbeings coexist in peace and such a paradise would last for 144 years.

An interesting anecdote about Fourier's life was that he would wait daily in a restaurant for a rich patron to finance his ideas but none came. His disciples were Albert Brisbane, Victor Consid'erant (1808–93) and Flora Tristan (1803–44) a feminist. He also influenced the Russian revolutionaries like Herzen, Petrachevsky and Cherayshevsky. Consid'erant[5] started a Fourierist journals entitled *La Phalanst'ere* (1832–34) and *La Phalange* (1836–49) and a model colony in Texas in the United States. Fourier's vision of workers colonies inspired the Swiss Jura, Shakers and similar experiments in Rumania, Russia and the United States like Oneida, New Icaria, the North American *Phalanx* and Trumball. The most ambitious enterprise was undertaken in America in 1850s which included the Brook Farm of Margaret Fuller (1818–50). However, without its founder many of these communes did not sustain themselves. Marx and Engels described Fourier's utopian community as 'fantastic blueprint despite its vein of true poetry and satirical depiction of bourgeois society'. In 1832 Fourier settled down in Paris permanently. He died on 10 October 1837.

The Ideal Society

The core of Fourier's philosophy was contained in his law of attraction, namely that there existed an all-pervading power in the world that united human individuals in common action. Momentarily anti-social actions eclipsed the power but once they were removed universal harmony would prevail and the wealth of humankind would increase enabling individuals to love their labour and eliminate the wastage under the present chaotic system. The basic quest was to establish a social organization which allowed for the full play and harmony of human passions. He accepted conflict as inevitable and that it would be useless to eliminate it, but desired reorganization of society in a manner that conflict would develop into harmony.

For Fourier the passionate code was the operating principle of the entire universe. He identified 12 passions (*a*) the five senses; (*b*) the four 'group passions' of friendship, love, family feeling and ambition, and (*c*) the three distributive passions which include the passions for planning, for change and for unity. All the 12 passions united into one, namely the passion of love for others in society. These were the cabalistic, butterfly and composite passions. Cabalistic was the passion for intrigue and competition. Butterfly was a passion for variety, and composite was the passion for complexity and required a combination of physical and spiritual pleasures for its satisfaction. The latter would keep the other nine in a state of perfect equilibrium and contribute to the formation of what Fourier called the passionate series, the groups which were the basic units of production in his vision of an ideal community.

Harmony was possible if men and women formed communities or *phalanxes*. Each *phalanx* would occupy a central building called *phalanstery*. Citizens would unite according to their tastes determined by the character of their 'passions'. The ideal size would be 1,600 to 1,800 members. Smaller units of seven to nine were called a 'series' and larger units were called 'groups'. Each group would undertake some specific kind of work like growing vegetables, while the series may look after specifics like, for example, potato growing. Individuals could join any series or group according to their liking and change from group to group at their will. This was done so that they do not find a particular task boring. The *phalanx* built public works projects, replanted depleted forests and irrigated fields.

The *phalanx* did not need policeman, lawyers or soldiers for it was a harmonious society without criminals, defaulters and cheats. There would be no need for separate kitchens, warehouses and stables, for common kitchens and storehouses increased in productivity leading to overall well-being. There would be a vast hall with three wings to govern material, social and intellectual concerns. There would be workshops, museums, libraries, salons and reception rooms. One segment of the palace would house a temple devoted to arts and gymnastics. There would be a temple of Unityism for instilling human cooperation by encouraging diversity. Each *phalanx* would have a tower of communication to signal others.

Each individual could think of working from his 18th to his 28th birthday and spend the rest of life in leisure and comfort. Instead of the individual adjusting to work Fourier proposed to reorganize society to suit human wants and desires. For Fourier cooperative production was more efficient making available a larger pool of resources for the greater enjoyment of everyone. Greater efficiency would be due to the elimination of wastage and because of planned production for that gave an opportunity for everyone to find an occupation that would lead to the enhancement of the passionate code. This would make work a source of greater happiness, giving an incentive to perform better and derive greater satisfaction.

Fourier, like the early socialists, rejected the individualist competitive society in favour of cooperative associations. While travelling from Rouen to Paris in 1798 he noticed the difference in the price of apples and that made him ponder over the harmful and destructive role of the middlemen. He was also moved by the misery, exploitation and the crisis of the working class. Though not a utilitarian he believed that human beings were guided by a passionate code which ought to be the basis of the societal organization guaranteeing satisfaction from the passion that activity gave them. He was convinced that complete sexual fulfillment would lead to social harmony and economic well-being. The passionate code was not attainable within a competitive society for human beings were at a state of war all the time with themselves and vis-à-vis others.

Unlike Saint Simon, Fourier did not demand abolition of unearned income. He desired that a sum was set aside for each member of the community from the product of industry. The surplus would be divided between labour, capital and talent, with labour getting five-twelfths, capital securing four-twelfths and talent procuring the remaining three-twelfths. He modified the Saint-Simonian dictum to read as follows, 'from each according to his capacity to each according to his labour, capital and talent'. He divided labour into three categories: necessary labour, useful labour and agreeable labour. The first received the highest reward and the last the least since it involved the least sacrifice.

The ideal was one in which each individual would be able to find the satisfaction of his desires in a manner that was useful to others. In a competitive society the individual worked out of compulsion, for work was boring, repetitive and limiting. It failed to satisfy the butterfly and composite passions, and instead concentrated heavily on the cabalistic ones. On the contrary, in an ideal society each individual would specialize in one task but would be a simultaneously proficient in 30 others, thereby making work delightful. In fact, the demarcation between work and play would break down for it would maximize physical and social freedom in the sense that all basic human wants would be taken care of.

In an ideal community, life would be communal but with a great deal of privacy. Private property, inheritance and economic inequality would be retained but they would lose their antagonistic character. The basic needs of individuals would be fulfilled for they would be rewarded according to their labour-contribution towards the total product. Public affairs would be organized on democratic principles and treated as routine administrative work. Individual rendered public service more out of love for one another. Fourier suggested that children perform household work and unpleasant chores like killing animals, cleaning sewers and drains since they loved to play with dirt.

The government of the *phalanx* would be elected. The *phalanx* head would be called *unarch* and the chief of the world *phalanxes* would be called an *omniarch*. The latter's headquarters would be in Constantinople. Fourier hoped that the community life would be based on peace and non-violence. It would be voluntary and not subjected to state control. It would be based on skilled agriculture which would also include stock-breeding and poultry-farming. Trade between communal settlements would be minimal.

Fourier realized that political liberty and personal freedom without a degree of economic equality was meaningless. He accepted inequality of talents and remuneration according to the work done but presupposed a gradual levelling of the privileges of the wealthy and the end of class antagonisms. He defended not only free choice but also guaranteed freedom from compulsion to work. He spoke of a 'social minimum', a guaranteed annual income. Everyone would have the right to work. He called for the satisfaction of both material and psychological desires in the human being.

Fourier was so fond of laying down meticulous details that there was hardly any room for improvisation and change; nor was there any respect for individual privacy. Though he tried to provide for attractive work that would enhance individual autonomy and self realization yet his system was regimented. Communal life was so tightly organized that it seemed more like a jail than a paradise. It seemed that Fourier was the master who orchestrated all the others like puppets.

The detail of Fourier's descriptions, the endless minutiae of arrangements covering every aspect of life in the state of harmony, mark the obsessive . . . Fourier was voicing the common pain of an age confronted by the breakdown of traditional forms, . . . The longing for order which he depicted with such poignancy was a cry from the soul of the early industrial society (Manuel and Manuel 1979: 644).

Marx felt that because of such detailed blueprints, the social systems of Saint Simon, Owen and Fourier were doomed to fail and become Fantasies. While Marx shared with them the ideal of the future, he differed in the method to achieve the ideal. For Marx, capitalism would be destroyed because it led to dehumanization and relative impoverishment. Socialism did not mean merely welfare but removal of conditions — competition and want — that made human beings rivals. It meant the abolition of estrangement between human beings. It signified human liberation.

Women and Family

Among the early socialists, it was Fourier who contributed most to the cause of women. Fourier condemned sexual activity that abused, injured or used a person against his will. He observed while rejecting the degradation and bondage of women and conjugal slavery in modern civilization that a slave was never more contemptible than when his blind submission convinced the oppressor that his victim was born for slavery. However, though women were free from the constraints imposed by patriarchy, in an ideal community they had to serve men both domestically and sexually. He dismissed marriage as boredom and described it as intensified prostitution. He equated women's emancipation with social progress and advocated collectivization of child-care and provided for liberalized play, equestrain training and a variety of musical instruments.

The transformation of a historical era can always be determined by the condition of progress of women towards liberty, because it is here, in the relation of women to men, of the weak to the strong, that the victory of human nature over

brutality appears more evident. The degree of female emancipation is the natural measure of general emancipation . . .
The humiliation of the female sex is an essential characteristic
of civilization as well as barbarism, only with the difference
that civilized order raises every vice, which barbarism practices in a simple manner, to a form of existence that is composite, ambiguous, deceptive and hypocritical. Nobody is hit
more profoundly than the man in being condemned to keep
women in slavery (Fourier 1901: 177).

Interestingly Fourier abolished nuclear families and monogamous marriages for both were disastrous to economic efficiency
and the fulfillment of the passionate code. He regarded love as a
compound emotion consisting of both physical and spiritual feelings, one that could not be confined within a marital relationship.
The emotion of love was universal providing the basis for individual satisfaction and social welfare. Within nuclear families there
was enormous wastage of resources. In Harmony, labour was voluntary and agreeable with communal education, communal living
and non-repressive sexuality. Similarly, complete sexual gratification would be guaranteed and, like a social minimum, there would
be a sexual minimum.
    Prior to the emergence of the ideal community there were seven
historical phases. In the fourth phase called *barbarism* women were
totally subjugated. In the fifth phase called *civilization*, which was
the contemporary society, there was monogamous marriage and
civil liberties for the wife but nevertheless women continued to be
oppressed for they were educated with the sole purpose of becoming mothers and wives. This led to the development of their faculties
in an one-dimensional way. Wives had to please their husbands
retarding their own sexual fulfillment. The final stage of Harmony
would be one of liberty where women would be equal with men
in both mental and intellectual abilities for there would be no co-
relationship between physical strength and body functions. Fourier,
like Plato, gave women full rights to participate in the administration of the *phalanstry*. Like James and J.S. Mill, Fourier judged civility
of a nation by the progressive role it gave to women.
    Inspired by Fourier, the Shakers established themselves in 1750
as a community. By 1850 there were 18 societies consisting of 58
families spread across the United States. The economic basis of the

society was agriculture. Labour was held as a sacred principle. Frequent changes in occupations were permitted to alleviate monotony and drudgery. Incidentally, Fourier regarded boredom as one of the greatest evils of modern civilization. Labour-saving devices were invented to make work more meaningful and playful. The Shakers believed in the power of the soul over the body, and that it was possible to overcome physical diseases through sheer will power. In England, the Shaker sect was founded by Jane Wardley who renounced sex altogether as lust of the flesh. She was succeeded by Ann Lee who along with seven members emigrated to North America. They denounced monogamous marriages though defended differentiated and traditional gender roles with women working indoors and men doing the heavy work outside. Both sexes, however, participated as equals in the process of political decision-making and governance.

Fourier, like Owen and the Utilitarians, believed that evil arose not out of human nature but was a product of social arrangements. Hence he advocated the liberation of society as a precondition to the emancipation of women. Socialism for him meant both class and gender equality.

Conclusion

Fourier was the most libertarian of all the socialists in nineteenth-century France. He was politically a conservative for he believed even monarchy to be compatible with his ideal, socially a reformist for he opposed revolution, and morally an anarchist for he believed in complete personal freedom. He was one of the earliest social ecologists for he conceived the universe as a vast living organism. He considered individuals and nature to be integral and inter-dependent. Behind the apparent chaos, there was an underlying harmony and the natural order was governed by an universal law. He disagreed with Saint Simon and Owen on the need to have complete levelling and equality for these were a mirage. He was a firm believer in social transformation though he ruled out force for this purpose.

Fourier was one of the foremost and virulent critics of the decadent Western civilization. Like Rousseau, he thought civilization made human beings in general worse off. Virtually everyone was poor for the passions remained unfulfilled and the natural instincts curbed. As a consequence, all were bored. He looked to market economy as one of deceit. He was critical of compulsive work and rejected the capitalistic work ethic. His libertarian and egalitarian perception also included animals and he spoke against cruelty to animals. He highlighted that exploitation and poverty were socially created and sustained by the modes of production, an aspect which Marx elaborated at length. He also pointed out the evils of small land holdings and the parasitic nature of trade in times of economic anarchy though he did not advocate abolition of private property and inheritance. His writings exerted considerable influence on factory and sanitary reforms. He emphasized the need to have political freedom along with social freedom. Though futuristic in his vision and plans, he eulogized the past for he looked to his society as one based on agriculture and trading rather than industry and technology.

Morris praised Fourier for making work pleasurable, aesthetic and attractive. He acknowledged that it was Fourier who convinced him of the necessity of socialism and its immediate realization. Fourier also sensitized one about the dark side of civilization, namely, cheating, oppression, theft, struggle and poverty. However, Morris found Fourierism to be regimented and dogmatic, and felt that it would not work despite the best intentions. The interesting thing that struck Morris about Fourier's ideal society was that it would be realized not through seizure of power or political reforms but by the act of a 'prince'.

Many of Fourier's disciples formed *The Society for the Propagation and Realization of the Theory of Fourier*. Several communities were started along the lines that Fourier laid down. One such experiment was the *familist'ere* which was a collective rural estate. Fourier inspired the cooperative movements which played an important role till 1914 and are still active in many parts of Third World. In the 1960s and 1970s, he was considered as a precursor of Sigmund Freud (1856–1939)[6] and on certain occasions he was glorified as the French prophet of new love. He was seen as a vital intellectual link between Marquis de Sade (1740–1814)[7] and Freud, the founder of psychoanalysis. Fourier's appeal was because of his romantic and utopian vision of socialism. His ideals attracted many during his own life time and immediately after his death. Contemporary communitarianism draw inspiration from Fourier and Owen.

Endnotes

1. See the section on Sorel in this book.
2. The bill contained three provisions. First no child should work until he was 10-years-old (Owen proposed 12). The second was that no child should be put to work at night (i.e., from 9 p.m. to 5.30 a.m.) until he is 18-years-old. And third was that no child should work more than ten-and-a-half hours a day until he turned 18.
3. William Thompson's tract *Appeal on Behalf of Women* (1825) was written following the failure of Benthamites to support women's suffrage and in general against their half-hearted campaign. The tract was inspired by the writings of Anna Wheeler Doyle (1785–1848), a close friend of Thompson though the latter did not acknowledge his source of inspiration in the same manner as J.S. Mill attributed *The Subjection* to Harriet Taylor. Wheeler in the *Rights of Women* (1830) attempted to reconcile Saint-Simonism, Owenism and Fourierism with Utilitarianism and contended that the greatest happiness of the greatest number could be best realized in a cooperative society. Thompson shared Wheeler's perception and argued that women's equality was possible only within socialism which accepted equality, mutuality and common good as its ordering principles. Thompson demanded end of sexual discrimination, equal educational opportunities for women, and right to vote and to contest political offices. Thompson and Wheeler focussed on the status of married women, single adult women and those women who did not have fathers or husbands.
4. See the section on Bebel in this book.
5. His major theoretical works included *La Destinee sociale* (1834), *Manifeste de l' Ecole Societaire* (1841) and *Le Socialism devant le vieux monde* (1848). Consid'erant desired the end of politics and creation of communities on a voluntary basis which he abandoned for 'social' point of view. In 1848 he was elected to the National Assembly and also participated in the Luxembourg Labour Commission of which Blanc was the president.
6. Freud in this theory of repression argued that social pressures denied direct expression of important instincts and consequently submerge to re-emerge in new and unexpected forms. It was not always harmful for in some cases Freud regarded it as a necessary process whereby primordial instincts were transformed into motivating force of civilization. Though Freud never applied his ideas to politics, yet it influenced political thought in a significant ways. His theory of unconscious determination, common to conservatism (Burke) and revolutionary (Marx) contended that the real motives of political action had to be found elsewhere than in the conscious reasons that was attributed to it.
7. Marquis de Sade's original name was Donatien Alphonse Francois. Comte raised some psychological and ethical questions regarding man's nature and undermined in the process preconceived notions about sexuality and the natural relations of the sexes. He insisted on the absolute equality between sexes and rejected laws as being detrimental to human passions. He looked to crime as an outcome of passions or want and believed that kindness and honour could provide an effective deterrent.

4

❖ *Nineteenth Century Marxists*

Karl Heinrich Marx

No thinker in the nineteenth century has had so direct, deliberate and powerful an influence upon mankind as Karl Marx. Both during his lifetime and after it he exercised an intellectual and moral ascendancy over his followers, the strength of which was unique even in that golden age of democratic nationalism, an age which saw the rise of great popular heroes and martyrs, romantic, almost legendary figures, whose lives and words dominated the imagination of the masses and created a new revolutionary tradition in Europe (Berlin 1939: 9).

Marx's views on technical change, exploitation, class struggle and belief formation retain an importance beyond the value they may have as instances of the Marxist method, if there is one . . . . Even today, not all of his insights have been exhausted (Elster 1986: 3).

Yet one must concede that with all the differences between Marx and Soviet Leninist communism, Leninism would have been inconceivable without Marx. Ironically it was in his various letters on Russia that Marx disregarded the possibilities open to its new theory, and here lies his major intellectual blunder. Though he thought of open historical alternatives nonetheless determined by identifiable and explicable causes, he overlooked the possibility that one of the alternatives to which the future development of his own theory was open might be the combination of his philosophical and historical theory with the Jacobin tradition of merely political, subjectivist revolutionary action: Leninism embodied such a combination. Thus, if Marx's point of departure was Hegelian, so was his blind spot: like Hegel himself he did not subject his own theory to a dialectical critique (Avineri 1976: 228).

Karl Heinrich Marx (1818–83) was truly the last of the great system builders in the Western intellectual tradition. His ideas exerted a decisive influence on all aspects of human endeavour — culture, economics, ethics, political science, philosophy, history and sociology. He transformed the study of society and history, and significantly changed philosophy, literature and arts. He established a link between economic and intellectual life. It would not be wrong therefore to say that in some sense we are all Marxists. Marx was a secular moralist, rationalist and a humanist thinker (Mills 1962: 25).

Marx was a revolutionary and a socialist but, above all, a humanist who believed that genuine emancipation and liberation of human beings would be brought about by their own efforts. He exuded the optimism of Victorian England for he had immense faith in the liberating and progressive role of science. He envisioned a humane and decent society free of exploitation, oppression, domination and injustice. It was this vision that captivated and attracted many to his ideas and method.

Some scholars differentiated between the young and the old Marx. The young Marx was concerned with alienation, human estrangement and morality while the old was more deterministic with his in-depth study of the workings of capitalism (McLellan 1971). The link between the two was the *Grundrisse* (1857–8) and the *Introduction to the Critique of Political Economy* (1859). Another crucial fact was that some of the most influential writings were in collaboration with Engels. After Marx's death Engels, as a disciple, edited and published some of his works raising questions relating to that which was original in Marx and that which was Engels' contribution. Engels acknowledged that while Marx was the genius, he was at best talented. Marx was the originator and Engels the popularizer.[1]

Marx described his socialism as 'scientific'. Having studied the laws of social development of capitalism, he believed that the destruction of capitalism was inevitable because of its inherent contradictions. He 'was the first spokesman for socialism to remove the earlier utopian fantasies and eccentricities, the first to present the socialist ideal not as a mere pleasing dream but as historically realizable goal, indeed as a goal that history had brought to the very threshold of possibility' (Howe 1972: 5). He disparagingly dubbed the socialists who preceded him as utopians though he was inspired and influenced by them. The relationship that Marx shared with the early socialists was similar to the one Plato shared with the Sophists. Like Plato, Marx underplayed his debt to the early socialists.

Marx inherited and integrated three legacies in his theoretical construct. From the German intellectual tradition he borrowed the Hegelian method of dialectics and applied it to the material world. From the French Revolutionary tradition he accepted the idea that apocalyptic change motivated by 'messianic' ideas was not only desirable but also feasible. He applied his method with a view to bring about large scale changes within the industrialized capitalist economy of which England was the classic model. He used the writings of the English classical economists to understand the dynamics of capitalism and industrial revolution (Nisbet 1969). Thus he drew upon German philosophy, French political thought and English economics (Howe 1972: 5).

Biographical Sketch

Marx was born on 5 March 1818 in a predominantly Catholic city of Trier in Rhineland, Germany, in a Jewish family. His father Heinrich was the son of Marx Levi, a rabbi in Trier. The surname Marx was the abbreviated form of Mordechai, later changed to Markus. His paternal side had an illustrious ancestry. His father was a successful lawyer. Heinrich converted himself to Lutheranism in 1817 but did not abandon his religion. His wife Henriette converted herself in 1825. Karl converted himself in 1824.

Marx studied law at the University of Bonn in 1835 and the University of Berlin in 1836. He changed his course to philosophy and came under the influence of Feuerbach, Bauer and the young Hegelian movement. He completed his doctorate in philosophy entitled *The Difference between the Democritean and Epicurean Philosophies of Nature* in 1841. He looked upon Epicurus (341–270 B.C.) as a genuinely radical and enlightened. In contrast to Democritus (469–370 B.C.) Epicurus provided energizing principles by emphasizing on absolute autonomy of the human spirit. He married his childhood sweetheart Jenny von Westaphalen, daughter of Baron von Westaphalen who had been his spiritual guide since his adolescence in 1843. Together they led hard but happy lives. In the early years of courtship Marx dedicated many of his poems to Jenny. About 60 of his poems were discovered and published by 1929, but Marxist scholars did not attach much importance to them for Marx disowned their significance for the purpose of revolutionary activity.

From 1842 to 1848 Marx edited radical publications in Rhineland, Belgium and France. On Hess' recommendation, he became an editor of the liberal *Rheinische Zeitung,* a post he held till 1843. In 1844 while in Paris Marx became interested in working class movement and was introduced to Engels' study of political economy. Marx and Engels began working on the *German Ideology* (1847) while living in Brussels. In 1848 they helped in the founding of the Communist League which lasted till 1850. In 1848 Marx was expelled from Prussian territories. He moved to London where he stayed till the end of his life.

Marx worked and studied in British Museum from 1850 to 1860. He wrote for the *New York Tribune* which paid one pound for each of his articles, and that was his only regular income. He was financially helped by Engels. Ironically he wrote critically about capitalism, business and finances but he knew two men intimately connected with it — his uncle Philips, the owner of the Philips company and his best friend Engels. He lived in poverty which was mainly due to financial mismanagement (Johnson 1988: 73). Three of his six children died of want. His own health was not very good. In 1881 Jenny died. She was extremely helpful editing his manuscripts and preparing them for publications. Marx himself died on 14 March 1883. He was buried at the High-gate cemetery in London. His death went unnoticed in Britain. It was the London correspondent in Paris who reported about his death which was subsequently featured in the *London Times.*

Marx's first full scale biographer Franz Mehring (1846–1919) conceded that Marx scored over his contemporaries as a scholar, writer and revolutionary but was harsh on his rivals, particularly Bakunin and Lassalle. He thought it was unfortunate that Marx's assessment of Lassalle after his death was so bitter ad unjust. This was because:

> Marx was never completely able to overcome his prejudice against the man whom the history of German Social Democracy will always mention in the same breadth with him and Engels and even the mitigating power of death had no permanent effect (Mehring 1936: xiii).

Dialectics

Marx made the Hegelian philosophy his starting point and then subsequently turned it upside down. The Hegelian philosophy was the dominant system in the 1830s and 40s as is evident from the following statement by Engels:

> ... the Hegelian system covered an incomparably greater domain than any earlier system and developed in this domain a wealth of thought which is astounding even today ... One can imagine what a tremendous effect this Hegelian system must have produced in the philosophy-tinged atmosphere of Germany. It was a triumphal procession which lasted for decades and which by no means came to a standstill on the death of Hegel. On the contrary, it was precisely from 1830 to 1840 that "Hegelianism" reigned most exclusively, and to a greater or lesser extent infected even its opponents (Engels, cited in Singer 1980: 11).

Dialectics was the key Hegelian idea. Engels regarded the ancient Greek philosopher Heraclitus (544–484 B.C.) as the originator of this idea for he asserted that everything was and was not, for everything was fluid, was constantly changing, constantly coming into being and passing away. All was flux and nothing stayed still. Nothing endured but change. Similarly Marx and Engels believed that social circumstances were constantly changing and hence no social system could last forever. Capitalism arose under certain historical circumstances and it would disappear in time.

In the Hegelian philosophy dialectics applied to the process, evolution and development of history. Hegel viewed history as the progressive manifestation of human reason, of the development of a historical spirit. History recorded the increasing awareness and greater rationality as exhibited in human affairs. Human consciousness and freedom expanded as a result of conflicting intellectual forces which were constantly under tension. He believed that from a rudimentary state of affairs there was a movement towards perfection.

The process of history for Hegel was marked by two kinds of causation: (a) the individual spirit which desired happiness and provided energy, and (b) the world spirit which strove for higher

freedom that came with the knowledge of the self. Hegel emphati-
cally believed that without the individual, each pursuing his own
goals whatever that may be, nothing was achieved in history. But
to know whether these actions were in conformity with the dialectic
of the universal 'the cunning of reason' played its role and 'sets
passions to work for itself'.

Marx agreed with Hegel that there was a constant movement in
the dialectical process but emphasized the real rather than the ideal,
the social rather than the intellectual, the matter rather than the
mind. For Marx the key idea was not the history of philosophy but
the history of economic production and the social relations that
accompanied it. He acknowledged Hegel's great contribution which
was to recognize world history as a process, as constant motion,
change, transformation, development and to understand the internal connections of this movement and development. From the latter
he also learnt that the various angles of the developmental process
could not be studied in isolation but ought to be considered in their
relation to one another and to the process as a whole. But while
Hegel was an idealist, Marx was a materialist for he believed that
consciousness was determined by life and not the other way round.
Unlike the latent conservatism of the Hegelian philosophy, Marxism
rejected the status-quo — capitalism — as intolerable. Thus Marx, like
Hegel, continued to believe that dialectics was a powerful tool. It
offered a law of social development and in that sense Marx's social
philosophy, like that of Hegel, was a philosophy of history. Both
perceived social change as inevitable.

Materialist Conception of History

Marx applied the dialectics to the material or the social world which
consisted of economic production and exchange. A study of the
productive process explained all other historical phenomena. He
noted that each generation inherited a mass of productive forces,
an accumulation of capital, and a set of social relations which reflected these productive forces. The new generation modified these
forces, but at the same time these forces prescribed certain forms
of life and shaped human character and thought in distinct ways.
The mode of production and exchange was the final cause of all
social changes and political revolutions which meant, for minds or
thoughts to change, society would have to change. Marx looked to

matter as active, capable of changing from within. It was not passive, needing an external stimulus for change, a conception found in Hobbes' theory.

> Our conception of history depends on our ability to expound the real processes of production, starting out from the simple material production of life, and to comprehend the form of intercourse connected with this and created by this (i.e. civil society in its various stages), as the basis of all history; further, to show it in its action as state, and so, from this starting point, to explain the whole mass of different theoretical products and forms of consciousness, religion, philosophy, ethics, etc., and trace their origins and growth (Marx 1977a: 35).

While Hegel looked to national cultures as the driving force of history, for Marx it was the social classes whose antagonism supplied the motive power for change. Both regarded historical course as a rational necessity consisting of a pattern of stages with each stage representing a step towards the predetermined goal. Both appealed to an emotion above self interest — in case of Hegel it was national pride and for Marx the loyalty among workers for a better future. Marx was initially enthused by Charles Darwin's *Origin of Species* (1859) but subsequently dismissed it as strictly an empirical generalization offering a causal theory of change with no implied idea of progress. Hegelian dialectics on the contrary offered a law with a definite beginning and an end, 'a conditions towards which society is progressing, a condition of complete harmony and integration in which man will discover his time fulfilled nature' (Caute 1967: 17).

It was the writings of Ludwig Andreas Feuerbach (1804–72) that influenced Marx in his attack of the formidable Hegelian philosophy. Feuerbach in *The Essence of Christianity* (1843) provided a critique of Christianity and expanded it to include the entire gamut of metaphysical tradition of philosophy whose final development was that of Hegel. He rejected the theory that subject and object conditioned each other declaring that comprehension of things was primarily sensual and passive, and only secondarily active and conceptual. Feuerbach saw religion as the basis of all social evils. The more the individual enriched the concept of God the more he impoverished himself. His later works went beyond the criticism of religion to the criticism of the Hegelian philosophy itself. Hegel had viewed the mind as the moving force of history and humans as manifestations of mind. This, according to Feuerbach, located the essence of humanity outside human beings and thus, like religion, served to alienate humanity from itself. He also insisted that philosophy had to begin with the finite and the material world. Thought did not precede existence, existence preceded thought. So for Feuerbach, neither God nor thought but the individual was at the centre of his philosophy.

Marx used Feuerbach's transformative method to turn Hegel upside down and proceeded beyond the former's conception. The material world was not to be merely understood but had to be transformed. The task of philosophy was to be critical and to participate in that transformation. As he observed in the *Theses on Feuerbach* (1845), 'The philosophers have only interpreted the world in various ways; the point, however is to change it' (Marx 1977a: 125).

Marx held that Feuerbach reduced religion to its secular origins but did not explain the duality in human existence and hence could not offer any effective cure. The mind could be freed from mystification only if the negativities of social life were removed through practical action. Marx began with a conception of socialized humanity rather than the civil society of old materialism. He rejected the Hegelian dichotomy between the civil society and the state. The state and the bureaucracy unlike in Hegelian conception did not, according to Marx, represent universal interests but promoted the welfare of the dominant economic class. He replaced God with money in *On the Jewish Question* (1848).

> Money is the universal, self contained value of all things. Hence it has robbed the whole world, the human world as well as nature, of its proper value. Money is the alienated essence of man's labour and life, and this alien essence dominated him as he worships it (Ibid.: 60).

Marx in his analysis of history mentioned the important role of ideology in perpetuating false consciousness among people and demarcated the stages which were necessary for reaching the goal of communism. In that sense, both the bourgeoisie and the proletariat were performing their historically destined roles. In spite of the deterministic interpretation of history, the individual played an active and a crucial role within the historical limits of his time and hastened the process to reach the destination.

Marx himself was a revolutionary with a belief in a philosophy of *praxis*. Implicit in this belief was an underlying assumption of a law operating all the time which led to Engels' formulation of the dialectics of nature. This alteration by Engels changed the very essence of Marx's method of arriving at a conclusion from a particular event or a happening to a general theory or general framework determining even the small happenings. Marx analyzed from the particular to the general, whereas Engels analyzed from the general to the particular.

Marx also had a very powerful moral content in his analysis and asserted that the progress was not merely inevitable but for the better and that the future ideal would create a society that would end alienation, fetishism and cater to human needs, irrespective of human capacities. Marx's materialistic conception of history emphasized that practical human activity rather than speculative thought was the moving force of history. The conception of alienation was crucial to the understanding of the materialist conception of history. In the famous funeral oration speech delivered on the occasion of Marx's death, Engels claimed that Marx had made two major discoveries, the 'law of development of human history' and 'the law of capitalist development'.

Economic Determinism

Marx developed the materialistic conception of history to explain the law of human development. In this context he looked to the mode of production which constituted the economic base. The mode of production consisted of the means or techniques of production and the relationships that people entered into with one another for production of goods and services. Each economic base had a corresponding superstructure which consisted of social, political, cultural, legal and spiritual dimensions of human life. The economic base conditioned and determined the superstructure. 'It is not the consciousness of men that determines their existence, but, on the contrary, their social existence determines their existence (Marx 1977a: 242).

With changes in the economic basis everything which was a part of the superstructure, including consciousness, changed.

At a certain stage of their development the material forces of production in society come into conflict with the existing relations of production, or—what is but a legal expression for the same thing—with the property relations within which they had been at work before. From forms of development of the forces of production these relations turn into their fetter. Then comes the period of social revolution. With the change of the economic foundation the entire superstructure is more or less rapidly transformed (Marx 1977a: 48).

Marx's materialism referred not only to matter but also economic and social relations. He referred to a conflict between the material forces and relations of production but did not explain the nature of that conflict other than alluding to the fact that it could be a moral one with the intention of creating a humane and a decent society free of exploitation, domination and oppression.

Marx identified five stages of economic development known to history. These were primitive communism, slavery, feudalism, capitalism and communism. In each of these stages, except for the final one, there were forces of contradiction which made revolutions inevitable. The given status-quo would be the thesis with conflicts in the form of an antithesis and a solution in the form of synthesis. The synthesis in turn would become the thesis and the process continued till the perfect society was reached. The difference between the earlier revolutions and the future socialist revolution was in the fact that the earlier ones were minority revolution while the socialist one would be majoritarian and democratic.

For Marx and Engels it was not merely enough to understand the general processes of history but also the way these processes worked themselves out in the present. If one desired to transform the world then a correct diagnosis of the prevailing social conditions was necessary. In the nineteenth century this meant an understanding of the working of the bourgeois society, a study of the sociology of capitalism. Capitalism in their perception had created unnecessary sufferings which ought to be negated, eliminated and opposed.

Class Struggle and Social Change

Marx articulated the idea of human distinct from political emancipation. The aim of human liberation was to bring forth the collective, generic character of human life which was real so that the society assumed a collective character which coincided with the life of the state. This would be possible if humans were freed from religion and private property. The proletariat by being the universal class in chains would liberate itself and the true human society would emerge. Relations of production in reality were class relations and class antagonisms were crucial to the workings of all societies. ' . . . the history of all hitherto existing society is the history of class struggles' (Marx 1977b: 109). In every society there were two classes, rich and poor. The rich owned the means of production and the poor sold their labour. During different historical phases these two classes were known by different names and enjoyed different legal status and privileges, but one thing was common — that in course of all these phases their relationship was one of exploitation and domination. 'Freeman and slave, patrician and plebeian, lord and serf, guild-master and journeyman, in a word, oppressor and oppressed, stood in constant opposition to one another' (Marx 1975).

Marx objected to the idea of the middle class historians that class struggle ended with the rise of the bourgeoisie just as he opposed the perceptions of the classical economists that capitalism was eternal and immutable. He harnessed the rising consciousness and power among the industrial proletariat and emphasized that it was their desire to bring about economic equality that kept alive class struggle and revolutionary change. He summed up his own contribution to the notion of class struggle in a letter to Josef Weydemeyer in 1852 wherein he confidently declared that class struggles would not be a permanent feature of society but was necessitated by the historical development of production. The class struggle would end with the destruction of capitalism for communism would be a classless society.

Class for Marx symbolized collective unity in the same manner as nation in Hegel's theory. Each class produced its own ideas and beliefs, and operated within a particular economic and social system. Mannheim's sociology of knowledge was an offshoot of this view which analyzed everything from a class perspective. The individual was important with respect to his membership within a class which determined his moral convictions, aesthetic preferences and reason.

Ideology

For both the Marxists and the non-Marxists, ideology connoted a distorted picture of reality. However, for Marx ideology was not merely a discredited concept but an important theoretical construct which shaped a particular kind of thought process. He used it in the inter-related sense of idealism and apology. However, like his theory of the state, his concept of ideology was never fully developed as its narration was restricted to the first part of the *German Ideology* and a few pages on the *Theses on Feuerbach*.

Not only ordinary human beings but even extraordinary thinkers like Hegel and the classical economists had an ideological content in their arguments. Ideological writers according to Marx belonged to two categories, those who were ideological unintentionally, and the vulgar writers who restricted their enquiry only to the surface of society because they dealt with abstractions without any critical and historical perspective. In this second category the most important theorist was Hegel as his entire philosophical project was unsatisfactory for it was positivistic and uncritical. He lacked clarity and his particularistic prescriptions did not match with his universalistic assertions.

For Marx a truly non-ideological framework of thought was possible with honest and impartial dissection of the internal structure of society. A scientific mind with a total comprehension of the complexities of society was also an essential requirement. The ideological and narrow bias of Hegel and the class economists was reflected in their restricted bourgeois view. But Marx did not look to the capitalist society from the point of the proletariat as contended by Lenin, Luk'acs, Gramsci and Althusser because that would also be a partisan view. Marx's non-ideological thought was based on science as he perceived himself to be a 'free agent of thought' (Parekh 1982). Believing in a theory of *praxis*, Marx thought that by exposing the ideological bias in thinkers he was able to correct the distortions that colour the image of the world which allow the ruling class to rule with ideological mystifications of even the classes that it exploited.

The ideas of the ruling class are in every epoch the ruling ideas: i.e., the class which is the ruling material force of society, is at the same time its ruling intellectual force. The class which has the means of material production as its disposal, has control at the same time over the means of mental production, so that thereby, generally speaking, the ideas of those who lack the means of mental production are a subject to it. The ruling ideas are nothing more than the ideal expression of the dominant material relationships, the dominant material relationships grasped to ideas; hence of the relationship which make the one class the ruling one, therefore the ideas of its dominance (Marx 1977a: 245).

The general framework of ideology developed by Marx in the *German Ideology* was refined in later writings, for instance, the conception of fetishism in the *Capital* by which social relationships between men assumed the relations between things, was an original contribution of Marx. Though the term ideology was coined by Antonio Claude Graf Destutt de Tracy (1754–1836) in 1796 it was Marx who made a skillful use of it. McLellan thinks that the problem with Marx's analysis was that instead of emerging a proletariat he remained a bourgeois as his faith in rationality, stress on science and technology and his essential euro-centricism arose out of Victorian capitalism (McLellan 1995: 18). Marx, with all his belief that he transcended the present reality, as also locally dated.

Analysis of Capitalism

Marx defined capitalism by two factors — first, by the use of wage labour. In the *Capital* (1867–94) he pointed out that capitalism arose only when the owners of the means of production and subsistence met in the market with the free labourer selling his labour power. The basis of capitalism was wage labour. The second defining characteristic of capitalism was the private ownership of the means of production and this was distinct from private property like household effects and home. The ownership of the means of production was the crucial feature of capitalism for it was restricted to a few. Those who did not own anything were forced to sell their labour power and become wage labourers. Unlike the medieval guildsmen they did not work for themselves but for others.

The man who possesses no other property than his labour power must, in all conditions of society and culture, be the slave of other men, who have made themselves the owners of the material conditions of labour. He can work only with their permission, hence live only with their permission (Marx 1977a: 228).

In the *Critique of the Gotha Programme* (1875) Marx implied that even if the state owned the means of production, wage labour would still continue. This was not real socialism but a new variation of capitalism — namely, state capitalism. Disgruntled and disillusioned socialists often argued that the erstwhile Soviet Union was not a true socialist state but a tyrannous form of state capitalism.

In *The Communist Manifesto* (1848) Marx paid handsome tributes to the bourgeoisie while highlighting its negative side. There were three reasons that made capitalism attractive. First it had brought about remarkable economic progress by revolutionizing the means of production and by developing technology as never before. It built and encouraged the growth of commerce and factories on the scale unknown before. It instituted cooperative, social production.

The bourgeoisie, during its rule of scare one hundred years, has created more massive and more colossal productive force than have all preceding generations together. Subjections of Nature's force to man, machinery, application of chemistry to industry and agriculture, steam-navigation, railways, electric telegraphs, clearing of whole continents for cultivation, canalization of rivers, whole populations, conjured out of the ground — what earlier century had even a presentiment that such productive forces slumbered in the lap of social labour? . . . It had accomplished wonders far surpassing Egyptian pyramids, Roman aqueducts and Gothic cathedrals; it has conducted expeditions that put in the shade all former exoduses of nations and crusades (Marx 1975: 35).

By the very range and extent of its activity capitalism made its second contribution. It undermined national barriers. In its search for markets and raw materials, capitalism and the bourgeoisie crossed national boundaries. They penetrated every corner of the world drawing the most backward nations into their fold. Capitalism was cosmopolitan and international.

Being world-wide, the third achievement of capitalism was within its territorial confines. It eliminated the distinctions between town and country and enabled the peasants to come out of what Marx called 'the idiocy of rural life'. In other words, capitalism revolutionized the techniques of economic production, reduced international barriers and created an urban civilization. In spite of these achievements, Marx contended that capitalism had outlived its use for it brought about immense sufferings and hardships and therefore had to yield itself to a new socialist organization of production.

Marx examined the sufferings within capitalism which were rooted in its origin: the eviction of peasants from their land, the loss of their sources of income, their vagabondage, their assembling in cities where they had become dependent at starvation wages. The proletariat was created.

> The historical movement which changes the producers into wage-workers appears, on the one hand, as their emancipation from serfdom and from the fetters of the guilds, and this side alone exists for our bourgeois historians. But, on the other hand, these new freedmen became sellers of themselves only after they had been robbed of all their own means of production, and of all the guarantees of existence afforded by the old feudal arrangements. And the history of this, their expropriation, is written in the annals of mankind in letters of blood and fire (Marx 1977b: 272).

The suffering required for the creation of the free wage labourer was the first cost of capitalism. The exploitation of the proletariat was described with reference to the notion of surplus value, a concept introduced in the *Capital*. Surplus value was the difference between the wage paid to the labourer and the price for which the product was sold. The rate of profit indicated the degree of exploitation. In the early stages the rate of profit increased. The capitalist squeezed the working class like a sponge to extract the last drop of profit from them. Exploitation was the second disadvantage of capitalism.

The third was the alienation of the worker. The human individual, being a worker, had to find his work satisfying and fulfilling, which was not the case under capitalism. The reasons for this were that the worker had no control over the productive process, did not decide when, how and where to work but had to obey the boss's commands. Division of labour and specialization of skills made the worker a specialist, preventing the full development of all his talents and thereby stifling his potential. The labourer did not control the final product of his labour. The nature of the productive process within capitalism divided workers and set them against one another. As a result, they did not conceive their work as a collective human project. All these criticisms rested on an implicit utopian premise: that men were fully human only when they developed and expressed their potential through satisfying labour. Linked with this premise was a second remarkable assumption that the modern industrial system afforded opportunities for all to engage in rewarding labour. In the socialist utopia, division of labour was abolished ending monotony and alienation.

Unlike the early liberals for whom inequality was never really a serious issue for the overall progress would percolate and raise the standards of living, Marx saw widening in the difference between the rich and the poor. He rejected capitalism for it encouraged inequality and consumerism leading to commodity fetishism. Marx looked to poverty and affluence as relative for human needs were social in nature.

A house may be large or small; as long as the surrounding houses are equally small it satisfies all social demands for a dwelling. But let a palace arise beside the little house, and it shrinks from a little house to a hut . . . however high it may shoot up in the course of civilization, if the neighbouring palace grows to an equal or even greater extent, the occupant of the relatively small house will feel more and more uncomfortable, dissatisfied and cramped within its four walls (Marx 1997b: 259).

For Marx exploitation and alienation made it possible for the revolutionary transformation of capitalism imperative. It was man as a producer who rebelled against society to end exploitation and oppression, which could be possible only with the abolition of private property. Socialism would see a transformation in human nature and the communist society would be a socialized humanity.

Capitalism divided society into two hostile camps. The proletariat increased in number, misery and impoverishment. The bourgeois shrank but became more prosperous. With polarization of society, class struggles became sharper making a revolution on a world scale inevitable, graphically stated in the *Manifesto* as 'Workers of the World Unite', a phrase borrowed from Karl Schapper. The proletariat was an agent and not as a tool in history and with its liberation came the liberation of society. Marx spoke of worldwide proletarian revolution for capitalism was global. He asserted that capitalism contained within itself seeds of its own destruction. Increase in monopolies led to growing exploitation, misery and pauperization of the working class. Simultaneously, as the working class increased in its numbers, it became better organized and acquired greater bargaining skill. This initiated a violent revolutionary process.

Marx's analysis of capitalism led him to predict the following: (*a*) the income gap between the capitalists and the workers would increase as more and more independent producers would be forced down into the proletariat leaving a few rich capitalists and a mass of poor workers; (*b*) workers' wages with short-lived expectations would remain at a subsistence level; (*c*) the rate of profit would fall; (*d*) capitalism would collapse because of its internal contradictions, and (*e*) proletarian revolutions will occur in the most industrially advanced countries (Singer 1980: 67).

Many, in fact, none of these predictions came true. Marx failed to take into consideration the changes within capitalism. He did not anticipate and comprehend capitalism's resilience for by the late nineteenth century it had stabilized itself. Marx's analysis was true of early nineteenth century capitalism (Dahl 1986: 9). Historical developments did not validate many of Marx's observations which became increasingly obsolete in the twentieth century. The operationalization of democracy, extensive social security cover and labour welfare laws improved the working conditions and the position of the working class. 'The proletarian class no longer exists in its previous stage. Workers have rights in developed countries, they are proprietors' (Djilas 1990: 7).

Marx spoke of monopolies, cartels and profits but neglected the risk factor in modern business. He pointed out to profits in business but never focused on losses. He romanticized the idea of work and thought it was degraded under capitalism which was why division of labour and specialization would cease under socialism. Not only Marx but even Fourier and Morris desired to go back to the medieval idea of craftsmanship which was equally specialized as labour under modern industry. Marx was obssessed with domination and exercise of political power but could not conceive as Saint Simon indicated and Parsons developed a theory of power which is equivalent to money.

Analysis of the State

Unlike Hegel who had worked out the details of a modern state by his distinction of the realm of the state and the realm of the civil society, Marx's account was sketchy. This was in spite of his professed aim to provide for an alternative to the Hegelian paradigm as outlined in his *Critique of Hegel's Philosophy of Right* (1844). His views of the state were largely determined by his perceptions and analyses of the French state, the Revolution of 1848 and the *coup d'etat* of Napoleon III. His ideas were the result of an elaborate misunderstanding of the French revolution, of the role of classes and of the very nature of the revolution. The Bolsheviks in Russia imitated France as seen through the prism of the writings of Marx which seemed to them more real than the actual French history (Wolfe 1969: 7–8). Keeping the French experience he advocated a violent revolutionary seizure of power and the establishment of the dictatorship of the proletariat. Interestingly, he accepted the possibility of peaceful and parliamentary transfer in England, America and Holland where the state was not so highly centralized and bureaucratic as in France. He, by and large, struck to the idea of violent revolution.

For Marx, the state was the superstructure and, in course of history, each mode of production gave rise to its specific political organization to further the interests of the economically dominant class. In the capitalist society, the state, as defined in the *Manifesto*, was 'the executive committee of the bourgeoisie' (Marx 1975). For Marx and Engels, the state expressed human alienation. It was an instrument of class exploitation and class oppression.

In the *Eighteenth Brumaire of Louis Bonaparte* (1852) Marx denounced the bureaucratic and the all-powerful state and advocated its destruction. Bonapartism was a regime in a capitalist society in which the executive branch of the state, under the rule of one individual, attained dictatorial power over all other parts of the state and society. Examples of such regimes during Marx's lifetime were that of Louis Bonaparte, the nephew of Napoleon I who became Napoleon III after his *coup d'etat* of December 1851. Engels found a similar parallel with Bismarck's rule in Germany. Bonapartism was the result of a situation where the ruling class in the capitalist society was no longer in a position to maintain its rule through constitutional and parliamentary means. Neither was the working class able to wrest control for themselves. It was a situation of temporary equilibrium between the rival warring classes. The independence of a Bonapartist state and its role as the 'ostensible mediator' between the rival classes did not mean that it was in a position of suspended animation. In reality, it ensured the safety and stability of the bourgeois society and guaranteed its rapid development. The relative autonomy of the state based on cancelling out the forces in a situation of temporary equilibrium developed by Marx here was later developed and elaborated by Gramsci. Both Marx and Engels were ambivalent about representative parliamentary institutions. In the light of severe restrictions on suffrage in their times, they had qualms about whether parliamentary means could act as an instrument or even as a catalyst for profound social and economic changes. Hence the *Manifesto* stressed on the need to introduce democratic institutions once the proletarian revolution was accomplished. The preliminary draft contended that the revolution would 'inaugurate a democratic constitution and thereby directly or indirectly the political rule of the proletariat' (Ibid.: 75).

For Marx and Engels the communist society would eliminate all forms of alienation for the human individual: from nature, from society and from humanity. Between the destruction of capitalism and attainment of communism was a transitional state called the *dictatorship of the proletariat*. Interestingly, one of the well known utopias was least delineated. Marx's cautions predictions have been imposed by his own epistemological premises (Avineri 1976: 221). Any discussion of the future which was not yet an existing reality meant philosophical idealism for it described an object that existed only in the consciousness of the thinking subject. Moreover Marx did not rival with those socialists whom he had branded as 'utopian' by constructing detailed blueprints for a communist society since for him the latter would be determined by the specific conditions under which it was established. In the *Critique of the Gotha Programme*, Marx wrote: 'What we have to deal with here is communist society not as it has developed on its foundations, but on the contrary just as it emerges for capitalist society' (Marx 1977c: 17).

In the *Civil War in France* similar sentiments were reiterated. 'The working class have no ideals to realize but to set free the elements of the new society with which the old bourgeois society itself is pregnant' (Marx 1977b: 224).

There were similar observations in the *German Ideology* and *Paris Manuscripts* (1844). Marx projected an image of the future society from the internal tensions of the existing capitalist society implying that, at the outset, the communist society would perfect and universalize the elements of the bourgeois society that could be universalized.

Dictatorship of the Proletariat

The controversial and ambiguous concept of the dictatorship of the proletariat emerged in the writings of Marx and Engels as a result of a debate with the German Social Democrats, the Anarchists and more significantly from the practical experiences of the Paris Commune of 1871. These observations had to be pieced together from remarks made solely *enpassant* and from different sources. The two major texts, however, were the *Civil War in France* and the *Critique of the Gotha Programme*. The concept of the dictatorship of the proletariat holds the key to the understanding of Marx's theory on the nature of the communist society and the role of the proletarian state. It was a concept that divided the Marxists and the Leninists from the Anarchists, on the one hand, and from the Social Democrats on the other.

The phrase as well as the idea of elimination of state power and machinery was mentioned in the *Manifesto*. Instead Marx and Engels spoke of the 'political rule of the proletariat' advising the workers to capture the state, destroy the privileges of the old class and prepare the basis for the eventual disappearance of the state.

We have seen above that the first step in the revolution by the working class is to raise the proletariat to the position of ruling class, to win the battle of democracy. . . . The proletariat

will use its political supremacy to wrest, by degrees, all capital
from the bourgeoisie, to centralize all instruments of production in the hands of the state, i.e., of the proletariat organized
as the ruling class; and to increase the total of productive
forces as rapidly as possible (Marx 1975: 74).

Marx and Engels were convinced that existing states, whether
as instruments of class domination and oppression, or bureaucratic
parasites on the whole of society, would grow inherently strong
and remain minority states representing the interests of the small
but dominant and powerful possessing class. Bearing in mind the
experiences of the French Revolution of 1789, he advised the proletariat to seize the state and make it democratic and majoritarian.
Whatever may be the form of the state, it was a powerful machinery
which the proletariat would have to contend with. The initial 'capture' thesis of the state, however, yielded to the 'smash' thesis subsequently. In a book review written around 1848–9 Marx observed
that the destruction of the state had only one implication for the
Communists, namely, the cessation of an organized power of one
class for the suppression of another class. (Draper 1977: 288).

In the *Manifesto* Marx described the nature of the Communist
society as a classless and 'an association, in which the free development of each is the condition for the free development of all'
(Marx 1975: 76). For the purpose of socializing the means of production a list of ten measures were outlined which included:
(1) abolition of property in land and application of all rents of land
to public purpose; (2) a heavy progressive or graduated income
tax; (3) abolition of all rights of inheritance; (4) confiscation of the
property of all emigrants and rebels; (5) centralization of credit in
the hands of the state; (6) centralization of the means of transport
in the hands of the state; (7) extension of factories and instruments
of production owned by the state; (8) equal liability of all to labour;
(9) combination of agriculture and industries, and gradual abolition of the distinction between town and country; and (10) free
education for all children in public schools (Ibid.: 74).

Marx modified his views on the state during 1848–52 as a result
of events in France and, more significantly, after 1871. Until March
1850, Marx and Engels did not apply the word 'dictatorship' to the
rule of the proletariat. Before that, they did not mention nor discuss
the Babouvist-Blanquist conception of educational dictatorship for

it contravened their vision of a proletarian revolution which was based on the faith they had in the masses to emancipate themselves. They did not feel the need for a period of educational rule by an enlightened minority or the postponement of democratic elections. The phrase was used as a tactical compromise slogan with the Blanquists and then as a polemical device against the Anarchists and assorted reformists (Hunt 1975: 334).

It was not Blanqui but Louis Eugene Cavaignac, a general and an arch antagonist of Blanqui, who helped Marx and Engels incorporate the word 'dictatorship' into their vocabulary. Engels clarified that dictatorship was necessary to fill the vacuum as a result of the destruction of the old order and till the creation of the new order. Marx accepted this formulation. Both were confident that it did not mean the permanent rule of one person or group. In March 1850 the phrase 'dictatorship of the proletariat' replaced the habitually used phrase 'rule of the proletariat'. Marx and Engels stressed on the notion of extraordinary power during an emergency for a limited period of time. It would be a constitutional dictatorship like the one suggested by Babeuf and Blanqui but differed from their conception insofar as it would not be educational. It did not mean the rule of a self-appointed committee on behalf of the masses, nor did they envisage the need for mass terror and liquidation.

Marx did not define any specific way as to what the dictatorship of the proletariat entailed and as to what was its relationship to the state. it was 'a social description, a statement of the class character of the political power. It was not a statement about the forms of government authority' (Draper 1977: 294). But for some the concept was both a statement of class character of political power and a description of political power itself. 'It is in fact the nature of political power which it describes which guarantees its class character' (Miliband 1965: 289–90). To Marx and Engels the dictatorship of the proletariat was of the entire class. In a series of articles written in *Neue Rheinische Zeitung,* later compiled under the title *The Class Struggles in France* (1848–50), Marx wrote:

> . . . the declaration of the permanence of the revolution, the class dictatorship of the proletariat as the necessary transit point to the abolition of class distinctions generally to the abolition of all relations of production on which they rest, to

the abolition of all social relations that correspond to these relations of production, to the revolutionizing of all the ideas that result from these social relations (Marx 1977a: 282).

The phrase 'dictatorship of the proletariat' was incorporated into the first of the six statues of the Universal Society. In a letter to Otta Luning, co-editor of *Neue Rheinische Zeitung*, Marx clarified that he did not find any significant departure of the idea of the dictatorship of the proletariat articulated in the *Class Struggles* to the one formulated in the *Manifesto*. The ambiguous compromise slogan 'dictatorship of the proletariat' would have died a natural death had the Marxists and the Blanquists not renewed their contacts in the aftermath of the Paris Commune (Hunt 1975: 305–6).

Meanwhile an important event that helped in the clarification of the concept was the Paris Commune which led to an amendment of the *Manifesto* in 1872. Marx felt that: 'One thing especially was proved by the Commune, viz. that the working class cannot simply lay hold of the ready-made state machinery and wield it for its own purpose' (Marx 1975: 8). Marx was enthused about the Commune, regarding it as the 'glorious harbinger of a new society', and observed in his letter to Kugelman in April 1871 that:

> If you look at the last chapter of my *Eighteen Brumaire*, you will find that I say that the next attempt of the French Revolution will no longer be, as before, to transfer the bureaucratic-military machine from one hand to another but to smash it and this is the precondition for every real people's revolution in the continent. And this is what our heroic party comrades in Paris are attempting (Marx 1977a: 240).

Marx saw the Paris Commune as the first major rebellion of the modern industrial proletariat. This was in consonance with his belief that France would set the example in the struggle between capital and labour. In his address to the General Council of The International Workingmen's Association or the First International (1864–76) in London, he outlined the importance of the commune and its lessons for future socialist movements. These were identified as follows: (*a*) abolition of the standing army and institution of the citizen's militia, (*b*) election of all officials subjecting them to recall, (*c*) removal of political attributes of the police, (*d*) abolition of monarchy, and (*e*) the role of the majority in directing and performing all functions of the state which was previously executed by a privileged minority. With regard to the last point, he emphasized on the following measures: (*a*) abolition of all representative allowances, all monetary benefits to officials and reducing the remuneration for officials to the level of 'workmen's wages', (*b*) abolition of the distance between the governed and the governors and erasing the label of 'high' dignitaries, (*c*) election of judges, and (*d*) universal suffrage exercised freely and frequently.

The commune was regarded as a working and not as a parliamentary body exercising legislative and executive power simultaneously. It would break down the power of the state and people would be organized on the basis of a decentralized federal system with the dissemination of power at the broadest and to the largest extent. Its real strength lay in the fact that it represented the working class and was 'the product of the struggle of the producing against the appropriating class, the political form at last discovered under which to work out the economic emancipation of labour' (Marx 1977a: 220–5).

Criticisms by the Anarchists and Social Democrats

To the Anarchists, the proletarian revolution ended all forms of coercive and superimposed organizations. They rejected the Marxist utopia — the dictatorship of the proletariat — for they feared that it may very well become a *status quo* giving rise to fresh set of inequities, privileges, oppression, terror and injustices. The dictatorship of the proletariat could become a dictatorship *on* the proletariat. They rejected statism outrightly for it stifled the initiative of the masses and their immediate organs of self government — factory committees and local communes. Not only did it undermine the libertarian and emancipatory elements of the revolution, it would also be inefficient for the central authorities would never be able to gauge pulse of the people at the local level.

Proudhon looked at the state as an evil. He located the origin of the state in human nature and family. His ideal was anarchy which meant reduction of political functions to industrial ones and that social order would resemble nothing more than transactions and exchanges. Proudhon repudiated class war, opposed trade unionism and did not advocate sudden expropriation of the bourgeoisie and abolition of the state. He looked to socialism as primarily a solution to a moral problem, namely, the deliverance of the individuals from the fetters imposed by the industrial system. He described communism as 'police despotism'. Bakunin in his *Statism and Anarchy* (1873) contended that the Marxist political order could turn out to be a rigid oligarchy of technocrats and officials. If such a state controlled all capital and the means of production, it would eventually lead to bureaucratization and to a government by the intelligentsia. 'It will be the reign of scientific intelligence, the most aristocratic, despotic, arrogant and elitists of all regimes' (Bakunin, cited in Dolgoff 1973: 319). Bakunin developed his arguments in detail and observed:

> One may well ask whether the proletariat would be in the position of a ruling class, and over whom it would? This means that yet another proletariat would emerge, which would be subject to the new sovereignty and new state. For instance, the Marxists, as is well known, are not yet well disposed towards the peasant rabble, who, being on the lowest cultural level, would doubtless be governed by the urban and factory proletariat . . . . What does raising the proletariat to the level of government mean? Surely, the whole proletariat is not going to head for administration? There are about forty million Germans. Does it mean that all forty million will be members of the government? In that case there will be no government and no state.
>
> This dilemma in the Marxist theory can easily be solved. A people's administration, according to them, must mean a people's administration by virtue of a small number of representatives chosen by the people. The universal right of each individual among all the people to elect so-called representatives and members of the government, that is the final word of the Marxists and of the democratic school, and it is deception which would conceal the despotism of a governing minority, all the more dangerous because it appears as a sham expression of the people's will. Those previous workers having become rulers or representatives of the people will cease being workers; they will look at the workers from their heights, they will represent not the people but themselves . . . if there are 'dedicated' or learned socialists, then the so-called

people's state will be nothing but a despotic control of populace by a new and not at all numerous aristocracy of real and pseudo-scientists. He who doubts it does not know human nature (Bakunin, cited in Lehning 1973: 268).

The task of the proletarian revolution would be not to transform the state but to abolish it. Bakunin perceived that, to Marx, the abolition of the state played no vital role. The latter wanted to capture the state and not destroy it in its entirety for he desired to 'liberaie from above' through the state. He held that true liberation must come only 'from below' through the individual. If, for Marx, the workers' state represented the entire people then:

> . . . why eliminate it? And if the state is needed to emancipate the workers, then the workers are not yet free, so why call it a People's state (Bakunin, cited in Dolgoff 1973: 331).

Marx argued that for Bakunin all states were evil since they were products of class-divided societies oppressing, exploiting and dominating the economically poor working class, thereby implying complete abstention from all politics. In *On Authority* (1872–73) Engels clarified that Anarchism was not the goal of Marxism. The impending social revolution abolished all forms of authority but not the state. In a classless society the state would cease to be an evil and would eventually 'wither' away. To this, Bakunin contended that power corrupted all those who wielded it.

The clash of the titans took place in the International Workingmen's Association, popularly known as the First International. Here Marx was involved in his polemics with Bakunin, Proudhon and Lassalle, and in particular with the first two. Bakunin joined the International in 1868 with a short speech which set the tone of the Anarchistic critique of the Marxist notion of the dictatorship of the proletariat and observed:

> I detest communism because it is the negation of liberty and I cannot conceive anything human without liberty. I am not a communist because communism concentrates all the powers of society and absorbs them into the hands of the state while I want to see the state abolished. I want the complete liberation of the authoritarian principle of state tutelage which has

always subjected, oppressed, exploited and depraved men while claiming to moralize and civilize them. I want society and collective or social property to be organized from the bottom up through free associations and not from the top down by authority of any kind ... in that sense I am a collectivist and not at all a communist (Bakunin, cited in Woodcock 1944: 41).

Bakunin, in contrast to the Marxist ideal, envisaged his future anarchist society to be one of abundance. Political power would have disappeared completely. It would be an equal society, for any kind of inequality would virtually amount to slavery for the proletariat. He demanded the complete and immediate abolition of the state and not merely the capture of political power by the victorious revolutionary forces.

The German Social Democrats following the views of Lassalle articulated the possibilities of using the existing state for the realization of socialism and enhancement of human freedom. They favoured reforms as opposed to a revolution and believed that the spread of suffrage enabled the workers to have a decisive role in parliament and the institutions of the state. These demands were incorporated in the Gotha programme adopted by the Social Democratic Party (SPD) in 1875.[2] In response to both the Anarchists and the German Social Democrats, Marx wrote the *Critique of the Gotha Programme* in which he emphasized the transitional nature of the dictatorship of the proletariat and outlined the two-phased development to full Communism which would be attained through a revolutionary transformation of society.

Between the capitalist society and communist society lies the period of the revolutionary transformation of the one into another. There corresponds to this also a political transition period in which the state can be nothing but the revolutionary dictatorship of the proletariat (Marx 1977c: 19).

According to Marx, the first or the lower phase would be still contain the remnants of capitalism from whose womb it emerged. The principle of distribution with regard to consumer goods would be one of performance. In the second phase, distribution would be on the basis of one's needs according to the principle 'from each according to his ability to each according to his needs' (Marx 1977c: 18–19). Lenin characterized these two phases as 'socialism' and 'communism', respectively.

In the second phase, the division of labour was abolished and each individual devoted himself to a single life task. In a Communist society Marx hoped that the individual could become whatever he wished, allowing a person to hunt in the morning, fish in the afternoon, rear cattle in the evening, criticize after dinner without ever becoming a hunter, fisherman, shepherd or critic. Individual and private ownership of property would cease to exist and would be replaced by social ownership. The antithesis between mental and physical labour would be abolished and labour would become not only a means of life but life's prime want (Ibid.: 19). Marx contrasted the higher form of communism with primitive or crude communism, the first stage in the process of historical materialism. The latter was signified by the necessity of all to labour, a levelling down of all individual talents and communal ownership of women, essentially indicating a negation of the human personality. All these features would be absent in the ideal communist society.

Marx did not specify the mechanisms of change from Stage I to Stage II in the post-revolutionary phase of human history casting serious doubts as to how Stage I would develop into Stage II and whether it would develop as intended (Avineri 1976: 329). Since this process was not explained, the ultimate aim of 'free development of each will lead to the free development of all' might not be realizable (Wilson 1941: 335–36). In *Anti Dühring*, Engels introduced the notion of the 'withering away of the state' and the fact that 'government of persons would be replaced by administration of things'. Both he and Marx accepted that the proletarian state would be centrally planned and directed without coercion and force, but they failed to resolve the possible conflict between centralized planning and individual freedom in the communist society.

Thus, Marx and Engels reacted sharply to Bakunin's criticism about the statist implications of their conception and Lassalle's free state. By 1875 it became clear that the German Social Democrats were thinking of using the existing state apparatus and had settled down for reformism while Marx advocated the revolutionary overthrow of the existing bureaucratic-military state and replacing it with the dictatorship of the proletariat which would be truly democratic and majoritarian for the revolution could only be truly democratic and majoritarian. Bakunin insisted on the immediate elimination of all forms of political authority and replacing it with spontaneous and voluntary organizations. Marx accepted the Anarchist demand of the abolition of the state but emphasized the majoritarian content of the transitional state purely as a temporary measure hoping to counter both his critics.

An examination of the development of the idea of the dictatorship of the proletariat revealed a tension between the concept's organizational necessity, may be of a transitory kind, with the larger Marxist hypothesis of enlargement of human freedom. Marx's handling of the crucial role of the theory of the state remained inadequate. In tackling the complexities of the modern state, the general descriptions of the ideal as realizing true democracy and communism proved to be simplistic in providing the essential institutions of a democratic state. His aversion to utopian blue-printing made him ignore the details that were necessary for managing a society based on equity, just reward and freedom. The phrases 'true democracy' and 'communism' hardly dealt with the complexities of the times (Dahl 1986). Marx never addressed himself to the issues of rights, political freedom, power and role of authority in the socialist society.

For all his libertarian vision, Marx himself was consummated by the idea of having absolute, total, concentrated state power, unrestrained and unlimited. He was contemptuous and, in fact, had very little faith in a constitution or law, dismissing it as a sham, a formal and a cover to conceal bourgeois oppression and domination. The attack on formal democracy by promising substantive democracy resulted in reducing formal democracy to the point of non-existence. Marx overlooked the protection that constitutional representative democracy and rule of law gave against arbitrary rule and the freedom these ensured against physical harm. He failed to understand the dynamics of democracy in empowering people being more revolutionary than a bloody violent revolution itself.

He profoundly underestimated the capacity of democratic societies to correct or mitigate the injustices that seemed to him built into capitalism. The concept of the 'class struggle', which is central in the thinking of all Marxists, seems largely irrelevant in America and Western Europe (Berlin 1939: xi).

Berlin's last observation about the obsolence of class struggle in advanced industrialized countries can be extended to the developing world now. There is no more any talk of revolutionary transformation of society or that 'East is Red'. Moreover the possibility of using democracy as a means of realizing socialism never moved to the centre stage of his analysis of the future society. 'The overall sweep of the Marxist historical scheme relegates democracy to a subsidiary role in the drama of human development (Harding 1981: 157).

This was where the Social Democrats scored over Marx because they and, in particular, Bernstein insisted on the need to combine democracy (representative parliamentary institutions with universal suffrage) with socialism bringing about a breach that could never be closed between German Marxism and Russian Communism (Plamentaz 1969).

The idea of the communist society being classless and equal remained a myth. Djilas in *The New Class* (1959) pointed to the presence of the *nomenklatura* in the former communist societies, namely, those who enjoyed privileges and special status because of their position within the hierarchy of the Communist Party thus confirming the fears of Bakunin that the dictatorship of the proletariat would create fresh inequities and new forms of oppression and domination. Perhaps no one has captured the myth of a classless society better than George Orwell (1903–50) in his satire *Animal Farm* (1945) and *Nineteen Eighty Four* (1949) made memorable by phrases 'all animals are equal but some are more equal than others' and 'the big brother is watching'.

In exploring the possibilities of a world proletarian revolution, Marx and Engels began to show interest in the non-European world. The Asiatic mode of production examined the relevance of Marxist concepts outside the European context. While they were convinced that socialism represented the zenith of capitalism and that the proletarian revolution would break out only in the advanced industrialized societies, they explored the possibilities of a revolution in semi-developed and backward areas with the view to fomenting a revolution in the developed areas. In this context, in 1882 they expressed the view that if a revolution in Tsarist Russia would occur it may complement the efforts of the proletariat in the advanced West. Russia's backwardness and the lack of a coherent theory of post-revolutionary society in Marx's concept attenuated Blanquism in Leninism and Stalinism. If Stalinism was an offshoot of Leninism, Leninism was inspired by Marxism.

Women and the Gender Question

Like in many other areas, with regard to the question of women, Marx made Hegel the starting point. Hegel regarded women as inferior with less reasoning abilities seeing the natural differences between men and women as immutable. Marx did not say much on the role and position of women. He took it for granted that socialism would bring about their emancipation. In *German Ideology* and *The Capital*, he spoke of the natural and spontaneous division of labour within the family. The natural relationship paved the way for a social one, and the first-property relationship was one when the man regarded his wife and children as his slaves. Man had the power over them and could do with their labour as he chose, though Marx did not explain how this came about. Marx did not focus his attention on the position and role of women.

Engels in the *Origins* provided a materialist account of the origin of patriarchy and linked women's subordination with the rise of private property. In the *Holy Family*, Marx and Engels observed that the degree of emancipation of women could be used as a standard by which one could measure general emancipation. Marx reiterated this view in a letter to Dr. L. Kugelmann in 1868 that social progress could be assessed exactly by the social position of women. In 1845 Marx warned against treating the family, regardless of its specific historic setting. In his criticisms of Max Stirner (1805–56) he observed it was a misconception to speak of the family without qualifications. Historically, the bourgeoisie endowed the family with the characteristics of the bourgeois family whose ties were boredom and money.

The Asiatic Mode of Production

Marx's views on the non-European world, like his overall political theorizing, also flowed from the Hegelian prescriptions. But in the evolution of these two basic themes, there was an interesting yet contradictory development. The contemporary analysis of Germany that Hegel offered was rejected on the basis of an universalistic criterion while the notion of the unchanging and static nature of the non-European world was accepted without any critical examination. Marx used the phrase 'Asiatic Mode of Production' to describe the non-European societies. In this formulation there was a clear 'discrepancy between the analytical and historical nature of the categories of ancient, feudal and bourgeois modes of production and the mere geographic designation of the Asiatic one' (Avineri 1969: 56).

Marx did not show any specific interest in the non-European world prior to 1852. His interest arose as a result of a series of articles that he penned for the *New York Daily Tribune* (1852–62). The Asiatic Mode of Production assumed importance subsequently within the theoretical and political debates within Marxist circles. 'The debates about the Asiatic Mode of Production has raised questions concerning not only the relevance of Marxist concepts outside the European context, but also the character of materialist explanations of class society, revolutionary change and world history (Bottomore 1983: 32).

The underlying assumption among many post Renaissance European thinkers who took an interest in the non-European world was that there was a marked and qualitative distinction between the advanced European cultures and other backward civilizations. Montesquieu was the pioneer of such a perception. Using climatic conditions as the yardstick, he noted that tropical climates were unsuited for democracies and individual freedoms. Adam Smith clubbed China, Egypt and India together for the special attention irrigation received in these societies. James Mill observed the difference between European feudalism and governmental arrangements in Asiatic societies. Richard Jones used the phrase 'Asiatic society' and J.S. Mill used the term 'Eastern society' in 1848. Others like Herbert Spencer (1820–1903), Vilfredo Pareto (1848–1923) and Emile Durkheim (1855–1917) analyzed Asiatic societies from a comparative perspective. Hegel was the most influential amongst these thinkers whose philosophy of history not only concurred with this prevailing European perception of the East but also influenced, to a very large extent, the left Hegelians with respect to looking to colonization as a modernizing force. For Hegel with his clear eurocentricism, India and China did not have any history. They were 'stationery and fixed'. This was true of all Asiatic societies. Hegel's point that the East lacked history influenced Marx.

Marx described the oriental societies of India and China as lacking in history, incapable of changing from within and essentially stagnant. Since, by themselves, they would block historical progress, the industrialized West, when it became socialistic, would be the agent of liberation in the less developed areas. In other words, European socialism would have to precede the national liberation movements in the Asian societies. Marx identified Europe with progress and the Orient with stagnation. He looked to the imperialist rule as being simultaneously destructive and constructive. It was degenerative because it destroyed indigenous institutions and practices, while it was regenerative because it created the modern techniques of production, brought political unity and social changes.

Marx and Engels concluded that the chief characteristic of Asiatic societies was the absence of private property, particularly private ownership of land. In contrast to the state in the European context which was an instrument of class domination and exploitation, the state in Asiatic societies controlled all classes. It did not belong to the superstructure but was decisive in the entire economic arena, building and managing water supply, the life breath of agriculture in arid areas. It performed economic and social functions for the entire society. Social privileges emanated from service to the state and not from the institution of private property as was the case in Europe. Asiatic societies had an over-developed state and an under-developed civil society. Military conquests and dynastic tussles ushered in changes periodically without affecting the economic organization because the state continued to be the real landlord. The unchanging nature of Asiatic societies was also buttressed by self-sufficient autarchic villages which sustained themselves through agriculture and handicrafts.

In the *Grundrisse*, Marx and Engels developed on these preliminary sketch of the Asiatic societies to highlight the key differences in the urban history of the West and the East. In the West, the existence of politically independent cities conducive to growth of the production of exchange values determined the development of a bourgeois class and industrial capitalism, whereas in the East, the city was artificially created by the state and remained a 'princely camp' subordinated to the countryside. The city was imposed on the economic structure of the society. Social unity represented by the state lay in the autarchic self-sufficient villages where land was communally owned. Stability was ensured by simplicity of production. The state appropriated the surplus in the form of taxes. Factors like free markets, private property, guilds and bourgeois law that led to the rise of the capitalist class in the West were absent in the Asiatic societies due to a centralized state that dominated and controlled the civil society. For Marx imperialism would act as a catalyst of change since these societies lacked the mechanisms for change. It was because of covert defence of imperialism that Marxists sought to dismantle the concept.

The Anarchists, and in particular Bakunin, defended the right of nations, including the predominantly peasant eastern nations, to self determination. The West was based on slavery and did not prove that it was superior to the 'barbarians of Orient'. He asserted that all states were constituted by its nature and the conditions of the purpose for which they existed, namely the absolute negation of human justice, freedom and morality. By this logic he did not distinguish between the uncouth Tsarist Russia and the advanced countries of North Europe, for the former did the same thing as the latter with the mask of hypocrisy.

The concept of the Asiatic Mode has had a chequered history. In the preface to *A Contribution to the Critique of Political Economy* (1859) Marx considered the Asiatic Mode as an one of the 'epochs marking progress in the economic development of society'. Engels did not refer to the Asiatic mode in *The Origins*. It was in the context of the discussions on revolutionary struggles in Russia that the concept figured once again. Different political strategies were devised in view of Russia being feudal, semi-capitalist, authoritarian and partly Asiatic. In 1853 Marx and Engels characterized Tsarist Russia as 'Semi-Asiatic'. In the *Anti Dühring* Engels (1952) viewed the Russia commune as the basis of oriental despotism. Between 1877 and 1882 Marx, in his letters to Zaulich and Engels as a member of the editorial board of *Otechestvenniye Zapiski*, examined the prospects of revolution in Russia and whether in such an eventuality the commune could provide the foundations of socialism.

In exploring the possibilities of a world proletarian revolution Marx and Engels began to show interest in the non-European world. The notion of the Asiatic Mode of Production examined the relevance of Marxist concepts outside the European context. While Marx and Engels were convinced that socialism represented the zenith of capitalism and that the proletarian revolution would break out only in the advanced industrialized societies, they pointed out in

1882 that if a revolution would break out in Tsarist Russia it would complement the efforts of the proletariat in the advanced west.

The Asiatic Mode paradigm undermined Marx's universalistic presumption that a ruling class could only be a proprietary class, i.e., a class that owned the means of production. The primary paradigm in the *Manifesto* and other writings did not focus on the class character of the state bureaucracy which could be one of the reasons why the Asiatic Mode in particular, and the theory of the state in general, remained so sketchy in the works of Marx and Engels (Gouldner 1980: 339–42).

On India

Analyzing India within the framework of the Asiatic Mode, Marx was convinced that Imperial Britain would establish the foundations of Western society in India for English imperialism represented the only social revolution in Asia. This belief rested on the logic that though colonialism was brutal yet it was dialectically important for the world proletarian revolution. Colonialism would unleash forces of modernization which would eventually lead to the emancipation of these areas. Marx's account of British imperialism led to the proposition that the more extensive the forms of imperialism, the more profound would be the consequences for modernization (Avineri 1969). Marx and Engels favoured colonialism as it was a catalyst for modernization though they did take note of the regressive and exploitative side also.

Marx noted that in India, England had a dual function, one destructive and the other regenerative. Colonialism as a regenerative force brought about political unification, introduced railways, free press, trained army, Western education, rational ways of thinking and abolished common land tenure. As for being destructive, British colonization destroyed indigenous industries and handicrafts. Marx mentioned the exploitative role played by the East India Company and the increasing resentment English capitalists had against its monopoly preventing the transfer of surplus British capital to India. All these changes profoundly affected the static nature of Indian society. In this context he mentioned superstitions and close mindedness which reinforced animal worship preventing development.

In spite of these insights, the fact remained that, like the Conservatives, Marx and Engels favoured colonialism. In the fierce controversy between Marx and Bakunin the question of the right of self determination was one of the major issues of disagreement. Moreover, the Marxist view of the non-European world and the dominant streams of twentieth century nationalist thought did not vindicate the Marxist thesis. Amilcar Lopes Cabral (1924–73)[3] rightly rejected this entire postulate of history starting with the emergence of class struggle and the consequent thesis that the continents of Africa, Asia and America did not have any history before the colonial period. The factor of nationalism that contributed to the liberation of the colonies was completely ignored by Marx.

Marx, in spite of his erudite scholarship, was a child of his times. He viewed the non-European world through the European perspective. His observations, however profound, reflected a great deal of prevailing Hegelian prejudices and euro-centricism. Many of the Indian Marxists did not accept Marx's formulations on the Asiatic Mode nor his observations on British imperialism in India.

Conclusion

Marx wrote in the optimistic environment of Victorian England where the gloomy predictions of Malthus were forgotten. He was a believer in the uninterrupted progress of human civilization and of industrial society. He did not recognize any limits to growth. He was generally hopeful of the liberating and progressive role of science and human rationality. For the sheer range and breadth of influence it would be appropriate to say that one could not write without taking into account his writings and without understanding the full import of his ideas.

Marx claimed that he had turned Hegel upside down and was initiating his own independent line of theorizing. Though he styled his brand of socialism as scientific, his exposition was not systematic and cogent. His observations and descriptions of the communist ideal lacked the details that were needed to project a blueprint. The general nature of the descriptions meant different things to different people. Unless one clearly and precisely stated the meaning of a just society, it was not possible to debate and reflect about it. Instead when

men range themselves under the banner as friends and enemies of the "revolution", the only important question which
is just and useful is kept out of sight and measures are judged
not by their real worth but by the analogy they seem to have
to an irrelevant abstraction (Lasky 1976: 573).

This failure to give details led to considerable confusion for the
same words conveyed different things to different people.' . . . Marx
sketched but never developed a systematic theory of the state and
hence the idea of a political economy remained overdetermined
and undescribed politically' (Wolin 1987: 469).

However, Marx was a revolutionary and a socialist but, above
all, he was a humanist who believed in genuine emancipation and
liberation of human beings. He registered protest against every
kind of domination. Though many of his predictions did not materialize, Marx's genius lay not merely in his ability to predict but in
the new modes of thinking about economic and political issues.

The doctrine which has survived and grown, and which has
had a greater and more lasting influence both on opinion and
on action than any other view put forward in modern times,
is his theory of the evolution and structure of capitalist society,
of which he nowhere gave a detailed exposition. This theory,
by asserting that the important question to be asked with regard to any phenomenon is concerned with the relation which
bears to the economic structure . . . has created new tools of
criticism and research whose use has altered the direction
and emphasis of the social sciences in our generation (Berlin
1939: xii).

Undoubtedly Marx was a genius but one should not overlook
his shortcomings. Weber in his famous essay *The Protestant Ethics
and the Spirit of Capitalism* (1904–5) points out that capitalism was
caused by the habits, beliefs and attitudes of Protestantism and
more specifically Calvinism and English Puritanism. For Weber,
ideas and economic motives were interests too, that 'material without ideal interests are empty, but ideals without material interests
are impotent' (Weber, cited in MacRae 1974: 58). Weber gave importance to concepts and values for they played a pivotal role in
social life.

According to Weber, Marx remained vague about the economic base. He conceded that within the parameters of non-economic factors, purely economic behaviour could occur. In fact, Marx's simplistic analysis precluded such considerations. Weber was not happy with Marx's clubbing of technology with the economic base for he believed that with any state of technology many economic orders were possible, and vice versa. He criticized Marx for being imprecise about what really constituted economic categories.

Weber criticized socialism for its attempt to replace the anarchy of the market and achieve greater equity through planning. This, he believed, would result in greater bureaucratization leading to a loss of freedom and enterpreneurship. Weber was clear that private property and market were necessary for guaranteeing plurality of social powers and individual freedom.

Marx did not foresee the rise of fascism, totalitarianism and the welfare state (Berlin 1939: xi). His analysis of capitalism was at best applicable to early nineteenth century capitalism and his criticism of contemporary capitalism as being wasteful, unequal and exploitative was true. However, his alternative of genuine democracy and full communism seemed more difficult to realize in practice for it did not accommodate a world which was becoming increasingly differentiated, stratified and functionally specialized.

Popper's (1945) critique of Marxism on the basis of falsification was equally true and difficult to refute for Marxism constantly adjusted theory in light of reality. He was suspicious of Marx's scientific predictions for a scientific theory was one that would not try and explain everything. Along with Plato and Hegel, Marx was seen as an enemy of the open society. Marxism claimed to have the laws of history on the basis of which it advocated total sweeping radical changes. Not only was it impossible to have first-hand knowledge based on some set of laws that governed society and individuals, but also Popper rejected Marx's social engineering as dangerous for it treated individuals as subservient to the interests of the whole. He rejected the historicism, holism and utopian social engineering of Marxism. In contrast, Popper advocated piece-meal social engineering where change would be gradual and modest- allowing rectification of lapses and errors for it was not possible to conceive of everything. It encouraged public discourse and participation making the process democratic and majoritarian.

Popper claimed that Marx's scientific socialism was not only wrong about society but also about science. The capitalism that Marx described never existed. Marx thought machines would become bigger and bigger whereas they actually became small due to the micro chip revolution. Marx made the economy all important ignoring factors like religion, nationality, friendship. Society was far more complex than what Marx described. In spite of exaggerating the influence of economics, it was a fact that: 'Marx brought into the social sciences and historical science the very important idea that economic conditions are of great importance in the life of society . . . . There was nothing like serious economic history before Marx' (Popper 1996: 20).

Cornforth in *The Open Philosophy and the Open Enemies* (1968) charged Popper for regarding capitalism and open society as coextensive and for believing that capitalism had changed fundamentally. For him, 'friends of the open society, who are organizing to get rid of capitalism, are its enemies; and the enemies of the open society, who are organizing to preserve capitalism are its friends'. The fight for an open society in reality was a fight against anything and everything that was done to prevent exploitation of man by man. He did not accept the charge that communism would destroy individual freedom, reinforce dogmatism, undermine science, arts, culture and eventually civilization. Communism did not stand for lawless tyranny and violence.

Cornforth's defence of Marxism against Popper was merely polemical without much substance. He ignored the fact that, unlike many other well known critics, Popper did not attack totalitarian Marxism at its weakest but from its strongest which led Berlin to acclaim that Popper provided the 'most scrupulous and formidable criticism of the philosophical and historical doctrines of Marxism by any living writer' (Berlin, cited in Magee 1984: 2). To this Magee observed 'I must confess I do not see how any rational man can have read Popper's critique of Marx and still be a Marxist' (Ibid.: 92).

Berlin rejected the deterministic outlook of Marxism and questioned the entire argument of providing a right goal for all individuals. The focus should be to concentrate on today rather than chase chimerical utopias of tomorrow. The idea of utopia for Berlin, like Popper, was philosophically dubious, hideously dangerous and logically incoherent. They ruled out finality in anything. While for

Berlin an utopian society meant lack of free choice and monist values, namely one idea of good life, for Popper a blueprint of a perfect ideal meant statism and arrested growth. It precluded what he called 'unplanned planning'.

Like Popper, Berlin attacked the historicism of Hegel and Marx which he developed in his essay *Historical Inevitability* (1954). Many of Berlin's arguments were similar to that of Popper except that Berlin was emphatic that the historicism of Hegel and Marx denied free human will which enabled them to absolve historians from censuring the villains in history. Historicism was some kind of metaphysical mystery. Both Hegel and Marx defined freedom as obedience to a rational will, namely the idea of positive liberty, rather than seeing freedom as choice as reflected in the writings of Locke, Hume and J.S. Mill. Choice implied conflict among rivalrous goods whereas rational will suggested one way of life, one life plan that would be same for most, if not all, the people.

Berlin's inherent faith in pluralism led him to defend freedom as choice or negative liberty for each individual, each culture and each nation. Each historical period would have its own goals, aspirations and conceptions of good life and it was impossible to unite them together into an overarching single theoretical system in which all ends would be realized without any clashes and conflict. For Berlin, values, however ultimate they may be, did and could exclude one another, and their incompatibility was to be reconciled through a constant process of compromise or trade off, instead of a false synthesis. Thus Berlin was a critic of enlightenment rationalism which suggested uninterrupted progress of history and the possibility of synthesizing all values. The master idea for Berlin was pluralism which suggested that there was no single grand idea, meaning that there were many conceptions of good life, a good society, and that these were often, at least sometimes, incommensurable and incompatible. A monist was compared to a hedgehog who knew one grand idea. Marx, Hegel and Plato were hedgehogs. A pluralist like a fox knew many things.

Rejecting monoism, Berlin attacked the metaphysical content behind positive liberty that everything could be explained with reference to a single homogenous principle and discoverable laws. This led to determinism and totalitarianism. He insisted that philosophy had to be humble. It could not offer a set of principles or a theory that would solve all the dilemmas of moral and political life nor could it straighten the 'crooked timber of humanity', a favourite phrase with him which he borrowed from Kant. He was opposed to philosophy proposing radical social reforms which explained his hostility towards Marxism. For Berlin, totalitarian ideologies and politics — Fascism, Nazism and Communism — did have different goals between them to pursue, but they shared certain common traits. They looked to the state as being superior to the individual giving it an overarching role over society and individual. It directed every aspect of the individual's life suggesting homogeneity and regarding any deviation as sacrilegious. 'It set out to refute the proposition that ideas decisively determine the course of history, but the very extent of its own influence on human affairs has weakened the force of its thesis (Berlin 1939: 234).

Habermas rejected specifically the nostalgic, romantic and utopian vision of socialism though he remained a committed socialist. He was clear that socialism will not rise again but it was still alive as a critique. He looked to socialism as a 'discourse in exile'. He examined Marx's theory of history by focusing on the relationship between crisis and critique and then on the concepts of reification and alienation. First Habermas raised doubts about Marx's Hegelian-inspired concept of labour as human being's self creative activity. Individuals learned to control the natural world and acquire technical knowledge but it was social interaction that established human capacity, namely the development of moral cognitive abilities. This, according to Habermas could not be explained by the increase in productive forces implying that class conflict is no longer a motive force in history. By focusing on production Marx failed to see the possibilities for freedom in the realm of social interaction. He mistook command of external nature of human freedom and ignored social repression of internal nature. Second, Habermas pointed out that societies were not totalities whose parts were in the end determined by the level of development of their productive forces. He distinguished between life-world and systems which in turn were divided into private and public spheres. The life-world was the realm of moral-practical knowledge or relations that existed within the families and workplaces (private) and political actions and opinions (public). It was coordinated through communicative action, namely action involving the self and that of others. In comparison, political (states) and economic (markets) systems were coordinated through the modicum of power and money. Habermas argued that Marx failed to see these distinctions, which was why he could not foresee the stability of capitalism nor the bankruptcy of socialism. Third, Marx defined history as progress rather than the development of universal principles of morality and justice. Though these did not represent the unfolding of reason in history yet 'Historicizing the knowledge of an essence . . . only replaces the teleology of Being with that of History. The secretly normative presuppositions of theories of history are naturalized in the form of evolutionary concepts of progress' (Habermas 1991: 35).

Habermas pointed out that the moral cognitive developments logically created a space for new forms of social organizations and that fundamental changes occurred when society demonstrated the capacity to adapt and grow. These changes indicated the meaning of freedom and ought to be defined by the participants themselves. Only with a convergence of knowing and doing and the self conscious creation of a socialist society could human exile end. The specific function of critical theory was to identify the formal conditions that made possible this emancipation. Habermas maintained that by visualizing humans as producers, societies as totalities and history as progress Marx went back to a Hegelian-inspired theology and anthropology. According to Habermas, state socialism became bankrupt but socialism still nurtured 'the hope that humanity can emancipate itself from self imposed tutelage'. It remained a 'doctrine in exile' for it nourished the possibility, according to Fischman, that 'people can be more human than their society permits' (Fischman 1991: 108).

Anthony Giddens observed 'In many respects Marx's writings exemplify features of nineteenth century thought which are plainly defective when looked at from the perspectives of our century' (Giddens 1995: 1) and concluded that 'Marx's materialist conception of history should be discarded once and for all' (Ibid.: 105). He pointed out that Marx's greatest failure has been the theory of nationalism for Marx was an archetypal modernist. Giddens distinguished between nationalism (symbols and beliefs) and the nation state (the administrative setup) which were two separate entities though sometimes they might converge. Nationalism was primordial sentiments 'found in tribal and traditional societies' while the nation state is a modern 'power container of time and space' (Ibid.: 193). Capitalism needed the nation-state as power structures promoted the aims of capitalism.

The collapse of Communism proved the serious shortcomings of Marxism both in theory and practice. It at best remained a critique rather than providing a serious alternative to liberal democracy (Harrington: cited in Heilbroner 1989: 10). However, its critique of exploitation and alienation, and the hope of creating a truly emancipated society that would allow for full flowering of human creativity would continue to be a starting point of any utopian project. In spite of Marx's utopia being truly generous it displayed a potential for being tyrannical, despotic and arbitrary. Centralization of power and absence of checks on absolute power was itself inimical to true human liberation and freedom. He 'offered no good reason to believe that the power politics of radicalism would prove to be less authoritarian in practice than the power politics of conservative nationalism' (Sabine 1973: 682). Commenting on the activities of his fellow comrades which were in a total negation to his ideals, Marx once proclaimed that he was not a Marxist. This proved to be a serious limitation of his theory even during his lifetime as it was after his death. He would be remembered at best a critic of early nineteenth century capitalism and politics. The limitations and inadequacies within the doctrine are a reminder that his blueprint was, as Koestler remarked, 'a God that failed'.

Friedrich Engels

Engels' contribution to the legacy of Marx culminated in the decisive role that he played in the tendency to transform Marx's views into a *Weltanschauung*, a philosophical system, an interpretation of the world (McLellan 1977: 72).

Engels' thought as a whole reflected certain fashions in nineteenth-century philosophy, among them system-building in the manner of Hegel and Dühring, the materialism and determinism of the physical sciences, evolutionism derived from Darwin, atheism arising from historical criticism of theology, and positivism in the view that theory arose from fact. Unlike Marx, who used some of these materials in a strikingly original and critical way, Engels was an autodidact and lacked the sophistication of a trained sceptic who could put awkward questions to himself and then strive, painfully, to answer them. Engels's philosophy was not merely scattered through various polemics, like Marx's but was in itself a meagre body of work, with many unexamined assumptions, undefined terms and unspecified relationships (Carver 1981: 71).

Engels had already reformulated the revolutionary credo of 1843–48 in a manner conducive to interpretations which brought it much close to positivism and its political corollary, democratic reformism (Lichtheim 1961: 265).

Friedrich Engels (1820–95) by accepting a secondary role made possible the famous Marx-Engels intellectual partnership. Though he himself acknowledged Marx's superior role in their relationship the fact remained that Marx was the originator and Engels was the popularizer as he coined most of the catchy phrases in Marxism. Engels was a remarkable man with tremendous interests and incisive insights into so many divergent aspects and varied subjects like natural history, chemistry, botany, physics, philosophy, political economy and military tactics. He was extremely well-versed. Marx described him as the most learned man in Europe. Kautsky referred to his encyclopedic knowledge and called him a laughing philosopher.

As a junior partner Engels helped in the elucidation and the development of Marxism, giving it a shape. He interpreted and popularized Marx's ideas. After the death of Marx he helped in editing and publishing many of Marx's works. He often conveyed the idea that he preferred a modest role in the famous partnership for he remarked in 1884 that all his life he was content to play second fiddle which he was supposed to do and was happy that he had Marx as the first violinist. Paul Lafargue (1842–1911) writing about Marx's admiration and his indebtedness to Engels had this to say:

Marx appreciated Engels' opinion more than anybody else's . . . I have seen him read whole volumes over and over to find the fact he needed to change Engels' opinion on some secondary point. Engels described Marx as a genius and himself as talented at best. Marx describes Engels as a "real encyclopedia, ready for work at every hour of the day or night, quick to write and busy as the devil" . . . he was a first-rate linguist, a distinguished military critic, at least the equal of Marx as a historian, a pioneer in anthropology and the acknowledged mentor of a dozen emergent Marxist parties (cited in McLellan 1977: 75).

Engels directed Marx's focus towards the study of economic categories by furnishing him with some of his basic concepts. His contribution to Marx's *Franco-German Annals* by his *Outline of a Critique of Political Economy* (1843) aroused Marx's interest in the science of political economy. Marx described it as a 'brilliant critical essay on economic categories' for it laid down some of the ideas which were basic to Marxism: factors governing economic growth, the phenomenon of trade cycles, the contrasts between growing wealth and affluence, on one side, and increasing impoverishment and pauperization of the working class, on the other, and the tendency of open competition to develop into a monopoly.

Biographical Sketch

Engels was born on 28 November 1820 in the German city of Barmen known as 'little Manchester'. He was the eldest son of a textile manufacturer in a family of eight. He was brought up as a devout Calvinist and trained to be a merchant. He was attracted to the study of literature and poetry though his father insisted that he enter the family business in Barmen. In 1838 he was sent to Hanseatic port of Bremen to continue his businessman's apprenticeship. However he was slowly influenced by the Hegelian philosophy and the young Hegelian movement that flourished in the 1830s around Bruno Bauer. He slowly moved away from religion and, on the suggestion of Hess, read the works of Saint Simon and Fourier and emerged as a communist.

In 1841 Engels left Bremen and was ready to go for his military service in Berlin to escape mercantile career. In October 1842 he went to Cologne to meet the editors of *Neue Rheinische Zeitung*. Here he also met Marx. In 1842 he moved to England to work in his father's firm in the city of Manchester. By now he had become a communist and his contacts with the factory workers in England made him distance himself from the Hegelian idealists and identified totally, instead with the left Hegelians. He looked to the industrial proletariat as a potential revolutionary class. This led him to write *The Condition of the Working Class in England* (1845) where he spoke of the 'brutal indifference, the unfeeling isolation of each in his private interest and the dissolution of mankind into monads of which each one has a separate principle, the world of atoms, is here carried out to its utmost extreme' (Engels 1977: 24).

Engels and Marx were involved with various political activities and workers movements. Their first joint work was *The Holy Family* (1845) followed by *The German Ideology* (1845). While Marx was busy with the theoretical portions of *The German Ideology* and re-futing Proudhon, Engels preoccupied himself with agitations. As early as 1843 he established contacts with the leaders of the German secret society in London, the League of the Just. Along with Hess he organized communist meetings in Rhineland till they were sup-pressed. By 1845 Engels had broken off with his father and was able to devote full time to political work with Marx in Brussels and Paris. They joined the German League of the Just, later renamed as the Communist League and co-authored *The Communist Manifesto*. After the 1848 revolutions Engels worked with Marx on the *Neue Rheinische Zeitung*.

In 1850 Engels returned to Germany after a year's stay in France with the purpose of organizing resistance to counter revolutionar-ies. From Germany he travelled to Switzerland and London and eventually settled down in Manchester in 1850 to rejoin the family firm. By then the Communist League had broken down. He began writing for the *New York Daily Tribune*. His father had died in 1860. He stayed on till 1870 financially supporting Marx and continuing with their political and intellectual collaboration. His mother died in 1873.

Engels moved to London and took over the daily operations of the First International from the ailing Marx. He also wrote and published extensively, establishing himself as a reputed scholar and a socialist. *The Anti Dürhing* (1877–78), *Socialism: Utopian and Scientific* (1884) influenced the new socialist movements between 1880 and 1914. *The Origin of Family, Private Property and the State* (1884) and *Ludwig Feuerbach and End of Classical German Philosophy* (1884) consolidated his position as an important thinker. He also established links between the materialist conception of history and developments in natural science in 1877–78 which remained un-finished till his death but was put together and published by Moscow in 1920 as *Dialectics of Nature*.

The *Anti-Dühring, Ludwig Feuerbach and the Outcome of Classical German Philosophy* and *The Dialectics of Nature* were the three main texts through which Engels contributed to the systematization of Marxist philosophy. In the first tract materialism and dialectics were the two main themes. He insisted man's material existence was the reality and that all knowledge was empirical. There were no 'eternal truths' either in science, history or ethics. Freedom was the recognition of necessity. In *Dialectics of Nature* Engels linked natural sciences with the dialectics. A truly dialectical view asserted the indestructible and uncreated nature of matter and that motion had no beginning and no end.

Engels became acquainted with Mary Burns, an Irish woman whom he got to know on his first visit to Manchester. He spent his week-ends and spare evenings with her at her house. He maintained a bachelor's lodgings where he entertained his business friends. He was heartbroken when Mary died unexpectedly in 1864. Subsequently Mary's sister Lizzie moved in to take her place. Lizzie died in 1878. Engels married her on her deathbed.

Engels was nicknamed 'General' by his friends. He was keenly interested in military writings and was an expert in military matters. He was an avid rider and fox hunter. He socialized extensively. He was cheerful by nature. He liked men who could mind their own business and women who did not mislay things. He believed in taking things easy. He was fond of long walks and would walk very fast. He was fond of drinking wine. He made it a point, like Gandhi, to reply to every letter that he received. He also supported Marx financially. It was rather ironical that Marx's collaborator and principal source of income while he wrote his trenchant criticisms of capitalism was a capitalist.

Besides his faith in and commitment to communism, Engels was fond of poetry and translated some of Shelly's poems. His favourite writer was Shakespeare. He regarded Beethoven as the best German composer and his favourites were the *Eroica* and the *Fifth Symphony*. He himself tried to compose operas in the 1840s. He was also fond of hunting, riding, swimming, skating and displayed an enormous zest for life. He was good with Greek language, literature and philosophy.

After the death of Marx in 1883, Engels devoted his time in editing and publishing second and third volume of the *Capital* in 1885 and 1895, respectively. He published his *Dialectics of Nature* (1873–83). While working on the fourth volume, he died. This was subsequently published as *Theories of Surplus Value*. His friends tried to convince him to move to Germany but he decided to stay behind in 122 Regent Park in London which provided him a peaceful asylum. The house remained open to all socialists and revolutionaries.

Engels devoted considerable time and energies to the German Social Democratic Party and influenced Liebkhecht, Bebel, Bernstein and Kautsky.

Engels kept poor health which hindered his work. He suffered from rheumatism, bronchitis and a weak eyesight. In spite of ailing he celebrated his seventieth birthday with gaiety and fun. In 1888 he visited the United States for two months. In 1892 he began his work for the Second International. He was the President for the Zurich Congress. In 1895 he wrote a *Preface* to Marx's *Class Struggles in France*.

Engels died of throat cancer on 5 August 1895. He left most of his £30,000 to Marx's daughters. Eleanor received the letters and manuscripts of Marx; the rest went to Bernstein and Bebel. As per his wishes his body was cremated and his ashes were scattered in the sea.

Understanding of History

Engels made a mark as a historian. His talent for descriptive writings, his wide interests in geography and chronology, his skillful use of language and his ability to use Marxist methods made him a first-rate historian. Though he covered an extensive area, his main contributions were in three major areas: his analysis of the English working class in the mid-1840s, his researches into pre-history and his efforts to lay down the principles of historical materialism in a systematic manner.

Soon after becoming a communist Engels wrote *The Condition of the Working Class in England*. In an article entitled *Outlines of a Critique of Political Economy* he furnished a critique of liberal economic theories. He analyzed concepts like trade, value, rent and population. He announced his intention of describing the factory system and also examined the social impact of industrialization. His main focus was on the industrial proletariat. Engels contended that economists who placed undue importance on the idea of private property and competition could never give a conceptual and a moral account of these notions. He concluded:

> . . . under normal conditions, large capital and large landed property swallow small capital and small landed property. . .

The middle classes must increasingly disappear until the world is divided into millionaires and paupers, into large landowners and poor farm labourers. Competition has penetrated into all human relationships and it has completed human bondage in all its aspects. Competition is still the great mainspring which repeatedly jerks our dying social order — or rather disorder — but with each newest effort competition also saps a part of the waning strength of our social system (Engels, cited in McLellan 1977: 28).

Engels devoted considerable space on the great towns beginning with London, major Yorkshire towns and concentrated on Manchester, the major industrial complex of England consisting of half a million of people. He concluded that the working class of the great cities varied in conditions, the best enjoying good wages and the worst suffering from bitter want, homelessness and death by starvation. He also narrated the diseases that affected them. Many of the children died before they reached the age of five. Illiteracy resulted in alcoholism leading to sexual immorality and increasing crime rates. He highlighted other evils like exploitation of women, child labour and the lack of hygienic conditions of work. In a similar vein, he focussed on mines and agriculture. Engels looked to increasing number of strikes as evidence of the 'decisive battle between the proletariat and the bourgeoisie' that was imminent. He discussed the attitude of the middle classes towards the workers, emphasizing their greed and hypocrisy as exemplified in the Poor Law. He concluded that only communism could eliminate class antagonisms and soften harsh social conflicts.

The noteworthy fact about *The Condition of the Working Class* was that it was the first of its kind combining modern geographical and sociological analyses and the fact that Engels was only twenty-four years old when he wrote it. Much of the information was based on first-hand account made possible by the fact that he was a businessman and an active socialist. He used government data and publications exceedingly well and disproved the impression that the working class was becoming better. The important fact about the book was its focus on the English working class as a whole. The drawbacks of the book related to its predictions. Engels spoke about the rapid collapse of society being 'as certain as a mathematical or mechanical demonstration' in the context of the worst slump of the 1840s that the nineteenth century witnessed. Ironically the slump was a prelude to the major boom in heavy industry mainly due to railway expansion.

Following the failure of 1848 revolutions, Engels wrote many significant articles on *The Peasant War in Germany* (1850) drawing parallels between the role of nobles and burghers in the sixteenth century to crush the peasants' revolt and the alliance between the bourgeoisie and the aristocracy in 1848 against a newly emerging proletariat. This was the first Marxist work on *history* (Carver 1981: 33). He claimed that behind religious struggles lay different interests, demands and requirements of the various classes. Similarly the French Revolution of 1789 was more than an intense debate on the advantages of constitutional monarchy over royal absolutism. The key issue involved the economic concerns of social classes.

Engels' historical interests was reflected in the *Anti Dühring* when he refuted the claim made by Eugen von Dühring (1833–1921)[4] that force was the fundamental factor in the development of history. He argued that force itself was dependent on the underlying economic conditions. Engels laid down three reasons for pursuing the writings of Dühring. The first reason was 'to prevent a new occasion for sectarian splitting and confusion developing within the SPD, which was still so young and had just achieved definite unity'. Many within the party were ready to accept the doctrine of Dühring and even the editorial policy of the party paper was getting tainted. The second reason was, as Engels called in 1878, the opportunity of putting across in a positive form his views on controversial issues which were of scientific and practical interest'. Third he warned his readers against other German systems of 'sublime nonsense' in which 'people write on every subject which they have not studied'. Dühring, according to Engels, was merely one of the 'most characteristic types' who promoted 'bumptious pseudo-science'.

Engels conceded to Dühring that Marxism relied heavily on Hegelianism for its laws of dialectics were universally valid. The difference between capitalism and socialism was due to the institution of private property. Once the proletariat assumed state power, it would socialize property and the means of production and, with that, all class distinctions, class antagonisms and the state would be abolished. The anarchy of capitalist production would be replaced by a planned model clearly making it more centralized, which would be far from the plank of decentralization that

Dühring's communes symbolized and the main reason for its attractions among the German social democrats.[5]

With the idea of publishing positive views, Engels observed in 1885 while writing the *Preface* to the second edition of the *Anti Dühring* that his polemic was transformed into a more or less connected exposition of the dialectical method and of the communist world-outlook. He developed his views on dialectics as one that comprehended things and 'their representations in their essential connection, motion, origin and ending and that Nature is proof of dialectics'. He then developed the notion of 'quantity and quality' and 'negation of the negation' as the two laws of dialectics. He defined dialectics as the science of the general laws of motion and development of nature, human society and thought. He linked his

> . . . dialectical view of science to the materialist conception of history by claiming that social forces work exactly like natural forces and that the final causes of all social changes and political revolutions are to be sought . . . in the changes in the modes of production and exchange . . . not in *philosophy* but in the *economics* of each particular epoch (Carver 1981: 49).

In the *Preface* to the second edition of *The Anti Dühring*, Engels explicitly linked his conception of dialectics with Marx's work on political economy and the development of the modern industrial society. He invented the phrase the materialist interpretation of 'history' (Avineri 1976; Lichtheim 1961). Not only did Engels invent the phrase but also used it effectively in the entire Marxist literature.

Engels also took great interest in military history and techniques and contributed innumerable articles on military matters to newspapers in America, Britain and Germany. He wrote about the American civil war and the Franco-Prussian War of 1870. Many of his historical writings influenced Lenin. He also outlined the history of German industry in the fourteenth and fifteenth centuries and contrasted with other models elsewhere in Europe.

> While in England and France the rise of commerce and industry had the effect of intertwining the interest of the entire country and thereby brought about political centralisation, Germany had not got any further than grouping interests by

provinces, and around merely local centres, which led to political division, a division that was soon made all the more final by Germany's exclusion from world commerce. In step with the disintegration of the *purely feudal* Empire, the bonds of imperial unity became completely dissolved, the major vassals of the Empire became almost independent sovereigns, and the cities of Empire, on the one hand, and the knights of the Empire, on the other, began entering into alliances either against each other or against the princes or the Emperor (Engels, cited in Carver 1981: 32).

In the *Dialectics of Nature* Engels tried to integrate Hegelian insights with modern science and suggested three laws: transformation of quantity into quality and vice versa, unity and interpenetration of opposites, and negation of negation. He described these laws as causal and invariable laws of motion which underwent a number of changes and could be observed in natural phenomena, human history and thought.

Women and Family

Engels researched into primitive societies relying on the work of Lewis Morgan's *Ancient Society* (1877) which formed the basis of his *Origin of the Family Private Property and State*. He felt that Morgan's conclusions were significant to anthropology in the same way as Darwin's for biology and Marx's for political economy. Using Morgan's account he contrasted the communal nature of primitive society with the exploitative ones that followed it. He paid attention to the role of the family and, in particular, to the position of women and thereby explained the rise of the state as an instrument of class exploitation and class domination.

Engels identified three kinds of marriage which paralleled the principal stages of human development. These were (1) group marriage in the period of savagery, (2) paired marriages for barbarism and (3) monogamy supported by adultery and prostitution for civilization. In the first phase, the woman enjoyed a position of supremacy. In the second period with the rise of agriculture and domestication of animals, man became more important. In the earlier phase, man was merely a provider of food and possessed weapons for that purpose but, in the second phase, he continued with his earlier duty but with an important difference that he owned cattle and later on slaves. Since inheritance was through the maternal side he found his children disinherited. Slowly the paternal law of inheritance and line of descent emerged. The establishment of patriarchy gave way to monogamous marriages with the man as the supreme source of authority within the family. Engels linked patriarchy and the subordination of women to the capitalist system and the institution of private property.

> The overthrow of mother right was the world historical defeat of the female sex . . . full freedom of marriage can therefore only be generally established when the abolition of capitalist production and of the property relations created by it has removed all the accompanying economic considerations which still exert such a powerful influence on the choice of marriage partner . . . what we can now conjecture about the way in which sexual relations will be ordered after the impending overthrow of capitalist production is mainly of a negative character, limited for the most part to what will disappear. But what will there be new? That will be answered when a new generation has grown up: a generation of men who never in their lives have known what it is to buy a woman's surrender with money or any other social instrument of power; a generation of women who have never known what it is to give themselves to a man from any other considerations than real love (Engels, cited in McLellan 1977: 35).

Engels traced the rise of the modern state, a distinct institution that was territorial in character, with public power derived from the people. Progressive division of labour and the institution of private property, which involved the sale and purchase of land, gave the state its distinct territorial character moving it away from kinship. He traced this process from ancient Greece to ancient Rome. The striking aspect of the work for the socialists was the point that, under primitive societies, productive and sexual relations were better. In particular it also raised questions with regard to the emancipation of women a theme that was lucidly and deftly handled by Bebel.[6] The major shortcoming in Engels' tract was its heavy reliance on the work of Morgan and the neglect of the systems in Asia and Africa. Like in Marx, there was a pronounced euro-centricism in Engels too. Moreover the section on the family was the weakest (Engels, cited in McLellan 1977: 37).

Politics

Engels, more than Marx, was forthcoming with regard to the nature of the future communist society. He described the latter as one where 'the government of persons would be replaced by administration of things', a phrase from Morris. In *On Authority* (1872) he stressed on the need for discipline within a society by using the model of a factory.

> . . . the automatic machinery of a bid factory is much more despotic than the small capitalists who employ workers over have been. At least with regard to the hours of work one may write up on the portals of these factories: *Lasciate ogni autonomia, voi che entrate* (meaning abandon all autonomy, ye who enter here!). If man, by dint of his knowledge and inventive genius, has subdued the forces of nature, the latter avenge themselves upon him by subjecting him, insofar as he employs them, to a veritable despotism independent of all social organization. Wanting to abolish authority in large-scale industry is tantamount to wanting to abolish industry itself, to destroy the power loom in order to return to the spinning wheel . . . a revolution is certainly the most authoritarian thing there is (Ibid.: 38).

In the communist society Engels believed that rationality, planning and the division of labour would remain and the productive process would be geared to ensure maximum output. Inspired by Darwin, he declared the 'withering away' rather than the abolition of the state as the goal of communism. The communist order would be one where human beings would find themselves in the realm of freedom rather than one of necessity.

In the later part of his life Engels was asked to furnish the basic principles of historical materialism, a phrase that he coined. In The *German Ideology*, the sages of communism argued that the nature of individuals depended on the material conditions determining their production. In the 1880s, on requests by German historians, Engels laid down the determining factors in history. In his replies, his main point was to stress the mutual interaction of forces, always emphasizing the economic. Many looked to these statements by Engels as suggesting some kind of revision of the basic principles of Marxism. Engels acknowledged that the superstructure at certain times may be temporarily the overall determining factor. He concluded:

> . . . according to the materialist conception of history, the ultimately determining element in history is the production and reproduction of real life. More than this neither Marx nor I have ever asserted. Hence if somebody twists this into saying that the economic element is the only determining one, he transforms that proposition into a meaningless, abstract, senseless phrase. The economic situation is the basis, but the various elements of the superstructure — political forms of the class struggle and its results, to wit: constitutions established by victorious class after a successful battle, etc., juridical forms, and then even the reflexes of all these actual struggles in the brains of the participants, political, juristic, philosophical theories, religious views and their further development in the systems of dogmas — also exercise their influence upon the course of the historical struggles and in many cases preponderate in determining their *form*. There is an interaction of all these elements in which, amid all the endless host of accidents (that is, things and events, whose inner connection is so remote, or so impossible of proof that we can regard it as non-existent, as negligible) the economic movement finally asserts itself as necessary (Engels, cited in McLellan 1977: 40).

Engels regarded communism as the general condition of modern civilization and not specific to any particular country. It concerned humanity as a whole and not just the working class. It transcended all classes for it appealed to the rational instincts of all individuals with a capacity for insight into the social process. Engels gave up his idealistic political principles in favour of social economic analysis once he began to collaborate with Marx in *The German Ideology*. He formulated the initial sketch of communism in his *Principles of Communism* (1847) which formed the basis of *The Communist Manifesto*.

Engels projected communism as the emancipation of the proletariat as a group which sold its labour in order to make a living. The proletariat and the bourgeoisie were the two main classes that the mechanized industrial revolution produced. The former grew in number due to the anarchic nature of the productive process and unbridled competition. These could be eliminated only if society was restructured with the purpose of securing general interests for all which would involve abolition of private property.

Once the proletariat became victorious, then they would essay out the following measures. An increase in productivity suggested sufficient goods for all and also the possibility of the abolition of division of labour. Communism meant independence and liberation for women and independence of children from their parents for private property was abolished. It would also overcome national boundaries and rendered religion obsolete. Social education would change with the elimination of the ruling class. Communism represented the most decisive and radical break with traditional ideas. Engels stressed on the forces of technology. The proletariat came into existence as a result of the industrial revolution which was made possible by technological revolution. While Marx emphasized the catastrophic nature of the productive forces, Engels emphasized their liberating and progressive character (Avineri 1976: 153; Lichtheim 1961: 59).

Engels regarded the battle for democracy as a transition to socialism. He was convinced that the revolution would be *social*. It would go beyond political institutions to economic life and the prevalent value system within society and hence observed that democracy or politics alone could be the battleground between the wealthy and the poor. The proletarian revolution would produce a democratic constitution resulting in the direct or indirect political rule of the proletariat. Direct rule would occur in England for the proletariat there was in a majority whereas it would be indirect in France and Germany for here the majority consisted of small peasants and burghers besides the industrial working class. Engels clarified that dictatorship of the proletariat[7] was necessary to fill the vacuum as a result of the destruction of the old order and till the creation of the new system which Marx accepted. He identified the commune as the prototype of the dictatorship of the proletariat in his 1891 edition of the *Civil War in France*.

Marx-Engels Relationship

In the entire history of ideas, the Marx-Engels relationship was unparalleled spanning over a period of four decades. Their unique friendship, total dedication to Marxism, and partnership both in scholarship and revolutionary activities were the fascinating facets in the growth and development of Marxist thought and practice. Engels' critical perception predated his acquaintance with Marx. In the period 1839–42 when he was a journalist, he emerged as a literary and political critic. The 1840s was a period of their closest scholarly partnership. During this period Marxism, emerged as a distinct branch of socialism.

In the 1880s, as Carver (1981) pointed out, the differences started manifesting themselves. Marx's 'guiding thread of history', the *Critique of Political Economy* (1889), became in Engels the materialist conception of history. In contrast to Marx, Engels developed a more rigid and positivist notion of science which led ultimately to his dialectical conception of nature. He was much more deterministic than Marx, which meant that even among the two originators of Marxism they had their differences.

Engels contributed many of the details of historical materialism in Marxism and argued that the theory of history and the subject matter that it applied exhibited the order of dialectic and hence he could be perceived as the originator of dialectical materialism. He added ideological superstructure to Marx's legal and political superstructure. He also introduced the notion of false consciousness and class interests to reduce the ideological content in scientific socialism with the purpose of explaining as to why superstructures appeared independent of or neutral between class interests when that was not the case, and why a scientific understanding of history differed from that of chroniclers and participants. In the *Anti Dühring* he extended the dialectical method beyond the description of human action and institutions to explain physical reality. In the *Dialectics of Nature* he gave the laws of dialectics to elaborate the term.

The First Revisionist?

In 1895 while writing the *Preface* to the *History of Class Struggles in France*, Engels came to believe in the positive and successful effect of universal suffrage and envisaged it as an entirely new strategy for working class struggle. This assertion by Engels meant the abandonment of the French Revolution which was the model for the proletarian revolution and also an acknowledgment that both he and Marx had erred in assuming during 1848 revolutions that the time was ripe for a socialist revolution.

> . . . the spell of the barricade is broken, street fighting belongs to the past . . . . And so it happened that the bourgeoisie and the government came to be much more afraid of the legal than the illegal action of the workers' party, of the results of elections than those of rebellion. The irony of world history turns everything upside down. We, the "revolutionaries", the rebels — we are thriving far better on legal methods than on illegal methods and revolt . . . . History has proved us and all those who thought like us wrong. It has made clear that the state of economic development on the continent at that time was not by a long way ripe for the elimination of capitalist production; it has proved this by the economic revolution, which, since 1848, has seized the whole of the continent . . . and has made Germany positively an industrial country of the first rank . . . (Engels 1977: 115).

Engels pointed out that not only had history some of their erroneous conceptions but transformed the conditions under which the proletariat had to fight. He called for revision of old tactics and adoption of new ones to accelerate the progress towards socialism made possible by the fact that capitalist development had reached its peak. He pointed to the astonishing growth of the German SPD increasing from 102,000 in 1871 to 352,000 in 1874, 493,000 in 1877, 550,000 in 1884, 763,000 in 1887 and 1,427,000 in 1890 which was possible due to universal suffrage. As a result the SPD could build itself as the strongest, disciplined and a rapidly growing socialist party. It also demonstrated to their fellow contemporaries the effectiveness of the right of vote which was no longer a means of deception but had become an instrument of emancipation. Engels' observations dispel the standard Leninist argument that it was Bernstein who was the first revisionist. On the contrary, it was Engels who was the first revisionist or the first social democrat[8] (Elliot 1973: 73).

Though Engels was hopeful of universal suffrage yet he cautioned against the total reliance on parliamentarism to the exclusion of the others. He envisioned a return to illegal and insurrectionary methods if necessary. He advocated armed uprising when the workers still had not achieved the support of a majority of the population and when they would have to face an army equipped with superior weapons. Engels was critical of the Erfurt Programme adopted by the SPD in 1891.

> One can suppose that the old society could peacefully develop into the new in countries where the representation of the people concentrated all power in itself, where a people could do constitutionally whatever was desired once a majority of people supported it: in democratic republics like France and America, in monarchies like England . . . where the dynasty was powerless against the popular will (Engels, cited in Hunley 1991: 102).

Interestingly in Germany, contrary to the revisionist perceptions, Engels continued to see the need for an armed insurrection since the government was still mighty and the legislature and other representative bodies were without real power. He dismissed the Erfurt programme of 1891 as 'opportunism'. Like Marx he continued to believe in the majoritarian notion of the proletarian revolution and to the humane liberation of the industrial working class.

Conclusion

Engels' intellectual legacy was the materialist interpretation of history. His views left an indelible mark on social theory and political practice. He was reasonably accurate, giving credit wherever it was due, and 'kept his claims and ambitions within the bounds of discipleship' (Carver 1981: 63). He transformed Marxism into a worldview and a system of philosophy which was necessary in light of the growing strength and numbers of the SPD and to the role of natural sciences as holding the key to human progress. He looked to the universe as dynamic, forever evolving and moving towards higher form yet it was diverse driven by inner conflict. His view was anti-mechanistic and naturalistic (Kolakowski 1981a: 399). He accepted the plurality of the universe which stemmed from his mistrust of philosophy and by his confidence in science and became the ' . . . doctrinal mentor for the emergent Marxist movement . . . . It was mainly with Engels and his successors that the notion of "scientific socialism" became narrowed and progressively emasculated' (McLellan 1977: 72–3). Later Marxists like Kautsky and Plekhanov accepted this link between natural and social sciences.

Engels contended that Marx's economics was a definite scientific advancement on classical political economy and held that Marx's contribution to history paralleled Darwin's to biological evolution. He believed that these discoveries coincided with those of natural science and demonstrate the truth of dialectical and materialist ontology, which was why he described Marxism as *scientific socialism*. Scientific socialism enabled the proletariat to pursue its class interests with the knowledge that its victory was inevitable since that was the direction of material progress. Engels made Marxism, quite naively and unintentionally a closed system intellectually.

August Bebel

In his book *Woman and Socialism* (1883) the most widely-read book to come out of the Social Democratic Movement, he (Bebel) painted an impressive picture of that age: a society enjoying perfect freedom and justice together with all the blessings of communal institutions, a society in which men could freely develop their creative potential in peace and harmony (Miller and Potthoff 1986: 51).

Bebel's book on the misery of woman under the system of bourgeois marriage, the bourgeois institution of prostitution, and woman's liberated position in a socialist society was one of the most popular socialist writings. It was one of the few great pieces of passionate feminism in German literature . . . Bebel's description is highly speculative and optimistic. He relies heavily on the spirit of solidarity created under socialist conditions and does not face the problem of authority in the large-scale organizations of modern industrialized society (Roth 1963: 235-6).

Bebel's book played a major role in the popularization of Marxism and in the development of a socialist analysis of sexual oppression; its continuing relevance and interest for those concerned with feminist issues should be self-evident (Donald 1988: i).

August Bebel (1840–1913) along with Wilhelm Liebknecht (1826–1900) was the outstanding spokesperson and founder of the German

Social Democratic Party. He was a German socialist theoretician and a leader who worked for the parliamentary road to socialism. A successful manufacturer, he remained a loyal Marxist of the peaceful evolutionary version. He was among the founding members of the Social Democratic Workers Party and helped in the founding and organization of the Second International.

Bebel was mainly remembered for his tract on women's emancipation and sexual equality. *His Woman in the Past, Present and Future* (1883) was rightly hailed as a classic in Marxist literature and the most authoritative text within the tradition of socialist feminism (Charvet: 1982). Initially it was known by the title *Woman and Socialism* and published in 1879. However, the changed title was more appropriate in light of the contents of the book. It examined the question of women's subjugation and oppression from a Marxist perspective. This in itself was important for the Marxists looked to gender equality within the framework of class equality.

Several million copies of Bebel's book were printed and it was translated into more than a dozen languages. It went into 58 editions in German alone, and 50 of these appeared between 1879 and 1910. The first English edition was published in 1885. It was widely read by the working class and was secretly distributed during the anti-socialist legislation in Germany. It was the most borrowed book from the German libraries in the late nineteenth and early part of the twentieth centuries. It inspired Engels to examine the position and role of women and family in the origins of modern society. Both Marx and Engels were impressed by its indepth and penetrating analysis.

Biographical Sketch

August Bebel was born in 1840. He was the son of a non-commissioned officer and was orphaned early in his life. He spent his childhood in poverty. He settled down in Leipzig as a woodturner and became active in the local industrial educational association. He started off as a liberal and was closely associated with the workmen's educational societies which organized in 1863 a federal league that opposed the views and movement of Lassalle. He worked in close cooperation with the bourgeois progressive parties and as supporter of the cooperative projects or *Schulze Delitzsch*.

Bebel became a socialist under the influence of Liebknecht in 1860s. He read and became acquainted with the theories of Marx. In 1865 he founded the 'League of German Workingmen's Association' in Leipzig along with Liebknecht. In 1886 the two of them founded the Saxon People's Party. In 1867 Bebel succeeded Dr. Max Hirsch as the Chairman of the Union of German Workers' Association. In the same year Liebknecht and Bebel were elected to North German Reichstag. The year 1875 saw the birth of the Social Democratic Workers' Party following an unity pact between the Lassalleans and Eisenachers. The Lassallenas strongly supported state socialism whereas the Eisenachers were orthodox Marxists.

Bebel was the editor of the *Vorwarts* (Forward) started on 1 October 1876. The first issue was published form Leipzig. In 1883, along with Kautsky and Liebknecht, he started a new theoretical journal of the SPD *Die Neue Zeit* in Stuttgart. As organizers of the SPD, both Bebel and Liebknecht helped Kautsky and Bernstein draft the Erfut Programme of 1891. He died on 13 August 1913.

Within a decade of Lassalle's death in 1864 there was a tussle regarding providing effective leadership of the growing working class movement leading to a serious division regarding the adoption of policy programme. Bebel and Liebknecht felt it would be right to support the progressive elements in the middle classes against the aristocracy and autocracy in the hope that a workers' victory would bring about after the collapse of autocracy and landlordism.

Supported by Marx and Engels, the Bebel-Liebknecht group made steady inroads in the local workers' societies. They reaffirmed the orthodox Marxist faith during the 1890s revisionist controversy. But interestingly when revisionism was voted down by the SPD they did nothing to expel its proponents and they themselves resumed their rightward movement (Cole 1954: 240). Like the revisionists, Bebel equated socialism with the attainment of equal rights on the grounds that the workers desired freedom and equality and not privileges. He cautioned the party not to lose sight of its higher objectives while focussing on detailed reform work. He saw the final struggle as imminent and accused the revisionists for undermining the socialist labour movement of its faith and its inspiration. His criticisms of revisionism was as severe as those offered by Kautsky and Luxemburg. He clung to Marx's assertion that capitalism would end with a severe and final economic crisis which would culminate in the breakdown of the present social order.

Socialism and the Gender Question

Bebel's most distinctive contribution to socialist thought was his in-depth and penetrating analysis of the women's question. It has been rightfully regarded as a pioneering work within the socialist tradition. While Engels' *Origin* was widely known yet it was Bebel's tract which was most popular at the time when it was published. It offered to the reader a fuller, broader and a comprehensive treatment than the tract by Engels. Both Marx and Engels considered it unnecessary to tackle the woman's question since Bebel had provided an exhaustive and a clear analysis on the subject (Meyer 1977: 76).

Bebel analyzed the question relating to the position and role of women. The first section *Woman in the Past* analyzed the relations between the sexes from an anthropological and historical perspective from ancient times to the reformation. This section was similar to the exposition that one finds in Engels. The second and the longest part of the book *Woman in the Present* presented in detail the legal, social, political and domestic situation of women in late nineteenth-century Europe and America. This section provided valuable insights backed with statistics and was of tremendous importance to historians and feminists interested in the history of women. The third and the shortest chapter *Woman and the Future* painted a vision of the future socialist society where women would be fully and truly free. Female emancipation was linked to the overall socialist ideal of human liberation. In this section he also disputed the findings and conclusions of the Malthusian theory, the issue of internationalism and overpopulation. His focus was the proletarian family to prove that women's emancipation and capitalism was basically incompatible.

Bebel believed that the collapse of capitalism would also mean a change in sexual and familial relationships that were sustained by it. However, the transition from capitalism to socialism had to be through parliamentarism and not revolution as espoused by Marx and Engels. It was necessary to go through the historical stages and acquire formal civil liberties before conceiving of socialism.

Accordingly, he sympathized with the demands of bourgeois feminism and held that suffrage was crucial to political education and participation. This enabled women to enter into professions that were traditionally held by men thereby dispelling the popular prejudice that they were of inferior minds and intellect. He accepted many of the arguments made by liberal feminists like Wollstonecraft and J.S. Mill but differed from them insofar in stressing the economic factors that sustained social and legal inequalities. He believed that women like men ought to enjoy equal rights and opportunities for employment. He ruled out accidents of birth and asserted that, given the same circumstances, people would differ very little. Like Mill, he believed that, given equal opportunities, women would excel.

> Geniuses do not fall from heaven, they must have opportunities to form and mature, and not only have such opportunities been hitherto almost denied to women but men have kept them for thousands of years in a state of the deepest subjection. It is just as mistaken to say that a woman can never become a genius, because people can discover no spark of genius among the tolerably large number of intellectual women that exist than to affirm that not more geniuses have been possible among men than the few who have been recognized as such thanks to the opportunities that were offered to them for development (Bebel 1988: 118).

Contemporary feminists found Bebel's arguments incomplete for they argued that dearth of women geniuses was due to two reasons, first lack of opportunities which Bebel acknowledged and second the non-recognition of female talents in a male dominated and centred society. Bebel like Engels made a historical survey of the women in the past in order to understand and analyze the present. He explored the possibility of women developing and realizing their latent capacities so that they could become equal members of a society that was non-exploitative and free from want. He thought it was important to dissect the woman's question because of past injustices, oppression, exploitation and deprivation that women have suffered and endured. He dismissed the bourgeois notion of formal legal equality for women as inadequate and was convinced that it was only with the abolition of both wage and sexual slavery that women could be truly independent. Emancipation of humanity was possible only if there was social equality and liberation of the sexes. Bebel began his exposition by observing and comparing the woman to a slave, an idea that one found in Mills *The Subjection*.

> . . . from the beginning of time oppression has been the common lot of woman and the labouring man . . . her position was even lower than his, an even by him was she regarded as an inferior and continues to be so to this day . . . *Woman was the first human being that tasted bondage. Woman was a slave before the slave existed* (Bebel 1988: 7).

Bebel described at great length the sexual form of oppression where the women were reduced to total dependency on their husbands. In particular, he took up the plight of those women who were seduced and subsequently abandoned both by the seducer and the state. Many of them relied on quacks for abortion or contracted sexual diseases. Sexual restrictions also manifested itself in form of unnatural expression leading to vice, to prostitution and neurosis. Unlike Engels, Bebel did not see the oppression and subjugation of women due to monogamous family and the institution of private property. Instead he pointed out that women were treated as the property of the horde or tribe, without the right of choice or refusal. They were made use of just like any other common belonging (Ibid.: 9). This observation was acceptable to critics who felt that Engels had overestimated the notion of equality within matrilineal societies. Both Bebel and Engels agreed that the development of the monogamous family and unequal sexual division of labour coincided with the rise of agriculture and family rather than the tribe as an unit of society. But for Bebel, sexual domination preceded private property because men desired to possess their women.

> It was doubtless a scarcity of women, or admiration of a particular woman, that first aroused in him the desire for permanent possession. Male egotism awaken. One man took possession of a woman with or without the consent of the

other men, who then followed this example . . . The foundations of private property, of the family, tribe and state, were thus laid . . . The possession of wife and children taught primeval man to regard a fixed abode as desirable . . . Now he built himself a hut, to which he returned after hunting and fishing. The division of labour began (Bebel 1988: 10–11).

Thus Bebel showed that the subjugation of women was brought about by an interplay between economic and non-economic factors. He was extremely critical of Christianity for its hostile and nega-tive attitude towards women. He observed that if women were better off it was not due to Christianity but due to the general 'ad-vancing civilization of the West, acting in spite of Christianity' (Ibid.: 26). Reformation released the priests from vows of celibacy and recognized that sexual impulses were natural. The puritan spirit of Protestantism accepted marriage as the only option and insisted on monogamous relationships as the only acceptable form. However, this did not improve the position of women in general. Matrimony was seen as the only available choice for them. An un-married woman was debarred from many trades and was treated unkindly by society. Married women were confined to domesticity with not much nourishment for their mental development other than being good wives and mothers. They in turn were expected to bring up their daughters in a similar way emphasizing on mean-ingless etiquette, charm and grace.

Thus, Bebel like Mill captured graphically the claustrophobic existence of mid-Victorian women. This, he agreed, had nothing to do with women having less intelligence or capabilities. He con-ceded that women were subjective, concerned with their dress and other external and frivolous things motivated by the desire to please, which he attributed to bad nurturing. He accepted that the brain of a woman was smaller than that of a man but did not agree that women were therefore less intelligent. He pointed out that the physical evolution of women's brains were affected by the ideals of beauty. Since Greek times it was considered that men with broad and high foreheads to be intelligent and handsome while women with low and narrow foreheads beautiful. As a result, many women who had high and broad foreheads styled their hair to conceal it. Bebel felt that it was important that men and women expressed their sexual desires naturally.

It is a law which every individual must fulfill as a sacred duty towards himself, if his development is to be healthy and normal, to neglect the exercise of no member of his body, to refuse gratification to no natural impulse. Each member must discharge the functions assigned to it by Nature, on pain of injuring and stunting the entire organism (Bebel 1988: 43–4).

Bebel supported his observations that physical and mental disorders were due to suppression of natural instincts with help of statistics. Celibate women could run the risk of contracting breast and ovarian cancer. The proportion of unmarried as opposed to married men and women in the lunatic asylums were much higher and their suicidal rates were higher. Since natural instincts needed an outlet for expression, he enquired as to which was better — the bourgeois marriage based on property or a socialist marriage based on free unfettered choice of love — and settled for the latter.

For Bebel it was the bourgeois women who suffered a great deal of sexual oppression. Their dress hampered their movement injuring their health. Their impoverished and restrictive lives, because of poor education, rendered them creatures of habit with little capacity for reason and self-development. Their dependence on their husbands subjected them to the latter's whims and fancies. Women vied with one another for marital status for that gave them property and standing in society. Most women sought marriage for it was a source of support. Men on their part were pleased to let the state of affairs continue for they were its beneficiaries. Their ego and pride was boosted because they were the masters and providers. They tended to see women under capitalism as a commodity, an article for profit and pleasure and it would be cutting against the grain if they acknowledged them as their equal. Men usually sought marriage with wealth in mind.

As a Marxist, Bebel viewed the subservience of women as a result of their lack of economic independence. Thus he gave a detailed historical explanation as to the cause of women's oppression rather than merely regarding it as an offshoot of the institution of private property as Engels did. Analyzing the proletarian family he saw poverty and insecurity as the bane of all relationships with women suffering a lot more for they had to take care of the domestic chores and be gainfully employed. As a result, they got totally exhausted leaving little time for child care. Being overburdened, their youth got destroyed making them ill-nourished. This led to poor health and poor children. As a result, women workers in comparison to their male counterparts did badly and became worse off. In fact, he argued that the number of women who died during childbirth equalled the number of men who died during a war and this itself was a sufficient reason for equality.

According to Bebel, since the material demands of a woman were less she was paid less wages. Since the cost of her labour was less the surplus value that could be extracted from her was much greater, hence making her attractive to her employer. Furthermore, in order to get employment and considering that during pregnancy and post-delivery period she would require rest, she would be willing to accept lower wages than men. She was also submissive because she needed to divert her attention towards her home and children. Her interest to participate in the working women's struggle was therefore lukewarm.

Bebel also pointed out that industries and factories that employed women did not provide any facilities for them. With increasing mechanization, women workers tended to suffer more because of low wages. He also anticipated the opening of newer opportunities for the middle class in jobs like teaching, higher education, clerical, sales and administration — all indicating the further proletarization of society. Women secured these jobs not because they agitated for it but because capitalism had an insatiable appetite for labour. So from the point of view of the proletarian family, the abolition of capitalism remained important. He did not see the competition between sexes as being an hindrance. Bebel like his liberal predecessors, Wollstonecraft and J.S. Mill hoped that men would help in educating and liberating women and enable them to come out of their narrow and impoverished lives. He believed that women led poor lives because they were trained and conditioned irrationally for domestic work.

Bebel described the future of family life by drawing heavily from Fourier. Work would be moderate, agreeable and freely chosen with vouchers instead of money. The state would have withered away placing control and management in the hands of elected administrators who would take into account the amount of socially necessary labour required from each person and then compute the supply and demand. Bebel thought that this would mean two hours of work per day leaving the rest of the day for leisure, arts, science and other creative activities. Production would be mechanized reducing wastage and poor quality of goods. Like the early socialists and Marx, he too was fascinated by the role and wonders of technology. In this he granted women an equal chance to become beneficiaries and narrated the particular advantage they would enjoy. He was convinced that men and women may differ physiologically and physically but that should not be the basis for denying women equal opportunities, rights and self-worth.

Bebel was particularly excited by the prospect of how technology could be applied to household chores providing much relief to women who were, by and large, beasts of burden. Like Marx, he conceded the historic role played by the bourgeoisie in liberating the productive forces and contended that what remained to be done was to establish common property for everyone to enjoy. He was excited about the idea of communal eating, the solidarity of sisterly food preparation and the possibility of extinction of single nuclear family. It was the drudgery of household work within the confines of private families, rather than domestic work per se, that oppressed women. 'The small private kitchen just like the workshop of the small master mechanic, a transitional stage, an arrangement by which time, power and material are senselessly squandered and wasted' (Bebel 1988: 29).

Bebel presumed somehow that sexual and familial relations, and patriarchal attitudes would change once the economic base underwent a transformation and hence it was disappointing that there was hardly any discussion of these in the future arrangements. Marx too was reticent about the future society offering very little but cautious descriptions about its institutional arrangements.

Bebel desired that children would be looked after by public officials. All would be provided with public education which would be supervised by women and men elected to boards of education. He did not see the prospect of parents devoting more time to their children since they would be relieved of the daily chores to a great extent. He accepted the continuation of the biological family in the future due to natural instincts rather than legal and economic imperatives. Since motherhood would be recognized as public service, it would be supported accordingly with the help of good nourishment, comfortable home and a decent environment. He was convinced, like Wollstonecraft and Mill, that women would opt for motherhood as a matter of choice despite the availability of newer opportunities. If women occupied high positions they would restrict the size of their families and that would help control population growth. Interestingly, he did not specify how this check would come about since he was against abstinence and unnatural preventives. The driving force for Bebel was the fact that, with economic affluence and social elevation, the size of the family would automatically be smaller and, in that sense, he was proved right.

Bebel saw future women as being socially and economically independent. They would receive, along with men, equal opportunities for education and employment. They would enjoy personal freedom to marry and divorce. He was convinced, like Engels, that in spite of these personal freedoms, relationships would remain monogamous and heterosexual. Free from child-care, unburdened by considerations of money and constraints of society, individuals would interact and associate with one another purely out of mutual love and respect.

Bebel did not visualize women doing the same thing in the future. In spite of having children their growth and development would not be hindered. They would be aided by nurses, teachers and friends, and would gain from the bond of sisterhood. He was somehow unable to free himself from natural prejudices that men harboured regarding women. He observed that women as compared to men were impulsive, naive and passionate which meant that in spite of his commitment to the women's cause he shared many of the prevailing prejudices against women. They were less reflective and were prone to lonesomeness which was due to physical differences in the brain. Without much analysis he concluded that it was only in Germany of the nineteenth century that the woman emerged as a fulfilled sexual being and as a social individual. His eurocentrism and German idealism was similar to Hegel's and Marx's bias toward Europe.

Social Democrats and the Gender Question

In 1869 the International Trade Cooperative of the Factory and Manual Workers of Saxony threw its doors open to women. The first German Weavers' Conference in Glauchau in 1871 adopted Bebel's resolution which enjoined all fellow workers to allow women to work on an equal basis. The Delegates Conference of the International, which held its meeting in 1871, ordered the opening of female branches within the working class. The Erfurt Workers' Congress in 1872, however, continued with its opposition to the induction of female labour in factories and workshops. In 1873 *Der Volksstaat*, the organ of the Social Democratic Workers' Party and the International Trade Union Cooperatives, noted:

> There are no objections to female and child labour in themselves, and Owen even regarded the latter as an integrative aspect of young people's education. But we are concerned with the contemporary mode of production, not with an ideal state which must be striven for; and as things stand at present, we must support every measure which aims to restrict women and children from working and to regulate the sanitary conditions of such work. Indeed as long as capitalism continues to rule, we have an obligation to strive to keep women and children out of bourgeois industry altogether, both in the interests of the women and children themselves, and in the interests of the proletariat in general (cited in Thonnessen 1969: 31).

This statement represented a step in the right direction for it took a positive attitude towards female labour even though it would be only in a socialist society. It failed, however, to take into account the contributions of female labour to the achievement of the 'ideal state'. The more progressive socialists supported female labour as an inevitability under capitalism, perceiving it to be a means for emancipating women and a fact that would undermine the old order. They championed greater reforms for female workers in the hope that this would bring about better working conditions for labour in general.

The Gotha Programme of 1875 granted equal, direct and voting rights for all men over 21 in all local and national elections and restricted female labour and prohibited child labour. Bebel insisted voting rights and education for women. His amendment proposing the right to vote for citizens of both sexes was rejected by 62 votes to 55 and instead general, equal an direct suffrage with secret and obligatory voting for all citizens over 20 years of age was included. Though an explicit reference to women was avoided, they were included under the category of citizens. Marx, in his critique of the

Gotha Programme, viewed female labour as 'unhealthy'. Bebel endorsed this view seeing female labour as unfeminine.

Bebel's formulations were developed by Clara Zetkin (1857–1933), Lily Braun (1867–1936) and Aleksandra Kollantai (1872–1952). All these were activist feminists who wrote extensively to support the causes they espoused. Their practical experiences helped them to articulate their theoretical concerns more clearly and intensely. As with the overall socialist movement, even the gender question by the end of the nineteenth century had a radical and a reformist perspective.

Zetkin in *The Question of Women Workers and Woman at the Present Time* (1889) devoted her attention exclusively to the position and plight of the female industrial workers seeing them as a part of a larger proletarian struggle against capital. The First World War brought a large number of women in the labour market making it necessary to focus on factory conditions. Unlike her colleagues, she felt socializing production rather denying women to work as a remedy for depressed wages for, if women were so denied then they would be dependent on their husbands. She also advocated male participation in domestic work and child rearing so that working women weren't overworked.

Zetkin was concerned about long working hours for mothers, lack of care and rest during and after childbirth. She demanded eight-hour day, free Saturday afternoons, infant and maternity welfare, six weeks leave after childbirth and prohibition of women in hazardous tasks, appointment of female factory inspectors to ensure observance of protection laws and improvement of wages for women. Protection for women was not demanded until 1877 and female suffrage only in 1895. It was not until 1891 that law protecting women workers was passed. The SPD was the only party committed to women's rights prior to the First World War.

Braun abandoned Zetkin's idea of class struggle and believed that socialist and bourgeois women could work together. She fought against sexism and patriarchy, demanded reform in women's clothing, proposed co-educational institutions like Wollstonecraft and the right of abortion, decriminalization of prostitutions, equal rights for single mothers and their children, kindergartens and day nurseries, people's kitchen, labour unions for domestic help, actresses, prostitutes and waitresses, communal housekeeping and maternity insurance. In her *Memoirs of a Socialist Woman* (1909) she criticized monogamous marriages and hoped that the proletarian revolution would be both social and personal. As a close ally of Bernstein, she emphasized on reforms holding the key to women's emancipation, and Bernstein extended his full support to Braun's proposals. Like her predecessors, she too glorified motherhood.

Kollantai agreed with Zetkin that the socialist movement must espouse the cause of women's suffrage and female labour including domestic help. Her insistence on the need to incorporate women's issues in the socialist movement was opposed by the mainstream leaders in Russia like Vera Zasulich (1852–1919) who dismissed it as divisive. However, Kollantai persisted and called for the abolition of all laws that subordinated women, the right of women to be elected to all institutions of self government on the basis of direct equal and secret vote, protection of female workers, forbidding night work, overtime and other hazardous conditions, female factory inspectors, maternity leave for eight weeks before and after childbirth and free medical care during pregnancy. Many of these proposals were adopted by the Russian Social Democratic Party in 1903.

In the *Social Bases of the Woman Question* (1909) Kollantai explored four broad themes: economic independence, marriage and family, care for pregnant women and women's political rights. She demanded equal pay for equal work, female enfranchisement, and public financing of child bearing and rearing. She attempted to reconcile feminism with socialism out of a conviction that the socialist revolution would lead to the emancipation of both the working class and women.

Kollantai's proposals were supported by Inessa Armand (1874–1920) and Nadezhda Krupskia Lenin (1869–1923) but were rejected by Lenin. Krupskia favoured birth control and the right of abortion. The communists did not visualize the withering away of the family nor the institution of marriage, including the role of mothers within it. They glorified motherhood. As the head of Zhenotdel, Kollantai tried to make women aware of their rights, to step out of their homes and take to political activity and help with their promotions into positions of leadership in government and the party. As a head of the Commissariat for Social Welfare, Kollantai wrote decrees that provided full state funding of maternity care, establishing legal and political equality of women and the need to reform marriage code. Stalin did not support the cause of women for he did not believe in the equality of women and men. His views on the family and women remained traditional.

An Assessment of Socialist Feminism

Socialist feminism, like liberal feminism, originated in the enlightenment doctrines of equality and liberty with the idea of extending the same to women. Both deplored sexual oppression and subjugation of women attributing it to lack of economic independence and dignity. It insisted that women had to be viewed primarily as persons both inside and outside marriage and home, and not merely as sexual beings. It opposed double standards with regard to sexual morality and condemned the perception that women and men differed by nature for otherwise, given the same opportunities, the two sexes would not develop properly and fully. Both schools were convinced that, in spite of equal opportunities, women would never give up their domestic responsibilities and were convinced that family and sexual relationships would improve if women were treated equally. Women's independence, dignity and emancipation would be guaranteed by equal opportunities in education, employment and suffrage. While the liberals desired the retention of capitalism with its institutions of private property, market and constitutional democracy as the framework for realizing women's emancipation, the socialists felt that it was under socialism that genuine emancipation was possible.

The liberals and the socialists differed on the question of the role of the family and marriage. For the liberals, the family was important as a school of civic values and moral virtues but it needed to be reformed with none being superior and domineering. Once women had the right to marriage, divorce, property, inheritance and custody of children, they would be legally equal with the men. The socialists desired the abolition of nuclear private families for they were wasteful, oppressive, inefficient and exploitative. Accepting anything collective to be elevating and cooperative they proposed communal households with common kitchens, dining, child rearing and sharing of domestic chores. They were convinced that the drudgery and monotony of household work would be obviated by technological innovations. In that sense they were prophetic. Bebel could think of most of the gadgets which have become domestic appliances in the late twentieth century to alleviate the misery and inequality of domestic chores.

Bebel, like Wollstonecraft and Mill, was a passionate exponent and defender of the principle of human and gender equality. He was confident that the proletarian marriage differed from the bourgeois marriage because it was based on personal reasons of love and care rather than property and material gain. True liberation was in the abolition of the institution of private property and market relations which was possible only under socialism. In spite of the optimism and conviction that women would be better off under socialism, he was unable to transcend the prejudices and limitations of his times.

In general, the socialists did not question the sexual division of labour and continued to support separate but equal spheres of work. Although they confronted the social function of motherhood and demanded social support and compensation for women's biological contributions, none of them , except for Zetkin, confronted the question of men's responsibilities with regard to domestic work and children. Motherhood continued to be encouraged as the most fulfilling and important of women's social functions. Even the liberals glorified motherhood, looking to child rearing as a woman's primary duty. However, they differed from the socialists in not denigrating household work and thereby respected the work that the majority of women did. Women rejected the communes and common households as being intrusive and demanding. Many of them shied away from them for the fear of hostile reactions from their husbands.

With regard to marriage, the socialists, like the liberals, criticized Victorian marriages as loveless. Unlike the liberals, the socialists spoke of free love which meant free choice but women understood it as permissiveness since they attacked monogamous relationships. Their emphasis on sexual fulfillment along with a social minimum was libertarian in intention but, in practice, turned out be one of control and regimentation. Replacing individualized personal experiences with communal ones was tantamount to disrespecting the moral worth and self-esteem of a person. In contrast, the liberals strongly defended the private space seeing the home as an expression of personal freedom and self-expression and never attempted to monitor or regulate the intimate lives of people. The socialists' acceptance of patriarchy and gendered political culture, which is essentially non-participatory like the dictatorship of the proletariat, belongs to lower civilization. If socialism is to represent a higher culture then gender equality and empowerment must be an integral part of it. This would mean going beyond the middle-class and proletarian women and elevating and empowering the wretched of the earth.

The socialist vision promised women a more equitable society free of oppression, injustice and domination but that remained a promise. As in case of the general theory of socialism even socialist feminism remained at best a corrective rather than an alternative to liberal feminism. In comparison, liberal feminism like its parent doctrine — liberal democracy — provided a more coherent, enduring and viable framework for the overall improvement and progress of women. However, in spite of this incompleteness within socialist feminism, the fact remains that it originated with Bebel and, in that sense, Bebel is to socialist feminism as Wollstoncraft is to liberal feminism.

Endnotes

1. See the section on Engels in this book.
2. See the sections on Lassalle and Bernstein in this book.
3. Cabral's most important contribution was his unique ability to combine pragmatism in politics with a persistent adherence to principles of human decency as a basic philosophy of political action. His belief in human rights and efforts to follow socialist policies without political opposition made him a rare revolutionary leader. For him Marxism was not an ideology but a methodology and this enabled him to be practical and creative. He questioned Marx's European bias in a memorable passage:

    > Does history begin only from the moment of the launching of the phenomenon of class, and consequently, of class struggle? To reply in the affirmative would be to place outside history the whole period of life of human groups from the discovery of hunting and later of nomadic and sedentary agriculture, to cattle raising and to the private appropriation of land. It would also be to consider — and this we refuse to accept — that various human groups in Africa, Asia and Latin America were living without history or outside history at the moment when they were subjected to the yoke of imperialism (Cabral 1983: 167).

4. Dühring as an exponent of a force theory emphasized the importance of political action and disagreed with Marx's rigid scheme of economic determinism for it dismissed political forms as irrelevant. Marx also erred in regarding economic relations as the exclusive determinant of all social and political actions.

Dühring felt that by a proper appraisal of this interdependency he would rectify the one-sidedness in Marx's analysis. His most important criticism was that of Hegelianism for that led to imprecise analysis. He also accused Marx for his failure to elaborate on communism the ultimate end of this process and, in particular, on the nature of property relationships. He also regarded Marx's theory of labour as false and challenged the theory of progressive pauperization for such pessimism was unnecessary and harmful to the socialist cause. Dühring contended that the destruction of capitalism would lead a network of autonomous and decentralized communes but never explained how this would come about. Dühring's analysis became very popular among the younger generation of socialists like Bebel, Bernstein, Kautsky, Liebknecht and Most.

5. Dühring responded to Engels' tract in detail. He characterized their version of communism as statist and protested at the enslavement of society by the state. He concluded that Marx's theocratic, authoritarian state was unjust, immoral and contrary to freedom. These criticisms were levelled by Bakunin a decade later. Dühring was forgotten by the social democrats not due to Engels' tract but because he abandoned social democracy. Moreover, the anti-socialist law of 1878 made radicalism highly impractical.

6. See the section on Bebel in this book.

7. For a fuller discussion and analysis of the concept, see the section on Marx.

8. See the section on Bernstein in this book.

5

❖ Social Democrats

Ferdinand Lassalle

In the development of German Socialism after the collapse of 1848 pride of place must be conceded, not to Marx, but to Ferdinand Lassalle . . . . The man who became the leading figure in German Socialism in that country was Lassalle (Cole 1956a: 71).

Apart from Proudhon, Marx's chief rival as a theoretician in the 1860s was Lassalle, who for many years outclassed him as far as ideological influence in Germany was concerned . . . . His inflated prophetic style exasperated Marx no less than their theoretical disagreements. Yet his practical success is beyond dispute: his insistence on an independent proletarian movement laid the foundations of organized socialism in Germany (Kolakowski 1981b: 238, 243-44).

After a fifteen year slumber Lassalle — to his undying credit — roused the labour movement in Germany to wakefulness once again (Marx, cited in Miller and Potthoff 1986: 18).

Kolakowski rightly called the period of the Second International (1889–1914) the 'golden age of Marxism'. During this period Marxism earned a distinction of its own, developed as a school of thought but 'was so rigidly codified or subjected to democratic orthodoxy as to rule out discussion or the advocacy of rival solutions to theoretical and tactical problems' (Kolakowski 1981b: 1). Except in Great Britain where the socialists drew their inspiration more from Owen, and Morris in Europe, socialist theory emerged mainly out of the writings and activities of people who identified themselves as Marxists though there was no Marxist orthodoxy and each thinker applied the theory in his own manner. True to the tradition left by the founders themselves, no distinction or compartmentalization was made between the theoreticians and practitioners and this applied even to the activists who were not intellectuals or theoreticians like Max Adler, Bebel and Turati. Because of this openness and enthusiasm,

> the general calibre of party leaders never again reached such a high level, either among social democrats or communists, Marxism seemed to be at the height of it intellectual impetus. It was not political movement; on the other hand, it had no means of silencing its opponents, and the facts of political life obliged it to defend its position in the realm of theory (Kolakowski 1981b: 2).

Marxism was taken seriously even by its adversaries and there were outstanding theoreticians on both sides. Amongst the defenders were Kautsky, Luxemburg, Plekhanov, Bernstein, Lenin, Adler, Bauer, Hilferding, Labroila and Pannekoek. Among its critics was Croce who exerted tremendous influence on Gramsci, Sombart, Siumel, Stamile, Gentile and Bohm-Bawerk. The influence of Marxism reached new heights and did not remain confined amongst the believers but reached a much larger audience of historians, economists, sociologists and philosophers (political science as an academic discipline developed later). Marxism in this period as it was before and after dealt primarily with the social, political and economic situations. However, in this 'golden age', the general problems of historical evolution from a materialistic point of view, the question of organization, imperialism, revisionism, aesthetics and art criticism was also taken up during this period.

The 1860s saw active socialist propaganda and campaigning in Germany. The question of German unity became of crucial importance to the workers since there was no other hope for a national movement. For the bourgeoisie, unity was an economic necessity. The two largest groups in the Reichstag were the General German Workers' Association (ADAV) established by Lassalle, and the League of German Workingmen's Association founded by Liebknecht and Bebel.

Lassalle was convinced that the battle for democracy had to be fought not with the help or by the liberal middle class but by the workers through workers' organizations or parties. Till the 1850s and early 1860s, it was the middle class which organized and led the working class. In 1863 Lassalle's calls for the establishment of a labour party independent of the middle class found resonance and support. He became not only the President of the ADAV but an idol of the working class.

Biographical Sketch

Lassalle was born on 11 April 1825. His father was a Jewish silk trader from Breslau. He studied philosophy and philology in Berlin and Breslau from 1843 to 1846. Lassalle's real name was Lassal. He intended to pursue a career in academics. He became a Hegelian, studied socialist literature and decided to become a philosopher with the hope of transforming the social conditions in Germany. Perhaps he would have attained his ambition had he not got involved in his own personal affairs.

Lassalle fell in love with Countess Sophie von Hatzfield who was twice his age, and for 10 years valiantly defended her financial interests vis-á-vis her estranged husband in German courts. In this connection he was arrested on charges of theft of certain documents in 1848. He was released six months later but imprisoned again in November for inflammatory speeches in support of the revolution. From 1849 to 1857, he lived in Dusseldorf. During this time he corresponded regularly with Marx whom he met in 1848 for the first time. He also wrote a long work on the Greek philosopher Heraclitus entitled *The Philosophy of Heraclitus the Obscure* which was published in 1857. It enabled him to discover the idea of absolute motion as a method for understanding philosophy and the process of society as well. Bernstein writing about Lassalle remarked that the latter had a passion for knowledge and science, righteousness and truth. In 1859 Lassalle published a historical drama, *Francs von Sickingen*, about a sixteenth century knight whose league pioneered the message of Reformation in Germany and his tragic death became a symbol of the defeat of the 1848 Revolution. This work contained patriotic sentiments with the intention of arousing faith in the German mission.

In 1860 Lassalle wrote a series of articles on Fichte and Lessing. In 1861 his most famous philosophical, historical and social treatise, *The System of Acquired Rights*, was published. It was received very well in academic circles. From 1862 Lassalle began to take an active interest in politics. Living in Berlin, he played an active role in the Prussian constitutional controversy criticizing the liberals of the Progressive party. In the spring of 1862 he published the *Arbeiterprogramm*, an address to the workers containing the core of his ideas. He also wrote a lecture on Fichte and the German constitution.

In 1863 Lassalle prepared an Open Letter which acquired the status of a charter of the first German working class socialist party, the *Allgemeiner Deutscher Arbeiterverein* established in May of that year. Bismarck, with whom Lassalle came in contact, described him as a man of intellect and a true patriot. The *Arbeiterverein* became successful after Lassalle's lifetime and became the first independent political vehicle of the German working class. In August 1864 Lassalle was killed in Geneva in a duel with his lover's ex-finance. His admirers described him as the new Robiespierre, a person with tremendous experience and maturity, a genius and a leader. Lassalle disliked Jews and literary persons, and, ironically, he was both. Marx refused to write an obituary and mocked Lassalle for being a 'modern saviour' and presuming that he had solutions to all the problems that confronted humanity. Engels too joined Marx in mocking Lassalle. The latter tried to reassure Marx and Engels of his orthodox credentials. Marx did not like the fact that Lassalle was the hero of a new generation of socialists and workers in Germany. The self proclaimed philosopher of the liberator of entire humanity could not rise above his prejudices, rivalry and jealously in his own personal life. Lassalle's important contributions and the role of social democracy was chronicled by Mehring in the *History of German Social Democracy* (1897-98) in which he appreciatively surveyed the political, social and intellectual developments in Germany in the nineteenth century.

Lassalle and Marx

Next only to Marx, Lassalle commanded enormous respect among the rank and file of socialist leaders, theoreticians and workers. Both, however, differed on practically every issue: economic doctrines, political tactics, their outlook towards the state, in general, and the Prussian state, in particular. Lassalle remained an ardent Hegelian idealist till the end. He never understood nor accepted

Marx for attacking Hegelianism from within. This was one of the reasons for their bitter rivalry.

On economic issues, Lassalle stated in his Open Letter of 1863 that the liberals were mistaken in assuming that they could liberate the working class with the help of insurance funds, cooperatives and the like. Here the similarity between Lassalle and Marx ended for Lassalle proceeded to prove with reference to the 'iron law of economics' that when wages were determined by the supply and demand of labour, they were bound to settle down in favour of a 'physiological minimum' that was needed to keep the workers and their families alive. If the wages arose, then the working class would have more children adding to the labour force and pushing down wages; if the wages fell below the minimum, then the workers would have fewer children, shrinking the supply of labour and increasing the wages. This vicious circle remained the determining factor as long as the wages were dependent on supply and demand. This was very similar to the Fabian economic theory propounded by G.B. Shaw.

In expounding this argument Lassalle was indebted to David Ricardo (1771-1823) and Thomas Robert Malthus (1766-1834) though Marx at times argued like Lassalle about the 'physiological minimum', he did not agree with Lassalle's supporting statements, namely, linking population growth with supply and demand of labour. Lassalle also asserted that the subsistence level in a society was determined by the minimum standards of living existing in a society at a particular period. Like Marx and Ricardo, he acknowledged the fact that subsistence level changed over a period of time with changes in production and social organization.

However, Lassalle seemed to contradict himself in the same document when he acknowledged social and cultural factors besides physiological in the notion of minimum needs. He conceded that the minimum needs went up with an increase in general progress and that it would not be possible to speak of improvement in worker's position in the context of the present by comparing it with the past for the workers earned more in absolute terms but were worse off in relation to their total needs. This position of Lassalle was akin to Marx's idea of relative pauperization.

Lassalle also differed from Marx in contending that the correct way to liberate the proletariat was through producers' cooperatives in which they would be paid wages equal to the value of the good they produced. Since the working class was not in a position to do it by its own efforts, he expected the state to help by providing credit. In order to get the state to provide credit facilities, he supported universal adult franchise for that would enable workers to exert political pressure. Lassalle's views on state-aided producers' cooperatives was similar to that of Proudhon. In articulating his views he rejected those of Hermann Schulze-Delitzsch who rejected state aid and advocated self-help measures in the form of consumer cooperatives, health and disability insurance schemes, savings bank and provident funds.

Lassalle, on the contrary, believed that the economic conditions of capitalism were not in a position to bring about lasting improvements for the working class. Moreover the laws of the market would continue to hold; there would be crises, bankruptcies and concentration of capital. Most often wages would never be equal to the value of goods produced, for a part of that value must be devoted to public needs, necessary unproductive work and building reserves. Lassalle insisted on the need to get the support of the state for raising loans to set up producers cooperatives. He was convinced that through working class pressure the liberal interventionist state would become a welfare state and fulfill its true mission of facilitating and securing the great cultural advances of humanity. Lassalle, unlike Marx, did not believe that the trade unions could effectively bring about substantive changes within capitalism and improve the position of the working class. This was in spite of his efforts to organize trade unions in connection with the General Union of German Workmen as subsidiary to the movement of political emancipation.

Concept of the State

Lassalle agreed with Marx and Engels on the situation of the workers in a capitalist society and the fact that the proletariat had a historic role to perform. But they differed with regard to the role of the state in the liberation of the proletariat, and their differences were fundamental and substantive. For Lassalle, socialism meant political democracy, universal suffrage, freedom of the press and of association, referendum, and trial by jury. The state represented the will of the people as a whole which was why he believed that suffrage would be the way by which people, including the workers, could advance their cause. From Hegelian perspective, he criticized the liberal theory by contending that the function of a state was not merely to protect individual freedom and property. He described the state as the highest form of human organization with the purpose of enabling the individuals to maximize and realize their freedom. It was a single moral entity intended to fulfill individual's destiny.

> Thus the purpose of the state is not simply to protect individual freedom and property . . . ; the purpose of the state is precisely to put individuals in a position, as a result of this association, to achieve ends and attain a level of existence that they could never achieve as individuals, to enable them to acquire a sum total of education, power, and freedom that they would all, as individuals, find utterly beyond their reach . . . . to bring about the positive unfolding and progressive development of man's nature, in other words, to realize the human purpose, i.e. the culture of which the human race is capable; it is the education and the development of the human race into freedom. The task and the purpose of the state consists exactly in its facilitating and mediating the great cultural progress of humanity. That is its job. That is why it exists; it has always served and always had to serve, this very purpose . . . . (Lassalle, cited in Grebing 1969: 33).

While writing these lines Lassalle had the Prussian state in mind and, being a true patriot, perceived the events of his time from a nationalist rather than an internationalist perspective as was the case with Marx. Lassalle regarded German unity to be crucial and hoped that Bismarck's policies would bring more benefits and gains. Since the true enemy of the proletariat was the bourgeois an alliance with the conservatives would not hurt. On this score also he differed from Marx who advocated an alliance with the liberal bourgeois in case of a conflict with conservatives. The Statute of the German General Workers' Association founded in 1863 in Leipzig contained the ideas of Lassalle in a nutshell.

> In the conviction that an adequate representation of the interests of the German working class and the abolition of the class conflict in society can only be achieved by universal,

equal and direct suffrage, the signatories hereby constitute an association for the German federal states, to be called *Allgemeiner Deutscher Arbetierverein*. Its purpose is to work by peaceful and legal means, particularly by influencing public opinion, towards the establishment of universal, equal and direct suffrage (Lassalle, cited in Grebing 1969: 34).

For Lassalle the state as it existed could continue to contribute to the enhancement of human freedom even after the emancipation of the proletariat. Therefore, he advocated the establishment of autonomous organizations, independent of the bourgeoisie; representation of the working class in the German legislative bodies through universal, equal and direct suffrage; the establishment of state-aided producers' cooperatives to counter-balance capitalism; will to freedom of the majority and appeal to the sense of equity.

Lassalle hoped that a social and a political society would be created through peaceful and legal means. Though he believed that the state would be the framework for the development of individuals into freedom he was ambiguous as to whether it would be a parliamentary democracy or a democratic order based on spontaneous popular will guided by the revolutionary act of the leader and the dictates of science. He had tremendous faith in the dictatorial role of the revolutionary leader, an idea that he borrowed from Fichte. Dictatorship, however, meant the dictatorship of reason. He believed that the mighty tasks during the transitional stage could not be fulfilled by different individuals bickering with one another. It was only possible by a great man whose determined action could unite the nation. However, by having a look at the organization of the German General Workers' Association one could conclude that in reality Lassalle desired the spontaneous expression of popular will guided by the acts of a revolutionary leader. He understood socialism to embody the interests of the entire community because it placed common good above the selfish demands of an individual or a group. Marx opposed this notion for society was neither homogenous nor an aggregate of private individuals. It was divided into conflicting classes whose interests were antagonistic.

For Lassalle, Fichte's conception of the state and nation symbolized a more concrete reality than the proletarian internationalism of Marx. 'In his glorification of the state, the organic unity of the nation, and the spiritual leadership of Germany he was, like Fichte before him, a pioneer of national socialism' (Kolakowski 1981b: 243). It was Fichte who inspired him on the issue of German nationalism. Fichte instructed the Germans to fulfill their mission and lead towards human progress. Germany was not only necessary part of world history but destined to be the sole champion of the idea of liberty. Reiterating Fichte, Lassalle wrote

> The metaphysical nation, the German nation, has had bestowed on it throughout its development and in the perfect accordance of its internal and external history, the supreme metaphysical destiny and the uttermost honour in world history—namely, that of creating a national territory out of the spiritual concept of a nation, and evolving its own being out of pure thought. To a metaphysical nation belongs a metaphysical task, an achievement no less than that of the divine creation. Pure spirit not only informs the reality presented to it but creates a territory, the very seat of its own existence. There has been nothing like this since the beginning of history (Lassalle 1920: 362).

Lassalle desired that the German working class organized itself on a national scale with universal direct suffrage as its first demand. Without universal suffrage nothing worthwhile could be attained, including improvement of the economic conditions of the working class. Suffrage would make the state serve the interests and aspirations of the working class. Lassalle insisted that the state everywhere and always was an instrument of general good and welfare of the people. In 1863 he instructed the working class to focus their undiluted attention on securing universal franchise and the secret ballot. Though no revolutionary changes were possible through the electoral process, mass pressure could persuade persons of stature and respect resulting in the dictatorship of the enlightened. Lassalle's views were similar to those of Bentham who also looked upon representative democracy and suffrage as the best mechanism of ensuring expertise and goodness in government.

Like Blanc, Lassalle used the term, 'universal suffrage' though he did not advocate rights for women. Both believed that suffrage could be the basis of organizing labour. Through the power of vote the workers could compel the state to establish national workshops. These workshops would be self-governing guaranteeing the workers the right to work and to the enjoyment of the full product of their labour. In content, the proposals of Blanc and Lassalle were similar. Blanc issued them contravening the Fourierist and the other advocates of the cooperative movement during the 1848 revolution while Lassalle articulated it in 1860s. Both were convinced that suffrage and state action were indispensable for the workers to achieve economic emancipation. Lassalle's views were articulated earlier by the Christian socialists and Owenites in England.

In the 1850s the German socialist and labour movement had two alternatives to choose from, the social democratic reformism of Lassalle based on the idea of a national state as the basis and source, the mother and root of the very concept of democracy, or the international revolutionary socialist ideal of Marx and Engels. Lassalle had in mind free and independent nationalities as the basis of democracy. He presented the workers with the task of winning democracy and striving for national freedom. In the context of Germany it meant German unification. The internationalism of the German Social Democrats called for a strong linkage with the claims of national obligations and, in that sense, they were a part of the 'liberal democratic German tradition' (Grebing 1969: 58).

In 1875 the Lassalleans of the All German Workers' Association and the Eisenachers of the Social Democratic Workers' Party founded by Liebknecht and Bebel in 1869 united. Both Liebknecht and Bebel did not agree with Marx and Engels' notion of the 'withering away of the state'. Liebknecht believed in the indissoluble link between democratic and socialist ideals. He regarded socialism as a function of democracy. He considered it the chief task of his party to prevent the Junkers from exploiting the class struggles between the working class and the bourgeoisie for their own selfish purposes. In the process, he allayed the suspicions against bourgeois democracy and kept the petty bourgeoisie on the side of the working class.

Like Lassalle, both Liebknecht and Bebel believed that the working class held the key to democratization. Political democracy would become social democracy and include the economic and social interests of the working class. In 1868 convention of the non-Lassallean Union of German Workingmen's Associations in Nuremberg, Liebknecht declared that democratic and socialist ideals were identical for him. In this he did not want to lose the support of the lower middle class groups whom he and Bebel had organized. Faced with continued pressures, they formed the Social Democratic Workers' Party in 1869 in Eisenach. Liebknecht was hesitant to accept the word 'worker's party' and did so under the pressure from the ex-Lassalleans. He tried to delink socialism from the working class per se and desired that it become the vision of the whole of society.

It was Lassalle's views that exerted considerable influence though both Bebel and Liebknecht played a pivotal role in the adoption of Marxist ideas within the SPD. Many of the social democrats considered themselves revolutionary because they desired a new kind of society but they did not subscribe to a Marxist theory of revolution. Liebknecht and Bebel accepted the Marxist assumptions on capitalism, class struggle and world revolution. They defended the notion of class-consciousness but denied that it would result in a revolutionary conspiracy. They defined the goal of the SPD in non-violent revolutionary terms. They refused to make concrete statements about the future revolution more as a tactic of self-preservation. During the unity congress at Gotha held on 23–27 May 1875, the SPD adopted a programme that revealed Lassalle's perceptions on the role and functions of the state for the party. '. . . fights by every lawful means for a Free State and a Socialist Society; it fights to annul the wage system and, its iron laws, to remove exploitation in every form and to abolish all social and political inequality' (Grebing 1969: 58).

The Gotha programme reiterated Lassalle's demand for universal, direct and equal suffrage, state-aided producers' cooperatives under the democratic control of the workers. The social democrats registered their favour for reforms as opposed to revolution. However, they also emphasized on the class character of the state which might result in a revolution. Though they did not talk of a democratic republic, the implications of their demands meant the realization of their demands through a democratic republic. They were convinced that a democratic state could grow out of the existing conditions provided certain political pre-requisites could be met. Marx in his criticisms on the consistencies of the Gotha programme observed:

Since we have not the courage — and wisely since the circumstances demand caution — to demand democratic republic as the French labour programmes under Louis Philippe and Louis Napoleon did — we also should not take refuge in the neither 'honourable' not 'worthy' subterfuge of demanding thing which only have meaning in a democratic republic, from a state, which is nothing else—though embellished with a parliamentary form of a government and intermingled with feudal relies—than a police guarded military despotism bureaucratically constructed and already influenced by the bourgeoisiè and moreover declared into the bargain to this state that we fondly imagine we shall be able to extort the same from it by legal means (Marx 1977c: 245).

Marx and Engels continued to reiterate that every state except the socialist state, by its very nature would remain an instrument of class suppression and domination and, even if wielded by the working class, it could be used only defensively to put down one's adversaries. In March 1875, Engels wrote to Bebel that as long as the proletariat used the state it would act in a manner that would be detrimental to its freedom and when the proletariat became conscious of its freedom, the state would cease to exist. For Marx and Engels, the ideal state that the Gotha programme spoke about was identical with the bourgeois state. In fact, the programme did not mention nor refer to the 'dictatorship of the proletariat'.

Property Rights

In the *System of Acquired Rights* Lassalle reviewed the Roman and Germanic laws of inheritance with the purpose of clarifying when and how did acquired rights lose their validity. The question had political overtones for the defenders of privilege invoked the classic rule that a law could not act retrospectively, and thereby helped Lassalle to deduce that new laws could not either erase the rights acquired under the earlier ones. He argued that acquired rights were created by an individual deliberately. Under the tacit agreement implicit in the law, these were valid as long as such rights were allowed in general by the legal system in force for the legal system derived its legitimacy from the consciousness of the nation as a whole. If a certain type of right or privilege was forbidden by later laws, the individual could contend that it was always there and make a claim. In doing so Lassalle defended and justified the legal basis to social change as a result of the abolition of privilege.

Lassalle discussed the system of property rights under different civilizations. The Roman law recognized the wishes of the dead person so the acts of his heir were regarded as acts carried out in pursuance of the dead person's will. In the German system it was not the individual but the family that was the source of will. Lassalle, in a true Hegelian fashion, explained social institutions in terms of the spirit of the people. This was because history was a chronicle of ideas in the minds of nations which was more real than the minds of individual persons. Unlike Marx who explained ideas in terms of material reality, Lassalle gave more importance to ideas seeing them as ' moving' forces in history.

Lassalle argued that a person had a right to that which was the result of his own voluntary action. All other rights were dependent on the claims recognized by the *Volksgeist*, and a change in the latter would mean a new set of rights. Therefore, within the legal system, there was nothing that would do away with prescriptive rights. Appropriately the validity of these rights was to be found in the consciousness of popular minds. Lassalle rejected the prescriptive claims of privileged classes.

Gender Question

Lassalle did not give much thought to the woman's issue. His attitude remained anti-women for he failed to understand the problem of female labour. His perception of the family remained bourgeois. Interestingly he demanded remunerative work for women at home rather than in the factory. This was evident from the 6th General Meeting of the General German Workers' Association held in 1867 which, in its resolution, observed:

> The employment of women in the workshop of modern industry is one of the most scandalous abuses of our times. Scandalous, because it does not improve the material situation of the working class but makes it worse, and because the destruction of the family in particular reduced the working class population to a wretched state in which even the last remnants of its ideal possessions are taken from it. This gives us all the more reason to reject the current efforts to increase even further the market for female labour. Only the abolition of the rule of capital can ensure the remedy, through which positive organic institutions will abolish the wage relationship

and give every worker the full proceeds of his labour (cited in Thonnessen 1969: 15).

In 1865 the 'General Association of German Women' was established by Luise Otto-Peters, an advocate of women's rights during the 1848 revolution. The organization dismissed by the social democrats as mere suffragettes demanded civil equality for women. Moritz Müller a manufacturer from Frankfurt championed the cause of women's education and employment at the third Conference of the German Workers' Association seeing the link between increase in female labour and mechanization within capitalism as an inevitable tendency. He recommended stoppage of female labour only if it was detrimental to health. The Congress stressed on the need to further women's intellectual development as it helped them to raise their children and manage their homes better. However, the advocates of female labour were not only in a minority but faced resistance on the grounds that female labour would lower wages, that women were unsuited for trade union activity and that the working class families would suffer neglect. The conservatives felt that the home was the rightful place for the woman and that it was sufficient if men worked. In spite of the resistance, the majority voted for Muller's resolution which proposed three items: (1) importance of mobilizing female labour power for political and economic reasons; (2) equal rights and equal status earned through serious work among committed work mates; and (3) establishing women's workers association to provide self help, moral and material assistance, and education.

The woman's issue did not figure in the Congress of the Workers' Associations in 1868. The International Workers' Association in its First Congress held in 1866 in Geneva present a draft statement on 'female and child labour' as one of the points on its agenda but it failed to obtain majority support. At the Eisenach Congress in 1869 the Lassalleans proposed 'universal, equal and direct suffrage for men about the age of twenty', and the Marxists demanded voting rights for all citizens. Only male suffrage was included in the final draft. The issue of female labour once again created controversies but finally a demand was made for restricting female labour and prohibiting child labour. For the first time the idea of 'equal pay for men and women' was advanced.

Conclusion

Lassalle's legacy to the development of socialism has been disputed by subsequent socialists. Mehring stressed on Marx's personal dislike for Lassalle and understated their differences. Kautsky pointed out that their socialisms were poles apart. It was beyond doubt that, for Lassalle, Germany dominated his theoretical orientations which explained his enormous and lasting political influence and success. Besides, the Marxists the Anarchists were critical of parliamentarism for it led to compromise and collaboration with the bourgeoisie. Bakunin contended that the SPD from its beginning stood for a compromise between socialism and liberal democracy for it accepted class collaboration.

Lassalle gave a socialist flavour to the Ricardian principles. He gave a thorough analysis of how most of the revenue of the state derived from indirect taxation was paid by the poor while political power was based on direct taxation of property. He highlighted the exploitative side of productive relationships and coined the expression 'iron law of wages'. He proposed producers' cooperatives to remedy the malady within contemporary capitalism, namely chaotic distribution and the separation of production and ownership.

Lassalle rejected the conception of nightwatchman state and favoured universal, direct and secret ballot for that would make the state reflective and responsive towards the workers' interests. Hence he was willing to negotiate with Bismarck directly for getting his proposals implemented. His perception of using the existing state and transforming it in the process formed the core of the social democratic philosophy. His perceptions suffered a temporary setback mainly because of the obstinacy of Bismarck's anti-socialist policies. The anti-socialist laws of 1878–90 weakened the case of Lassallean socialism which depended heavily on state support, thus reinforcing the left orthodox opposition to his policies. With the relaxation of anti socialist laws Lassalle's demands echoed in the SPD's Erfurt programme of 1891. Bernstein developed and expanded Lassalle's ideas, thus stating the core ideas of social democracy.

Eduard Bernstein

Bernstein rejected all the fundamental cannons of Marxism including the theory of the state as a class institution. Analogically the view of Bernstein is similar to that of the democratic pluralist view of our time which believes that in the advanced capitalist countries 'all active and legitimate groups in the population can make themselves heard at some crucial stage in the process of decision (Dahl 1986: 89).

It there had been no Bernstein, it would have been necessary to invent him. Political and economic conditions in Germany demanded a reformist doctrine around the turn of the century . . . . It was his commitment to both socialism and democracy that made him a social democrat in the exact sense of the word (Gay 1979: 110, 244).

His (Bernstein) strength lay in the detailed observation of contemporary trends and his strong moral sense. But at the same time he was an extremely eclectic thinker and incapable of interpreting his observations in the light of any coherent and systematic theory (McLellan 1977: 40).

One of the most important reasons for the varied meanings that were attached to Marx's writings and his world view was the fact that his contemporaries, which included his close associate Engels as well as his numerous disciples and followers, said and did a lot of things which were very different from Marx's presumptions, but always presented these to be totally in consonance with his precepts both in letter and in spirit. This was true of practically all the Marxists after Marx which include Kautsky, Lenin, Luxemburg, Trotsky and Mao. The only probable exception was Eduard Bernstein (1850–1932) who had the honesty to admit that his thesis was quite at variance from the one propounded by Marx and, as such, openly called it 'revisionism'.

Bernstein till date remains the best and finest exponent of revisionism, a doctrine that openly announced the obsolence of many of the Marxist ideas and the need to humanize socialism to an age of democracy and industrialized capitalism. As an important and influential member of the German Social Democratic Part (SPD), the largest socialist party in Europe in the latter part of the nineteenth century, he served it tirelessly and with utmost devotion. His life paralleled and became an integral part of the story of SPD.

Besides being an eminent theoretician and an intellectual with rare insights, Bernstein was a man known for his humane qualities, impeccable integrity of character and courage of conviction. He was described as fearlessly honest and scrupulous, committed to truth and never resorting to expediency. He was, in all sense of the term, a true scholar — well-read, intelligent, witty and, above all, honest. His unflinching search for truth made him renounce Marxism, and his search for an alternative in revisionism made him give up close friendships and even the party that he had served all his life.

Bernstein was convinced of the need to realize both socialism and democracy in a gradual, piecemeal and non-violent manner. In his commitment, he never wavered. He looked to violence for its own sake as utter barbarism. This became apparent and evident in his critique of Bolshevism. He also believed that means and ends were intimately related and that imperfect means could undermine a movement that used them, no matter how much it professed human needs. Equally attractive of his revisionism was its non-dogmatic and non-doctrinaire approach to social, economic and political analysis.

The modifications that Bernstein brought about within Marxism had far reaching implications for the doctrine both at the level of theory and practice. His emphasis on democratic and parliamentary brand of socialism which lay at the heart of revisionism was not a lone voice in the history of socialist thought and movements. The English Fabians had done the same. However, he was certainly the first to stress and reconcile socialized means of production with parliamentary democracy, nationalized industries with civil liberties. He realized that true socialism would have to eschew all dictatorial, authoritarian and conspiratorial methods and remain steadfast in its realization of democracy and civic freedoms. In short, the statement of Oscar Wilde that 'anybody can write history, only a great man can make it' is an apt description for Bernstein.

If Edmund Burke (1729–97) was the rallying point of those who were critical of the French revolution, it was Bernstein who became the main spokesman of the new revisionist thesis. This fact assumed added significance because he was not just an ordinary unknown critic but was a close associate of Engels and one of two executors to the latter's literary will implying that 'his track record was that of an eminent and orthodox Marxist' (Tudor 1988: xi). This was evident from his pioneering Marxist analysis of the English civil war and the revolution of the seventeenth century written during his years of exile in England in 1895. He analyzed this event as a social and economic phenomena laying stress on the growth of dynamic and aggressive upper middle class and vividly portrayed its conflict with both the nobility and the workers. He also showed how the commercial financiers and the industrial capitalists were drastically altering old institutions. On this basis, he looked to the contemporary social and political philosophy of the period, including that of Hobbes and Harrington, the Levellers and the Diggers as emerging out of the class between a dying feudalism and an emerging youthful capitalism. He felt reassured and pleased that the journal of an extremely radical party, the Levellers was called *The Moderate*. His analysis made a remarkable use of the approach of materialistic interpretation of history and he was probably the first analyst who highlighted the important role of Winstanley in this period. In fact it was due to Bernstein and Kautsky's analyses that Marxist historians were comfortably informed about seventeenth century English social history. So both as an activist as well as a Marxist theoretician, Bernstein occupied an important place in the socialist theory and practice. However, it was his dissection and critique of Marxism after the death of Marx that was crucial to the understanding of the revisionist doctrine.

By 1875 it became clear that the German Social Democrats were thinking of using the existing state apparatus. Though they still remained committed to the principles of revolutionary Marxism at the level of theory, they were settling down to a mood of reformism at the level of practice. The historical setting of the SPD within Germany created a serious dilemma for the party which was not in a position to challenge the armed might of the state. Moreover, the prospect of parliamentary activity at that point of time seemed bright and hopeful. In response to this dilemma, Engels argued that the capitalist societies had structural defects which could only be rectified with an overthrow of the system when the proletariat captured power and created the material basis for socialism. Engels clarified that though this may be the final aim, he would have no objections if the party actively participated in the parliamentary process for that would enhance its strength and principles. He projected parliamentary activity as an immediate and a tactical move within a broad and long term revolutionary strategy.

The 1890s saw important changes in German politics with Kaiser favouring a policy of reconciliation with the working class which was opposed by Bismarck leading to the latter's resignation. The anti-socialist law was also allowed to lapse after twelve years since it came into existence in 1878 giving the SPD relative freedom to function. The latter's clandestine operations ceased and its paper *Social Demokrat* with Bernstein as its editor resumed its publication. During the time of the anti-socialist law, the party held its congresses outside Germany and its paper was published from Zurich. The next five years 1890–95 were crucial for the SPD, and a watershed and turning point in the outlook and perceptions of Bernstein.

Biographical Sketch

Bernstein was born on 6 January 1850 in Berlin. His father Jakob was a plumber's apprentice in Danzig and then an engine driver in Berlin. His mother Johanna Rosenberg was a hardworking woman who bore fifteen children, five of whom died at an early age. His family was Jewish though they did not practice their religion. He was a sickly child and a fairly good student. At the age of sixteen he left his studies and joined the Berlin bank as an apprentice. His formal education ended though he continued to study on his own, which enabled him to emerge as one of the most outstanding intellectuals of his time.

Bernstein completed his apprenticeship in 1869. He found a job as a clerk in S & L Rothchild Bank in Berlin which he left in 1878. He entered the social democratic movement at the age of twenty-two in 1872 by joining the Social Democratic Workers' Party. For the next six years till 1878, a period which he described as his 'Social Democratic apprenticeship', he acquired skills as a political leader, interacted with more experienced party leaders and began to read social theory. He undertook extensive speaking tours which usually began on a Saturday night and carried on the whole of Sunday. It was a hectic schedule that consisted of three talks or participation in three debates in as many localities as possible. He found the suburbs of Berlin particularly challenging and when he felt satisfied there, he moved to the capital. On many occasions there were fist fights but most violence was usually confined to verbal exchanges only. Like many of his contemporaries, he was influenced by Marx's *The Civil War in France* and Dühring's *Cursus der National-und Sozialokonomie* (1872). Soon Bernstein was able to establish his reputation and popularity within the SPD that was formed following the unity talks between the two wings, Eisenacheis and Lassalleans in 1875.

Bernstein's Berlin phase drew to a close following the repressive measures which included the anti-socialist bill undertaken by Bismarck. The bill became a law on 19 October 1878 and remained in force for the next 12 years. He moved to Switzerland on 12 October 1878 and became private secretary to Karl Hochberg, a wealthy young socialist and a supporter of SPD. He returned to Germany after 20 years.

In 1879 Bernstein got acquainted with Marxism after reading Engels' *Anti Dühring*. Dühring's criticisms prompted Bernstein to make a detailed study of his objections to Marx. He was also attracted to the liberal element in Dühring's socialism for he viewed with alarm the growing emphasis on statism within socialism.

> What especially attracted me to Dühring was his strong emphasis on the liberal element in socialism. Opposition to the liberal parties had caused many socialists to attribute unseen virtues to the state, which might well be attributed to the state in theory, but which the state with which we had to deal did not exhibit. There were indeed socialists who were conscious of the dangers which this cult of the state could have in the political struggle and, with a view towards them, fought against it. But this rejection for reasons of political expediency did not satisfy me. It occurred to me to warn the workers to expect from the conquering state that it would soon develop the whole economic machinery of the modern state to the highest productivity from above down by means of laws, regulations and central organs (Bernstein 1961: 11–12).

Bernstein pointed out that he was not aware of Marx's views on the Paris Commune till he read the *Civil War in France* where Marx emphasized on the need for decentralization, but as with representative parliamentary democracy even the theme of decentralization never moved to the centre stage of Marx's analysis.[1]

While planning the publication of a *Yearbook for Social Science*, Bernstein wrote to Engels with the purpose of eliciting his opinion. The latter, Marx, Liebknecht and Bebel were critical of the issue. In 1880 Bernstein decided to pay Marx and Engels a personal visit with two purposes, to mend fences and to choose a new editor of

the *Sozialdemokrat* since Georg von Vollmar (1850–1922) had decided to quit the post on 1 January 1881. Liebknect supported Hirch
for the post while Bebel hoped that Bernstein could get it, which
meant that the party leaders would have to change their minds
about him. The former in his reminiscences wrote that: 'Marx and
Engels . . . were strongly hostile to him, and I wanted to show them
that he was not the terrible fellow that the two old ones believed
him to be' (Bebel, cited in Gay 1979: 33).

Bernstein's London visit was a spectacular success for he secured the editorship of the *Sozialdemokrat* in January 1881. Initially
separated from his family he felt lonesome but gradually overcame
it by making new friends and by achieving success in journalism.
Moreover he was filled with the charms of Zurich landscape which
he never failed to mention to his readers. Zurich next to London
became the centre for the international socialist movement since
socialist activity in both the cities was legal and active.

It was the editorship of the party newspaper rather than the
party congresses that engaged Bernstein's interests, energy and
time. This meant corresponding with Engels on a regular basis,
with the latter playing the role of a critic, guide and admirer. Even
though he wanted to leave the job, Engels asked him to reconsider
his decision. Both Bebel and Liebknecht also praised his efforts.
Not only did Bernstein continue with the newspaper but became
its permanent editor. Thus, in his 30s he occupied a key post,
enjoyed better relations with Marx and Engels and was close to
Bebel and Liebknecht. Under his editorship, Engels felt that the
newspaper had become the best that the party had ever had. It was
around this time that Bernstein met and developed a lifelong friendship with Kautsky, though for many years they never spoke or
corresponded with one another. The latter was a regular contribu-
tor to the newspaper. Meanwhile Engels assumed the mantle of
the chief advisor of the party on the death of Marx in 1883.

In August 1886 Bernstein married Regina Zadek a widow, with
two children. He lived happily with her for the next thirty seven
years until her death in 1923. He went into exile in 1888 following
the measures launched by Bismarck to dislodge the Zurich centre
of the party. He moved to London where he continued to publish
the newspaper. He wrote an epilogue to Webb's *History of British
Trade Unionism* which was translated into German by his wife
Regina. In this he hinted at the obsolence of a socialist revolution.

It was in London that Bernstein attempted the revision of Marxism and published his masterpiece on the English civil war of the seventeenth century. He developed his theory of revisionism in detail in the 1890s and nearly all the work he undertook upon his return to Germany in 1901 was directed towards elaborating and expounding the doctrine. While in London he came into close contact with the members of the Fabian society — Graham Wallas, Shaw, Sidney and Beatrice Webb, Stewart Headlam, Keir Hardie, John Burns and Ramsay MacDonald. Engels was aware of these contacts but still made Bernstein one of the executors of his literary will.

By 1900 Bernstein's conversion to revisionism and his renunciation of orthodox Marxism was complete. He was allowed to stay on within the party for Bebel feared that his expulsion may mean loss of many others who would have gone along with him. During the First World War, the SPD voted for war credits. Bernstein supported it for he was firmly convinced that Russia was behind the Serbian crisis. On 31 July 1914 Jean Leon Juares (1859–1914) was murdered, which reinforced his belief that war with Russia was inevitable and even desirable. For their decision, the German socialists were criticized and hated by the whole socialist world. This made Bernstein search for the truth about the war which he did single-handedly. At this time he decided to renew contacts with his old friend Kautsky with whom he had not spoken for several years and on whose help he knew he could count. He defended the right of any country to defend its independence while in danger.

During the second rounds of voting on war credits, Bernstein abstained for he disliked war and only recognized defensive ones. He realized that Germany was forced into the war on account of her ambition and stupidity. He left the party with which he had spent forty years, serving it and being intimately associated with it, on 24 March 1916, and joined the Independent Social Democratic Party (USPD) but never took a prominent part in its deliberations. His literary activity kept him busy. He still hoped to unite the socialist factions, which was made possible by the German revolution that broke out in 1918. He became Assistant to Dr. Schiffer, Secretary of State for the Treasury, and remained in that post till February 1919. He rejoined the SPD without giving up his USPD membership with the purpose of demonstrating the fundamental unity within the German working class. But this strategy did not work. There were objections against dual membership, which meant he had to renounce his USPD affiliation. However, he never regained his earlier influence.

Bernstein was extremely critical of the Bolsheviks for they did all that he abhorred. He spent his last years in isolation. Though not so involved within the party, he spent his time in journalism. He wrote articles and gave lectures in the university. He helped young people with their problems, helped foreigners to obtain their residence permits in Germany, advised upcoming authors and provided financial help to his party colleagues. All these increased more after his wife's death for it accentuated his loneliness.

In the 1920s Bernstein became sympathetic to the Zionist colonization in Palestine and was held in high esteem by the Zionist labour movement. In 1928 he joined the Socialist Committee for a Workers' Palestine. He reacted sharply to Kautsky's denunciations and stressed on the positive achievements of 'cooperative Jewish labour' in Palestine 'under the most difficult conditions'. He argued that the rise of national socialism and difficulties of emigration to other countries made a Jewish national home in Palestine the most important need of the hour. The German Left found it difficult to combat the rise of new wave of racism.

In 1925 Bernstein suffered two strokes but he continued to serve in the Reichstag for three more years. His mind remained alert till the very last. In a letter written to Kautsky shortly after his 82 birthday, he expressed his concern over the economic depression and the party's prospects. He died on 18 December 1932. His funeral was well-attended.

The Erfurt Programme

In the 1880s Germany witnessed uninterrupted economic development and industrial expansion, thus benefitting from what was referred to as a 'golden era of world economy'.[2] The overall economic growth made the workers relatively prosperous, thereby signaling better times for the SPD. The latter grew in strength and electoral support.[3] With increase in votes, parliamentarism gained a new lease of life. This becomes evident from the Erfurt programme that the party adopted in 1891. The programme redrew and reaffirmed its commitment to Marxism but in practice became more committed to parliamentary activity. The first and the theoretical part of the programme was prepared by Kautsky, the chief exponent of Marxism in Germany and the editor of party's theoretical monthly *Die Neue Zeit*. It adhered faithfully to the doctrines of Marx and Engels as stated in the *Capital*. Its very first sentence stressed on the 'natural necessity' of economic development of the bourgeois society towards the socialization of the means of production.

The second and the practical part of the programme was prepared by Bernstein. It acknowledged the need to use the existing state for improving the social and economic conditions of the working class. It demanded universal suffrage, equal rights for women, proportional representation, freedom of expression, freedom of association, free schooling, secularization of schools, free legal assistance, medical care, local self-government, direct legislation by means of proposal and rejection, election of magistrates, eighthour day and prohibition of employment for women and children whereever possible. Nowhere was the need to achieve these aims through revolutionary violence mentioned.

This dualism in the Erfurt programme indicated what Marx considered reform versus revolutionary goals. Kautsky clarified that SPD was a revolutionary but not a revolution-making party. The programme did not mention the controversial Marxist concept of the 'dictatorship of the proletariat' nor the 'democratic republic' though Engels in his critique of the programme added that the democratic republic would be the specific form that the dictatorship of the proletariat would assume (Engels 1977: 435).

The Erfurt programme indicated the commitment of SPD to achieve socialist goals through constitutional and parliamentary methods echoing the sentiments of Lassalle. The German social democrats were convinced following the repeal of the anti-socialist law that the capitalist society had reached a stage when it could evolve into a socialist society peacefully and gradually.

The revisionists demanded renunciation of revolutionary slogans and stressed on the need to embrace a social democratic reformist programme keeping in tune with the prevailing mood and reality. The radicals, on the other hand, dismissed the parliamentary system as opportunism and continued to stress on spontaneous revolutionary upsurge. The leadership of SPD was unable to tilt in favour of either side. It did not want to lose its right-wing support that was reformist, nor abandon the left which still remained devoted to revolution. It took Bebel's diplomatic skill to keep both the groups satisfied and within the party. The Janus-faced nature of SPD which became apparent in the Erfurt programme was finally resolved in 1959 in the Bad Godsberg programme when it formally renounced its revolutionary goals even at the level of theory.[4]

Bernstein's Revisionism

Bernstein's conversion from orthodox Marxism to revisionism ought to be understood in the context of the observations that Engels made and perhaps with the knowledge of the latter. In fact, Engels was aware of the close links that Bernstein maintained with the English Fabians.[5] The significance of revisionism was that Bernstein was the first to realize an open cleavage between the Marxist theory and the social, economic and political realities within the late nineteenth century capitalism. While conceding that Marx was a genius, he stressed on the need to critically assess the 'development and elaboration of the Marxist doctrine' (Bernstein 1961: 25).

> The theory which the *Communist Manifesto* sets forth of the evolution of modern society was correct as far as it characterized the general tendencies of that evolution. But it was mistaken in several deductions, above all in the estimate of the time the evolution would take . . . the further development and elaboration of the Marxist doctrine must begin with criticism of it . . . The mistakes of a theory can only be considered as overcome when they are recognized as such by the advocates of that theory. Such recognition does not necessarily signify the destruction of the theory. It may rather appear after subtraction of what is acknowledged to be mistaken . . . that it is Marx finally who carries the point against (Bernstein 1961: xxiv, 25, 26–7).

Bernstein in 1898 wrote to Bebel that he was studying the teachings of Marx, and tried to match the same with practical realities and, in the process realized, that all the predictions had not materialized. He asserted that Marx had faulted on some observations with regard to the late nineteenth century capitalist societies. He contended that, contrary to Marx's predictions, the rate of profit had not fallen, the wages had not gone down nor were there any signs of an imminent collapse of capitalism. Most important of all, the working class did not show any desire or inclination to make a revolution. Instead of concentration, there was diffusion of wealth making peaceful transition to socialism desirable. His attempt to revise Marxism was with the intention of preventing Marxism from becoming obsolete.

Bernstein acknowledged the significant differences between his world-view and that of Marx. Without mincing words he honestly termed it 'Revisionism'.[6] He did this 'without renouncing his allegiance to the socialist movement and its ideals' (Hook 1961: vii–viii). His refusal to admit that he had abandoned Marxism was due to the tremendous influence which the theory had on him. In fact, he often reminded his followers and critics that both Marx and Engels were revisionists in their own time within the socialist theory and practice (Ibid.: ix). 'Revisionism was far more than a patchwork of "corrections" or "improvements" on Orthodox Marxism. In the hands of its chief proponent it evolved into a full-scale attack on Marx's system' (Gay 1979: 131).

From 1896 Bernstein began to publish a series of articles in *Die Neue Zeit* called *Problems of Socialism* which formed the basis of *The Premises of Socialism and the Tasks of Social Democracy* (1899). Following Engels' insistence on the need to revise tactics, Bernstein pointed that it was not merely tactics but the entire premises of theoretical Marxism that needed revision. In 1899, writing to Victor Adler, he conceded that the Marxist doctrine was way behind the practical developments, at least that was the case in Germany. He found 'excessive abstraction' to be the main shortcoming in Marxism.

Philosophical Basis of Revisionism

Bernstein acknowledged that he doubted Marxism not because he questioned its whole structure but because events falsified some of its important predictions. He felt that it was the method that led to errors. He accepted that Marxism was not a sacred doctrine and was uncomfortable with adhering to a faulty method. This was because the 'Hegelian-dialectical method was a "snare" for it had totally abandoned the empirical world for idle speculation' (Bernstein 1961: 51). Moreover, under the Hegelian influence, Marx relied heavily in force and violence to realize socialism. He felt the need to minimize the influence of the dialectical method in a letter to Kautsky,

I had not turned from the fundamental concepts of the Marxian view of history, but had always merely opposed certain interpretations and applications. Further I had sought to explain hasty conclusions of Marx and Engels as the consequence of their being seduced by the Hegelian dialectic, which after all is not integrally connected with theory (Bernstein, cited in Gay 1979: 136).

Bernstein regarded evolutionism as the core of Marxism for both Marx and Engels visualized socialism not as an utopian idea but a tendency within the economic processes of capitalism thereby giving the 'labour movement its greatest impetus and its solid foundations' (Bernstein 1961: 15). Such a perception was 'organic' whereas by perceiving historical change as a result of a struggle of the opposites, it would give undue importance to violence and hence would be 'unorganic'.

I am not of the opinion that the struggle of opposites is the basis of all development. The cooperation of related forces is of great significance as well. It becomes necessary, therefore, to view social evolution as a gradual growth into socialism. True, class antagonisms continue, but they diminish in force; immediate work *within* the state takes the place of intransigent opposition to it (Ibid.: 335, 347).

Bernstein, following Lassalle, found Marxism to be very deterministic and ideological, limiting the range of individual's ethical thinking. By introducing the ethical dimension into socialism, he made it morally desirable which could be realized by human will. Like Fichte, he looked upon the individual as incomplete and in constant search and pursuit of transcending limitations. He was categorical that socialism was not a matter of scientific prediction. He abandoned Hegelianism and relied on Kantianism to furnish the philosophical foundations of revisionism. A socialist theory without an ethical content would be sterile for socialism is 'a never ending task. The world is never finished, never perfect; the reformer's work like the housewife's is never done' (Bernstein, cited in Gay 1979: 155).

Economic Doctrines of Revisionism

Bernstein questioned Kautsky's optimistic observations and conclusions on three grounds. Against the alleged tendencies of the capitalist development outlined in the Erfurt programme, he pointed out that: (a) The peasantry and the middle class were not disappearing. Small business organizations were not being eliminated and the industrial working class did not constitute the overwhelming majority of the population. Instead, the substantial portion of the population continued to be neither bourgeoisie nor proletarian, and their preferences, perceptions and politics were of crucial significance for socialist politics. He observed, 'peasants do not sink, middle class does not disappear, crises do not grow ever larger, misery and serfdom do not increase' (Bernstein 1961: 56). (b) Even amongst the working class, the rapid growth in membership and votes for social democracy did not necessarily indicate any desire for socialism. The workers voted and joined social democrats for many reasons and not purely out of a commitment for socialism. In this context, he cited the British example where an industrial development under capitalism did not commensurably lead to the growth of socialist consciousness among the workers. (c) He also questioned the present capacity of the working class to take control of the entire means of production. He reiterated Sidney Webb's views on industrial democracy for he pointed out that the poor performance of the cooperatives, once they had grown fairly large in size, was because of their democratic character on the one hand, and the need for functional differentiation and hierarchy of authority on the other. Webb thereby concluded that cooperative management was not possible if the unit of production was reasonably big. In a similar vein, Bernstein asserted the impossibility of the idea of the manager being 'the employee of those he manages, that he should be dependent for his position on their favour and their bad temper' (Ibid.: 65).

Revisionism attacked Marxian economics just as it questioned Marxian philosophical premises. Bernstein accepted that though there was concentration and centralization, small independent enterprises and innumerable industrial establishments continued. 'Modern capitalism does not simplify its class relations but differentiates them to an ever greater degree' (Ibid.: 89). With help of statistics obtained from England and Germany, he proved that small- and medium-sized enterprises were not growing at the rate of big industries but proved to be viable. In many sectors, giant enterprises were not growing at the rate of big industries though division of labour enabled them to give semi-finished goods to the big industries which in turn prepared them as products for the market. The more important factor was that these small and medium-sized firms had direct access to the consumers and were in a better position to compete with the big industries. But this process of centralization did not succeed in commerce, transport and agriculture. Interestingly, Kautsky agreed with Bernstein on this point for he contended that it was difficult to say when all the small businesses would disappear. However, in 1924 when the German industries witnessed intense cartelization and centralization Bernstein was too old to take this into account for the 'new facts would have compelled him to revise his view drastically' (Gay 1979: 163).

Bernstein vehemently opposed the Marxist proposition with regard to the concentration of wealth in fewer hands. He did not question the claim that social differences were disappearing but rejected the categorical assertion of Marx that middle class was vanishing and that the number of property-holders was decreasing. On the contrary, their number was on the increase. He used income statistics as proof of widespread shareholding in corporations. He studied the tax returns in industrialized societies of Europe which revealed that a sizable number of people were enjoying respectable incomes. There was no indication of any deterioration.

> Social conditions have not reached that acute tension which the *Communist Manifesto* had predicted. Not only would be useless it would be the height of folly to conceal this from ourselves. The number of propertied persons has not diminished but become larger. The enormous increase in social wealth is accompanied not by a shrinking number of capitalist magnates but by a growing number of capitalists of all ranges of wealth. The middle classes change their character but they do not disappear from the social scale . . . the number of propertied is growing absolutely and relatively (Bernstein 1961: 88).

Bernstein pointed out that the new middle class consisted of technical personnel, 'white collar workers', office and sales clerks and government employees. These categories increased along with the mounting bureaucratization of monopoly capitalism. Their incomes were higher than those of wage labourers but, in their social standing, they were with the bourgeoisie. He recognized that the working class by itself was not homogenous anticipating Poulantaz's differentiation between working class consisting of productive labourers that was separate from the white-collar supervisory workers.

In 1899 Bernstein published his most famous *Evolutionary Socialism: a Criticism and Affirmation* considered to be the 'Bible of revisionism'. Impressed by the progress of the democratic state, he felt that the workers could use the ballot box effectively to press forward their cause. Conversely, in the changed situation, Marx's clarion call for revolutionary overthrow of capitalism was neither practicable nor desirable. He reiterated Lassalle's reformist outlook that socialism could develop as a result of gradual process of social reform. Capitalism was stabilizing itself through the creation of monopolies and cartels, through the credit system, through the growth of world market coupled with tremendous improvements in communications and transportation, and increased wealth of industrialized states in Western Europe. The ownership in the joint stock companies was spreading widely. The real wages of the workers were rising and the middle class was expanding. Contrary to the popular view, trade unions safeguarded the rights and interests of the workers. All these made modern capitalism adaptable and immune to depressions and growing misery. He was confident that the advance of capitalism paved way for socialism. Trusts and cartels were organized in a manner that socialists could deflect its working for the benefit of the society. Workers were steadily growing in size, power and social importance. They were steadily claiming and securing citizenship rights and had the power to seize them if denied or withdrawn.

Mass Strike

Bernstein rejected the idea of mass strike intent upon starving the bourgeoisie into submission as utopian and nonsensical. Equally absurd was the Sorelian view of the 'general strike' as the supreme myth of the working class. The political mass strike was a tactical weapon. It could be used both offensively and defensively only if rights and liberties that were previously granted stood threatened. In that case, without any utopian trappings, its aim would be to exert the strongest political and moral pressure upon government and public opinion. The possibilities of its success were limited and hence he advised its sparing use. Unlike a revolution, it could not be instigated nor could one hope for its spontaneity. The chances of its success would depend on wrongs and misdeeds of the ruling class. He stated that the weapon of mass strike would be outmoded in a full-fledged democracy. But even if it was to be used as a defensive tactic, it would have to be peaceful. This clearly proved that he still hoped to arrive at socialism through parliamentary means without violence and bloodshed. The moral component was important for that would reflect the public support it could muster. It was for this reason that mass strike was defined as 'an economic weapon with an ethical object' (Bernstein, cited in Gay 1979: 234).

Bernstein clarified that mass strike need not involve universal stoppage of work. If the workers failed to show up in the vital areas of the economy like transport and communications, light and power, and food establishments, it was enough to bring the total work to a halt. The organizers would have to ensure that the workers' families did not suffer more in the general disorder than the ruling groups. Besides Bernstein, Kautsky and Bebel also rejected the idea of a general strike as the expression of the highest for of revolutionary activity in the context of Germany. They favoured political mass strikes by individual trades and regions but regarded the exercise of the right to strike as the ultimate resort in an extreme situation when there was a threat of disenfranchisement.

> For Bernstein's theory of political tactics his approach to the mass strike was a refreshing amendment. It recognized that nonviolence may be supremely desirable but also completely impossible when certain line-ups of social forces exist and when the machinery for peaceful social change is but a disguise for enforced social standstill. It is to be regretted that he never fully integrated and this insight with his constitutionalism. Had he done so, he would have been in a far stronger logical position against both the intractable revolutionists of the left as well as the feverish legalists on the right who preferred the destruction of their movement to defensive action

that might violate the sacred principles of law and order (Ibid.: 238).

Political Aspects of Revisionism

For Bernstein, socialism and democracy had to be realized simultaneously. These were the two final values in revisionism. Democracy meant the absence of class government, minority rights, political equality, greatest possible freedom and equal rights for all. Socialism meant self-organization of the people. Therefore, looking to the prospects for democracy which Bernstein felt was bright and hopeful, he objected to the use of the phrase 'dictatorship of the proletariat'. 'If Democracy is not to exceed centralized absolutism in the breeding of bureaucracies, it must be built upon an elaborately organized self-government with a corresponding economic, personal responsibility of all the units of administration as well as of the adult citizens of the state' (Bernstein 1961: 155).

Bernstein regarded socialism as the final goal but could foresee a lengthy period of transition characterized by minimum of violence and maximum of rational planning. Essentially pragmatic, he emphasized on the need for piecemeal but effective measures for gradual change towards socialism. He rejected the idea of 'final conflict', a 'messianic mission' and a 'total apocalypse'. Instead, he relied on reforms. It was in this sense that he asserted that the 'movement is everything, the final aim, nothing' (Ibid.: xii–iv).

Bernstein compared and contrasted the revolutionary and democratic roads to political power. While revolution was a quicker way of removing privileges and obstacles, democratic reform would offer long-term and lasting solutions. He was emphatic in defending democracy and democratic political and social institutions as an indispensable condition for realizing socialism. 'Democracy is at the same time means and end. It is the means of the struggle for socialism and it is the form socialism will take once it has been realized' (Ibid.: 244–5).

Bernstein looked upon democracy as an educational and a moral institution. Democracy would be parliamentary and not plebiscitarian, representative and not direct. Its bureaucracy would be permanent and professional. The remedy for excesses of parliamentarism would be local self-government. It had to be self-governing and self-regulatory. It had to be federal and decentralized in nature, delegating the maximum possible power to the local communities. Unlike Lassalle, he acknowledged social democracy's indebtedness to liberalism for he regarded socialism as its spiritual and legitimate heir. He was emphatic that democracy could be achieved only democratically. 'But a national central government is indispensable for an efficient carrying on of public business; to dissolve all its institutions and to delegate its functions to local communities would be sheer utopianism' (Bernstein 1961: 189–98).

Bernstein was convinced that the gradual road to socialism could be attained only under democracy. In support of his contention, he quoted statements of Marx and Engels on the lessons learnt from the Paris Commune of 1871 which, according to him, was the workers' need for democracy. He believed that, as a result of universal suffrage, the workers could become equal partners in a democratic society. He was confident that the existing political institutions, however limited in scope, could be changed and developed and need not be destroyed. Though classes existed in contemporary society, yet it did not automatically imply a class government. For Bernstein, the dynamics of universal suffrage would, in the long run, subordinate the state to popular control. In this assertion, he cited the example of the Prussian anti-socialist laws and their subsequent repeal. Initially, Bismarck had used franchise as a tool but was finally compelled to treat it as a goal. Hopeful of the tremendous potential of democracy, he rejected the idea of the dictatorship of the proletariat as essentially barbaric, an atavism belonging to lower culture and civilization. It reminded him of irrational Blanquism. He was categorical that socialism ought to eschew any form of proletarian dictatorship in the name of a class or party. 'Is there any sense in holding to the phrase 'dictatorship of the proletariat' at a time in which Social Democracy has in practice put itself on the basis of parliamentarism, equitable popular representation, and popular legislation, all of which contradict dictatorship' (Ibid.: 182).

Bernstein's idea of a proletarian society was one of universal citizenship, a self-organized people without the need for a centralized absolute authority of the bureaucracy. Such a society would be representative, democratic and equal. He contended that the need for democracy in every sphere of human activity was the principal lesson of the Paris Commune. He also rejected the notion of the 'withering away of the state' and thus made a final break with orthodox Marxism (Gay 1979: 286). Along with that, he rejected the idea of workers' fatherland that the *Communist Manifesto* espoused. He rejected socialization of everything as unwise and instead proposed an economic criterion: ' . . . where the state operates less efficiently than private industry it would be un-socialist to give preference to the state over private management' (Bernstein 1961: 92).

Bernstein accepted equality as the core of socialism which could be realized through nationalization, social insurance, housing and food distribution. He recommended a shift in the distribution of the national income and a levelling of differences in living stand-ards. He also defended the right of disposal over property through social legislation.

It is noteworthy that Bernstein condemned protectionism and defended free trade, and here he differed from Marx and argued more like the utilitarians. The Benthamite-Cobdenite viewpoint believed that while conflict prevailed between states, a natural harmony existed among people and nations; that free trade and peace were one and the same; freedom and civilization were served better by peace, trade and public education than by government; that diplomacy and war were outmoded and detrimental to human happiness; that arbitration, disarmament and non-intervention were desirable goals and world government would be brought about by free trade and peace. Intervention would only be for pro-tection of liberty. Due to a similarity in the views of Bernstein and the utilitarians, Fletcher (1983) placed him in the tradition of Cobdenite radicalism.

Impact of Revisionism

Thus, the writings of Bernstein represented the first coherent cri-tique of Marxism from within the Marxist camp and the first sus-tained effort to move the SPD away from revolutionary Marxist theory to one of reformism. This was made possible by the social, economic and political conditions of Germany in the 1890s. Even though Bernstein challenged the very essence of Marx's theory of social change, he acknowledged the greatness of Marx.

But it is not every epoch that produces a Marx, and even for a man of equal genius the working class movement of today is too great to enable him to occupy the position which Marx fill its history. Today it needs, in addition to the fighting spirit, the coordinating and constructive thinkers who are intellectually enough advanced to be able to separate the chaff from the wheat, who are great enough in their mode of thinking to recognize also the little plant that has grown on another soil than theirs, and who, perhaps though not kings, are warm hearted republicans in the domain of socialist thought (Bernstein 1961: 224).

Like the Fabians, Bernstein rejected the fundamental cannons of Marxism, including the theory of the state as a class institution. He found class war and violence as unacceptable. He displayed tremendous faith in the inevitability of gradualism, which was why Luxemburg accused him of seeing the world through the English spectacles. Revisionism differed from general reformism through its emphasis on an intellectual critique of Marxism and attempted to establish an alternative ethical view. The Reformists in contrast abandoned Marxism and with it socialism and internationalism.

Bernstein's Revisionism was opposed by the German Radical Left led by Luxemburg. The affirmation of the Marxist orthodoxy was led by four different groups constituting the 'generation of four'. These were (*a*) the German-Polish group led by Karl Liebknecht Luxemburg, Karl Radek (1885–1939) and I. Helphand 'Parvus' (1869–1924); (*b*) the Austro Marxists,[7] (*c*) the Menshevik group of which Trotsky was a de facto member, and (*d*) the Bolsheviks around Lenin. The issues that concerned these groups were revolution and imperialism.

In an influential lecture *How is Scientific Socialism Possible?* (1901), Bernstein rejected the scientific content of Marxism by arguing that socialism was not the inevitable outcome of capitalism. Rather it was a moral ideal for those who were committed for it must struggle.

Bernstein in 1920s

Bernstein during the 1918–19 revolution within Germany considered himself to be the mediator of the two social democratic parties, the SAG (Social Democratic Working Group) and the USPD (Independent Social Democratic Party). He approved of parliamentary democracy even though in 1916 he considered it to be the govern-mental system of the social capitalists. He regarded the council movement, the most original innovation of the German revolution, as a transitory mechanism in convening the National Assembly though he dismissed Liebknecht's demand 'All Power to the Coun-cils' as a provocation for counter-revolution.

Bernstein was a vociferous critic of Russian Bolsheviks and warned his colleagues against imitating the Russian model. In his opinion the Bolsheviks had 'combined an amateurishly experi-mental economic policy with a system of the most brutal violence contemptuous of all civilized development, and by throttling nec-essary economic drives caused production to decline' (Bernstein, cited in Fletcher 1987: 100). He branded the Bolsheviks as counter-revolutionaries and declared at the Berne International Socialist Congress of 1919 that their 'system is in fact the death of the achievements of the revolution' (Ibid.). He castigated the Bolsheviks for resorting to violence and for distorting the early writings of Marx. He accused them of ignoring Marxian economics by attempt-ing to create socialism in Russia where the capitalist development was far lower than that of any western country. He concluded that the Bolsheviks had 'brutalized' the Marxist doctrine. In a similar vein he distanced himself from Luxemburg's council system pro-posed in 1918 and sought to combat Bolshevism in Germany. 'The decisive challenge to the reformism of Social Democracy came from the Bolshevik Revolution in Russia which led to the creation of communism as a world wide revolutionary movement' (Howe 1972: 11).

In 1929 when he was eighty, a lowered voice Bernstein acknowl-edged that the Bolsheviks were not unjustified in claiming Marx as their own. In fact, Marx himself had a Bolshevik streak in him (Bernstein, cited in Hook 1933: 43n).

Conclusion

Bernstein's commitment to the parliamentary process, faith in the value of democratic processes even in times of crisis, his abhor-rence of violence as an act of barbarism made him and unrelenting critic of authoritarian socialism and Leninism. By doing so he proved his unflinching devotion to 'liberal parliamentarianism' (Gay 1979: 299). Moreover, his position was strongly opposed to that of the dogmatic revisionists for 'he would have refused to impose the will of his party upon a hostile country and he was anxious to arrive at the desired end — socialism — only with the proper means — democracy. In other words, he was unwilling to kill for the sake of logic' (Gay 1979: 299–300). The important contribution of the revisionists was their unshakable faith in the immense potentialities of parliamentary democratic socialism. In this, they were not alone. The English Fabian society too articulated a similar viewpoint. Engels was not pleased with Bernstein's enthusiastic response towards Fabianism but he never doubted his commitment to the cause of socialism. The revisionists and Fabians were strikingly similar in their ideas, and even to a layman they seemed 'like brothers, if not twins' (Ibid.: 104).

Bernstein rejected the theory of the inevitable breakdown and the collapse of the capitalist system. He rightly asserted that the theoretical model outlined by Marx was dated in the context of increasing tranquillity, and prosperity of workers in advanced capitalist countries. Politically the steady consolidation of parliamentary representative democracy with universal suffrage ensured the possibilities for a non-violent and evolutionary transformation of society. Bernstein's commitment to non-violence and gradualism without sacrificing democratic norms and practices remained firm. He explored the 'contradiction' between *political equality* and *social inequality*; appealed to the inalienable individual rights as proclaimed by the French Assembly; emphasized natural law as the underlying basis to his ethical socialism; accepted liberalism as the essence of modern democracy and believed that parliamentary government and representative state would mitigate the tensions arising out of class differences (Colletti 1969: 103).

According to Hook (1961), there were three important arguments in Bernstein's revisionism. The first was his rejection that capitalism would collapse catastrophically because of its internal contradictions. He also discounted the thesis of widespread misery, and theory of collective ownership of all major means of production, distribution and exchange. Second, his conception of socialism was the fulfillment of both the theory and practice of democracy not only in the political sphere but also socially. This meant abolition of class privileges, elimination of arbitrary power, discrimination and inequality. Third, the socialist movement had to shed its utopianism and be more pragmatic. History was not deterministic for man had the moral will to overcome class antagonisms and realize socialism peacefully. Socialism could be realized through democratic and parliamentary methods. Social legislation could raise the proletariat to the level of the middle class. All this meant renunciation of revolution and class struggle as inevitable. Bernstein's revisionism was based on the acceptance of the foundational concept of democracy with emphasis on discussion and rational deliberations within an overall democratic framework. He emphasized the importance of civility and tolerance.

The major criticisms that were levelled against Bernstein was his failure to grasp the subsequent course of German history. The First World War and its depressing conditions, and the rise of fascism repudiated some of the assumptions of revisionism. Germany also witnessed an abortive insurrection in the form of Spartacus uprising. But this was just temporary for, in the long run, the vision that Bernstein espoused that socialism could be realized through non-violent, evolutionary, gradualist and democratic methods became the guiding force for not only the advanced capitalist countries of the West but also for the developing world in the later half of the twentieth century. He 'promised socialism without the tears of revolution' (Dunn 1988: 25). It was also alleged that there is hardly any originality in Bernstein. The fact that is often forgotten is that Bernstein himself did not claim any originality and accepted the fact that his role at that particular moment was to be factually correct rather than to be theoretically original. But still due credit is to be given for establishing closeness between democracy and socialism, and insisting that realizing one without the other would always be incomplete. Bernstein cherished both democracy and socialism. Means and ends were both inter-related. He denounced every form of dogmatism. Accepting plurality of goals and purposes he asserted that 'it is impossible to declare one conception right and the other absolutely wrong' (Bernstein, cited in Gay 1979: 209).

Hook (1961) dismissed the charge of Bernstein being a ritualistic liberal because of his total commitment to civil rights. In the *Preface* to the English edition of *Evolutionary Socialism* published in 1909 Bernstein wrote:

The present book has not only had its history, it has also in some way made a little history . . . . Opponents of socialism

declared it to be the most crushing testimony of the unsound-
ness of the socialist theory and criticism of capitalist society
and socialist writers . . . . Unable to believe in finalities at all,
I cannot believe in a final aim of socialism. But I strongly believe in the socialist movement, the march forward of the
working classes, who step by step must work their emancipation by changing society from the domain of a commercial
landholding oligarchy to a real democracy which in all its
department is guided by the interests of those who work and
create (Bernstein 1961: xxi–ii).

The point that Bernstein was making echoed in 1977 when
Miliband, writing during the de-Stalinization phase, acknowledged
that civil liberties were not given but had to be earned after centuries
of unremitting struggle and that a socialist society ought to incorporate these and extend them further.

Bernstein's credit was in interpreting Marxism as a critique of
early nineteenth-century capitalism and that it had become outmoded by the end of the nineteenth century and more so by the
turn of the twentieth century. Berlin credits him for pointing out in
clear and categorical terms the non-fulfillment of the various Marxist prophecies and the fact that none before him had done so.
Bernstein could see the resilience of capitalism and its capacity for
adaptability and change more than his ideological rivals like
Kautsky and Luxemburg. The failure of revisionism in Germany
was not his own failure but rather the failure of Germany. In sharp
contrast to Germany was the success of the British Labour party. It
is difficult to remain a Marxist after reading his account.

It was his faith in democratic culture and non-dogmatic approach
that enabled Bernstein to provide the most desired changes within
Marxist orthodoxy in the 1890s. He accepted that his doctrine too
was subject to criticism and was willing to rename his philosophy
'Critical Socialism'. A major reason for resentment against revisionism was because Bernstein questioned the 'accepted comforts
of revolution'.

It may seem strange to speak of a revolutionary doctrine as
comfortable, but there is comfort in routine belief irrespective
of *content*; Bernstein was proposing changes in outlook and
policy which must radically alter many of the accepted

notions on which the party's whole rhythm of life was based. To this extent Bernstein, with all his denial of violence and advocacy of reform, was the revolutionary, while the accepted doctrine provided the shelter of conservative tradition (Nettl 1966: 150).

Bernstein's revisionism was the 'child of its time' as all major political theories are (Gay 1979: 302). However, what emerged as a child of its time became in due course the guiding force for both the developed and developing worlds. Interestingly his early critics subsequently rejected the Bolshevik claim that their revolution was a socialist one precisely because of its disregard and blatant violation of democratic norms and culture. The immediate impact of revisionism was negligible. None of Bernstein's supporters understood the full import of his ideas to develop it further. Instead they converted his ideas into a conservative doctrine interpreting gradualism to be or to do as little and as slowly as possible. However, ultimately 'it was he (Bernstein) and his line of thinking that triumphed all along the line' (Schmidt, cited in Fletcher 1983: 25).

George Douglas Howard Cole

Mr. G.D.H. Cole
is a bit of a puzzle;
A curious role
that of G.D.H. Cole,
with a Bolshevik soul
in a Fabian Muzzle;
Mr G.D.H. Cole
Is a bit of a puzzle
(Reckitt 1919: 3).

He was a prophet who sought to identify and work with progressive forces, rather than a dogmatic utopian who stated his ideal without regard to the means to be used in obtaining it (Carpenter 1973: 13).

The writings of G.D.H. Cole are of especial interest. This is not because of their volume but because they illustrate with particular force how guild socialism, which seemed such a radical rejection of the modern state, provided an intermediary position for those who wished to accept that state and to get on with their business within it confines and in terms of its responsibilities (Barker 1978: 101).

One of the most important characteristics of the British political development since the beginning of the nineteenth century was the colossal extension of governmental activities at all levels. It was a total reversal from a minimalist state which was essentially libertarian and individualistic towards a collectivistic setup. There were a number of reasons for this change, namely, war which enhanced governmental activity quickly and extensively, preparation for war even during peace time, enhanced industrial development which necessitated protection of labour and their working/living conditions, legislations and controls, maintenance of full employment, education, scientific research and planning. All these ultimately led to the triumph of the Keynesian revolution.

This drive towards collectivism was demonstrated in diverse and even contradictory schools of political thought like Utilitarianism, Positivism, Darwinism, Marxism and Green's emphasis on common good. It was also strengthened by existing inequalities and exploitation which needed partial redressal by philanthrophic and religious acts, and a consequent realization that personal charity was not by itself enough and needed extensive relief measures which only a state could provide to make it meaningful. This increase in state activity which led to a schism between collectivism and libertarianism was a significant facet of British political life of the last 150 years (Greenleaf 1973b). This conflict was reflected in the emergence of different kinds of political creeds revolving broadly around two themes: *collectivism* and *libertarianism*. In the initial phase, Smith contented that collectivism would impede natural development and progress led to the influential creed of *laissez faireism*. Cobden and Spencer provided the two different dimensions of classical liberalism. The change in this classical form was first reflected in J.S. Mill and then in Green.

J.S. Mill distinguished between two categories of socialists. There were those who conceived a new social order of free and small self-governing associations as opposed to those who advocated a more comprehensive scheme to efficiently manage the entire resources with help of a strong centralized state authority. Mill preferred the first school, seeing it as British while the second one reflected characteristics of socialists in continental Europe. In this, he was mistaken for both these categories existed among socialists in England as evident from the divergence between the collectivistic Fabian led by the Sydney Webb (1859–1947) and Beatrice Potter

Webb (1858–1943) and the libertarian Guild Socialists led by George Douglas Howard Cole (1889–1959).

The Guild socialist movement consisting of dissident Fabians and other intellectuals espoused a moderate version of 'syndicalist' ideas by discarding the idea that manual workers alone could and would administer industry. It asserted that the governance of industry would cover all those concerned with production, including the managerial and professional ones. Not only was this a sensible version of syndicalism but also a corrective to Fabian emphasis on state ownership and bureaucratic management (Lichtheim 1975: 233). Syndicalism derived from the French word *syndicate*, meaning trade union, was a synthesis of Proudhonism and Marxism. It was Fernand Pelloutier (1867–1901), a follower of Jules Guesde (1845–1922), the leader of the Marxist wing of the French socialist movement along with Victor Griffuelhes (1874–1923), Emile Pouget (1860–1932) and Paul Delassalle, anarchists by conviction who delineated the outlines of syndicalism. Common to all of them was a contempt for parliamentarism and doctrinaire nature of Marxism. They bestowed faith in the general strike by which they meant complete cessation of all labour which would lead to their emancipation.[8] Syndicalism meant workers' control and commanded huge following in France and Belgium. In Italy and Spain it managed to disown its pure anarchist beliefs. In Britain, inspired by American syndicalism of the Socialist Labour Party, James Connolly founded a wing with the same title in 1903. Cole was the chief theoretician of the English version of Guild Socialism which, unlike the Continental Syndicalists, was based firmly within the democratic framework.

Biographical Sketch

Cole was born on 25 September 1889. He was the youngest in the family. His father George was an estate agent and was self-made. Later on, his father became a Tory and a member of the Church of England. The young Cole was educated at St. Paul School and was well-versed in Greek, Latin and classical history. He won prizes in English essays, verse, history and Latin prose. He edited the school newspaper *The Pauline* and became a perfect. During this time his interests were mainly in literary and artistic subjects. In 1908 he joined a socialist organization just before going to Oxford.

In 1905 Cole was introduced to Morris from whom he learnt that work was an expression of one's whole life which became the basis for his philosophy of industrial democracy and Guild Social- ism. He understood work with another phrase of Morris which he loved to quote 'Fellowship is heaven, and lack of fellowship is hell' (Cole 1934: 212). Armed with this faith, Cole sought to improve the world. Morris's egalitarian and libertarian ideas inspired Cole to become a socialist and enter the Labour movement with tre- mendous idealism.

> I became a Socialist because, as soon as the case for a society of equals, set free from the twin evils of riches and poverty, mastership and subjection, was put to me, I knew that to be the only kind of society that could be consistent with human decency and fellowship and that in no other society could I have the right to be content. The society William Morris im- agined to me to embody the right sort of human relations, and to be altogether beautiful and admirable . . . (Cole 1956b: 5).

Socialism for Cole became a moral way of life, different and superior, and did not mean a set of political and economic ideas. His socialist convictions made him realize that freedom was possi- ble only within socialism. Right from the outset, the libertarian strand of socialism predominated. Morris also impressed upon Cole to regard the socialist movement as a whole and not in its narrow and sectarian manifestations. It was this that refrained him from criticizing the former USSR even after the Hungarian invasion in 1956, though at the same time he shunned all those socialists who harbored non-libertarian tendencies. This support to the Hungarian invasion was indeed a serious aberration in Cole, considering that the invasion brutally, inhumanely and imperiously trampled a popular uprising. He was emphatic that the socialists had to unite together and reconstruct society along socialistic lines. Throughout his life, he looked upon himself as the custodian of socialism.

Though Cole disagreed considerably with the Fabians, he shared many common points with them. Like the Fabians, he stressed on collection of facts and devoted most of his time and energy in the Fabian Research Department, various study circles, social history, the New Fabian Research Bureau and the Nuffield College Social

Reconstruction Survey for this purpose. Not only did he have a gargantuan appetite for facts, he was also insistent on verifying their accuracy and honesty. Like the Fabians, he was pragmatic and shunned doctrinal consistency. He combined judgement about facts and values in a manner that was integrative. Cole moved between his idealistic beliefs and practicality.

While at Oxford Cole joined the Fabian society on 5 March 1909. He also joined the Oxford Socialist Friends group, edited the *Oxford Socialist* along with F.K. Griffith, and subsequently the *Oxford Reformer*. In the last one, Cole found a forum to express his views on issues that preoccupied him. He passed with a double-first, a rare distinction, from Balliol in Classical Moderations and *Literae Humaniores* and secured a seven-year fellowship at Magdalen upon graduation. A.D. Lindsay's lectures exerted considerable influence on him and introduced him to political pluralism, and to a functional conception of the state, which gave place to social and economic associations.

Webbs looked upon Cole as their heir and Cole too regarded the Webbs as his mentor. However the discipleship ended when Cole reacted against the paternalistic and statist conception of Webbs' collectivism. Cole made an extensive study of labour unrests of 1912 and published *The World of Labour* in 1913 along the lines of Webbs' *Industrial Democracy* of 1897. It made a comparative study of labour unions in Britain with its counterparts in Europe and America. He rejected the idea of general strike as an inefficient way of fomenting a revolution for capitalism could not be destroyed by direct industrial action. He also rejected the collectivistic models of the Marxists and Fabians for both armed the state with enormous powers. This was also the time when political and legal theorists like Maitland, Barker, Lindsay and others, though not socialists, were developing the pluralist theory which suggested that collective groups had a real will and personality and were logically and historically prior to the state and not created by it. All these helped Cole at a time when he was developing the outlines of Guild Socialism.

In May 1915 Cole resigned from the Fabian society but helped to revise the Labour Party's constitution in 1918. In 1920 he resigned from many of its advisory committees also. By 1921 he was in political wilderness and regained his influence after he founded the New Fabian Research Bureau in 1931. Between 1917 to 1923 he became the leading exponent of Guild Socialism. His major treatise, *Guild Socialism Restated* was published in 1920. His other published works, to mention a few, were *Chaos and Order in Industry*, (1923), *The Life of William Cobbett* (1924), *A Short History of the British Working Class Movement: Robert Owen* (1925), *The Intelligent Man's Guide Through World Chaos* (1932), *Chartist Portraits* (1940), *The Common People* (1940) and *The Meaning of Marxism* (1948). His encyclopedic work was the *A History of Socialist Thought* in six volumes. It remains till date an unparalleled account of socialism both in terms of analysis and details. He married Margaret in 1919. Together they edited *The Guildsman* and *The Guild Socialist*. Margaret also helped Cole with his writings. Cole was a prolific writer who could write 3000 words a day and a distinguished labour historian. He died in 1959.

Guild Socialism vs Fabian Collectivism

Cole, like the pluralists and unlike the collectivists, wanted a decentralized social and political structure. He differed from the pluralists for he was committed to industrial democracy which meant self-government both for and within the group. Guild socialism was a theory of democracy appropriate for modern industrial civilization and, in evolving this theory, he was influenced by Rousseau and Morris. Cole hoped to improve on Rousseau's ideas and envisaged a participatory democratic model in contemporary mass societies. 'From Fousseau and Morris in their different ways Cole developed his conception of a community founded upon the co-operation of self governing associations, a cooperation which found its source in a genuine community consciousness, a real general will (Wright 1979: 24).

The possibility and desirability of realizing democracy at the grassroots led Cole to disagree with Fabian collectivism. They differed because Cole, like Owen, identified slavery rather than poverty as the primary evil of, and enemy within, society because the former was the disease and the latter its symptom (Cole 1917: 34). By slavery he meant any practice which made men's life subject to the will of leaders, bosses or managers who were not responsible to them. Freedom was the condition of self-determination which applied to all phases of life. It meant self-government. Cole understood freedom as a means and an end. The emphasis on self-government meant democracy which was not only a political practice but a moral relationship between men, enabling them to realize their creativity.

Cole favoured a radical perception of power when he argued that a social order rested on a series of power relationships and that socialism was primarily a programme of harmonizing these relationships. But in this formulation, he was not repeating the fears either of the liberal individualists or the anarchists. It was not merely a philosophy to protect the individual from an all powerful state. Rather it was a philosophy of participatory democracy in which an average individual had personal access to social power. Democracy in industry would ensure that power did not remain remote or, for that matter, external for it would be realized within the workplace itself.

The major thrust of Cole's critique of Fabian collectivism was that it ignored the problem of social power and he felt a failure to tackle this crucial problem would make it difficult to realize the 'conditions of reasonable human association and government' (Cole 1920a: 27). This was true even in situations where present class formations did not exist. Instead of providing a democratic solution to the question of social power, collectivism ensured 'the completion of the present tendency towards state sovereignty by the piling of fresh powers and duties on the great Leviathan' (Ibid.: 27). On the question of democracy both the socialist schools – Fabian and Guild – developed different theories which revealed 'the existence of fundamentally different approaches to social analysis and to social action' (Wright 1979: 51). This cleavage was reflected in a controversy between the Webbs and Cole which led to a lively theoretical debate that remained unparalleled in English socialist thought, wherein Cole launched 'a sustained intellectual critique of Fabian democracy which forced Fabianism back to fundamentals in search for a satisfactory formulation of its position' (Ibid.: 51). Both Webb's *Constitution for the Socialist Commonwealth of Great Britain* and Cole's *Guild Socialism Re-stated* appeared in 1920 stating the two alternatives representing 'the high water mark in optimistic social engineering in a modern context' (Ibid.: 52).

The origin of this divergence could be found in the Guild Socialists' rejection of the Fabian plank in identifying collectivism with socialism.[9] They refused to agree with the Fabian assumption that efficiency of production and justice of distribution were the two most important foundations of a socialist society. This objection stemmed from the fact that the Fabian model would merely replace a capitalist state by a bureaucratic state, which might provide distributive justice but would be immensely harmful to society as the individual in this scheme would become a passive recipient rather remain an active participant in policy formulation and execution. This mistake regarding the basis of social formation emerged from the early Fabian assumption of identifying individualism as the most important enemy and regarding democracy as a means to reach the goal of social collectivism. In such a scheme, the individual would not have any meaningful role in the decision-making process. The Fabians wanted nationalization without socialization, which meant transformation of state capitalism into state socialism undermining individual initiative. In this sense, the Guild Socialists and Cole shared the anguish of the Expressionist movement at the hollowness of the individual under the pressure of the modern industrial civilization most succinctly expressed as follows:

> We are the hollow men,
> We are the stuffed men
> leaning together,
> Headpiece filled with straw, Alas!
> (Eliot 1975: 77).

Industrial Democracy

In order to meet this challenge, the Guild Socialists provided a theory of participatory socialist democracy which would revolutionize and completely change the arena and mode of social activity. In this scheme, the most important transformation would come at the place of work where the workers spent bulk of their meaningful and productive years. The purpose of socialism was to prevent loss of individual personality and, since this was not achieved either in capitalism or state socialism, both were rejected. Its aim in the context of present-day industrial society was the socialization of Rousseau's individual through a participatory democratic order.

For the Webbs, the objection to authority was not a socialist but a radical one. Society was a revolving organism which manifested itself by organic differentiation of functions. Efficient management was essential both in the political and the economic scene. Representation of authority and power was a necessity both in the political and the industrial world. This had to be contrasted with primitive democracy which suffered from legislative instability and administrative weaknesses. Webbs further argued that economic differentiation was a necessity because of increasing specialization. Following Adam Smith, they argued that division of labour was an important and essential component of the modern production process. This logically led to the identification of the individual in relationship to a larger whole. On the basis of this plank, Webbs' model of social reconstruction was based on the primacy of social efficiency and a scheme of distributive justice. Centralization and extreme specialization became inevitable in the Webbian scheme which followed the principle identified by Shaw and the Fabian policy statement.

We have the distinctive term Social Democrat indicating the man or women who desires through democracy together the whole people into the state so that the state may be trusted with the rent of the country, and finally with the land, the capital, and the organization of the national industry with all the sources of production (Shaw 1889: 216).

However, the Webbs conceded that this professionalization of representation did mean that the representative would lose 'that vivid appreciation of the feelings of the man at the bench or the forge' which he accepted as the 'cruel irony'.

This specific understanding and unchallenged acceptance was questioned by Cole and the Guild Socialists. Society was an unique organization and since there was no other parallel to it, it had to be understood and analyzed in terms of this uniqueness. Two important considerations were to form the basis of social analysis — the first was the question of human needs and second the will of the people who composed it. Emphasizing the idealist and voluntarist basis of his theory, Cole criticized the 'deadening determinism' of Marx. He was equally emphatic on the role of ideas and theories because 'only an idea can slay another idea' and 'until the workers are animated with the desire to be their own masters they cannot supplant the idea that their class is born form wage slavery' (Cole 1917: 162).

Unlike the Fabian Socialists, their Guild counterparts did not accept the inevitability of the wage system, division of labour, separation between art and work, and industrial elitism. These were far from natural happenings and positively detrimental to individual development and social cohesion. They were as virulent critics of the early twentieth-century capitalism as Marx was of nineteenth century capitalism. The present hierarchy had to be replaced by a democratic social, economic and political structure based on the dignity and active participation of the average person. However, Fabian collectivism was based on some very different assumptions which the Guild Socialists termed as the 'heresy of distrust' questioning the capacity and character of the average person. The Fabian theory rested on the assumption of individual and group selfishness which would lead to the exploitation of each other unless there were social safeguards. Sydney Webb commented:

> I often wonder when I hear my Guild Socialist friends talk about the right of the workman to control his own, to exercise authority over his own sphere, when we shall have a revolt of the technician, the electrician, the chemist, the artist, the designer, the manager. We, too, want to have self-determination, we want to have control over our working life (Webb 1919: 7).

Webbs pointed to the dangers of sectional selfishness and, in particular, that of the manual workers. They referred to the lessons of history and gave instances of selfishness both from the medieval guilds as well as modern organizations. Apart from this, group selfishness of the producers in their own relationships, industrial democracy violated the interests of the consumers. However, it ought be pointed out that the Guild Socialists did not want to dismantle the institutional safeguards which they used as devices that ensured protection to the consumers. While the Webbs believed that no person could be trusted in judging his own case, Cole's perceived everybody to be a natural democrat with dignity, creativity and capacity for self-development. For the Webbs, democracy required 'assent to results' whereas Cole emphasized on the close link between the process and the result. The average person's association in the process of social decision-making was both rational and necessary and, since in the modern social set-up total representation was impossible, it was all the more necessary to have continuous participation in the decision-making process itself. For Cole, the denial of industrial democracy led to servility while for the Webbs, independence meant freedom from unproductive and non-productive work.

For Webb, the entire emphasis was on maximizing efficiency. For Cole, the realization of democracy at the grassroots, at the workplace would pave for ultimately efficiency, harmony and unity of purpose, the idea being that functional democracy instead of being separate was integrative and hence more desirable than the Webbian model which was essentially a passive state. In Cole's plan, active participation would lead to the creation of a community of interest synthesizing individual and collective good. Fellowship provided the real basis for his theory of democracy and society. He did not attempt to provide an elaborate and well-laid-out blueprint for the constitution of a socialist society but only emphasized the necessity of accepting democracy in the largest and the broadest sense. He also took up the question of the special interest groups. The democratic principle would apply 'not only or mainly to some special sphere of social action known as "politics" but to any and every form of social action' (Cole 1920b: 12).

Along with this philosophy of active social democracy, Cole considered participation and freedom at the workplace as vital. Regarding the Fabian apprehension of the inherent tendency of organized sections to exploit the consumers, Cole did not perceive any such threat and merely thought that just by communicating consumer needs and desires to be guild of producers, such problems could be tackled. This optimism emerged from the fact that the Guild Socialist man was essentially socialistic with a natural tendency for fellowship. Human nature as it reflected in the contemporary situation was because of the existence of a very imperfect and divisive institutional arrangement in society, and this reflection need not be the basis for projecting the future of a socialistic commonwealth. In taking up this position, Cole was on stronger philosophical grounds as he refused to accept the contemporary person as a prototype for all times. The Webbian logic was akin to Hobbes who presumed that the seventeenth-century Englishman as the universal person. Furthermore, the inherent elitism of Webbs led them to think quite poorly of the average person. Even after the Guild socialist challenge to their position became intense,

Sydney Webb commented in 1919 that democracy of the geographical type

> . . . inevitably means the submerging of the active spirits in what the French call the apathetic mass. The great mass of people will always be found apathetic, dense, unreceptive to any unfamiliar ideas, and your eager active spirit with the unfamiliar idea . . . frets and fumes at being held in check by this apathetic mass. But, after all, the apathetic mass are individually God's creatures, and entitled to have a vote, and it is no use kicking against their apathy and denseness. You have got to work your governmental machine in some way that will enable you to get on notwithstanding theirs (Webb 1919: 5).

Cole, unlike Webb, did not think poorly of the average person and hence worked out the theory of participatory democracy based on functional representation for realizing the principles of participatory democracy. Modern democratic theory rested on the principle that one person could represent another which was not acceptable. What really could be represented were particular functions which people shared in common. The concept of functions was 'the real and vital principle' (Code 1918b: 201).

Cole rejected the theory of state sovereignty and stressed the associational and functional nature of all kinds of organizations. A genuine democracy was supposed to be based on a system of co-ordinated functional representation. Representation as such had to be 'specific and functional' and not merely 'general and inclusive'. The present parliament 'professes to represent all citizens in all things, and therefore as a rule represents none of them anything' (Cole 1920a: 108). This theory of representing functions was similar to that of Burke who wanted to institutionalize an anti-democratic oligarchic power structure with a natural aristocracy at the helm. Cole, on the other hand, desired to make democracy alive in every sphere of social, economic and political activity. There were significant differences between the Webbs and Cole with regard to the theory of representation. For Webb, 'the supreme paradox' of democracy was reflected in the fact:

> . . . that every man is a servant in respect of the matters of which he possesses the most intimate knowledge, and for

> which he shows the most expert proficiency, namely the pro-
> fessional craft to which he devotes his working hours; and he
> is a master over that on which he knows no more than any-
> body else, namely, the general interests of the community as
> a whole. In this paradox . . . lies at once the justification and
> the strength of democracy (Webb 1920: 108).

But, for Cole, the failure of this was manifested in its acceptance
by all the classes and depriving the ordinary worker and an average
citizen of any meaningful role in determining his social environment. The individual 'in learning to control his own industry would
learn also to control the political machine' (Cole 1917: 185).

For the Webbs, the lesson of history was that self-government
in industry could not be successful. The relationship between the
manager and the workers could not be worked out on the basis of
democratic control. But for Cole, the instances of failure of self-
governed industries was not due to their inherent weaknesses but
mainly because of the overall capitalistic environment in which
they functioned. Both in the analysis of human nature as well as in
social formation, there was a wide divergence between the Webbs
and Cole. In industrial democracy, workers' urge for participation
and social plurality were the very essential conditions for a life
worth living and, since Fabian collectivism was silent or unable to
provide any basis for achieving them, it was grossly an inadequate
scheme of social reconstruction. Cole and the Webbs analyzed that
question of participation from two different perspectives. The
Webbs entertained a nostalgia for direct or primitive democracy
within a modern mass industrial society. Cole, on the other hand,
regarded democracy as the real issue and explored the possibility
of its realization within modern industrial society preserving the
primacy of the individual and his active participation. Commenting
on Webb's perception of the individual, Cole wrote in 1918:

> He still conceives the mass of men as persons who ought to
> be decently treated, not as persons who ought freely to or-
> ganize their own conditions of life; in short his conception of
> a new social order is still that of an order that is ordained
> from without, and not realized from within (Cole 1918a: 154).

The sustained criticism of the Guild Socialists had its impact on
Webb who admitted in 1919 that the 'socialist have contributed so

far very little to the theory of practice of democracy' and had accepted 'uncritically the ordinary Radical idea of democracy' (Webb 1919: 2). Accepting that there was a revolution in democratic theorizing in the early twentieth century, Webb accepted trade union participation in management reversing this earlier total opposition to producer participation in industrial management. This was a distinctive change from their earlier formulation of the division of the world in A (anarchists) and B (bureaucrats).

It was mainly Cole's efforts in 1939 that prohibited the Fabian Society from expressing collective opinion in policy matters beyond a general commitment to socialism and the Labour party, which enabled the society to survive in a meaningful and open way. Fabianism, over the years, became an integral part and parcel of the British socialist tradition, first by producing intellectuals like Shaw, Webbs and Wells, and then bringing under its fold Tawney,[10] Cole, Laski and, after the Second World War, incorporating the philosophers of the welfare state, Titmuss, Townsend and Crosland. Though the Fabian society occasionally faced crises at the beginning of this century because of the failure of the society to go beyond a 'little dribble of activities', it had always been able to attract newer members all the time. The serious limitation of early Fabian socialism was its elitism and defence of imperialism. As exponents of 'directional socialism', according to Oakeshott, the basic purpose of the Fabians was to convince the educated middle class and, in that sense, they tailored their policies and programmes for that group. This attitude made them dissociate from mass political activities and organizations. Webbs' collectivism led them to admire Stalin's Russia in the early thirties.[11] They hailed the Russian revolution as pure Fabianism for Lenin and Stalin realized the inevitability of gradualism. They were critical of Guild socialism on the premise that cooperatives were incapable of providing management, skills and discipline at the workplace. However, in spite of such limitations, Fabian socialism exerted considerable influence both within and outside the British socialist movement.

Freedom and Individuality

In Cole's theoretical construst, individual, freedom, fellowship and democracy were core values and intimately linked to the idea of industrial democracy and workers' control. Together, they defined his conception of goodlife. He regarded individuals as the ultimate reality and an ethical end and thus instinctively insisted on a pluralistic approach to social theory. 'Every individual is in this nature universal; his actions and courses of action, his purposes and desires are specific because he makes them so; but he himself is not, and cannot be, made specific . . . ' (Cole 1920b: 49).

Cole retained the traditional liberal attitude towards private life and distinguished between acts that were private from those that were social. However, he looked upon the individuals as social creatures, thus implying that the distinction was not between individual and society but between individual acts that were personal as opposed to those that were social. He looked to this distinction not in absolute sense enabling him to safeguard and cherish personal activity while focusing on participation and organization. 'As long as human life remains, most of the best things in it will remain outside the bounds and scope of organization as to afford the fullest opportunity for the development of those human experiences to which organization is the cold touch of death' (Ibid.: 31–2).

Cole considered existence of classes as the greatest threat to individuality. He disliked capitalism for it generated classes denying people their full individuality. He insisted that a true individual had to be freed from class barriers. This led him towards the principle of political pluralism and the principle of function. Society had to be organized around the essential functions which individuals performed and it should not try and organize the individual as a whole. His insistence of recognition of function led him to deny the idea of a sovereign state. A social organization had to allow the expression of the personality of those who composed it for individuals were the ends rather than the means. The supreme importance given to individuality and human will led him to give a firm commitment to freedom. Freedom for Cole was a means to the development for individual. He distinguished between liberty associated to individual qua individual and liberty associated to institutions and groups with which the individual was concerned.

This is not the familiar distinction between "civil" and "political" or even "social" liberty as it is ordinarily drawn; for a liberty attached to the individual qua individual may be political or economic in its content as well as civil. It is a distinction, not in the *content* of the liberty, but in its form of expression, between the liberty of personal freedom and the liberty of free and self governing associations (Cole 1920a: 181).

Unlike the liberals, Cole was confident that self governing groups would not restrict personal freedom. He did not see a conflict between the two definitions of liberty for he understood democracy as equality, fellowship and self-government rather than majority rule and electoral procedures. He desired a societal arrangement that would preserve the two conceptions of freedom, for it was complementary since one could not exist without the other, and gave the individual the greatest opportunity for self-determination.

When, therefore, we seek to bring personal and social liberty into a complementary relation, what we are really doing is to seek that relation between them which will secure the greatest liberty for all the individuals in a community, both severally and in association. It is not a question of striking a balance between the claims and counter-claims of the individual and of society, but of determining what amount of organization and what absence of organization will secure to the individual the greatest liberty as the result of a blending of personal and social liberties (Ibid.: 184–85).

For Cole, personal liberty denoted expression of one's personality without any hindrance. Within its realm were important civil liberties and Cole supported freedom of speech, of conscience and of taste. In 1930s he staunchly defended these liberties. He contended that the idea of personal liberty had a negative connotation in a class society but once the class privileges were removed then it would become complementary to social liberties. This position set Cole apart from the Marxists and idealists of his time who desired an abolition of personal liberties because they were abstract. By defending the importance of personal liberties *per se*, Cole remained a libertarian socialist. He also believed that freedom had a positive value by which he meant the freedom to do something and create collective ways for self-expression and self-development. His defence of liberty made him desire minimum laws and self-government.

Self-government meant three things. First, the individual had to be free to establish and join any association that would articulate his will. Second, an association created in this way had to be free 'from external dictation in respect of its manner of performing its function' (Cole 1920a: 182). Third, each function had to be organized separately and represented. Freedom led to democracy and the two were inter-dependent. Cole demanded equality of status along with equality of opportunity to avoid the danger of creating a meritocracy. Economic equality was necessary to sustain democracy.

Conclusion

In bringing about this important change of perception in Fabian collectivism, Cole's transformative criticism played a very crucial role in its intensity and intellectual level and could be compared easily with the well-known transformative criticism of Feuerbach by Marx. If Marx found Feuerbach mechanical, Cole found Fabian collectivism to be rigid and unmindful of the needs and aspirations of the average person. Cole was a precursor of the late twentieth century advocates of participatory democracy by championing the fact that work experience and environment were the most decisive factors in moulding man. In this context it should be noted that though Mill spoke of participatory ideal it was the work of socialists like Cole focussed on the democratic participation in daily industrial life (Lively: 1980). His industrial democracy tried to restore meaning and control to the work. Inspired by Morris, he modernized Morris to the requirements of the modern industrial society. He understood democracy in the social sense and believed in the ideal of active citizenship. This meant rejection of statist, collectivist and centralized socialism and treating labour as a creative force within industry.

The apprehensions of the Guild socialists was vindicated in the late 1940s and early 1950s when large scale nationalization was introduced in Britain. Cole, like Kautsky, was able to see very clearly the dangers of excessive bureaucratic control and the need for democratic norms and culture. In comparison to the pluralists who championed the associational character of the modern society, Guild socialists like Cole went a step ahead by advocating freedom both for the group as well as for the individual within the group.

In that sense they were pioneers in raising questions about the nature and content of what constituted the essence of democracy. By pointing out the moral and human dimensions, Cole not only humanized socialism but also raised questions concerning freedom, democracy and socialism. He summed his ideal most succinctly while concluding his *A History of Socialist Thought* in 1960,

> I am neither a communist nor a social democrat, because I regard both as creeds of centralization and bureaucracy, whereas I feel sure that a socialist society that is to be true to its equalitarian principles of human brotherhood must rest on the widest possible diffusion of power and responsibility, so as to enlist the active participation of as many as possible of its citizens in the tasks of democratic self-government (Cole 1960: 337).

Guild socialism was the non-communist, non-statist, pluralist and libertarian version of socialism. Though Cole was not its originator, for there were others like Arthur Penty, S.G. Hobson and A.R. Orage, he was its most erudite exponent Russell (1916: 72) acknowledged that it was Cole who recognized the importance of independent organizations vis-à-vis the state in maintaining order and satisfying a necessary minimum. Among the Guild Socialists, he was the one whom Russell (1918) mentioned appreciatively. Cole provided Guild socialism with a distinctive political theory and related theory with practical programmes and that was his enduring contribution.

Endnotes

1. See the section on Marx in this book.
2. The number of workers doubled between 1887–1914. The percentage of unemployed remained steady at 2 per cent. Real wages rose rapidly in comparison to other industrial countries in the pèriod 1885 to 1910 in the range of 100 per cent. Average wages rose by 37.5 per cent between 1895–1907. The cost of living increased by 22.5 per cent. Till 1900 about five-and-a-half million were covered by insurance. In 1891 the Workers' Protection Act replaced the Imperial Industrial Act providing for regulations to prevent danger to life and health, ordinances relating to hours of work in a day, Sunday being a day-off for industrial work, women to work for 11 hours in a day'and the young for 10 hours, prohibition of night shifts for both the young and women, and a

ban on child labour under 13 in industrial occupations. This was followed by many more legislations relating to protection of children, young and women. Industrial tribunals were established in 1890 to settle disputes between the workers and employers. The German Civil Code of 1900 provided for the legal basis of all work contracts. Non-manual employees were also given adequate protection at the turn of the twentieth century.

3. The votes for the Social Democrats was 6.1 per cent in 1881. It rose to 9.7 per cent in 1884 and to 19.7 per cent in 1890.

4. The Bad Godesberg programme identified five criteria which constituted the core values of social democracy: political liberalism, mixed economy, welfare state, Keynesian economics and a belief in equality. These were formally embodied in German, Austrian and Scandinavian parties.

5. The Fabians were a small group of London-based intellectuals who organized themselves with the aim of creating a nucleus of a future planned socialist society in 1884. It emerged as the Fellowship of the New Life which was started by a civil servant, Percival Chubb, and a mystic, Thomas Davidson, in 1883 and decided to adopt its new name at a meeting on 4 January 1884 in the London home of Edward Pease, a young solicitor. Davidson taught his associates to practice a life of simplicity without wealth and advocated a new life based on love, wisdom and unselfishness. Though Davidson himself did not advocate socialism, the initial Fabian philosophy emerged largely out of his views. The Fabians included Sydney Webb, Beatrice Potter Webb, and George Bernard Shaw (1856–1950). Other important Fabians were H.G. Wells, Graham Wallas, Annie Besant G.D.H. Cole and R.H. Tawney. The basic principles of Fabianism were worked out in the period 1884–89. During this time a distinctive economic theory was developed out Shaw's theory of exploitation. Its basic thrust was that unearned income in any form was immoral. For the Fabians, socialism implied a moral transformation to be brought about by a change of opinion through democratic means. The emphasis was on gradualism and permeation which was why they took their name from Roman general Quintus Fabius, known as Cunctator from his strategy of delaying until the right moment the main thrust of his attack. The early society had the tortoise as its symbol and the slogan 'when I strike, I strike hard'. Like the Marxists, the Fabians also looked to socialism as inevitable but believed it had to be peaceful through constitutional measures like extension of franchise. They sought to make socialism respectable among the middle class.

6. Besides Bernstein, the other revisionists were Kurt Kisner, an ethical socialist and neo-Kantian, Vollmar, Ignaz Auer, Gustov Noske, Friedrich Ebert and Joseph Block, all of whom were party practitioners within the SPD.

7. Austro Marxists, a term coined by Louis Boudin, an American sociologist believed that Marxism could be a rigorous and undogmatic science while retaining its revolutionary fervour. It included Max Adler (1873–1937), Otto Bauer (1881–1938), Rudolf Hilferding (1877–1941) and Karl Renner (1870–1950). Hilferding and Bauer were among the foremost contributors of Austro Marxism. Hilferding's *Finance Capital* (1910) dealt with the problems of circulation and the process of capitalist production. He considered the rise of joint stock companies as altering the structure of capitalism for it led to centralization of capital in few hands. The fusion of industrial and bank capital led to

the emergence of 'finance capital', a term that Lenin borrowed and incorporated in his theory of imperialism. As a result, cartels, trusts and monopolies were formed making suppression of competition and planned organization of the world economy inevitable. Capitalist states became powerful and aggressive heightening international tension. They vied with one another to monopolize markets and sources of raw materials and carved out potential markets endangering freedom, equality and democracy. In this context, revolutionary politics made it necessary to seize state power. Bauer believed that the state was not always an organ of the bourgeoisie and, contrary to Marx's observations, it was becoming more and more autonomous due to an equilibrium of class struggle. He supported slow revolution when socialism would be gradually constructed after the working class conquered political power through radical reforms. He criticized the Russian revolution for it led to the establishment of a minority dictatorship. Adler contended that Bolshevism was in reality the dictatorial rule by the party. Renner's views were similar to that of Bernstein and he believed that if the workers could gain greater control over the institutions of state, they would get the state to perform greater public functions.

8. See the section on Sorel in this book.

9. Paradoxically in spite of the emphasis on collectivism and centralized bureaucratic management, the Webbs extolled the virtues of localism and considered local autonomy as crucial to English liberty. They retained the constitutional monarchy as part of the new institutional arrangement for a socialist Britain. They castigated the reforms since 1830 as responsible for giving rise to capitalist interests over English local institutions. They supported state control and regulation of society and never developed a proper relationship between the state and the civil society. The Webbs endorsed the Benthamite principle of 'greatest happiness of the greatest number' which was realizable within a collectivistic society rather than within capitalism. A national minimum of civilized life which included income standards of health, housing was due to all. Such measures would realize equality of condition which they viewed as the ultimate goal of a compassionate society.

10. Richard Henry Tawney (1880–1962) was regarded as the most influential and authentic voice of English socialism in the early twentieth century. It was socialism which did not speak of class power, economic determinism or historical inevitability, and tried to relate itself with general human values. He was critical of contemporary capitalism and socialism and observed that in general society was sick because of the absence of a moral ideal. His ideal was the notion of functional property and common social purpose as a remedy for the existing moral vacuum. In *Equality* (1931) he understood equality as equal worth and desired a society that would enhance liberty, promote self-development and create the conditions of common culture. He strove to create a just society based on equality and fellowship as an alternative to capitalism. He also desired that the educated and the privileged would use their talents in the service of the working class. Interestingly Rawls reiterated this argument in *A Theory of Justice* (1971) when he held that incentives to the well-off would be given so that they could work towards the elevation of the disadvantaged. In *The Acquisitive Society* (1921) the focus was on production

rather than consumption. Tawney pleaded that the goal of economic gain, increased productivity and individual self-interest had to be subordinated to a higher set of values. He also observed that capitalism brought in a schism between ownership and the actual management of businesses, that the greater part of the income was derived from ownership constituting 'functionless wealth', and the need to reorganize society so that functions could be rewarded rather than allowing the passive owners of capital to amass huge wealth created by others. Tawney thought the individualist idea of property as developed since the seventeenth century was responsible for all the contemporary social ills. While absolute right to property was necessary in the struggle against feudalism and absolutism, it was the bane of modern industrial society. He conceded that capital ought to earn a return but that would be a fixed rate. In *Religion and Rise of Capitalism* (1926) Tawney appealed to the Christian doctrine of social responsibility to launch a strident criticism of capitalism. He discussed the role of religion in the origins of capitalism and was critical of Weber's emphasis on the unique contribution of Calvinism for the latter was not so clear cut as Weber suggested. In fact, puritan individualism was more conducive to growth of business and commerce.

11. The Webbs looked upon the Russian revolution as a victory of democracy though they were subsequently unhappy with the repressive nature of the regime. They described their tour as a pilgrimage 'to the Mecca of the equalitarian state' and were confident that future belonged to the former USSR and that it would win the ideological battle with the US. They were impressed with the state farms, the cosmosols and considered the Communist Party to be a spiritual order. Interestingly, when the *Soviet Communism: A New Civilization?* (1935) went into its second edition, the question mark was deleted, much to the annoyance of their friends like Laski and Beveridge. In the *Truth about Soviet Russia*, Beatrice denied that Stalin was a dictator. Russell correctly attributed the praise the Webbs had for Soviet communism to their elitist and undemocratic view of the government.

6

❖ Twentieth Century Marxists

Karl Johann Kautsky

After Engels' death, the mantle of intellectual leadership in the European Social Democracy fell to Karl Kautsky, a man of scholarly inclinations but slight intellectual originality. Enormously influential among all European socialist at least until 1914 he was admired even by Lenin—Kautsky guided the socialist parties along with the ambiguous, yet at least partially fruitful, road of continuing to speak in behalf of revolution while defining the forthcoming revolution not as a complete political rupture or an insurrectionary apocalypse but as a process of historical and social transformation that might occur through democratic means. Trying to maintain this "centrist" course Kautsky found himself challenged from two directions: on the left by Rosa Luxemburg and the right by Eduard Bernstein, both of them figures of greater intellectual brilliance than himself (Howe 1972: 8–9).

In the aftermath of the Russian Revolution, Karl Kautsky became the principal theoretical antagonist of Bolshevism (Cole 1958: 245).

The fact that Kautsky, the most respected of them all, actually came to provide a theoretical validation of a state of affairs which was essentially static in an un-Marxist sense—and all in the name of Marxism—is one of the great ironies of Socialist history. It was not, . . . without a logic of its own, not accidental or treacherous, but implicit and inevitable—and above all unconscious. That was to be why Kautsky remained the Communist bogeyman for many years, long after he had ceased to be important (Nettl 1966: 149).

Karl Johann Kautsky (1854–1938) was a friend of both Marx and Engels and, along with Bernstein, was regarded as their direct successor. Known popularly as the 'Pope of Marxism', he was undoubtedly the most important Marxist thinker of the period of the Second International, for about two decades from the death of Engels in 1895 to the beginning of the First World War in 1914. 'Luxemburg, Lenin, Trotsky and Stalin, all sat at his feet' (McLellan 1983: 25). Kautsky was the editor of the SPD journal *Die Neue Zeit* for over 30 years, occupying a pivotal and a coveted position among contemporary Marxists. He was the leading and the most authoritative interpreter of Marxism after the death of Engels, referred to as SPD's 'party professor' by the Bavarian socialist leader Vollmar.

Kautsky's intellectual evolution and political thinking remained by and large consistent. He retained his belief in the labour theory of value, capital concentration, class polarization and increasing class antagonism. Long before 1910 he envisaged the possibility of a non-violent revolution and a democratic dictatorship of the proletariat. His attitude towards mass strike was ambivalent and his support for revolution was nothing more than organization and education. He rejected a voluntaristic model of social change and continually insisted on the need for objective preconditions for a successful revolutionary action.

Kautsky's views epitomized the outlook of his generation that faults were not of an individual as they had a social origin. His assessment of the German situation in 1914 was more realistic than most of his critics. However, his defence of the Marxian theories of immiseration and capitalist crisis, and his predictions of class conflict, revolution and war were never vindicated in the Europe of 1890–1930. His conviction that democracy and socialism were inseparable and that any attempt to realize one without the other would only intensify terror and brutality prophetically came true, as evident from the events in the former Soviet Union subsequently. It speaks of his immense courage of conviction that at the age of sixty-three he could lift his pen and write of a critique of the Bolshevik experiment. He was also the earliest to discern the similarities between the totalitarian experiments of the fascist leaders, Mussolini and Hitler, and those of Stalin, for all of them blatantly disregarded constitutional and parliamentary democracy and rule of law perpetuating unprecedented exercise of terror and brutality. Till the end, he retained his conviction of the need to combine both democracy and socialism for realizing a more free, equal and a just society.

Biographical Sketch

Kautsky was born on the 16 October 1854 in Prague. He was the son of an artist father and a mother who was at first an actress and then a writer of popularly read socialist novels. Even Engels had read and appreciated these novels. Kautsky studied history, philosophy and economics at the University of Vienna. In 1875 he joined the Austrian Social Democratic Party and published articles in its various journals while he was still a graduate student. He attempted to earn a living by being an actor and a writer but those ventures failed. One of his plays was performed in 1878 in Vienna and his novel remained unpublished. He began writing for a socialist press in Leipzig and in the process came into contact with the German Labour Movement. From 1879 he began to work on Hochberg's newspaper *Der Sozialdemokrat* in Zurich where he met and befriended Bernstein four years his senior. From 1881 he devoted his time and energy to the service of German Social Democracy. He travelled to London in 1881 to meet Marx and Engels and, for the next five years, lived in London and collaborated with Engels. He became better acquainted and friendly with Engels than with Marx.

In 1883 Kautsky launched what became the most prestigious of all international Marxist journals, *Die Neue* Zeit (The New Age). His task was made easier because the Prussian censor which banned subversive literature did not mind the 'scientific' nature of the journal. He remained its editor till 1917. The journal became a reputed and a leading one both nationally and internationally with the aim to disseminate the views of Marx. He returned to Germany following the repeal of the anti-socialist law. He became a leading figure of the Social Democratic Party. He wrote the theoretical section of the Erfurt programme of 1891.

Kautsky was the leading theorist of the Second International from 1899 to 1914. His rise to prominence was due to the power and presence of the SPD's organization as being the largest socialist party in the world. Once the anti-socialist law was repealed, the SPD was able to build a massive organization structure with innumerable paid functionaries. It published over seventy newspapers and provided for a range of facilities, including insurance schemes and advice on legal issues affecting the workers. The party also ran a host of ancillary organizations, including gymnastics associations, choral societies, soccer, stamp-collecting, educational associations, cyclist organizations and even smoking clubs. In the process, a sub-culture was created in the large industrial cities in Germany.

By 1914, the SPD had over one million individual paying members, of whom 80 to 95 per cent were manual workers though predominantly they were skilled labourers. The party did very well electorally. In 1877 elections it gained 9.1 per cent of the total votes cast, 23.3 per cent in 1893 and 34.2 per cent in 1912. In spite of such an electoral performance, the party did enjoy political power for real power was placed constitutionally outside the elected representatives in the Reichstag. The SPD consisted of diverse groups and outlooks.

Kautsky translated and edited various works of Marx and became the foremost spokesman and defender of Marxist orthodoxy. In the 1890s, with full support of Bebel, he led an orthodox attack on works of his former friend and one-time Marxist, Bernstein. Kautsky was successful for revisionism was rejected in a overwhelming way at the party conference of 1903 in Dresden. He played an equally important role in the debates on mass strikes during 1905–12 supporting the concept in principle, but was very critical of its advocates like Luxemburg and Pannekoek for its use in Germany. When the First World War broke out, he instructed the SPD to abstain from voting for the government war credits and by 1915 opposed the annexationist aims of the Reich and advocated peace. Though initially supportive of the efforts of the Bolsheviks, he became one of their most virulent critics. In his support for parliamentary democracy he was one of the foremost critics of the Leninist experiment of the revolutionary dictatorship of the proletariat. He admonished Lenin for betraying socialism, inviting the latter's wrath and getting dubbed as a 'renegade' in the process.

In 1917 the SPD split. Kautsky's restraint on the issue of mass strike made him a centrist and, as a result, he got increasingly isolated. The SPD's support for the German war effort discredited the party, and with it Kautsky, in the eyes of the revolutionary left. An Independent Social Democratic Party (USPD) was formed and Kautsky was its founding member. The split also meant the loss of editorship of the *Die Neue Zeit*, his major platform. Increasingly marginalized, he rejoined the SPD in 1922. The communists were severe with him for being critical of Lenin. He helped in the drafting

SPD's Heidelberg programme in 1825 but realized that his popularity had waned.

In 1924 Kautsky went to Vienna to be with his three sons. He witnessed the defeat of German socialism at the hands of Hitler and the annihilation of Austrian social democracy in the civil war of 1934. In *The Limits of Force* he repeated his optimistic announcement that history was on his side. When the Germans annexed Austria, he fled to Amsterdam. Most of his works were banned by the Nazis. He virtually spent most part of his later years out of public life. He emigrated to Prague in 1934 and died in exile in Amsterdam on 17 October 1938.

Initiation to Marxism

Kautsky became a Marxist under Bernstein's influence and in 1881 visited Marx and Engels. The initiation of *Die Zeue Zeit* in 1883 as a monthly (it became a weekly in 1890) enabled Marxism to crystallize into a school of thought. Since its inception he continued to be its editor till 1917 and published contributions of socialist thinkers from all over the world. In the period 1885–90 he was in London and maintained close contacts with Engels. In 1887 he published *The Economic Doctrines of Karl Marx* which went into many German and foreign editions and was largely responsible for the rapid spread of Marxism in the late nineteenth century. Like Bernstein who analyzed the evolution of seventeenth century English history by applying the Marxist method, he produced original and startling historical studies like *Thomas More and His Utopia* (1888) and *Foundations of Christianity* (1908). He also published a book in 1889 on class conflicts during the French Revolution. Emphasizing the complexities of social conflicts, he modified the very formulation of the class struggle by pointing to divisions within the classes, which subsequently became a very important component of his thought.

The decade 1890s was the most important period in Kautsky's evolution as a Marxist theoretician. In 1891 at the SPD Congress at Erfurt, the programme adopted was divided into two parts, (*a*) formulation of theory in which he played the most important role, and (*b*) a plan of action largely drawn up by Bernstein. The first part reiterated the traditional Marxist theories of a drive towards monopoly, the decline of the middle class, the continued and steady impoverishment of the proletariat and the inevitability of socialization of the means of production in a future socialist class-less society. The second part dealt with immediate demands like universal suffrage, freedom of expression, free schooling and implementation of a progressive income tax. Writing about the programme and its fulfillment, Kautsky observed:

> We do not wish to say that the abolition of private property or the expropriation of the means of production will occur by itself, that the irresistible development through natural necessity will take place without human action. Nor do we wish to say that all social reforms are useless or that those who suffer the consequences of the contradiction between productive forces and the existing relations of production have nothing to do other than stand idly with their hands in their pockets waiting for this contradiction to be overcome (Kautsky 1964: 101).

Kautsky believed that the working class was on the right side of history and far from being passive should make an effort to get the masses on its side and bring about capitalism.

Kautsky wrote an extended commentary on the Erfurt programme — *The Class Struggle* (1892). In the background of considerable prosperity of Germany in the 1890s from which the working class also benefitted, he argued that socialism was the inevitable product of capitalist development with economic consequences that would lead to the decline of the peasantry and the urban petty bourgeoisie. Concentration of capitalist production would swell the organized working class into a majority. The political consequences of this sea change in the social fabric would be reflected in the irreconcilability of the interests of the proletariat and the bourgeoisie.

> Sooner or later in every capitalist country the participation of the working class in politics must lead to the formation of an independent party, a labour party. . . . And, once formed, such a party must have for its purpose the conquest of the government in the interests of the class which it represents. Economic development will lead naturally to the accomplishment of this purpose (Kautsky 1971: 189).

This theory of the emergence of a labour party which would provide the necessary leadership to the working class anticipated Lenin's thesis in *What is to be done?* (1902) for Kautsky argued that the working class by itself would be able to develop only trade union consciousness. He recommended workers participation in parliamentary struggle for that would have an impact on both the government and the working class. The opportunity to use freedom of press, right of organization and universal ballot would enable them to develop class consciousness. The growing numerical strength and political maturity of the working class would eventually make it the majority within the parliament.

Kautsky envisaged a socialist transformation with the emergence of a parliamentary majority for the socialists with popular support. In his scheme of things there was no place for violence or bloodshed nor any strategy of alliance with the radical bourgeoisie, the peasantry, the intelligentsia and the petty bourgeoisie. Such alliances in the short run was dangerous and in the long run unnecessary as the working class would become the overwhelming majority and an unbeatable socialist political force in due course of time.

Emergence as the Leading Theoretician

Kautsky's support to orthodox Marxism coupled with his disagreements with his mentor, Bernstein, established him as the leading theoretician after Engels not only within Germany but also outside. He became responsible for countering revisionism and symbolized the high glory of SPD.

Kautsky participated in one of the most widely discussed topics in Marxist thought, namely, the question of the breakdown of the capitalistic system. In 1902 he published his most important contribution to the crisis theory in form of a review article criticizing Tugen's book *Theory and History of Commercial Crises in England.* He questioned as to 'whether and to what extent the character of the crises is changing, whether they display a tendency to disappear or to become milder, as several revisionists in agreement with liberal optimists still insisted two or three years ago' (Kautsky 1971: 209). In an answer using Tugen's statistics and descriptive information he stated 'one can say in general that crises are becoming even more severe and extensive in scope' (Ibid.: 209). He also asserted that capitalism was heading for a period of chronic depression.

According to our theory this development is a necessity, and it is proved by this alone that the capitalist method of production has limits beyond which it cannot go. There must come a time, and it may be very soon, when it will be impossible for the world market even temporarily to expand more rapidly than society's productive forces, a time when over production is chronic for all industrial nations. Even then up and downswings of economic life are possible and probable; a series of technical revolutions, which devalue a mass of existing means of production and call forth large scale creation of new means of production, the rediscovery of rich new gold fields, etc., can even then for a while speed up the pace of business. But capitalist production requires uninterrupted, rapid expansion if unemployment and poverty for the workers and insecurity for the small capitalists are not to attain an extremely high pitch. The continued existence of capitalist production remains possible, of course, even in such a state of chronic depression, but it becomes completely intolerable for the masses of the population; the latter are forced to seek a way out of the general misery, and they can find it only in socialism . . . . I regard this situation (Zwangslage) as unavoidable if *economic development proceeds as before,* but I expect that the victory of the proletariat will intervene in time to turn the development in another direction before the forced situation in question arrives, so that it will be possible to avoid the latter (Kautsky 1964: 57).

During this time Kautsky analyzed imperialism and that remains one of his major theoretical innovations in Marxism. He pointed out that the annexation of overseas territories was linked with underconsumption, namely, insufficient home markets creating a need for new markets in colonies. Coupled with this essential factor, the military, bureaucracy and capitalists helped in the export of surplus goods and provided the capital to buy them. The export of capital had two-fold purpose, that of limiting productivity and stabilizing the system. Kautsky also pointed out the imbalance in the expansion between the agricultural and industrial sectors in the world market. The slow growth of industries impeded the supply of raw material to agriculture. At first he argued that war was the logical culmination of imperialism. However, by 1912, with the emergence of a more peaceful and cooperative international situation, he argued that the colonial system was detrimental to the capitalistic system itself. Furthermore capitalism needed peace to develop and the capitalists, being conscious of their own interests, could prevent the arms race and war by entering a phase of what he termed as 'ultra-imperialism'. As such, he did not consider imperialism inevitable, nor did he assert with Lenin that imperialism was the last stage of capitalism. Unlike Hilferding and Lenin, but like Schumpeter, Kautsky did not consider imperialism as a product of industrial capitalism but of pre-industrial, especially aristocratic, segments that remained strong and influential in modern society. He supported his contention with help of history when nomadic conquerors of peasant societies aimed for unlimited territorial expansion (Kautsky 1961).

In 1902 Kautsky wrote *The Social Revolution* in which he distinguished between the political and social revolutions. The political revolution—the conquest of state power—was seen as a matter of strategy. The social revolution would occur as a result of the unfolding of the objective contradictions within capitalism. In 1909 Kautsky's *The Road to Power* was published in which he emphasized the need of the working class to undertake direct revolutionary action against the power of the state. Here he propounded the interesting theory that there was a possibility of an alliance between the working class of the imperial countries with the national liberation movements in the colonies. In the following years he was criticized by the very vocal German Left led by Luxemburg on the question of the mass strike. In contrast to her earlier polemics against Bernstein, where her defence followed the line envisaged by Kautsky regarding the role of mass strike, there was a wide gulf between the two. In the background of the success of the Russian revolution of 1905, Luxemburg looked to the mass strike as the embodiment of spontaneity, and this formed the core of her theory of revolution.

In theory, Kautsky at least was one of the earliest proponents and defenders of mass strike but, in actual practice, he never recommended its use until certain preconditions like the participation of all workers, general disaffection of all members of society and a weak government were fulfilled. For him, like most of the SPD leadership, mass strike was at best a defensive weapon to be used with extreme caution as the last resort if the democratic rights of the working class was endangered. In the context of Germany of that time, the views of Luxemburg was clearly over-optimistic while Kautsky's caution was closer to reality and right (McLellan 1979 and 1983). Incidentally even Lenin endorsed Kautsky's stand as more realistic.

Kautsky believed that the socialist movement was becoming more democratic, shedding its Blanquist tendencies while retaining its revolutionary ardour. Revolution meant a complete alteration in the class structure, introduction of full democracy but not the dictatorship of the few. He was willing to accept the notion of a majoritarian conception of the dictatorship of the proletariat but not the Jacobin-Blanquist notion which was unworkable in an industrialized society. During his debate with the revisionists and Bernstein, he supported their intrinsic faith in parliamentary democracy as the best means for realizing proletarian demands.

Both Kautsky and Bernstein saw parliamentary democracy as necessary for the political maturity of the proletariat and as an instrument whereby the proletariat could control state power with the help of popular support. Kautsky also regarded democracy as indispensable for preparing the proletariat for the imminent social revolution for he was convinced that genuine democracy would be achieved with socialism. After 1918 he was categorical that democracy was not only a means of strengthening the proletariat politically till the advent of the socialist society but also as a necessary life breath for a society.

Events in Russia

Kautsky hailed the February (Kerensky) Revolution of 1917 in Russia and was hopeful that it would inaugurate 'a new epoch for all Europe' since it represented 'a powerful advance of the political forces of toiling masses throughout the capitalist world'. The revolution embodied the proletarian spirit and aspirations. 'The consolidation of the conditions of the new state order strictly depends on this question: rule of the proletariat or the rule of the bourgeoisie?' (Kautsky, cited in Salvadori 1979: 218). The need of the hour for the proletariat was the realization of both democracy and socialism in equal measure for 'social production without democracy would become a most oppressive bond. Democracy without socialism would allow the persistence of the economic dependence of the proletariat' (Kautsky, cited in Salvadori 1979: 219). Kautsky advised the proletariat to combine democracy and socialism as both were inter-related and indispensable.

The Kerensky Revolution failed because of its inability to achieve peace and convene a constituent assembly and these ultimately contributed to the Bolshevik victory. Since the Russian situation was a complicated one within an overall and general backwardness, Kautsky was quite supportive of the Bolsheviks during the initial phases of the revolution. Actually he advised them to act decisively with the purpose of bringing about the required social changes and initiate political democracy.

> Now we will see whether the fears about their rise were justified. They do not lack energy. In their ranks are extremely intelligent comrades, rich in experience. But inherent difficulties of the real conditions are enormous. If they succeed in overcoming them, it will be something extraordinary. A new epoch of world history is beginning (Ibid.: 224).

On the Bolshevik promise of convening the constituent assembly, Kautsky pleaded for a parliament linked to the masses and based on the principle of decentralization.

> The introduction of a parliament is one aspect of democratization but it not sufficient in itself. Important as the dependence of the government on parliament may be, it leads to democratization only when it is accompanied by the growing dependence of the parliament on the popular masses. A parliament is deprived of strength when it cannot rely on the mass of the people (Ibid.: 224).

The dissolution of constituent assembly and the abolition of universal suffrage in the Soviet Union was a turning point in Kautsky's perceptions of the Bolshevik revolution. The insurrection which he initially supported had 'assumed the character of a coup d' etat in his eyes' (Ibid.: 225). This led to the publication of *The Dictatorship of the Proletariat* in 1918 written as a frontal attack on the practice of Bolsheviks. He denounced any attempt to introduce socialism in a backward society by violence and minority action. He thought this to be a betrayal of Marxism and democracy and was convinced that ultimately it would lead to dictatorship and eventual collapse.

Kautsky explained the meaning of the dictatorship of proletariat, a notion that was not only controversial but very sketchy in the writings of Marx and Engels. The dictatorship of the proletariat according to Kautsky meant: (a) power obtained by the working class through the conquest of a majority in parliament, namely through the exercise of democratic freedoms in competition with all other parties; (b) the reliance of a socialist government in transforming the social base of the state in a parliament that represented all political forces and controlled by a socialist majority; (c) a regime that would not suppress political and civil rights of the citizens; (d) a regime that would be prepared to obtain popular consent through periodic elections; (e) a regime that would use violence only against the advocates of counter-revolution, against those who refused to accept the reality of socialist majority constituted in a legal government. By dictatorship of the proletariat he meant the radical and democratic transformation of the state. He rejected the claim of the Bolsheviks that their government was the dictatorship of the proletariat that Marx and Engels spoke about. On the contrary, he described the regime as 'barrack socialism'.

Kautsky was categorical that socialism imposed by a revolutionary minority was a contradiction in itself. Socialism was majoritarianism with respect to the rights of the minority and the dissenters. Kautsky, like Bernstein, considered socialism and democracy to be complementary for socialism could become a reality only if there were proper conditions. This made him critically assess the October revolution and the Leninist interpretation of the dictatorship of the proletariat.

Kautsky argued that Lenin was wrong in claiming Marx's support and regarding the dictatorship of the proletariat as a form of government opposed to democratic norms and culture. For Marx and Engels, the dictatorship of the proletariat meant not just a government but a society. It was the social content of a transitional society that they emphasized. By dictatorship Marx meant the hegemony or the dominance of the working class to be democratically constituted and imposed—a dictatorship of the majority—a class rule by the proletariat. However, Marx never moved democracy to the centre-stage of his political analysis and remained ambivalent on role of parliamentary institutions as the framework for realizing socialism so the Jacobin tendencies within the doctrine became magnified under Leninism and got distorted under Stalinism.[1]

In spite of other substantive theoretical differences, Kautsky and Luxemburg shared a similar notion of proletarian democracy. Luxemburg specifically interpreted Marx's concept as implying a majoritarian model of socialism. Kautsky joined Luxemburg in emphasizing the need for creating a radical democratic foundation on which socialism could eventually be built. Dictatorship of the proletariat in this sense meant a dictatorship of the majority and not, as in class societies, a dictatorship imposed by concerted elites upon the masses. Majoritarian proletariat dictatorship for both was a pre-requisite for the transitional stage towards full communism. Interestingly the East European dissidents and humanists subsequently made this notion of a majoritarian democratic socialism their central feature in their critique of the erstwhile Soviet model. For Kautsky, the constituent assembly provided the link between the rulers and the people and was a guarantee against abuse of power for

> ... the introduction of a parliament is one aspect of democratization, but it is not sufficient in itself. Important as the dependence of the government on parliament may be, it leads to democratization only when it is accompanied by the growing dependence of parliament on the popular masses. A Parliament is deprived of strength when it cannot rely on the mass of people (Kautsky 1964: 24).

Kautsky contended that socialism based on minority despotism and imposed by force would only intensify the rule of terror. 'Tartar Socialism' he observed prophetically would lead to bureaucratization and militarization of society and finally the autocratic rule of a single individual. Democratic institutions were not only compatible with the proletarian rule but its essential pre-requisite.

> Democracy and socialism do not differ in the sense that one is a means and other an end; both are means to the same end .... For us socialism is unthinkable without democracy. By modern socialism we mean not only a social organization of production, but also a democratic organization of society,

for socialism is indissolubly linked to democracy. There is no socialism without democracy (Kautsky 1964: 4–5).

Kautsky argued that socialism was not an end in itself but the elimination of every kind of exploitation and oppression whether of a class, party, race or sex. Socialism could only be attained if the proletariat had the will, numbers and maturity to realize it. He contended that an advanced capitalist state which was democratic offered the best training ground for the working class. Once the proletariat had the will to achieve socialism then only a democratic method could give it its content. To seize power without testing the will among the proletarian masses would amount to a *coup d'etat* and not a social revolution. He realized the difficulty in situations like Russia where the proletariat had the will but constituted a minority in terms of the overall population. In his opinion Bolshevism's 'original sin' was its pre-mature birth. The Bolsheviks had a misconception that they were acting in accordance with history by establishing democracy for the proletariat.

The achievements of the Bolsheviks according to Kautsky had been to accelerate the process of degeneration of the entire system of power, inevitably transforming the proletariat into an armed aristocracy incapable of emancipating the rest of society by itself. Besides the dissolution of the constituent assembly and the withdrawal of universal suffrage, other measures like the introduction of a system of different weighing of the votes of industrial workers and of peasants, the election of the highest leading bodies through various levels by indirect suffrage, the construction of a bureaucratic-police machine to control the majority of the population which was denied any real power in the political process constituted successive steps culminating and consolidating Bolshevik despotism. It was not the dictatorship of the proletariat but the dictatorship of the party, politically and economically, which was more oppressive for the working class than that of capitalism itself (Salvadori 1979: 258).

Kautsky's arguments in the *Dictatorship of the Proletariat* emphasized that socialism could be reached only through democratic means and demonstrated the consequences of a minority dictatorship. Democracy to him meant majority rule, civil liberties and the protection of minorities for these would create possibilities and conditions for political groups to work out alliances, sort out their differences in an open way and ensure changes, if any, in the party of government. He was hostile to bureaucratic rule for he was convinced that it would lead to arbitrariness, suppression of minorities, and general social and economic stagnation. He was convinced that a parliament would be able to exercise greater effective control over government bureaucracy. Pointing out the enormous advantages of democracy for the working class, he contended that it would give a clear indication of the relative strength of the classes and parties while, in an absolutist system, both the ruling and the revolutionary classes would be waging a battle in darkness.

Kautsky distinguished between the rule of classes and governance by political parties to differentiate between the dictatorship of the proletariat and the dictatorship of the party. The former referred to a situation in a democracy when the working class gained and became the ruling class eventually. This, according to him, was a distinct possibility for the numbers within the working class were on the increase. It was in this connection that he, like Bernstein, referred to the lessons of the Paris Commune. Since the classes rule, but do not govern, the dictatorship of a *class* cannot be equated with the dominance of a particular *party*.

For Kautsky, if the proletariat constituted the majority, there was no need to interfere with the democratic process. It was only when the proletariat was in the minority that dictatorship would become a necessity as it was in the case Tsarist Russia. He was optimistic and confident that capitalism would logically develop into socialism for it would have created an enormous working class and the conditions for a democratic transformation to socialism. He warned prophetically of the disastrous consequences if a minority seized power and tried to bring about socialism because such an attempt would be premature and unnecessary.

Kautsky, like Bernstein, analyzed the democratic process and prospects for democracy in a general manner without relating it to any particular class. Lenin, on the contrary, distinguished between the bourgeois and the proletarian democracy. The latter insisted that the principal lesson of the Paris Commune was not that the working class needed democracy in general but that it needed popular democracy in particular. Both Kautsky and Bernstein, unlike Lenin, regarded democracy as important because of its potential. They were not so much concerned with its class character. Lenin, on the other hand, regarded parliamentary institutions as detrimental to the interests of the working class and hence insisted on the need to smash the bourgeois state apparatus. The principal lesson of the Paris Commune was that it was not a parliamentary institution. Democracy for Lenin meant popular control and mass participation. However, he never sketched the institutional and procedural basis of such a system and left it undefined.

Lenin, who had earlier called Kautsky 'the chief of German revolutionaries' and praised him for his method of scientific analysis in which the method of Marx lived again, now turned against him. Lenin and Trotsky castigated him to be a 'renegade' for having betrayed not only the revolutionary conceptions of Marx and Engels but even his past as well. They accused him of arguing like a liberal thinker and not as a Marxist. Lenin turned virulent when the prospects of a revolution in Germany and other parts of Europe failed. In the *Proletarian Revolution and Renegade Kautsky* (1918) he clarified that the dictatorship of the proletariat did not mean the absence of democracy. He insisted that for a Marxist the class connotation of a regime was important.

> However limited the effectiveness of parliamentary control may be, there is a point to Kautsky's argument that is evaded in Lenin's essentialist rejection of parliamentary institutions as a form of bourgeois dictatorship. It is all very well to talk of dispensing with parliamentary-bureaucratic forms of state organization when some alternative forms of popular control and self organization have been developed. Otherwise it amounts to proposing that we dismantle even the limited form of popular control over the bureaucratic state machinery that parliament represents (Hindess 1983: 34).

For Kautsky the remnants of an absolute state could be destroyed by the proletarian revolution, thereby laying the foundations for the attainment of full parliamentarism under a democratic republic. The commune to him was a symbol of democratic pluralism. Though he paid tributes to the 'great and glorious history of soviet organization', he did not characterize it as the dictatorship of the proletariat. He considered the commune to be superior to the soviets for the former was the government of the entire working class. In Russia, the Bolsheviks had gained power by fighting the other socialist parties and, moreover, they represented only a fraction of the proletariat.

Kautsky rejected the Bolshevik characterization of the soviets as the commune, for a political system that did not draw sustenance from universal suffrage was not a majoritarian system nor the dictatorship of the proletariat. The Soviet state continued and reinforced the vestiges of the old Tsarist state. It failed to create a constitutional state based on rule of law and respect for individual rights.

> The Commune demands the abolition of the army and in its place had advocated a militia, while the soviet government began with the dissolution of the old army but latter created the Red Army. The old police was destroyed to be replaced by a new one — the *cheka* — a political police much harsher than that of Russian tsarism and Bonapartism. The Commune and Marx demanded the replacement of the state bureaucracy with functionaries elected by the people through universal suffrage but the Soviet Republic had destroyed the old Tsarist bureaucracy, but in its place has created a new equally centralized bureaucracy with more extensive powers. On only one respect the Bolsheviks remained faithful to the Commune — in their unification of legislative and executive (Kautsky 1964: 20–21, 36–39).

Kautsky in *Terrorism and Communism* (1920) contended that any attempt to establish socialism without accompanying democratic norms and institutions would be premature. He characterized the Bolshevik regime politically as a 'bureaucratic dictatorship' and economically as a 'state capitalist order' (Ibid.: 132–33).

Trotsky furnished a reply and argued that any one who repudiated terrorism in principle, namely the measures of suppression and intimidation of an armed counter revolution[2] must renounce any idea of the political supremacy of the working class and reject its revolutionary dictatorship. He made a virtue of necessity and argued for the use of these methods as essential for the protection and advancement of socialism within Russia. Subsequently, Trotsky castigated the Stalinist regime for having betrayed the revolutionary ideals without shouldering responsibility for being among the originators of a system that produced a Stalin.

The Lenin-Trotsky criticism of Kautsky was "exceedingly frail" as for the positions that Kautsky developed precisely during the period in which Lenin considered him a "master" and the "chief of German revolutionaries" were all such as to lead him inevitably to the sharpest opposition both to the tactics and strategy of the Bolsheviks in the seizure of power and to the manner in which they established their dictatorship after it (Salvadori 1979: 253).

The charge of 'renegade' by Lenin and Trotsky was made to defend their indefensible positions. They even went to the extent of doubting Kautsky's commitment to democratic values in spite of his explicit reference to the importance of democracy.

Our final goal correctly understood, consists not in socialism but in the abolition of any form of exploitation and oppression, be it directed against a class or a party, nation or race . . . . we propose the socialist form of production as a goal in this struggle because given present technical and economic conditions, it appears the only means to attain our goal. If it could be shown that we are mistaken, that the liberation of the proletariat, and of humanity in general could be achieved only, or more similarly, on the basis of private property in the means of production, as Proudhon thought at one time, then we would have to reject socialism, without it any way renouncing our final goal, but rather in the very interest of this goal (Kautsky 1964: 4).

Kautsky was sanguine that socialism would be the method to abolish exploitation and oppression. However, he was equally sure that if any other method other than democracy was followed in the name of socialism then that would mean introduction of a system leading to large scale abuse of power.

Critique of Fascism

Kautsky's commitment to both democracy and socialism made him oppose fascism. He considered the fascist phase to be an abnormal one. To confront the danger realistically, he suggested the unity of the proletariat with bourgeois forces opposing fascism. He argued correctly, confidently and convincingly that countries with a long history of parliamentary democracy would never turn fascist.

> Fascism will not cross the Rhine or the North Sea. In France, England and America it will remain the folly of a handful of braggarts of no political significance. . .The rise of dictatorship in some states signals a local transitory interruption of a process that has been under way for more than a century in the entire civilized world. It is a consequence of the world. We must not fear that it may become so general and persistent as a lead to the "decadence of the West" that has been prophesied by one of the leaders of National Socialism (Kautsky, cited in Salvadori 1979: 351–2).

Kautsky admitted that though Germany was in a position to attain the goal of parliamentary democracy, the aberration in the form of national socialism would remain localized for ultimately the logical course within a modern industrial society was parliamentary democracy. It was this hope that sustained his optimism of realizing democracy and socialism simultaneously and eventually. He considered fascism to be a serious lapse, a 'parenthesis', a phenomenon which was grave but was also destined to be a passing phase. In his optimism, there was a great deal of similarity between the position that he and Gramsci took. Remaining faithfully to democratic ideals, he rejected any idea of replacing the fascist dictatorship with a Marxist one, as 'whoever asserts that democracy has failed asserts that the proletariat itself is not yet capable of liberating itself' (Ibid.: 357).

Kautsky was aware of the vast difference between the modern dictatorships and the ancient ones. He conceded that the modern dictatorships were something new, unprecedented in history. He even accused the Bolsheviks of attenuating dictatorship for they had blatantly and brutally dissolved the fabric of democracy and civic freedom. Kautsky anticipated the phenomenon of totalitarianism which was unprecedented and unrivalled in terms of nature and exercise of power and control.

> Bolshevik methods were closely studied and imitated not only by the communists but also by the capitalists and reactionaries. The techniques of oppression first developed over the

course of years by the Bolsheviks, technique which not even Mussolini had found ready-made, have now been completed and utilized with maximum intensity by the National Social-ists . . . . the first condition for overcoming the new dictator-ships is to overcome those factors which have dragged broad sectors of the proletariat to such a low moral and intellectual level . . . but one thing we can do — above all and in all circum-stances remain faithful to ourselves. We must not become worshippers of the success of the movement; we must not at one stroke jettison the ideals for which so many workers and socialists of all countries have placed their lives and liberty in jeopardy for a century, just because in special condition our enemies have done a brisk political business in the past few years with opposite methods and goals (Kautsky, cited in Salvadori 1979: 356, 362).

With optimism and courage, Kautsky declared:

We who believe in the capacity for development and the fu-ture of the working class put our full faith in democracy. The toiling masses have been struggling for democracy for a cen-tury and a half now. Many have seen their defeats, but they have never been demoralized. Those who have fought for democracy have never lost faith in it; democracy has always been reborn . . . . A single defeat must not induce us to abandon this embattled front, which alone can lead our party to vic-tory and liberate toiling humanity for ever (Ibid.: 365, 366).

Kautsky believed that both Fascism and Bolshevism were un-stable political systems for they would be unable to create a just and a rational society. It might seem inadvertent that he also did not point out the 'obvious' differences between the two competing systems but it was not an oversight for both the regimes used ter-ror so systematically with the help of a messianic ideology to jus-tify their brutality and in their futile efforts to create a new social and economic order that they were similar.

Conclusion

Kautsky's Marxism was determinist and evolutionary. He remained steadfast to the belief structure of orthodox Marxism. He believed in the imminence of the collapse of capitalism and, to prove this, he pointed out that the appearance of monopolies and cartels represented the final stage of capitalism. Serious crises within it was brought about under-consumption reducing the growing middle class to that of the proletariat and that would bring about the final collapse of the system.

Kautsky displayed remarkable consistency in his social analysis of 50 years during a very turbulent epoch of European history. His conviction that democracy and socialism were inter-linked remained unshaken even during the dark years of fascist rule. He perceived Marxism to be a single unified theory that explained and covered the totality of human experience. He refused to distinguish between natural and social world. He was interested in anthropology, ecology and demography, fields that blurred the distinction between natural and social sciences. He incorporated this approach in a non-Marxian book on the influence of population growth on the progress of society (1880), in a later work on reproduction and development in nature and society (1910) and in *Are Jews a Race?* (1914). The most important work exemplifying this method was his seminal work on the materialist conception of history (1927). He remained a Darwinian for he believed that there was a close link between social evolution and natural evolution. He was convinced of the scientific character of Marxism for it offered universal laws and a value-free approach. He also argued that technology was fundamentally effected by the particular natural environment in which a group found itself. He found that in agriculture there was no evidence of large ones replacing the small ones and that larger enterprises were generally more productive. Hence he favoured a socialist programme that converted large estates into communal ones in the hope that individual peasants would eventually from such large cooperatives.

Kautsky combined revolutionary goals with reformist methods but ruled out insurrection. He agreed with the revisionists that socialism would have to be realized with the help of democracy but diverged from them for, unlike them, he did not expect democracy to come about peacefully. He denounced any efforts by a violent minority to create a revolution in a backward society for that would betray Marxism and democracy and slide into a dictatorship which would eventually collapse. Had Lenin heeded to this advice by one whom he acknowledged the 'master', Russia could have avoided the bloodshed of millions of innocent, brutal repression and mindless violence.

Kautsky, like Gramsci, believed that fascism would not be able to create a stable system of power but, unlike Gramsci, did not extend the same argument to communism. Gramsci could grasp the incompleteness of the Leninist model but did not share Kautsky's intrinsic faith in democracy which remained unshakable even during the years of totalitarian fascism and communism. Kautsky's life and teaching also remind us of an important aspect of German socialism that all its leading theoreticians, the revisionist Bernstein, the radical Luxemburg and the cautious Kautsky never conceived of building socialism without basic democratic institutions and civil liberties. It was because of this essential commitment that they remain relevant even today when Lenin and Stalin have been dismissed as pre-modern and irrelevant in an age of democracy. In this unequivocal assertion there was a great similarity between the socialist stalwarts of the early and the late twentieth century like Miliband and Sweezy. Lichtheim (1975) aptly observed that the modern era demonstrated that while either democracy or socialism was attainable, the unfinished task was to achieve both and, in that context, pioneers like Kautsky are still relevant and could provide a starting point for bringing about a political synthesis.

Georgii Valentinovich Plekhanov

Plekhanov's most important contribution was the laying down of an orthodox Marxist perspective for the development of the revolution in Russia. As the most "Westernizing" of the Russian Marxists, Plekhanov saw no fundamental difference between Russia and the West (McLellan 1979: 68).

Plekhanov ranks with Kautsky in the importance of his role in the history of Marxism and the dissemination of Marxist doctrine (Kolakowski 1981b: 329).

Plekhanov effected that enduring fusion of Populism and Marxism which was to be the secret of Lenin's "national" appeal. And it was on the strength of his later philosophical essays, which in the 1890s were influential in expounding Marx's historical materialism and, rather less fortunately, Engels' dialectical materialism (so described by Plekhanov himself, who is the inventor of the term), that Lenin regarded Plekhanov as his teacher and stressed the importance of his work, even after he had parted company politically. Soviet Marxism on its philosophical side represents the legacy of Plekhanov: a circumstance duly stressed in all official pronouncements down to the present day . . . one of the world's greatest thinkers (Lichtheim 1975: 154).

Georgii Valentinovich Plekhanov (1856–1918) occupies an important position in the history of socialist thought as the father of Russian Marxism. He was the first to make a systematic break with Populism which was the predominant revolutionary movement in Russia in the 1860s and 1870s. In the process, he inspired a whole generation of Marxist thinkers in Russia and popularized the Marxist doctrine in that country. Plekhanov's importance was in the fact that his political philosophy was a bridge between Populism and Marxism. After the death of Engels, Plekhanov along with Kautsky was the spokesman and advocate or orthodox Marxism. He played an active role in countering Bernstein's Revisionism.

Plekhanov's shift to Marxism was on the premise that Russia was already a capitalist country with a sizable proletariat. He expressed tremendous faith in the ability of the Russian workers to bring about a revolution. However, he asked his Marxist followers to wait till the process of industrial development was over and warned against any attempt to establish socialism prematurely. This seemed like a prophetic warning which went unheeded. Plekhanov was not a supporter of the Bolsheviks for he wondered whether he had acted hastily in introducing Marxism in a backward Asiatic society. He did not approve of the methods and the strategy that the Bolsheviks used in making the revolution and in establishing the workers state. Fortunately for him, he did not live enough to see the degeneration.

Russian historians argued that the state in Russia, far from being an instrument of class domination, created social classes from above, a point that most Russian Marxists did not accept. Plekhanov and Trotsky conceded that the Russian state was far more independent than its counterparts in Europe. Plekhanov spoke of Russia's Asiatic nature which led him to emphasize decentralization in his political proposals. 'All major economic changes in Russian history have been effected from above by means of state power' (Kolakowski 1981b: 306). If socialism was to make any difference, then this over-centralized state had to be dismantled and replaced by a plural decentralized structure. Interestingly,

Lenin rejected this line of thinking in the *State and Revolution* as anarchistic and categorically stated that a socialist state had to be centralized.

Biographical Sketch

Plekhanov was born on 29 November 1856 in the Russian province of Tambov. He was the son of a conservative landed gentleman of the local gentry whose estate was halved after the emancipation of the serfs. His mother was a distant relative of Vissarion Grigorievich Belinsky (1811–48), the critic and friend of Alexander Ivanovich Herzen (1812–70), known as the father of Russian socialism. After the death of his father Plekhanov and his 12 siblings were raised by their mother single-handedly.

In 1873 Plekhanov enrolled himself as a student in a military school in Petersburg. After 1874 he joined the mining school and became attracted to Populism. He joined the *Zemlya y Volya* and in 1876 organized an illegal protest demonstration in front of the Kazan Cathedral. Consequently he fled abroad. He returned a year later with the help of forged papers and joined the *Cherny Peredel*. He went abroad in 1880 and settled down in Geneva from where he observed the assassination of Tsar Alexander II in 1891. He engaged in polemics with the surviving Bakunists and with Peter Pyotr Nikitich Tkachev (1844–86). He translated the *Communist Manifesto* in Russian. He wrote a number of books and pamphlets elaborating Marxist theory. Besides politics, he also wrote extensively on other subjects like law, economics, science, aesthetics and political philosophy in a lucid, witty and polemical style.

In the 1880s Plekhanov established himself as the foremost Russian Marxist abroad. Along with Zasulich and Paul B. Axelrod (1850–1928), he formed the first Russian Marxist organization called the 'Emancipation of Labour' in 1883 in Geneva. He played an active role in refuting the main heresies of leading European socialists like Bernstein. Along with Lenin and Martov, he founded the Russian Social Democratic Labour Party's journal *Iskra* (the spark). Following the heated debates within the party regarding the organizational questions, he joined its Menshevik wing after the split in 1903. When he returned to Petersburg in 1917 after thirty-seven years of exile, he became a democrat in the Western sense. He was ready to support the provisional government, much against the wishes of Lenin. Ten weeks after the Bolsheviks captured power in the fall of 1917, Plekhanov's journal *Edinstvo* (Unity) was banned. He died on 30 May 1918 in a Finnish Sanitarium.

Origins of Russian Socialism

The revolutionary movement in Russia goes back to Napolenic times known as the Decembrist uprising of 1825. Russian democratic thought from the beginning was socialist in nature. Political opposition to absolutism was part of wider opposition of not only to serfdom but also to nascent capitalism. Subsequently, a radical movement which developed in Russia after 1862 came to be known as 'populism' (*narodnichestvo*), and the populists or *narodniks* regarded the need to stop the development of capitalism in Russia for it was intrinsically retrograde. They regarded the peasant commune, the *obshchina*, as a self-contained institution for it ignored class differences. It represented in essence a just and an equal society. They felt that the intelligentsia could be an independent force capable of imparting to history whatever it decided. However, the link between the intelligentsia and political institutions on the one hand, and the class interests of the Russian society on the other hand was not perceived. Social justice and equality were the goals of populism.

The populists took from Herzen the idea that the Russian commune (*mir*) with its communal property could be the basis for the future socialist society and enable Russia to escape from the evils of capitalism. They cherished the aim of an agrarian revolution and in 1874 staged a 'go to the people' movement only to realize that young intellectuals were not at all interested in socialism. All they wanted was more land. It became clear to them that the peasants were not ready for a revolution but that did not deter them from looking to the villages as possible centres for revolution-making.

Herzen's socialism resembled that of Blanc and Proudhon. He admired the English for their institutions which guaranteed political liberty. He opposed capitalism and westernization for it promoted a cult of excessive materialism and led to poverty, exploitation and misery. He insisted that western institutions were not suitable for Russia. He believed that the cause of socialism was bound up with the national development of the Slav peoples, above all the Russians. He envisioned a democratic revolution which, starting from the basis of the village commune, would realize socialism. Herzen's importance in the history of socialism was due to the fact that he drew attention of the radical intelligentsia to the importance of the village commune. He believed in the supremacy and intrinsic quality of human beings and held that social institutions had to enhance it in every way. Western civilization was too competitive destroying the spontaneous unity among human beings. Herzen's critique of capitalism was from an aristocratic rather than socialist perspective (Kolakowski 1981b: 312). He agreed with Bakunin that the state was a necessary evil but he was cautious on the issue of revolution.

Bakunin, like Herzen, felt that Russia had a special part to play, that of the leader of the Slav nations in the long march toward self-determination and socialism. This was only possible with the destruction of Tsardom and getting rid of its ancient past since the Tsars encouraged only hatred for the Russians among the Slavs, in particular among the Poles. It has to be noted that libertarian socialism was West European idea whereas in Russia the radical populists wavered between terrorism and faith in a peasant revolt. In either case, they realized the need for conspiratorial methods and they did their best to provide one. They saw themselves as followers of Bakunin, and the latter's denouncement of intellectuals and experts for they led to tyrannies on the ordinary people influenced them tremendously.

The populists proceeded to ignite a popular uprising by a self-appointed group of what would be later called 'professional revolutionaries' drawn from the radical intelligentsia. They obtained the support of Bakunin for this programme. A revolutionary was defined as one who disliked public opinion and had the sole aim of annihilating the existing society totally and recreating a new one. Bakunin advocated and defended the destruction of state authority and political power. His passion for destruction which he characterized as 'creative joy' did not contradict his benevolent view and faith that he had in the essential goodness of human beings. He did not however despise the latter. Like Feuerbach, he was a humanist regarding the individual as the highest being and it was for this purpose that the oppressors of the human individual had to be eliminated. It was from total destruction that revolution could become a liberating experience. The state, the church and private property had to be uprooted if the world was to be free from oppression. He had faith in self-renewal since the social community was essentially harmonious and the individual was good. He, however, failed because of his 'inability to establish plausible connection between the two extreme poles of his *Weltanschauung:* liberty on the one hand, conspiracy on the other' (Lichtheim 1969: 134–35).

Radical populism found in Nicholas Gavrilovich Chernyshevsky (1828–89) a new patron saint. It remained faithful to Bakunin but dismissed Herzen as a liberal constitutionalist. Chernyshevsky, a radical materialist, provided them what it was searching for, namely, the devotion to the cause of revolution. Though not an anarchist, he conceived of the state as an organizer and protector of free associations of peasants and workers. It guaranteed order, efficiency, equality and individual liberty. All of them believed that once the revolution destroyed autocracy, inequality and exploitation, a new, natural, harmonious and just order would emerge and attain perfection if guided benignly by the enlightened revolutionaries. The basis of this claim was their belief in the genuine goodness of human beings.

Chernyshevsky accepted the basic tenets of liberalism and desired the overthrow of autocracy and the enthronement of freedom, universal education and emancipation of the peasants. He was keen that Russia enjoy industrial progress and liberalism without renouncing its communist aspirations that was latent in *Obshchina* so that the nightmares of capitalism could be averted. During his two-year imprisonment from 1862–64, he wrote his celebrated novel *What is to be done?* — a phrase that became a catechism with the young revolutionaries in Russia and was immortalized by Lenin in 1903 by using it as a title to his pamphlet on the party organization. Chernyshevsky believed that art, like science, was relevant if it was socially useful. The novel instilled in the youth a sense of dedication to people's cause and other-worldiness.

P.L. Lavrov (1823–1900), N.K. Mikhailovsky (1842–1904) and P.N. Tkachov (1844–85) contributed significantly to the radical cause in the 1870s. Lavrov gave a prominent place to the intelligentsia for they could provided moral leadership. He was confident that once economic backwardness was overcome, the workers would make the revolution for they would be sufficiently imbibed with socialist values. Mikhailovsky felt that capitalism was not necessary in Russia and, like Lavrov, was confident that the village commune epitomized the essence of socialism and cooperatives. For Tkachov, revolution would end inequality, elite culture and mass misery.

The failure of the populist movement led to a new revolutionary party called *Zemlya y Volya* (Land and Liberty) which split into those who stood for terrorism called the *Narodnaya Volya* (People's Will) and those who believed in educating the peasant called the *Chernyi Peredel* (General Redivision). Both groups, however, remained faithful to Chernyshevsky. The latter saw the *obshchina* as the basis of socialism but rejected Herzen and Bakunin's faith in a Russian national destiny. The *obshchina* could become a socialist community but only if Western Europe showed the way. In 1882 this view was incorporated in the second Russian edition of the *Communist Manifesto* by Marx and Engels.

The 1880s saw the advent of Marxist ideas in Russia as a result of a constant debate with the populists. Marx's ideas were well known in Russia. His *Poverty of Philosophy* and *Capital* were translated into Russian. The populists accepted Marx's sociological analysis and the critique of capitalism but not the materialistic outlook and conviction in the proletarian revolution. They did not see the relevance of Marxist ideas to Russia.

Both Marx and Engels were also ambivalent as far as Russia was concerned. They studied the Russian developments in detail, and in particular the peasant commune. Engels was enthused about the establishment of communal ownership and hoped for its transformation into a higher one. With the establishment of *Zemlya y Volya*, Marx became more sympathetic to the populists accepting that the community was the mainspring of Russia's social arrangements. In 1882 both Marx and Engels expressed the possibility that if there was a outbreak of a revolution in Russia, it might set into motion similar movements in the West.

From Populism to Marxism

The Emancipation of Labour under the leadership of Plekhanov made a transition from Populism to Marxism. Contrary to the expectations, the assassination of the Tsar in 1881 did not lead to the fall of the autocracy. It became even more oppressive. The People's

Will Organization was in disarray following the arrests or executions of its leaders. The *Cheryny Peredel* had a chance to succeed had it not adopted the Bakuninist strategy for it proved ineffective as an instrument of political combat.

The bankruptcy of the policy of terrorism after 1881 led Plekhanov to re-examine the basic tenet of the populist creed — the belief in the revolutionary potential of the peasantry in Russia. Armed with Marxist teachings, he warned the populists that without the creation of an economically independent class that was capable of limiting the power of the tsar, the revolution would not succeed and their heroism would be wasted. Though they may succeed in killing one Tsar after another, Tsarism as an institution would continue. Meanwhile, in 1894 Engels believed that the development of capitalism in Russia destroyed the revolutionary potential of the commune and any revolution at that point in time would hasten the victory of the modern industrial proletariat.

For the Russian Marxists, the central problem was the nature of the impending revolution. It was Plekhanov who made this the key issue and was confident that the proletariat rather than the peasantry would make the revolution. The intellectual shift to Marxism did not mean the marginalization or death of populism for many of their ideas were championed by other groups.

The populists were convinced that the death of the peasant commune would mean death, or any rate a vast setback to freedom and equality in Russia; the Left Socialist-Revolutionaries, who were their direct descendants, transformed this into a demand for a form of decentralized, democratic, self-government among the peasants, which Lenin adopted when he concluded his temporary alliance with them in October 1917. In due course the Bolsheviks repudiated this programme, and transformed the cells of dedicated revolutionaries — perhaps the most original contribution of populism to revolutionary practice — into the hierarchy of centralized political power, which the populists had steadily and fiercely denounced until they were themselves finally, in the form of Socialist Revolutionary Party, proscribed and annihilated. Communist practice owed much, as Lenin was always ready to admit, to the populist movement; for it borrowed the technique of its rival and adapted it with conspicuous success to serve the precise purpose which it had been invented to resist (Berlin 1979: 237).

Plekhanov's Ideas

Plekhanov's political ideas were elaborated in *Socialism and the Political Struggle* (1883), a tract that contained the core of his views. Like Kautsky, he believed that social processes could be studied as objectively as natural phenomena for human history was subject to universal laws of change. He contended that, in a backward country like Russia, if a revolutionary socialist party seized power it would face a dilemma of either to organize production along the lines of modern socialism or fall into a patriarchal and authoritarian model. In case the latter happened, which in all probability would be the case, people would be reduced to obeying the centralized supreme command and its bureaucratic agents. Far from being educated for socialism they would become subservient to a far more powerful state than the one the tsars had established. They would lose their capacity for progress towards freedom, democracy and socialism.

For a decade-and-a-half, Plekhanov's observations were a gospel for Lenin and were treated with similar reverence that Marx, Engels and Kautsky commanded. Even after Plekhanov's break with Bolshevism over revolutionary tactics, Lenin still regarded himself as an adherent to his overall strategy. This perception did not change even after the Bolsheviks captured power. In the former Soviet Union texts gave Plekhanov a prominent place among its intellectual founders. Even Trotsky, the first major theorist to break away from Plekhanov and whose personal relations with his senior was never cordial, defended the important attributes of Plekhanov's political economy against the party critics in 1922.

Plekhanov accepted the scientific quality of Marxism but his focus was more on understanding the implications of ascendancy of capitalism rather than the causes for its malfunctioning. Therefore he never spoke of breakdown of capitalism. Being multi-linearist, he accepted that it was not necessary that every society was destined to follow the same path of stages of development. In this context, he stressed on three general considerations. First was the importance of geographical or natural conditions in determining economic development. In view of this, he accounted for the semi-

Asiatic, pre-capitalist condition of Russia which differentiated it from others, especially those in Western Europe. Second, the different sub-systems — political, social, economic, cultural, etc. — within a complex society were relatively autonomous. He accorded a crucial role to human consciousness and political organization in determining the course of historical development. Third, he held that international events exerted tremendous influence on domestic policies, particularly in backward societies. It was due to external influence that Russia was catapulted into capitalist development.

Lenin reiterated many of Plekhanov's views concerning industrialization of Russia and the need for a 'bourgeois democratic revolution' before commencing on a struggle for socialism. Plekhanov rejected the view of the populists that the bourgeoise was inherently reactionary. The populists thought in terms of replacing tsarist absolutism with socialism. However, Plekhanov spoke of revolution in two stages.

In the first stage, Russia would be transformed into a modern European country by eliminating the vestiges of feudalism and expanding the industrial base. A liberal democratic republic with full political and civil rights would replace Tsarism. Plekhanov emphasized that, with the emancipation of the serfs, Russia would become capitalist with manufacturing industries, commodity market and wage labour. This meant that the proletariat would emerge as an oppositional force and lead the democratic revolution since the bourgeois could not be trusted to complete the process. The underlying assumption was that, despite the reluctance and hesitations of the bourgeois class, its interests were incompatible with that of the autocracy. However, Plekhanov did not focus on this aspect in detail. He studied the development of capitalism in agriculture but did not make a similar enquiry into the dynamics of industry though he assigned to the urban bourgeoisie a crucial revolutionary role. Since he did not theorize from the historically specific conditions of Russian industrialization, he was unable to analyze the politics of the bourgeoisie.

The proletariat organized into a social democratic party would acquire the necessary political experience needed for their future role as governors. With improved strength, it would secure political preponderance that would enable it to inaugurate socialism. The experience of Western Europe in general and Germany in particular in 1848 demonstrated for Plekhanov the unreliability of the bourgeoisie as a revolutionary class and placed a greater responsibility on the radical intelligentsia to provide the initiative and leadership to the proletariat. In the second stage, with the socialist revolution, the means of production and distribution would be nationalized and the political system would be one of the dictatorship of the proletariat. Reiterating Marx, he claimed that it implied the rule of the vast majority of the proletariat over the tiny minority of exploiters. He described this situation as *panarchy*.

Plekhanov tacitly admitted the fundamental similarity between the historical destiny of the West and Russia. He was equally perceptive to realize the differences. Anticipating Trotsky and Lenin's law of uneven development, he introduced certain modifications. The most significant was the need to establish an organic connection between the two revolutions — the bourgeois and the socialist. He predicted a period of transition during which the proletarian class-consciousness would be awakened at the earliest and encouraged to fight for the attainment of socialism.

Plekhanov did not suggest the machinery through which the masses could exercise their dictatorship, the safeguards needed against the abuses of power and the methods that could be used for dealing with opponents and detractors. Neither did he articulate clearly his views on the nature of reforms that the bourgeois democratic revolution would accomplish, and this evasion made his followers take the view that democracy, freedom and rule of law were simply part of the paraphernalia of middle class rule which could be dispensed with according to the dictates of expediency. His followers came to regard the first stage of the revolution as merely a stepping stone for the second, considering economic liberation as the goal and political movement as a means to achieve the goal. Plekhanov made the same mistake that Marx committed by not outlining the details of his conception and, by remaining sufficiently vague and general, he allowed his followers to have their own interpretation, creating more confusion rather than clarity.

Plekhanov was also ambiguous about the chronology of the revolution. His theory implied a lengthy interval between the two phases to enable the Russian workers to become sufficiently conscious. He advised them to wage a prolonged open struggle against their employers and endure hardships and miseries. He also stated that he did not see the possibility of socialism in Russia in the near future and warned against any efforts to combine the two revolutions for that would lead to disorder and instability. However, he was also confident that capitalism in Russia would fade out sooner than predicted if there was a proletarian revolution in the West or if the middle class declined.

> Plekhanov was caught in a conflict between his head and his heart. Reason taught him that the Russian workers still had far to go before they could draw level with those of the West in numbers or experience; emotion demanded some assurance that the promised land of socialism might after all be not so far away. His populist critics seized upon the flaw in his revolutionary strategy; if Russian middle class were so feeble, how could the coming revolution be branded as bourgeois (Keep 1963: 23).

In trying to answer this riddle, the Marxists were forced to resort to 'intellectual contortions' until Axelrod propounded that the proletariat had to exercise 'hegemony' as distinct from dictatorship in the first phase of the revolution. He argued that the problem of confronting the Russian Marxists was of greater and different dimension and depth than those faced by their counterparts in the West. The latter had to merely lead the workers against the bourgeois system whereas in Russia the workers were simultaneously allied with and opposed to the bourgeoisie in a common struggle against the tsarist autocracy. They had to simultaneously accomplish both the democratic and socialist revolutions, neither of which could be neglected. Exclusive attention to socialist revolution would leave the broader task of winning liberty to the moderates which might result in a democratic revolution that may solely benefit the middle class. Moreover, a one-sided emphasis on the furtherance of workers' economic interests would antagonize the liberals, thereby undermining the democratic alliance. The only way out would be for the party to preserve its own independence and mobilize the masses under its own leadership. Once it attained strength, it could force its allies to accept its hegemony.

Plekhanov expected that the Tsarist regime would give way to a democratic political order in 1905 rather than a pseudo-parliamentary system that existed during Bismarck's time in Germany. With great resoluteness, he fought against revisionism in western socialism but his efforts were futile. He envisaged under a Russian bourgeois democratic regime, a social democratic party embracing the largest possible number of workers, engaging in political campaigns and parliamentary activities, fostering the growth of trade unions and maintaining close contacts between the party and labour organizations. He emphasized the desirability of social reforms, the possibility of securing favourable social legislations. Nevertheless, he staunchly denied that these circumstances prevented the increase in the proletarian class consciousness for that was inevitable as long as society remained divided into classes.

Plekhanov published his *Defence of Materialism* psuedonymously as *On the Question of the Development of the Monist View of History* (1884). This was the first attempt to systematically expound the principles of historical materialism in Russia. This also established his reputation in the West. We presented Marxism as the inheritor of all the positive traits that were latent in the eighteenth century French materialism, utopian socialism and German idealism. He also attributed the influence of geographical factors to historical developments and applied the historical materialistic perspective to the study of aesthetics. Along with Mehring[3] and Lafargue, he pointed out that art depended and reflected class values and hence it was the content and the form that had to be the basis of judgement. He did not distinguish between western and Russian brand of socialism.

Conclusion

Plekhanov was an extremely influential interpreter of Marxism as a system of philosophy and provided the doctrine with internal cohesion. As a result, he gained enormous popularity not only in Russia but also in the West. It was due to his interpretation that Marxism reached a wider public. His understanding of dialectical materialism constituted the philosophical foundations of the Soviet official ideology. Luk'acs regarded Plekhanov along with Engels as commentators of Marx and took the former's interpretation as a starting point for his analysis of Marx's ideas.

Plekhanov broke away from Narodism and became a Marxist on the plea that a new revolutionary movement was needed to deal with Russia that was developing into a capitalist society. He projected Narodism as the Russian equivalent of western utopian socialism. Like most of the Russian revolutionaries of his time, Plekhanov looked to the West for inspiration. Initially, he remained neutral in the debate between the Mensheviks and Bolsheviks on the party organization but subsequently supported Lenin and the Bolsheviks.

Plekhanov accepted that capitalism was the unavoidable prerequisite of socialism and that it would be morally difficult for the revolutionaries to endorse the coming of capitalism since it would result in mass misery for those whom they desired to liberate. He pointed out that the Marxists could awaken proletarian consciousness though he warned that imposition of socialism would result in a patriarchal and authoritarian communism, which was worse than capitalism.

Plekhanov acted as a bridge between Chernyshevsky and Lenin. He did not abandon his faith in the village community and approved of the relevant remarks made by Marx and Engels in the *Manifesto*. But he contended that socio-economic forces in Russia conformed to Marx's theory of history: capitalism was developing fast and could not be set aside. In spite of his caution against premature socialism, he was never opposed to the idea of employing revolutionary means to seize and exercise power. He wanted the revolutionary class to use all its dominance and wield against the power of the state. It reflected shades of Bakuninism rather than Jacobinism. In *Our Differences* (1884) he bestowed faith in the revolutionary intelligentsia and looked upon it as being able to exercise a powerful and decisive influence on the people. Lenin read this work in 1889, giving him the necessary introduction to Marxism. By then Lenin was already a committed Jacobin-Blanquist, a commitment which he never wavered. He was convinced that without terror and violence the dictatorship of the proletariat would be an empty phrase.

For all the warning against a minority revolution, Plekhanov entertained the possibilities of realizing socialism in Russia at the earliest. He argued that the Leninist conception of the party independent of spontaneity would lead to the dominance of intellectual and professional revolutionaries and that such a notion was at variance with the Marxist conception of class struggle. He accused Bolshevism of displaying Jacobin-Blanquist tendencies trying to force social development through conspiratorial methods. It was an irony that Plekhanov's opposition to revisionism led to the rise of Leninism though subsequently his criticisms of Leninism brought him closer to revisionism (Baron: 1963). This was because of his unflinching faith that the West European model of development was applicable to Russia. Within this framework he regarded the Bolsheviks as followers of Bakunin rather than Marx. But Plekhanov did help eventually in the establishment of the Marxist state in Russia.

In 1903 during a debate within the RSDLP over the Leninist conception of the party, a question was posed as to whether such a conception would not be incompatible with socialism, civil liberties and dignity of the individual. To this Plekhanov replied that if the revolution demanded it then democracy, freedom and individual would be sacrificed to it. He castigated the Bolsheviks and Lenin after the Bolshevik seizure of power for acting too hastily, but he himself was not prepared to wait and endure with patience for the right moment. He looked to the Bolshevik seizure of power as an act of madness. He also insisted that a true revolution had to be a democratic one even though he was out to destroy Bernstein totally during the revisionist controversy. He contended that if socialism was imposed through force, it would be politically deformed, a renewed Tsarist dictatorship with a Communist visage. In 1918, a dying man, he felt responsibility for what Lenin had done. He told an old colleague with whom he spent his last hours in a tone of regret that he probably had not done the right thing by beginning a propaganda of Marxism too early in a country that was backward and pre-modern. This summed up the dilemma and the subsequent distortion of Soviet Marxism both at the level of theory and practice.

Vladimir Ilyich Ulyanov Lenin

In fact Lenin had no *political* philosophy covering a post-revolutionary period, no notion that a proletarian democracy might require any system of sanctions to control its representatives. The gap was filled by authoritarian expediency (Conquest 1972: 122).

When I met Lenin, I had much less impression of a great man than I expected; my most vivid impressions were of bigotry and Mongolian cruelty . . . and again his guffaw at the thought of those massacred made my blood run cold (Russell 1948: 35–44; 1950: 171).

Lenin applies Marxism to the age of imperialism; he restates the Marxian theory of the state, placing the doctrine of the dictatorship of the proletariat in the centre of all things; apart from the theory of socialism, he provides a tactical handbook for the use of all revolutionaries (Gray 1946: 461).

In the twentieth century, Vladimir Ilyich Ulyanov Lenin (1870–1924) occupies an important position as one of its makers. He had led the October Revolution of 1917 and established the first communist state in Russia. He was primarily a strategist with a keen purpose of fomenting a social revolution, and secondarily a theoretician. Most of his tracts were in response to issues that confronted him as a revolutionary tactician. He ensured the success of the regime through a bloody civil war, founded the Communist International and subsequently initiated the new economic policy to sustain the system in the erstwhile Soviet Union. In deference, the communist party invented the term Marxism-Leninism and refused to bury his corpse. The latter was embalmed, placed in the glass case in a mausoleum outside the Kremlin in Red Square for public viewing. On his death, he was hailed as the greatest genius of mankind, creator of the Communist Party of the Soviet Union, founder of the Union of Soviet Socialist Republics, the leader and teacher of the peoples of the whole world. However, 70 years later when the communist system collapsed in the Soviet Union, the deification gave way to frustration, anger and even total rejection of the Leninist heritage.

Lenin rejected the social democratic approach of continual reforms within capitalism for that was the result of economic advantages that skilled workers, 'the aristocracy of labour', enjoyed, thereby losing their class solidarity. Therefore, he advocated staging of a revolution by subjective action with the help of a body of professional revolutionaries. He was the first to lay down the ground rules with regard to mass mobilization and manipulation that was emulated by others like Mussolini, Hitler, Stalin and Mao.

Lenin resurrected the controversial and ambiguous Marxist concept of the dictatorship of the proletariat which he regarded as the necessary transitional period from capitalism to socialism. His most important contribution was his conception of the Vanguard Party consisting of highly disciplined and committed Marxists who would guide, educate and produce a revolution on behalf of the working class who were unable to transcend their narrow economic interests.

Leninism was criticized by Kautsky, Luxemburg, Julius Martov (1873–1923) and Bernstein. All his critics pointed to the lack of democratic norms and culture in the Bolshevik experiment. Lenin attempted half-heartedly to liberalize the Soviet system during the phase of the new economic policy but that was confined only to the economic field. The failure to liberalize politically led to the rise of Stalinism. If the latter was a malignant form of Leninism, then Leninism itself was an authoritarian offshoot of Marxism.

For the Russian Marxists, the central problem was the nature of the impending revolution. Plekhanov cautioned against the establishment of premature socialism in a relatively backward and autocratic country like the Tsarist Russia. Lenin regarded Plekhanov's observations as a gospel and reiterated his views on the industrialization of Russia and the need for a bourgeois democratic revolution before commencing on a struggle to bring about socialism. He justified the October Revolution as socialistic and the February Kerensky Revolution as bourgeois democratic.

Biographical Sketch

Vladimir Ilyich Ulyanov, later and popularly known as Lenin since 1901, was born on 22 April 1870 in Simbirsk on the Volga. The city represented the confluence of both European and Asiatic cultures. Lenin was brought up in an Europeanizing ambiance. He was the second son and the third child of Ilya Nikolayevich Ulyanov and Maria. His father was a school inspector who had achieved the status of minor nobility.

Lenin was expelled from the Kazan University in 1887 for student radicalism and subsequently passed the law exam in 1891 by studying on his own. In 1887 his elder brother Alexander Ulyanov was arrested and executed for attempted assassination of Alexander III. Soon he was attracted to revolutionary activity and joined the Marxist group in the Russian capital of St. Petersburg in the early part of 1890. He became a lawyer and pursued his studies of Marxist literature. During this time he met Martov and they became good friends.

In the mid-1890s, Marxist ideas were extremely popular among the Russian intelligentsia. During this time Lenin wrote *The Development of Capitalism in Russia* (1899), considered to be the bulkiest and his best published work. From 1893 to 1900 Lenin's Marxism was orthodox. In 1895 he was allowed to go abroad for treatment of his pneumonia. While in Geneva he met Plekhanov, Zasulich and Axelrod who had been there, setting up as Russia's first Marxist study group (the Emancipation of Labour group), since 1893. Though he was in broad agreement with their ideas, he found them inclined towards the liberals forgetting that such an approach had to be tactical rather than a principled alliance. In spite of his reservations, he agreed to extend and broaden the organization to Russia.

On his return to Russia, he resumed his contacts and, with the help of Martov and others, founded the Petersburg League of Struggle for the Emancipation of the Working Class. They also prepared an illegal newspaper. In December 1895 he was arrested with most of the other members and sent to Siberia. 'It was here that he read of, and reacted to, events which were to bring to an end to his more or less gradualist and orthodox phase of Marxism and lead to the Leninist version proper' (Conquest 1972: 25). He was released in 1900 and, except for two years from November 1905 to December 1907, he remained in exile up to the revolution of 1917. It was during his exile that intra-party struggles were fought within the Russian Social Democratic Labour Party founded in 1898.

During his exile Bernstein's *Evolutionary Socialism* (1899) was published. Fearing that the latter's observations on trade unionism or economism of the working class could be true, Lenin chose to insist on the need for voluntary and decisive individual action. By the turn of the century he became the co-editor of the Marxist journal *Iskra* (the Spark) and what came to be known as Leninism became evident in his *What is to be done?* (1902). Here he defended the need for a highly disciplined and organized communist party that would act as the vanguard of the working class. The party would be based on the principles of secrecy, centralization, specialization and exclusivity. This all-encompassing and powerful role of the party was the most important post-Marx development within Marxism. In 1903 Lenin lead a successful struggle to split the fledging Russian Social Democratic Labour Party (RSDLP) at its London Conference with Lenin's followers adopting the name of 'Bolsheviks' which meant *majority* in Russian. The others were Mensheviks which meant *minority*.

During the next decade Lenin attempted to instill rigid centralism within the Bolshevik movement, edited several new journals and founded the *Pravda* in 1912. He returned to Russia in April 1917 and plunged into revolutionary politics arguing that all power ought to pass from the newly formed liberal provisional government to the Soviet of Soldiers and Workers Deputies. In the fall of 1917, the Bolsheviks came into power in a second revolution and for the next seven years attempted to establish a viable worker-peasant state while awaiting a Western socialist revolution that would end Russia's new isolation. Lenin was known to be generous and open with his family and friends though he was highly intolerant. Unlike other tyrants, he did not desire riches nor amass wealth. He remained modest, working for 16 hours in a day and reading extensively. Like Marx, he was fond of total power and, unlike Marx, enjoyed it too.

On 26 May 1922 Lenin suffered his first stroke which forced him to withdraw from active politics. On 9 March 1923 he suffered a final stroke which left him paralyzed. He finally died on 21 January 1924.

The Party Organization

From the Emancipation of Labour emerged the RSDLP in 1898. It was founded in Minsk. The former's original founders, Plekhanov, Axelrod and Zaulich, were joined by Lenin, Martov and A.N. Potresov, and the six of them jointly edited a journal called *Iskra* (Spark). In 1903, while debating on the nature of the organization of the RSDLP, Lenin proposed a 'narrow' party to be composed as far as possible of trained revolutionaries as opposed to an 'open' party of mere sympathizers. Lenin considered economism as a serious threat to the maintenance of a revolutionary spirit among the Russian workers.

In his attack on economism Lenin pointed out the similarites between economism and Bernstein's revisionism and the fact that socialism could not develop out of trade union struggles. For Lenin the immediate fight was against economism and revisionism as is evident from the startling change he made from his earlier articulated views in the *Development of Capitalism in Russia*. This change was perhaps due to the fact that he feared Bernstein to be right, which implied that the domestication of the working class was because of trade unions thus rendering the Marxist prophecy of a proletarian revolution as redundant. Unlike Bernstein, Lenin felt that strong subjective action should be undertaken to prevent this social tendency. Through a series of articles in the *Iskra* Lenin developed his view which formed the text of *What is to be done?* This pamphlet can be rightly regarded as the key document of Leninism and Lenin's most original contribution.

> The working class exclusively by its own efforts is able to develop only trade-union consciousness . . . . Modern socialist consciousness can only be brought to them from without . . . can arise only on the basis of profound scientific knowledge. The bearers of science are not the proletariat but the bourgeois intelligentsia. It is out of the heads of members of this stratum that modern socialism originated . . . Pure and simple trade unionism means the ideological subordination of the workers to the bourgeoisie . . . . Our task is to bring the labour movement under the wing of revolutionary Social-democracy (Lenin, cited in Conquest 1972: 38–9).

This clearly reflected a change and an abandonment of the earlier view that Lenin upheld in the 1890s. Here he espoused a more orthodox position:

> The task of the party does not consist in thinking up out of its head any kind of modern methods of helping the workers, but in linking itself with the labour movement . . . The workers acquire an understanding of all this (class consciousness) by constantly drawing it from the very struggle which they are beginning to wage against the factory owners . . . The struggle of the workers against the factory owners for their daily needs of itself and inevitably forces the workers to think about the state, about political questions (Ibid.: 24–5).

In the changed perspective, Lenin combined the elite revolutionism of Chernyshevsky and the rest with the majoritarian workers movement that Marx emphasized. A point to be noted was that there was an agreement on the need for a conscious party leadership acting in unison with the masses on the outside but the disagreement between what came to be known as 'Bolshevism' and 'Menshevism' was with regard to the nature of the party organization.

Luxemburg agreed with Lenin but did not assent to his blunt rejection of 'spontaneous working class movement'. The differences in the perceptions of Bernstein, Lenin and Luxemburg can be summarized as follows:

> ... while Lenin dealt with this situation by retaining revolutionary Marxism and renouncing democracy, since he believed that the proletariat unaided from "without" could not attain revolutionary class consciousness just as Robespierre believed that the "people could not express their 'real will' without proper enlightenment". Bernstein dealt with this situation by renouncing revolutionary Marxism and retaining democracy. Luxemburg held on to both—revolutionary Marxism and democracy (Elliot 1967: 86).

While Luxemburg's attempt failed, Lenin's succeeded which was because he saw, and she did not, the necessity of dealing with a non-revolutionary proletariat. On the eve of the Spartacus uprising in Germany, Luxemburg delared that the proletariat need not resort to terrorism for it had the 'historical necessity' on its side. Lenin, on the contrary, argued that even though 'historical necessity' was on the side of the proletariat it would not be adequate in assisting the workers to seize political power. Since the working class refused to adopt the Marxist revolutionary myth, this 'consciousness' must be thrust upon it 'from without'. Luxemburg refused to accept Lenin's contention. Perhaps the common point between Lenin and Bernstein was the acceptance of the fact that the industrial proletariat was overwhelmingly rejecting revolutionary Marxism though their remedial measures were poles apart. More than Bernstein, it was Lenin who introduced a 'profound revision' in the Marxist doctrine (Lipset 1963a: 65).

The RSDLP headed for a split on the issue of party membership and the degree of commitment of the party members. The Bolsheviks desired only those members who took an active part in the activities of the organization and the Mensheviks were content to have on rolls anyone who lent continuous personal support to the organizations' activities. The former won the issue with Plekhanov rallying behind Lenin's proposals carrying with him a sizable number of votes.

The RSDLP in its programme reiterated the notion of the dictatorship of the proletariat which was defined as the conquest of political power by the proletariat. It called for the overthrow of the tsarist autocracy and setting up of a constituent assembly by the whole people as a first step towards realizing socialism. This pro- gramme remained the party policy till 1919. Thus the 'years 1901– 03 marked a new stage in the development of Russian Marxism and Russian social democracy. During this time the foundations were laid of the Leninist variant of Marxism, the novelty and spe- cific character of which were visible only in degrees' (Kolakowski 1981c: 329).

Bolsheviks and Mensheviks

Lenin and the Bolsheviks called for an immediate establishment of a proletarian dictatorship while the Mensheviks, along with the other Right-wingers led by Lev Borisovich Kamnev (1883–1936), urged that a longer period of parliamentary government was nec- essary to enable the proletariat to prepare itself for power.

For the Bolsheviks, the Marxist Party would have to act like the *avant-garde* of the industrial proletariat in leading it to its predes- tined path. The Mensheviks believed that a party must be a mass organization, built from below. It must be a collection of autono- mous units. Lenin, on the other hand, believed that the party must fulfill the following: strict discipline, absolute control of the party authorities over its organizations and a clear dividing line between the party and the working class. It would be organized on the prin- ciple of democratic centralism with democracy at each level but not between the various layers. The lower cell would be allowed to make its decisions but it would be subject to scrutiny and veto by the immediate next cell. The party organization would resemble a pyramid with the central committee as the supreme decision- making body. The critics of Lenin feared that such an organization might degenerate into an autocracy and eventually result in the personalized rule of one person.

Lenin tried to counter these criticisms by asserting that this was not the case, but subsequently clarified that he did not mind even if it was. He rebuked Bukharin in 1921 for failing to understand the need to subordinate formal democracy to revolutionary expe- diency. In March 1918 he asserted that: 'there is no absolutely no contradiction in principle between soviet democratism and the use of dictatorial power by single individuals. . .how can the strictest unity of will be ensured? By the subordination of the will of thousands to the will of one' (Lenin, cited in Conquest 1972: 46).

In 1920 Lenin went to the extent of asserting that the 'will of the class is sometimes given effect by a dictator, who sometimes does more alone, and often is more necessary'. Luxemburg dismissed Lenin's principles as amounting to ultra-centralism with the Central Committee appearing to be the real active nucleus of the party and all other organizations merely as its executive organs. She rightly observed: 'Nothing will more surely enslave a young labour movement to an intellectual elite hungry for power than this bureaucratic straitjacket, which will immobilize the movement and turn it into an automaton manipulated by the Central Committee' (Luxemburg, cited in Conquest 1972: 47).

Axelrod feared that if the workers were subordinated to the revolutionary intelligentsia then they might be used in the ensuing revolution as mere cannon-fodders. Trotsky prophetically proclaimed that the Leninist party organization would lead to centralization and despotism.[4]

The Mensheviks maintained that the Russian revolution at first would have to be a bourgeois revolution led by the bourgeoisie and resulting in the establishment of a bourgeois democratic government. Lenin accepted their claim but rejected their view that the bourgeoisie would lead the revolution. In his view, a revolution would only succeed if it was directed against the bourgeoisie and made possible through an alliance between the proletariat and the peasantry. This would culminate in the establishment of a revolutionary and a democratic dictatorship of the proletariat and the peasantry.

The Mensheviks emphasized trade union activity and the intrinsic value of any improvements the working class might secure by legislation or by strike action. To Lenin, all such activity was valuable only in so far as it helped to prepare the working class for the final conflict. The former regarded democratic freedoms as valuable in themselves while to Lenin these were tactical weapons that might serve the party under particular circumstances.

Besides the Mensheviks and the Bolsheviks, there was a third position articulated by Trotsky. As opposed to the Mensheviks, Trotsky was in favour of seizure of power by the proletariat and was opposed to any collaboration with the bourgeoisie. He agreed with Lenin about the lack of revolutionary potential in the liberal bourgeoisie but asserted that Lenin had over-estimated the prospects of an independent revolutionary republic with the proletariat and peasantry in alliance. Consequently, Trotsky was confident that the proletariat would have a predominant and decisive influence in the revolutionary government. He rejected any such alliance for he did not trust the peasantry which was inherently conservative, and for the fact that the proletariat was still numerically weak. He felt that a revolution in Russia would only succeed provided there were similar revolutions in advanced capitalist countries. Once in power, the proletariat would initiate radical reforms with regard to property rights and would fight to defend its rule.

From 1905 to 1917

For Lenin, the bourgeois democratic revolution in Russia had to be effected through a revolutionary alliance between the proletariat and the peasantry. This would establish a bourgeois state and develop a capitalist economy since Russia was not ready for a socialist revolution. He worked out a concept of democratic dictatorship of the proletariat and the peasantry. Unlike Marx, he believed in the revolutionary potential of the peasantry, a theme that is expanded and developed by Mao.

The *Two Tactics of Social Democracy* (1905) explicitly and formally rejected the Paris Commune of 1871 as a model for the Russian revolution. According to Lenin, the commune went wrong because it was unable to distinguish between the elements of a democratic revolution and a socialist revolution by confusing the tasks of fighting for a republic with those of fighting for socialism. He did not regard the Paris Commune as the dictatorship of the proletariat but as the participation of working class representatives with a poorly developed class consciousness in a government of petty bourgeois democracy.

The *Two Tactics of Social Democracy* reveals with extraordinary clarity the tension in Lenin's mind between his rich, revolutionary realism and the limitations imposed in him by the straitjacket of what was called "orthodox Marxism". On the one hand, we find it illuminating and penetrating analyses of the incapacity of the Russian bourgeoisie to lead successfully to a democratic revolution, which can be carried out only by a worker–peasant alliance exercising its revolutionary dictatorship; he even speaks of leading role of the proletariat in this alliance and at times seems to put his finger on the idea of an uninterrupted transition towards socialism: this dictatorship will be unable to affect the foundations of capitalism (Lowy 1976: 7).

However, on the eve of the downfall of Russian Tsarism, in the *April Theses* (1917) which became the basis for his pamphlet *State and Revolution* (1917), Lenin drew a parallel between the Soviets and the Paris Commune. In the first tract he called for a commune state and defended the Paris Commune on the lines similar to those of Marx.

In *Imperialism, the Highest Stage of Capitalism* (1916), Lenin asserted in a scientific manner that imperialism would spell doom for capitalism for it would create the objective condition for a world revolution. He maintained that capitalism had entered a new and final epoch in which competition was replaced by monopoly attenuating concentration of capital and class divisions in society. Export of goods was replaced by export of capital, finance capital, and the entire world was subjected to the parasitic exploitation of the most powerful capitalist states. During the imperial phase capitalism became militaristic, parasitic, oppressive and decadent. Because of concentrated production in trusts and cartels and capital in the banks, the whole economy was brought under social control and ownership. This in itself created the 'complete material basis for socialism'.

Lenin laid down five characteristics of imperialism: (1) the 'export of capital' became the prime objective along with export of commodities; (2) production and distribution became centralized through great trusts and cartels; (3) there was merger of bank and industrial capital which was termed as 'finance capital'; (4) the world was divided into spheres of influence by the capitalist powers, and (5) there was a further re-division bringing forth intercapitalist struggle and rivalry. Lenin's theory followed from Marx' theory of accumulation which looked to capital as expansionary. He looked to the snapping of the weakest link, thereby triggering off a world proletarian revolution. He looked to Russia as that weakest link. In doing so, he accepted that Marx's prediction of a world proletarian revolution in advanced countries had not taken place nor would it take place.

Lenin dealt at length with the colonial situation in his *Thesis on the Colonial Question*. He prepared an advance draft thesis on the national and colonial question for the Second World Congress of the Communist International (Comintern) in July-August 1920. Before the Congress officially met, Lenin circulated his arguments among the delegates for dissensions, comments and criticisms.[5]

Proletarian State and Socialist Democracy

The *State and Revolution* written on the eve of the October Revolution is considered as one of the most authoritative texts written on the nature of the proletarian state and socialist democracy. Prior to this tract, the theory of the state and the concept of the dictatorship of the proletariat never found detailed ramifications in the Classical Marxist Political Theory (Chang 1965: 11; Miliband 1977: 138–9). The core argument of the *State and Revolution* was an affirmation of the revolution as a modicum of destructive violence and of its creative genius. It accepted that 'the revolution cannot be restricted to the seizure of power, it must also be the destruction of the old state' (Colletti 1969: 219). Historically the *State and Revolution* was Lenin's response to what he regarded as an act of treason on the part of German Social Democrats led by Kautsky in supporting Germany's entry into the First World War by voting for war credits (Carnoy 1984: 57).

The origins of the *State and Revolution* lay in the debate between Lenin and Bukharin in 1916 on the nature of the state in the postproletarian revolution phase. 'Lenin's position in 1917 arose from a personal reappraisal of Marxist theory, rather than from a purely tactical grasp of the revolutionary possibilities entailed by the collapse of the Tsarist Russia. *State and Revolution* was the product of both a determinate political conjuncture and a determinate theoretical conjunction' (Sawer 1977: 209). Contrary to Bukharin who reiterated the Anarchist ideal of the withering away of the state, Lenin, reiterating Kautsky, argued that the proletariat must capture the state structure and create socialism but differed from the latter in proposing a revolutionary and violent overthrow of the bourgeoisie.

Lenin, initially averse to Bukharin's views changed his position. This change was occasioned by the spontaneous outgrowth of the Soviets with the onset of the February Revolution. He re-read Marx's writings on the Paris Commune in order to counter Bukharin. He thereby identified the Soviets as the prototype of the dictatorship of the proletariat. In the *April Thesis* he had already advocated the need to establish a Commune State shifting from the position articulated in the *Two Tactics*.

Replying to Bukharin, Lenin in an article published in *Spornik Sotsiak-Democrata* argued that the socialists were in favour of using the present state and its institutions in the struggle for the emancipation of the working class for the state in the form of the dictatorship of the proletariat was the specific form of transition from capitalism to socialism. He also added that the anarchists want to 'abolish' the state, 'blow it up' as Comrade Bukharin expressed it in one place. He also expressed similar sentiments in his notebook which became the main theme in the *State and Revolution*.

Bukharin raised the question of the withering away of the state in the Seventh Party Congress in March 1918 to which Lenin replied, 'one may well wonder when the state will begin to wither away . . . to proclaim this withering away in advance is to violate historical perspective' (Lenin, cited in Sawer 1977: 215). Moreover, during this period Lenin repudiated his earlier positions on the workers' state. His replies affirmed Bukharin's views which he felt were closer to truth than those articulated by Kautsky (Ibid.: 216–18).

Dictatorship of the Proletariat

Lenin regarded the dictatorship of the proletariat as the core of the Marxist thought. In the *Proletarian Revolution and Renegade Kautsky* (1918) he regarded the dictatorship as the 'very essence of the proletarian revolution' (Lenin 1977: 30) ' . . . . only he is a Marxist who extends the recognition of the class struggle to the recognition of the dictatorship of the proletariat. This is what constituted the most profound distinction between the Marxist and ordinary petty (as well as big) bourgeoisie' (Ibid.: 35).

In the *State and Revolution* Lenin reviewed the ideas of Marx and Engels on the state and examined the views of other contemporary Marxist scholars on the subject. Using the model of the Paris Commune, he argued that the proletarian revolution would destroy the bourgeois state and establish the dictatorship of the proletariat for that was the most appropriate political form during the transitional phase. Lenin argued that the bourgeois state with all its democratic instruments was controlled by the bourgeois class and its primary function was direct coercion. Therefore, it had to be destroyed totally. He contrasted the meaning and implication of Engels' notion of the withering away of the state with the anarchist notion of the abolition of the state. The difference for him lay in the fact that the proletarian state would wither away whereas the bourgeois state would be abolished and destroyed.

Lenin defined the state as a special organization of force, an instrument of violence for the suppression of one class, namely the bourgeoisie. He emphasized that the socialist revolution would lead to the political rule of the proletariat and its dictatorship. The proletarian state would wield coercive force but of a different kind; coercion would be exercised by the majority over the minority which was just the reverse of a bourgeois state. The *raison d'être* of the state after the revolution was to crush the resistance of the exploiters and build up a socialist democracy, which he believed could be accomplished only by the proletariat. This transitional state would, for the first time, create democracy for all. Lenin, like Marx, was critical of the representative parliamentary democracy as being a shell to conceal the exploitation of the working class by the bourgeoisie and that it was illusory for it gave the people the impression that they were free and sovereign while in reality they were free and sovereign only during the time when government had to be elected. It was a refinement of Rousseau's indictment of indirect parliamentary democracy as practiced in Britain. The dictatorship of the proletariat would not provisionally but permanently abolish the parliamentary system and the separation of legislature and executive. It was a total rejection of the process of modern constitutional development which began in the USA after the American Revolution of 1776.

Lenin outlined the two-stage development to the attainment of communist society. The first or the lower stage — the socialist phase — would retain the vestiges of the old bourgeois order in which exploitation would continue. The state as a coercive force would continue but, as he remarked, it would be a 'bourgeois state without the bourgeoisie'. The second phase would dawn when the imperative need for the state machinery would have completely disappeared, when society would adopt the rule of 'from each according to his ability to each according to his needs' and when the 'government is replaced by the administration of things'. The antithesis between mental and physical labour would also disappear. The proletarian state would be like the Paris Commune where the workers directly participated and managed the state affairs without a bureaucracy and a standing army. In *Left Wing Communism* (1920) he described the tactics to be employed by the dictatorship of the proletariat.

Lenin christened the first and the second phase as 'socialism' and 'communism', respectively, and since then the two phrases have been used in common parlance. He faithfully reproduced the observations of Marx and Engels on the dictatorship of the proletariat and the communist society and, in the process, added a 'permanent ideology to Marxism, namely, that the attainment of the communist society would be two-phased' (Sabine 1973: 762). For Lenin, the dictatorship of the proletariat would be a political concept, 'a rule won and maintained by violence by the proletariat against the bourgeois rule unrestricted by any laws' (Lenin 1977: 117). It would be viable only through the vanguard of the proletariat, the Workers' Party, for he had very little faith in the industrial proletariat as a mass.

> The proletariat needs state power, the centralized organization of force, the organization of violence, both for the purpose of crushing the resistance of the exploiters and for the purpose of guiding the great mass of the population . . . in the work of organizing socialist economy. By educating a workers' party, Marxism educated the vanguard of the proletariat, capable of directing and organizing the new order, or being a teacher, guide and leader of all toiling and exploited in the task of building up their social life without the bourgeoisie and against the bourgeoisie (Ibid.: 28).

Miliband (1977: 179–80) correctly commented that the Leninist model was illusory for if the revolution of the kind as in Russia had to succeed what was needed was the creation of a 'proper' state. Such a state had to be strong for it had to organize the process of transition from capitalism to a communist society. The concept of the dictatorship of the proletariat as used and understood by Marx was of little help for it meant the exercise of political power directly through representative institutions, strictly subordinated to the people. Such a power was always popular. Unlike Marx who conceived of a majoritarian revolution, Lenin spoke of a minority revolution made by the vanguard party on behalf of the proletarian mass. Therefore, given the scheme of minority revolution, a majoritarian popular government in the meaning that was assigned to it was not feasible. Moreover, the proletarian state, for Lenin, would continue to be the state. The revolution would end the bourgeois state but not the state as such the difference being that in the bourgeois democratic state it was the interests of the bourgeois minority that would be protected while the proletarian state promoted and furthered the interests of the proletarian majority. The latter represented the quintessence of true democracy.

The *State and Revolution*, however, neglected the problem of political articulation and political organization. This meant more an avoidance rather than the resolution of the question. It became all the more tricky, given Lenin's emphasis on the need and role of the vanguard party (Miliband 1977: 182). Lenin's conception of a minority revolution to be led by the vanguard party of the workers defeated the majoritarian connotations of the transitional state as outlined in the *State and Revolution*. Even more tricky was the role of the soviets and workers' councils which represented spontaneity. He was skeptical of their role till the eve of the revolution. The *State and Revolution* did not examine the relationship between the soviets and the vanguard party. It was when Kautsky accused the Bolshevik regime of violating democracy that Lenin described the role of the soviets.

> The Soviets are the Russian form of the proletarian dictatorship . . . . it created the most all embracing form of proletarian organization, for it embraced all workers. In 1905 they were only local bodies; in 1917 they became a national organization. The Soviets are the direct organization of the working class and exploited people themselves, which helps them to organize and administer their own state in every possible way . . . . Soviet power is a million times more

democratic than the most democratic republic (Lenin 1977: 127–8, 137).

However, in a short period of time, after the revolution, the regime in the Soviet Union became the dictatorship of the Bolshevik Party. The party came to enjoy an irretrievable and an irrevocable position largely because of the failure to:

distinguish between the dictatorship of the proletariat and the dictatorship of the party is a proof of an unbelievable and inextricable confusion of thought. In 1921 Lenin bluntly asserted against the criticisms of workers' opposition, and declared that the dictatorship of the proletariat is impossible except through the Communist Party (Carr 1979: 230).

Critics of Leninism

The Russian Revolution and the Leninist experiment were severely criticized both within and outside Russia. Most of his critics unanimously concurred that it amounted to an absence of democracy and the lack of sufficient institutional checks against abuse of power. From a social democratic standpoint, Bernstein dubbed the revolution as a counter-revolution and regarded Bolshevism as a 'brutalized' version of Marxism for it relied on terror and violence and was contemptuous of civilized behaviour. It was a continuation of his earlier theoretical posture and personal conviction that socialism ought to eschew all forms of dictatorship and violence.

Martov and the Mensheviks contended that Russia was not ready for a socialist revolution in view of her general backwardness. Martov was skeptical of the methods and tactics of the Bolsheviks and felt that Russia was not yet ready for a socialist revolution in view of its backwardness. He upheld Plekhanov's theory of bourgeois revolution and warned against the consequences of a premature socialist revolution. He insisted that Russia was still economically and socially backward and, therefore, lacked the prerequisites for a socialist revolution. Its petty-bourgeois masses lacked the will for socialism. In such a situation the social democrats had no right to seize and employ state power to 'neutralize the resistance of the petty bourgeois to the socialist aspirations of the proletariat'.

Following Marx's advice, Martov viewed the role of the social democrats as a militant revolutionary opposition. He instructed them to get entrenched in the 'organs of revolutionary self government' such as the Soviets, trade unions, workers' clubs, cooperatives, and pressurize the official bourgeois democratic government to implement democratic policies. Subsequently, he called for a coalition of a socialist government in view of the failure of the bourgeois parties to capitalize on the situation between February and October 1917. This coalition, he hoped, would accomplish the bourgeois revolution by establishing a democratic republic, capitalist economy and social reforms.

Martov rejected the Leninist conception of a minority revolution led by a disciplined well organized workers' party with covert or overt mass support on the grounds that it would only institutionalize dictatorship or 'commissarocracy'. He regarded the Leninist model as a flagrant departure from the majoritarian perceptions of Marx and Engels as they had visualized in their scheme of the dictatorship of the proletariat. He claimed that, for Marx, the dictatorship of the proletariat meant the conscious will of the proletarian majority directing its revolutionary power against the capitalist minority with the view to neutralize their resistance. It meant the transfer of political power to the working class legally. In his view, Lenin had imposed the will of a 'conscious revolutionary minority' on an unconscious majority reducing the latter to a position of passive object of social experimentation.

For Martov, the distinguishing feature between the revolutionary Marxists and the social democrats was their commitment with regard to state power of the toiling masses. The Bolsheviks or the revolutionary Marxists or the communists articulated a view of minority dictatorship and also created institutions that would reinforce dictatorship on a permanent basis. In view of Russia's backwardness, socialism would be one of 'barrack socialism'. The social democrats, on the other hand, were committed to realizing both socialism and democracy. Martov's position coincided with that of Kautsky.

The Mensheviks and Martov regarded the October Revolution as a *coup d'etat*. Subsequently, Martov and some of the Mensheviks lent their support to the Bolsheviks during the civil war while the others participated in the anti-Soviet actions of the imperial West. Martov continued to believe that the working class organization and consciousness could be developed gradually through the growth of productive forces and democratic institutions, thus preparing the material basis for socialism.

Trotsky, in his reply to Martov, contended that the Russian revolution would trigger off revolutions in the advanced West and the latter would rescue the former from its backwardness. But he had no convincing answer to the query as to what would happen if a revolution in the advanced West failed to materialize. Interestingly, Trotsky in the 1930s feared that it was the very backwardness of Russia that would subsume the socialist ideals of the October Revolution.

Lenin's reply to Martov was also weak. In his pamphlet *Will the Bolsheviks Retain State Power* he wrote that if 130,000 landowners were able to govern Russia in the past, why could not 240,000 members of the Bolsheviks party govern it now? To this, Martov and others replied that 'Yes, you may be able to stay in power with your 240,000 members but only insofar as you approach and then exceed the repressive measures of the 130,000 landowners'. In response, Lenin retreated partially and launched the new economic policy (NEP) acknowledging that more time would be needed to build socialism, and tried to liberalize the economy. This was attempted without bringing about political democracy and civil liberties. The lack of political liberalization only strengthened the autocracy under Stalin who introduced forced collectivism, industrialization, nationalization and also simultaneously increased mass terror, mass murders and purges, thus confirming the worst fears harboured by Martov.

The suspension of the constituent assembly and the suppression of universal suffrage provoked both Kautsky and Luxemburg to virulently denounce the revolution and Leninism. Both castigated Lenin for disregarding democratic norms and procedures and feared that the minority revolution would lead to militarization and bureaucratization. Luxemburg was sanguine that the abandonment of spontaneity would only encourage centralization and personal dictatorship.[6]

Kropotkin, like Luxemburg, felt that party dictatorship would eventually deaden spontaneous creativity of the masses and impressed upon Lenin that local initiative could be brought about only by local forces. The party bosses would only destroy the soviets and the anarchists feared that the centralized party would subvert popular revolution. The anarchists considered the destruction of the provisional government by the masses in February 1917 and not the Bolshevik Revolution of October 1917 as the real revolution. In fact, Kropotkin was delighted when the Tsarist autocracy fell though he rejected a cabinet post of minister of education that Kerensky offered.

Kropotkin met Lenin in 1919 to caution him about the worst excesses committed by the Bolshevik regime. He complained of the persecution of the cooperatives and the local authorities. He felt that the Bolsheviks replicated a centralized state that closely resembled the one that Babeuf proposed with full dictatorial powers. Such a state in his opinion would paralyze the reconstruction work of the people undermining success totally. Lenin impatiently dismissed these observations as 'stupid' and the views of one who did not know much about politics.[7]

Reply to and Denouncement of Kautsky

Lenin, along with Trotsky, castigated Kautsky to be a 'renegade'[8] for having betrayed not only the revolutionary conceptions of Marx and Engels but even of his own past as well. Beyond this he was not particularly worried about the repercussions of Kautsky's attack for political forces within Russia were clearly drawn but was more concerned about its effects on the impending German revolution. Since Kautsky was a venerable figure within the socialist movement and his views were at variance with those of the Bolsheviks, Lenin felt it would be futile to provide a detailed critique. But by November 1918 the fate of German revolution was decided. Since Lenin's expectations of a world revolution did not materialize and the fact that the European proletariat, particularly in Germany, followed the tactics of Kautsky rather than those prescribed by Lenin, the latter realized that there was a need to furnish a reply to Kautsky within a Marxist paradigm.

Lenin in his *Proletarian Revolution and Renegade Kautsky* pointed out that the fundamental question which Kautsky discussed concerned the very essence of the proletarian revolution, namely, the dictatorship of the proletariat. The contrast between the Bolshevik and the non-Bolshevik socialist movement was a contrast between two diametrically opposite methods, dictatorial and democratic. For Lenin, the question of the dictatorship of the proletariat was with regard to the relationship of the proletarian state to the bourgeois states, of the proletarian democracy to the bourgeois democracy, a fact that Kautsky had overlooked.

Lenin vehemently reacted to the remark by Kautsky that Marx had used the phrase 'dictatorship of the proletariat' only once. In fact, Kautsky himself had called it a 'little word' (*wortchen*). Lenin clarified that dictatorship did not mean the absence of democracy. To a Marxist, Lenin contended, the class connotation of a regime was of crucial importance. 'Dictatorship does not mean the abolition of democracy for the class that exercises the dictatorship over other classes; but it does mean the abolition of democracy for the class over which, or against which, the dictatorship is exercised' (Lenin 1977: 116).

Lenin dismissed Kautsky's assertion that democracy was compatible with and a precondition to proletarian rule as nonsense. He argued that since the proletariat was governing, it must govern by force, and dictatorship was a government by force and not by law. 'Dictatorship is rule based directly upon force and not by law. The revolutionary dictatorship of the proletariat is rule won and maintained by the use of violence by the proletariat against the bourgeoisie, rule that is restricted by any laws' (Ibid.: 117).

Lenin's other refutations were not that substantive. He merely contended that Kautsky displayed his ignorance and did not argue like a true Marxist. Furthermore, he pointed out that Kautsky's opposition to the conversion of the soviets into state organization and for his refusal to recognize in them the dictatorship of the proletariat lay in his rejection of revolutionary violence under the militaristic-bureaucratic conditions of imperialistic capitalism.

> For Lenin the revolution is not only the transfer of power from one class to another, it is also the passage from one type of power to another; for him the two things go together because the working class that seizes power is the working class that governs itself. For Kautsky the seizure of power does not mean the construction of new power but simply the promotion to the use of the old power of the political personnel who represent the working class but are not the working class themselves (Colletti 1969: 219).

In the post-1917 period Kautsky interpreted dictatorship of the proletariat as the dictatorship of the proletarian majority. Socialism did not mean management of power in the name of the masses but an exercise of power by the masses.

Conclusion

The important gaps left by Marx in his theory of the state created controversies and generated debates in the first two decades of the twentieth century. As far as the basic principles were concerned there was a considerable disagreement between Bernstein, Kautsky, Lenin and Luxemburg. Within the camp of the Russian Marxists too, there were significant differences.

The opposing views of Russian Marxists led by Lenin and the Western Marxists reflected two very different situations. In Germany where the followers of Marxism were the largest and with the existence of the powerful Social Democratic Party, the lot of the working class was improving rather than deteriorating, and this was contrary to Marx's predictions. The collapse of capitalism did not seem imminent. The working class also had lost its revolutionary spirit. The majority of the SPD members concentrated on utilizing the existing state structure to secure practical benefits in hope of reforming and transcending its bourgeois class basis and evolve gradually but definitely towards an egalitarian, democratic, socialist and an emancipatory society. The Labour Party in Britain was also working towards that direction. The situation in France was similar. All these indicators meant that the 'Marx's apocalyptic vision of capitalism in its last throes bore little relevance to conditions in the most industrialized countries' (Grenville 1980: 246).

Instead of analyzing the social and economic basis of what he contemptuously referred to as 'revisionism', Lenin believed that through positive subjective action rooted in a violent revolutionary seizure of power the social developments that the revisionists spoke about would be surmounted. ' . . . Lenin tacitly admitted that Marxism, that product of thought and conditions of the 1840s and 1850s needed a thorough revision. But *his* revisionism Lenin was to proclaim as orthodoxy' (Ulam 1922: 203).

The majority of the socialists were against Lenin and thought that he was dividing the rank and file of socialists. Even among the Russian socialists up to the revolution of 1917, his following was only among the minority. As such, the entire thrust of Marx's concept of a majoritarian and democratic revolutionary transformation was set aside by Lenin's conspiratorial tactics and strategy that the vanguard party would pursue and this at best could be described as insurrectionist politics. Lenin justified his advocacy of utmost centralization and secrecy with autonomy at the local level but subject to the right of veto by the central committee of the party due to the repressive conditions in Tsarist Russia, to the backwardness of the Russian working class and the woolly mindedness of the Russian intelligentsia. Though it was first enunciated by Kautsky, the notion of the Communist Party was distinctive to Leninism and original to Marxism. It had become since the prototype for future revolutionary party organizations.

Lenin, the chief spokesman of Bolshevism, looked to theory for explanation, justification and defence of a practice. His entire persona was devoted to organizing revolutionary activity. In fact

> virtually the total force of his personality was concentrated on the broadly political — to a far greater degree than Marx's had been. Everything else in his life appears as no more than mild, brief and absentminded relaxation. Where some truly non-political matter really took his time and energy, he gave it up, as with chess . . . . his life and character appear as not just predominantly, but almost totally, political (Conquest 1972: 32–33).

Once he returned from exile (1897–1900) and resumed political activity, he was concerned about the ability of the working class to develop socialist consciousness. This concern became more serious from 1902–03 thus sparking off a debate within the RSDLP on the need for a vanguard party of professional revolutionaries to act on the behest of the working class. In 1917, on the eve of the October Revolution, he was confident of the spontaneous role of the workers, which explained his libertarian outlook in the *State and Revolution* as opposed to the authoritarianism of *What is to be done*? This change was due to the spontaneous growth of soviets. Theoretically also, he had to meet the challenge posed by Bukharin who advocated the need to smash rather than capture, as Lenin did, the existing state apparatus in a situation of revolutionary seizure of power.

The concept of the dictatorship of the proletariat would have ceased to be controversial had not Lenin resurrected it in his campaign against Bukharin. The *State and Revolution* has been regarded as the most substantive contribution of Lenin to political theory (Colletti 1969). With the imminence of a proletarian revolution, it became imperative to define the post-revolutionary state and the nature and form that socialist democracy would assume.

For Lenin, the dictatorship of the proletariat represented both a *regime* and a *form* of government. He distinguished bourgeois democracy, which in his opinion was narrow and formal, from the proletarian counterpart characterized as truly and fully participatory and free, and regarded the transitional state as necessary for removing the vestiges of the old order and for creating and ushering in the new society. This meant that the proletarian revolution did not destroy the state altogether, for some kind of state does continue under the dictatorship of the proletariat but this would be a qualitatively a different state.

In reality, the Leninist revolution was a minority revolution. The Bolsheviks following Lenin displayed very little faith or confidence in the masses. As Gorky noted of Lenin that he 'had no pity for the mass of the people' and that 'the working class are to Lenin what minerals are to a metallurgist'. Economically, Russia was backward, semi-industrialized and predominantly agrarian. Politically, she was authoritarian with a lack of democratic culture and civil liberties. Lenin himself acknowledged that lack of culture and the fact that they did not know how to rule as the chief deficiencies of the Soviet political system. He was also equally unaware of the need of a political regime in the post-revolutionary phase to have a set of rules which would enable him to deal with problems of real politics. Marx was hardly helpful on this issue. As Djilas aptly pointed out, Marxism lacked a theory of political liberty. Having visualized his classless communist society as a non-conflictive and a harmonious one, Marx could never comprehend the dynamics of the democratic functioning of a modern society and the fact that individuals function rarely as isolated creatures but very often through group(s) which serve to articulate and represent the plural and diverse interests in society. Marx's mistake was to assume that a classless society would necessarily mean a homogenous and unitarian one. This fallacy, coupled with the Leninist emphasis on a vanguard party, led to the emergence of a monolithic party system in the erstwhile USSR that straddled and terrorized all aspects of civil society. The monopolistic position that the CPSU held, as given to it by Article 6 of the Soviet Constitution, was never really examined at any point when political reforms were contemplated and initiated. It was finally revoked in 1989–90 in the wake of de-Leninisation and that led to the mushrooming of diverse political groups.

In the absence of a philosophy for the post-revolutionary phase, coupled with the backwardness of Russia and the absence of a democratic culture both within Tsarist Russia and the Leninist model, the minority nature of the Bolshevik Revolution reconstructed the state with total power under the guidance of the vanguard party. This was inevitable if the revolution had to succeed and, given its essential minority character, it was impossible to conceive of a majoritarian government.

Gramsci rightly pointed out that an advanced state ruled by perfecting the ideological apparatus rather than through repressive measures like force and terror. He understood the tenacity and strength of societal forces within advanced capitalism where the capitalist class asserted its hegemony, making a genuine communist revolution virtually impossible unless it was carried out in a Leninist manner. The Leninist model would never serve the democratic aspirations of communism. It was for this reason that Gramsci remarked that in the Soviet Union 'the state was everything and civil society, nothing', implying that enormous differences existed between backward Russia and advanced capitalism.

It would be easy, and perhaps misleading, to attribute the transformation of the dictatorship of the proletariat into a dictatorship by the party to the particularly trying circumstances Russia found herself in 1917, namely, foreign intervention, civil war, the international isolation of the Soviet regime and massive deprivation. But there was no denying of the fact that Lenin and his followers, right from the beginning, justified the use of force and terror. Immediately after capturing power in January 1918, the constituent assembly was dissolved for which the Bolsheviks had secured only 25 per cent of the votes and were in a minority. The slogan 'all power to the soviets' lost its essence in the midst of the civil war and militarization of public life. Slowly the soviets faded out of existence. The Mensheviks, in spite of their growing support were suppressed. In fact, any sign of anti-Bolshevism was denounced as counter-revolutionary and all opposition parties were suppressed. One-man management was re-introduced. Trade unions became totally subordinated to political authority. In June 1918, Lenin exclaimed that 'the energy and mass nature of the terror must be encouraged'. The extensive use of terror was resorted to in order to deal with 'crafty and cunning counter-revolutionaries' or those who engaged in a 'plot of intrigue against the Soviet'. In 1919 Lenin remarked: 'We recognize neither freedom, nor equality, nor labour democracy if they are opposed to the interests of the emancipation of labour from the oppression of capital (Lenin, cited in Conquest 1972: 104).

In 1920 Lenin defended the increased use of 'revolutionary violence' as necessary against the unrestrained and faltering sections within the working class itself. In December 1917 the secret police or the 'cheka' was formed. One example of the senseless use of terror was when the members of the royal family were executed which included their doctor, their nurse and their dog. The climax of Leninist authoritarianian was in March 1921 at the Tenth Party Congress which met a few weeks after the brutal suppression of Kronstadt rebellion, a rebellion spearheaded by those who had wholeheartedly supported the October Revolution.

At this Congress Lenin initiated two proposals, first 'the immediate dissolution of all groups without exception', and second that 'only the political party of the working class, i.e., the Communist Party, was capable of uniting, training and organizing a vanguard of the proletariat and of the whole mass of the working people. It alone would be capable of withstanding the inevitable petty bourgeois vacillations of this mass, and the inevitable traditions and relapses of narrow craft unionism or craft prejudices among the proletariat'. This phase of Lenin 'marked the break. It was war on the *idea* of libertarian radical socialism and on proletarian democracy. On the other side, there remained only the idea of the party. Lenin's party, cut off from its social justification, now rested on dogma alone. He assumed that popular or proletarian support could be dispensed with and that the mere integrity of motive would be adequate, would justify everything in the long run' (Ibid.: 104–5).

At the Tenth Party Congress, Stalin became the General Secretary of the party. After the Congress, the deification of the party was intensified, ending all voluntaristic and libertarian aspects of the Revolution of 1917. One-party rule inevitably degenerated into the personalized rule of one person under Stalin. As Solzhenitsyn rightly commented: 'There never was any such thing as Stalinism (either as a doctrine, or a path of national life, or as a state system). Stalin was a very consistent and faithful — if also very untalented — heir to the spirit of Lenin's teaching' (Solzhenitsyn, cited in Keane 1988: 267). In the final analysis, Leninism itself was an offshoot of Marxism. Marx's major intellectual deficiency was disregarding the different possibilities emerging from his theory. A combination of his philosophical and historical theory based on Jacobinism with 'political, subjectivist revolutionary action' led to the theory of Leninism (Avineri 1976: 228).

The adoption of the NEP and the abandonment of crash socialization meant accepting that the Mensheviks were right all along. At this juncture the choice was clear. Either tighten the dictatorship, suppress all other parties and silence the critics of communism or reconcile differences with the Mensheviks and accept that there would be democratic and workers groups within the communist system.

> In 1921 the fate of the country lay in the hands of Lenin. He had a chance of burying past enmities and of carrying the vast majority of the country with him in an attempt to build up ruined Russia on the basis of co-operation and legal order, and not of the dictatorship of an unpopular minority (Schapiro, cited in Conquest 1972: 106).

Lenin preferred total and immediate suppression of the Mensheviks and the social revolutionaries culminating in the trials of some of their leaders in 1922. He invented artificial famines and used them as political weapons. He dismantled free press and suppressed civil liberties. Gorbachev who called himself a 'confirmed Leninist' confessed that cruelty was Lenin's main problem (cited in Remnick 1998). It was a cruel fact of history that just as the Russian Tsar threw away a golden opportunity of transforming Russia into a working constitutional state by cooperating with the moderate liberal opinion after the revolution of 1905, Lenin repeated the same mistake by not attempting to create a constitutional government. The establishment of a repressive and an authoritarian state and the subjugation of civil society logically followed such a denial. Moreover, while under the tsar one was condemned for own actions, under communism any deviating thought was dubbed as counter-revolutionary and dealt with dire conse-quences. Thus, the Tsarist state reincarnated as the Leninist state in a more repressive form. Like Marx, even Lenin never 'spoke of a law governed state ... because they considered that the state would inevitably wither away' (Djilas 1990: 7). Instead of with-ering away, the Soviet State became omnipotent and eventually straddled all aspects of individual and societal life.

In 1946 George Kennan commented that the 'Marxist dogma' was the fig leaf covering the brutal realities of the Soviet policy, the origin of that brutality could be traced back to the originators themselves. This charge could be substantiated by the fact that the communist culture that dominated the former Soviet Union for the next seventy years emerged with the Bolsheviks with Lenin as their most important leader, tactician and theoretician. After realizing that Marx's prediction of a world proletarian revolution was neither inevitable nor imminent, Lenin invented the Communist Party with its mission of revolutionary seizure of power, and once in power, to impose its will from above. The fact that such an experiment would fail was pointed by all the critics of Bolshevism.

For the collapse of communism, the originators themselves can-not escape the major responsibility as they never provided a blue-print for actualizing the realization of true democracy and communism. A well-developed Marxist theory of the state with a view to provide a functional model based on equity, just reward and freedom that could have been an alternative to the liberal demo-cratic theory of the state eluded all important Marxists, including Lenin. The Leninist state was inherently authoritarian with very little regard for the rule of law. The legacy of communist rule in the USSR after the collapse of communism was aptly captured in a headline in *Moscow News Weekly* in 1990 'Seventy Years: A Journey to Nowhere'.

Rosa Luxemburg

Rosa Luxemburg ... was the prophet par excellence of the uninstitutionalized revolution. She preached the primacy of action and the relationship between a revolutionary situation and the participation of growing masses of the "proletariat". Having no experience of the post-revolutionary socialist state and of the problems of continued alienation which this has been seen to entail, her focus was primarily on the evils of the present society and the necessity of transforming it. She knew better than any how close must be the relationship between personal commitment and action, between action and class-consciousness, between class-consciousness and revolution (Nettl 1966: xxxix–xi).

Her criticisms were of an elementary democratic kind; had they been headed by the Leninist, the world might have been saved incalculable grief and oceans of blood (Howe 1990b: 134).

Rosa Luxemburg is an outstanding example of a type of mind that is often met with in the history of Marxism and appears to be specially attracted by the Marxist outlook. It is characterized by slavish submission to authority, together with a belief that in that submission the values of scientific thought can be preserved. No doctrine was so well-suited as Marxism to satisfy both these attitudes, or to provide a mystification combining extreme dogmatism with the cult of "scientific" thinking, in which the disciple could find mental and spiritual peace. Marxism thus played the part of a religion for the intelligentsia, which did not prevent some of them, like Rosa Luxemburg herself, from trying to improve the deposit of faith by reverting to first principles, thus strengthening their own belief that they were independent of dogma (Kolakowski 1981b: 94–95).

Rosa Luxemburg (1870–1919) was an articulate spokesperson and theoretician of the German Left and one of the founding members of the German Communist Party. There were two things that stood out in her as a person. The first was her total commitment to an idealized version of Marxist theory of revolution and the second when she challenged Lenin by defending democracy against the claims of the Russian communists. In spite of her virulent criticisms, she was referred to, by Lenin in 1922 as an 'eagle of the proletarian revolution' whereas others, which included his venerable master Kautsky, were hens who knew only to cackle at the mistakes committed by others. Luxemburg represented in the trust sense the democratic tradition within revolutionary Marxism. She was equally a valiant defender of orthodox Marxism against revisionism or social democracy seeing her mission as the destruction of Bernstein's deviation from Marx's teachings.

Luxemburg, in her career, combined the roles of an activist and a theoretician of socialism in general, and of the left-wing variant in particular. Socialism to her was ultimately a moral vision, a spiritual transformation not just the success of dialectical materialism but the emancipation of the humankind. Luxemburg was not an orthodox Marxist. Marx to her was no more than the best interpreter of reality which explained her non-polemical and innocent style of writing. This was evident from her analysis of imperialism. Since capitalism did not show any internal signs of collapse she began to search for an explanation externally.

Luxemburg's critique of Leninism goes back to the early part of the twentieth century when she, like Trotsky, rejected Lenin's model of party organization. This was in contrast to the other critics who disagreed or drifted from Lenin only after the Bolshevik Revolution, sometime after 1917. It was for this reason that her criticisms could not be dismissed as irrelevant before 1917 nor could she be condemned as a renegade as was done by Lenin in case of Kautsky. She provided a critical support to the regime for she insisted that people desired a combination of revolutionary spirit with enthusiasm. Revolution to her was as real as it was to Lenin, symbolizing the idea of uninstitutionalized and spontaneous revolution. People's participation was the key issue, whether it was related to organizing a revolution or governing a system. She stressed on a close relationship between activists and intellectuals for she herself was a personification of this belief. In her perception, a distinction was made between an intellectual and a bureaucrat and not between an intellectual and an activist because for her an intellectual, like an activist and unlike a bureaucrat, was not opposed to change. The Weberian elaboration of the utmost necessity of bureaucracy in the modern capitalistic legal-rational structure had no influence on her.

Biographical Sketch

Luxemburg was born on 5 March 1871. She was the youngest of the five children, three boys and two girls, and was born to Elias (or Eduard) and Line Luxemburg. Zamosc was her birthplace. After being partitioned from Poland, it was first under Austrian rule until 1809 and then came under Russian rule in 1815. It was predominantly a Jewish township and found itself at the cultural crossroads of Austria, Poland and Russia. The Jews of this town were among the most cultured communities in Poland. The Luxemburg family did not lead a conscientious Jewish life. Within their home, they spoke and read German and all of Rosa's siblings had German names—Maximilian, Josef and Anna.

Luxemburg was a quiet child and was a voracious reader. She was familiar with both German and Polish classical literature. In

1873 the family moved to Warsaw. Here she developed disease of the hip which was wrongly diagonized as tuberculosis and, as a result, wrongly treated. Bedridden for a whole year, she used the time productively by teaching herself to read and write. The illness left a permanent deformation of the hip which made her limp. She developed a keen interest in literature. At the age of nine, she had translated German poems and prose into Polish. At the age of thirteen, she wrote a poem to felicitate the visit of the German Emperor William I to Warsaw.

In 1884 Luxemburg joined the second girls' high school in Warsaw. This was primarily a Russian-speaking school. The 1880s saw the zenith of socialist activity. She became acquainted with the writings of Marx and Engels in 1887. She moved to Zurich in 1889 when she enrolled herself at the university to study philosophy, natural sciences and mathematics. In 1892 she moved to the faculty of law. She graduated with two doctorates from the University of Zurich, one in law and the other in philosophy. In her doctoral thesis *The Industrial Development of Poland* (1898), she argued that the development of industrial capitalism in Poland was heavily dependent on Russian market and the Polish economy would remain a part of the Russian economy. The analysis of this book formed the basis of the political programme of the Polish Social Democratic Party.

During this time Luxemburg was deeply involved in the socialist movement, and Zurich at that time was one of important centres of Russian revolutionary Marxism. She worked closely with the Russian exiles such as Plekhanov, Axelrod and Lenin. By this time, she met Leo Jogiches, a Polish exile and a radical who arrived in Zurich in 1890 and within two months got to know Luxemburg very well. Soon an intimate relationship developed between the two. In 1897 Luxemburg married a German Gustav Luebeck in order to escape her designation as a foreigner but the marriage ended very soon. It took five years for her to obtain a divorce. In 1897–98 she visited Paris and Berlin.

Luxemburg's visit to Germany was momentous for she became associated with German Social Democracy for the next 20 years. In the revisionist debate within the SPD, she was one of the most articulate defenders of the German Left. She contributed to the German Communist Party's theoretical organ *Neue Zeit* and later became an assistant to its founder and editor, Kautsky. She also edited several radical provincial dailies and the party's daily paper *Vorwarts*. She became a teacher of Marxian economics at the Central Party Primary School.

Luxemburg was actively involved with the 1905 Russian Revolution. Temporarily she became close to Lenin for both viewed the 1905 revolution as a bourgeois one to be carried under the proletarian leadership. She laid down the tasks for the Polish and the Russian proletariat and translated these revolutionary events for the benefit of the German socialists. From 1905–1919 as a leader of the extreme left-wing of the German Marxist movement she opposed Germany's entry into the First World War and later, during the Spartacus uprising in Germany, the centralizing tendencies of the German Communist Movement. Outvoted by her party, she hesitantly supported a doomed putsch which had neither the arms nor the popular support required for its success.

Luxemburg refused to leave Germany. While in hiding for two years she tried to reconstruct the party but was seized and arrested with Karl Liebknecht and Wilhelm Pieck. Along with Liebknecht she was brutally murdered by the Prussian officers on 15 January 1919 while being taken to the prison.[9] Though the murderers were known, nothing was done to arrest and chargesheet them. Jogiches stayed back in Berlin to bring the culprits to book. However, two months later he too was murdered.

Luxemburg was a small built, fastidious person. She was tidy, conscious of her appearance, which included her clothes and shoes, and careful about her walking style. Her house reflected these traits in her. Her book shelves were neatly arranged, labelled and easily accessible. Her paintings, ornaments and botanical collections were also organized similarly. From 1903 she had her own neatly embossed note-paper which she used for special occasions. Her home was her private sphere though many people stayed there for long periods of time as her guests. In her house management, she displayed her German traits like being meticulous, clean and orderly. She was a cautious spender. Her holidays were spent mostly in Switzerland though she was keen on visiting places like Corsica, Africa and the East. She visited none of these, except Corsica. Thus in spite of her reputation as 'Red Rosa', she remained self consciously a woman. She was against the woman's liberation movement of her time though she shared an intimate friendship with Zetkin, the chief spokesperson for women's cause.

Luxemburg was not an easy person to get along with. Being passionate, she developed quick attachments which made her touchy too. In morals, her position was quite rigid. She cherished privacy. She felt drawn only towards intelligent persons. She was not fond of Kautsky, Wilhelm Liebkhecht, Plekhanov and Trotsky. She was harsh on those who displayed personal weaknesses. Her tastes were conservative and classical. She liked Mozart and Beethoven among musicians, and Titian and Rembrandt among painters. He favourite composer was Hugo Wolf. She preferred the writings of Goethe, Morike and Lessing. She was fluent in Polish, Russian, German, French and spoke English and Italian very well. Though her family did not share her socialist convictions yet they did everything for her whenever she was in prison or hiding from the police. Her death brought a vacuum within the German Communist Party. She was truly among the last of the great socialist leaders of her time and perhaps a very 'civilized voice in the cause of international socialism' (Geras 1976: 300).

Critique of Revisionism

In her critique of revisionism and reaffirmation of orthodox Marxism, she raised the key issue of whether socialism could be achieved through reforms in a gradual manner or was revolutionary action the only possible way. In other words, the option was between reform and revolution, and she opted for revolution. In accordance with this theoretical framework, she accused the social democrats for equating reforms with revolutionary class struggle and for positing social reform as the sole and final aim thus departing from the main essence of socialism.

Luxemburg considered Bernstein's views to be important for their potential to move away revolutionary authoritarian socialism but also cautioned against their opportunistic character. The quintessence of her criticism as articulated in *Social Reform or Revolution* (1899) was that if Bernstein was right, then socialism had no *raison d'être*. She rejected the latter's revisionism on three grounds: (1) that trade unions were incapable of making structural changes, (2) that social reforms were not the means by which the workers gained control of society, and (3) that the capitalist class was strengthening its rule by tariff protection and militarism. 'And by the final goal I do not mean this or that conception of some future state, but which must necessarily precede the establishment of any future socialist society, i.e., the conquest of political power by the proletariat' (Luxemburg 1971: 127). Such a goal, Luxemburg contended, was necessary to give the proletariat a sense of purpose in its struggle against capitalism. Like Sorel, she understood the need for a myth in creating proletarian consciousness. Though not a opponent of reforms, she regarded them as the means for preparing the working class for a revolution for it gave them practical experience, the education to realize the need to overthrow the capitalist state and free themselves from the bonds of wage-slavery.

Luxemburg was confident that daily reforms would not automatically ensure socialism. She contended that Bernstein's equation of democracy with socialism was wrong for democracy was the device used by the capitalists to conceal the real and true nature of the exploitation of the masses. She agreed with Lenin's emphasis on spontaneity after the 1905 revolution in Tsarist Russia whereby the proletariat would directly struggle against the capitalist state machinery. She was critical of the policy of the English trade unions for they lacked the consciousness to achieve socialism. Luxemburg asserted that the efforts of the trade unions to improve working class conditions and parliamentary struggle for democratic reforms would be socialistic only if their final aim was socialism.

Disagreeing with Bernstein she observed that the credit system, far from strengthening capitalism, only aggravated internal contradictions. This led to concentration of capital in the form of joint stock companies and commercial credit and weakened the competitive potential of small companies. Regarding cartels and trusts, she admitted that not much research had been done. It was clear that they would reduce capitalist anarchy only if they could become the general productive form. Their role in raising profits in one area of industry at the costs of the others was successful within the domestic markets but it intensified competition and anarchy in the international market.

> If the capitalist market begins to shrink because of the utmost development and exhaustion of the world market by the competing capitalist countries — and it obviously cannot be denied that such a situation is bound to arise sooner or

later—then the forced partial idleness of capital will reach such dimensions that the medicine will suddenly change into the illness itself, and the capital, already heavily socialized (*vergesellschaftet*) through regulation, will revert to its private form . . . (cartels and trusts) exacerbate the contradiction between the international character of the capitalist world-economy and the national character of the capitalist state because they are accompanied by a general tariff war, which carries to extremes of the antagonisms (among the individual capitalist states) (Luxemburg 1971: 65).

In *The Accumulation of Capital* (1913) she analyzed the conditions of economic growth under capitalism. She contended that pure capitalism by itself could not generate conditions required for its development. It was the expansion into non-capitalist areas that sustained capitalist production necessitated due to accumulation of capital which was the result of lack of demand to absorb the increasing supply of goods. During the imperialist phase of capitalism this difficulty was solved by production of arms which not only absorbed domestic capital but created new markets in the colonies. The customs and tax policies of a state played an important role in the economic development of capitalism, especially during its imperialist phase. She criticized Marx for ignoring the historical conditions that affected the accumulation of capital. She contended that Marx analyzed the historical conditions that led to the rise of capitalism and concentrated on private accumulation. She believed that the relationship between capitalism and pre-capitalism constituted a source of tension and international conflict. This led to a series of wars and social revolutions which started the process of the decline of capitalism.

Bauer, Bukharin, Hilferding, Kautsky, Lenin and Pannekoek[10] rejected the major arguments of the book and even questioned whether the problems raised by Luxemburg were important ones. The Marxists took the view that though capitalism would be destroyed by its multiple contradictions, it was difficult to forecast the exact circumstances in which this would happen. Many, and in particular her Leninist critics, doubted whether there could be an automatic collapse of capitalism. If that happened then it would inculcate a passivity in the proletariat and the party. Paradoxically, the Keynesian revolution which highlighted the lack of purchasing power as responsible for the breakdown of capitalism rehabilitated Luxemburg's thesis (Kowalik 1968: 497).

Luxemburg considered trade unions as necessary for protecting the standard of living of the working class and shielding them from the immanent tendencies within capitalism, namely, impoverishment and unemployment, but her theoretical insights compelled her to spell out the limits of trade union struggle.

Thanks to objective processes at work in capitalist society, (the trade unions struggle) is transformed into a kind of labour of Sisyphus. However, this labour of Sisyphus is indispensable if the worker is to obtain at all the wage-rate due to him in the given situation of the labour market, if the capitalist law of wages is to operate, and if the effectiveness of the depressive tendency of economic development is to be paralyzed, or to be more exact, weakened. But a proposed transformation of the trade unions into an instrument or gradual reduction of profits in favour of wages presupposes, above all, the following social conditions: first, a halt to the proletarization of the middle strata of society and to the growth of the working class; second, a halt to the growth of the working class; second, a halt to the growth of labour productivity, i.e., in both cases . . . *a reverse to precapitalist conditions* (Luxemburg 1971: 67).

Luxemburg considered the institution of democracy as a product of historical processes, though not as 'the great fundamental law of all historical development' like Bernstein did. In fact, she dismissed democracy as superficial, a mechanical generalization of the features of one small stage in developments since 1870 and even petit bourgeois in spirit. She did not find any intrinsic relationship between capitalism and democracy. She regarded, contrary to the reformists, that parliamentarism was on the decline and that it was a 'historical form of the class rule of the bourgeoisie' and would remain alive only as long as the bourgeoisie was in conflict with the feudal elements. Interestingly she considered parliamentarism as a powerful tool for encouraging socialist propaganda and for increasing the influence of socialist ideas among the masses but insisted that it need not be restricted merely to agitation. It ought to devote itself to the task of positive legislative work.

Social democracy, in order to remain an opposition force, would have to derive its strength from the proletarian masses and abandon the illusion of empowering the capitalist state by majoritarianism in parliament.

Luxemburg summed up her criticisms of revisionism by pointing out that its philosophical basis was similar to that of vulgar bourgeois economics. Its theory and tactics would not lead to a triumph of socialism because Bernstein was not choosing 'a more tranquil, calmer and slower role to the same goal but a different goal, not the realization of socialism but reform of capitalism' (Ibid.: 130). This crucial distinction between reform and revolution was the most important point in Luxemburg's critique of evolutionary socialism because it was this important difference that distinguished social democratic movement from both bourgeois democratic ideas and bourgeois radicalism. This ultimate revolutionary goal had to be harmonized and embodied in the social democratic activity. Similarly, ideals were inseparable from trade union struggle and the struggle for social reforms and democratic rights. This was of utmost necessity for Luxemburg because otherwise the socialist dream would never materialize.

Luxemburg refused to concede that reforms were valuable in themselves and she mistrusted any spectacular success that the workers had achieved in their economic struggles. As a result, her assessment was negative and pessimistic. Unlike Bernstein and Eduard David (1863–1930), she regarded English working class as being corrupted by temporary gains. In 1899 she declared that the English workers abandoned their class perspective and compromised with capitalism. Luxemburg, like Marx, did not clarify which would come first, that capitalism could not be reformed and the working class would inevitably destroy it through a revolution. In her polemics with the revisionists, she relied on the first statement and her theory of accumulation supported her contention. However, she did not clarify as to how would that lead to a proletarian revolution. In fact, she believed that the revolutionary consciousness of the proletariat would increase without observing social reality which was why she hoped for a spontaneous rather than organized action by the party (Kolakowski 1981b: 81–2). She remained committed throughout her life, like Marx, to a conscious majoritarian revolution which did not need the help of either an elite or a party.

Critique of the Leninist Model of Party

Luxemburg made spontaneity vs. party organization the main focus of her critique of the Leninist model of party in *Organization Questions of Russian Social Democracy* (1904). Central to her conception of revolution was the notion of 'spontaneity'. By spontaneity she did not mean blind impulse shorn of ideological self-awareness. She never denied the need for creative leadership. To her, the socialist revolution could only occur through the cooperation and comradeship between the revolutionary masses and leaders like herself who did not impose on the workers their own 'correct' vision of political struggle. She desired a dialectical reciprocity between the spontaneity of the masses, the intellectuals and the political leaders. This was very similar to the Gramscian conception of proletarian intellectuals which meant total amalgamation of the intellectuals in the proletarian struggle. A similar trait could be found in Fanon also.

Furthermore, Luxemburg added that the great historical hour itself created the forms that would carry the revolutionary movements to its successful outcome. The Russian revolution of 1905 convinced her that mass strikes were the most effective form of revolutionary action. Kautsky disagreed with Luxemburg for assuming that a few months of accidental, disorganized strikes without an unifying idea of plan could teach the workers more than thirty years of systematic work by parties and trade unions. But the latter was confident in the spontaneous uprising of the workers and rejected the Leninist conception of the need for a vanguard party as the *avant-garde* of the proletariat. The task of a proletarian party was to awaken the revolutionary consciousness in the masses and kindle a desire for socialism, but this could not be done by conspiratorial methods.

Luxemburg was critical of Lenin's extraordinary faith in ultra centralism, his implicit contempt of the working class — its own creative impulses and purposes — his distrust of all spontaneous developments and of spontaneity itself. She visualized his future party as one in which the central committee could and would perpetuate itself, dictate to the party and have the party dictate to the masses. The central committee would be 'the only thinking element', reducing the entire party and the masses to 'mere executing limbs'. She pleaded for the autonomy of the masses, respect for their spontaneity and creativity, respect for their right to make their own mistakes and to be helped by them. Her polemic ended with words so often quoted, 'Historically, the errors committed by a truly revolutionary movement are infinitely more fruitful than the infallibility of the cleverest central committee' (Luxemburg 1961: 108).

This was the core of Luxemburg's theory of non-authoritarian majoritarian socialism. For although she criticized Lenin's conception of the vanguard party, she did not object, as Kautsky did, to the Leninist notion that revolutionary consciousness would be instilled in the workers movement from without. She accepted this idea as she believed that the party would become the vehicle of proletarian class consciousness and that its task was to turn theory into practice by creating a spontaneous movement. For Luxemburg, the party was the self-organizing proletariat, not the proletariat organized by professional functionaries of the revolution. Marxism for her was not merely a theory of the:

> historical process but an articulation of the consciousness, latent though it might be as yet, of an actual workers movement. When that consciousness took shape, i.e. when the spontaneous movement achieved theoretical self-knowledge, the distinction between theory and practice would cease to exist, the theory would become a material force, not in the sense of being a weapon in the struggle but as an organic part of it (Kolakowski 1981b: 84).

Mass Strike

Initially the German social democrats were sceptical of the idea of mass strike owing to its anarchist origins but with the relative success of mass strikes in 1903–1904 – in particular in Belgium – they paid more attention to the idea. Even Bernstein conceded that mass strike could be the answer for assaults on universal suffrage. Kautsky cautiously accepted it after the success of the method in Russia in 1905. At the Jena Congress held in 1905, the SPD adopted Bebel's resolution on the mass strike as a defensive tactic. But subsequently the emphasis on mass strike was toned down following the failure of the 1905 Russian revolution and the opposition from the trade union leaders who did not want their gradual gains endangered. At the Cologne Congress of 1905 the technique of mass strike was condemned and with it the radical wing of the party.

It was in this context that Luxemburg wrote her *Mass Strike, Party and Trade Unions* with the purpose of narrowing the gap between the economic reformism of the trade unions and revolutionary political action. She clarified that mass strike was no longer an anarchist technique. To counter the trade union opposition she insisted that the principle lesson of the 1905 Russian Revolution was that mass strike was a historical phenomenon, a historical necessity that arose out of social relations at a given point of time. She presented a sociological analysis of the motives forces of a social revolution on the one hand, and the role or the masses, organization and the leader an the other. She regarded general strike as spontaneous and a basic weapon in the hands of the working class struggling for power. A proletarian revolution would consist of strikes, demonstrations, marches, meetings—all spontaneous, guided and inspired, but never dominated or controlled by a party.

Luxemburg analyzed the role of mass strikes and drew three main conclusions. First, that it was not an isolated action but 'the sign, the totality-concept of a whole period of the class struggle lasting for years, perhaps decades (Luxemburg 1971: 231). Second, within a mass strike the economic and political aspects were integrated and interdependent.

> The economic struggle is that which leads the political struggle from one nodal point to another; the political struggle is that which periodically fertilizes the soil for the economic struggle. Cause and effect here continually change places. Thus, far from being completely separated or even mutually exclusive, as the pedantic schema sees it, the economic and political moments in the mass strike period form only two interlacing sides of the proletarian class struggle in Russia. And their unity is precisely the mass strike (Ibid.: 237).

Third, mass strike would not lead to a revolution but the reverse was possible since a revolution would create conditions that would fuse economic and political factors in the mass strike. Summarizing her views on this idea, Luxemburg wrote:

If the mass strike does not signify a single act but a whole period of class struggles, and if this period is identical with a period of revolution, then it is clear that the mass strike cannot be called at will, even if the decision to call it comes from the highest committee of the strongest Social Democratic party. As long as Social Democracy is not capable of staging and countermanding revolutions according to its own estimation of the situation, then even the greatest enthusiasm and impatience of the Social Democratic troops will not suffice to call into being a true period of mass strikes as a living, powerful movement of the people (Luxemburg 1971: 244).

For Luxemburg all the Russian strikes were spontaneous not because the proletariat there was 'unschooled' but because 'revolutions allowed no one to play schoolmaster to them' (Ibid.: 245). However, this did not rule out the importance of leadership.

To give the slogans, the direction of the struggle; to organize the tactics of the political struggle in such a way that in every phase and in every moment of the struggle the whole sum of the available and already released active power of the proletariat will be realized and find expression in the battle stance of the party; to see that the resoluteness and acuteness of the tactics of the Social Democracy never fall below the level of the actual relation of forces but rather rise above it — that is the most important task of the "leadership" in the period of the mass strike (Ibid.: 247).

Finally, Luxemburg contended that the relative success of mass strikes in Russia was not due to Russia's backwardness because the economic and social conditions in Russia and Germany was identical. The German trade unions could not argue that they were not sufficiently organized to attempt a mass strike. They neglected the crucial point of class consciousness.

The class consciousness implanted in the enlightened German worker by Social Democracy is theoretical and latent: in the period of domination of bourgeois parliamentarism it cannot, as a rule, become active as direct action of the masses . . . In the revolution, where the masses themselves enter the political arena, class consciousness becomes practical and active (Luxemburg 1971: 200).

Luxemburg also argued that it was a fallacy to equate trade unions with the party. Though trade unions were a part of the whole movement, they could not be identified with the party which embodied the consciousness of the proletariat. In her view of the trade unions there was similarity between Lenin and Luxemburg as both were sceptical of these being able to transcend their narrow economic interests and whether they could develop revolutionary consciousness.

Imperialism

In Luxemburg's scheme of ideas, the concept of mass strike was closely connected to the idea of imperialism. Most left-wing radicals looked to imperialism and militarism increasing the power of the bureaucracy and reducing that of the parliament which was why they advocated direct action. She contended that capitalism would grow just as long as they were pre-capitalist societies to be exploited and, once all these societies had been absorbed into the process of the capitalist accumulation, the capitalism system would collapse since it proceeded by assimilating the very conditions which alone ensured its existence.

> . . . the more ruthlessly capital sets about the destruction of non-capitalist strata at home and in the outside world, the more it lowers the standard of living for workers as a whole, the greater also the change in the day-to-day history of capital. It becomes a string of political and social disasters and convulsions, and under these conditions, punctuated by periodical economic catastrophes or crises, accumulation can go on no longer . . . At a certain stage of development there will be no other way out than the application of socialist principles (Ibid.: 466).

Luxemburg's conclusions were criticized and not accepted by Marxist economists. Her criticisms of Marx were looked as being misguided. Moreover there was considerable ambiguity in her analysis on the automatic process of the breakdown of capitalism.

Whatever may be the ambiguities in her analysis, she was perceptive to observe and lay down the devastating impact that economic
imperialism had on underdeveloped societies, which were, by and
large, relevant.

By 1912 Luxemburg and her followers emerged as a cohesive
group emphasizing mass strikes and imperialism. As the First
World War progressed, the SPD split when the left radicals and
others who opposed the war were expelled from the party. As a
consequence, an independent German Socialist Party came into
existence which included Luxemburg's Spartacists, Kautsky and
even Bernstein. As in its earlier phase, the leftists did not believe in
any compromise as exemplified by Luxemburg's analysis of the
collapse of the Second International. Her opposition to the war was
total whose origin she attributed it to the imperialist rivalry of the
capitalist classes in the different imperialist countries. She advocated internationalism and mass action to combat these forces. Her
criticisms of Bolshevism came out of this presumption.

Initially Luxemburg supported Lenin's thesis of the possibility
of a bourgeois revolution led by the proletariat.

> The party of Lenin was the only one which grasped the man-
> date and duty of a truly revolutionary party; with the slogan —
> "all power in the hands of the proletariat and peasantry" —
> they ensured the continued move forward of the revolution.
> Thereby the Bolsheviks solved the famous problem of
> "winning a majority of the people" which has always weighed
> on the German Social Democracy like a nightmare . . .
> (Luxemburg, cited in Geras 1975: 21).

In spite of such praise, Luxemburg was critical of the Bolshevik
actions, mainly their seizure and distribution of land to the peasantry rather than nationalization, promise of national self determination and the dissolution of the constituent assembly.

Critique of Bolshevism

Luxemburg's belief that the workers movement would not be manipulated or forced into a tactical mould by the party leaders was
at the heart of her criticisms of the Bolshevik regime. She regarded
the Bolshevik revolution as the most important outcome of the First

World War yet she criticized the regime from the standpoint of her ultimate Marxist faith — the spontaneity of the masses in the *Russian Revolution* (1918) which was published posthumously in 1922. She rejected the arguments of Kautsky and the Mensheviks that, in view of Russia's economic backwardness, a coalition with the liberals and the bourgeoisie had to be forged. Instead, she agreed with Lenin and Trotsky that the party had to seize power when it was politically feasible. She also rejected the social democratic principle that the party gain a majority and then think about capturing power. The proper method was to use revolutionary tactics to gain a majority, and not the other way around.

Luxemburg was categorical that the party, having seized power, could not maintain itself by terror and reject all forms of political freedom and representation. The turning point of the Russian revolution was the dissolution of the constituent assembly. Lenin and Trotsky abolished general elections altogether, basing their power on the soviets. The latter declared that the assembly summoned before the October Revolution was reactionary and that universal suffrage was unnecessary as it did not properly reflect the true feelings of the masses.

Luxemburg reproached Lenin not with the neglect or contempt of direct, rank and file democracy, but rather with the exact opposite, namely, the exclusive reliance on council democracy and the complete elimination of representative democracy (dissolution of the constituent assembly in favour of the soviets alone). Her arguments, in reply to Trotsky's explanations, were that the masses could influence their representatives after the elections were over and make them change course. The more democratic the system, the more effective would such pressure be. Though democratic institutions in themselves may not be perfect, to abolish them would be to paralyze and eventually eliminate public life. The restrictions on the press, on suffrage and on the right of assembly made the rule of masses a mockery.

> Freedom for the supporters of the government, only for the members of one party — however, numerous they may be — is no freedom at all. Freedom is always and exclusively freedom for the one who thinks differently. Not because of any fanatical conception of 'justice' but because all that is instructive, wholesome and purifying in political freedom depends

on this essential characteristic; and its effectiveness vanishes when "freedom" becomes a special privilege . . . . Lenin is completely mistaken in the means he employs. Decree, dictatorial force of the factory overseer, draconic penalties, rule by terror, all these things are but palliatives. The only way to rebirth is the school of public life itself, the most unlimited, the broadest democracy and public opinion. It is rule by terror which demoralises (Luxemburg 1961: 69).

Socialism could not be replaced by administrative decrees for it had to be a live historical movement. If public life was not properly controlled, it would become the province of a narrow clique of officials, and this was bound to lead to corruption in political life. Socialism involved the spiritual transformation of the masses which could not be brought about by terrorism. There was a need for flowering of democracy, a free public opinion, freedom of elections and press, and the right to hold meetings and form associations. Otherwise, it would lead to the entrenchment of the bureaucracy, and the soviets, considered to be the true representatives of the labouring class, would be further crippled and eventually impotent. The dictatorship of the proletariat would be replaced by the dictatorship of a clique (Ibid.: 71–72).

Luxemburg was of the opinion that the basic error in the theory of Lenin and Trotsky, and also of Kautsky, was to consider democracy antithetical to dictatorship. Kautsky, in fact, had decided in favour of bourgeois democracy and the Bolsheviks for the dictatorship of a handful of people. The proletariat was supposed to exercise their dictatorship as a class and not as a party or as a clique.

If we have revealed the bitter kernel of inequality and slavery beneath the husk of formal equality and freedom, it is not in order to throw the husk away, but to persuade the working class not to be satisfied with it but to press on to the conquest of political power and fill it with a new social content . . . by conquering political powers, to create a socialist democracy to replace — not eliminate — democracy altogether . . . socialist democracy begins simultaneously with the beginnings of the destruction of class rule and of the construction of socialism. It begins at the very moment of the seizure of power by the socialist party. It is the same thing as the dictatorship of the proletariat — Yes dictatorship. But this dictatorship consists in the manner of applying democracy, not in its elimination, in energetic resolute attacks upon the well entrenched rights and economic relationships of bourgeois society, without with a socialist transformation cannot be accomplished. But this dictatorship must be the work of the class and not a little leading minority in the name of the class . . . (Luxemburg 1961: 77–78).

Luxemburg argued that it was true that the Bolsheviks had come to power under circumstances in which full democracy was impossible. But having seized power they made a virtue of necessity by seeking to impose their own tactics on the whole of the worker's movement, turning the distortion of an exceptional situation into an universal rule. They were to be commended for seizing power in Russia but the socialist cause was a matter for the whole world and not for a single country.

The mass of the proletariat is called upon not merely to define the aims and direction of the revolution with the clear understanding. It must itself, through it own activity, nurse socialist, step by step, to life. The essence of socialist society is that the great working mass ceases to be a ruled mass and instead lives and controls its own political and economic life in conscious and free self-determination. Thus, from the highest offices of the state down to the smallest municipality, the proletarian mass must replace the outdated organs of the bourgeois class rule — the federal councils, parliaments, municipal councils with their own class organs: the workers' and soldiers' councils. Further, the proletarian mass must fill all posts, supervise all functions and measure all state's requirements against their own class interests and against the tasks of socialism. And only in a constant active interrelation between masses' activity fill the state with socialist spirit . . . In tenacious hand-to-hand struggle against capitalism in every firm and factory, through the direct pressure of the masses and through strikes and by creating their one representative organs, the workers can gain control over production and ultimately the actual leadership . . . All . . . socialist civic virtues, together with the knowledge and ability to manage socialist operations, can be acquired by the working class only through their own activity, their own experience . . . the socialization of society can be realized only by the stubborn and untiring struggle of the working class on all fronts . . . the liberation of the working class must be the work of the working class (Luxemburg 1961: 277–78).

This raised the question regarding the scope of democratic rights and liberties within the dictatorship of the proletariat. Luxemburg considered proletarian dictatorship as a more direct and extensive form of democracy which would involve comprehensive democratic procedures and freedoms, elections, freedom of the press, of opinion and of assembly. She criticized the Bolshevik policy of dividing large landholdings among peasants, for that created a new and powerful class of proprietors as enemies of socialism.

Luxemburg also disproved of their policy towards nationalities, an issue that remained unresolved in Marxism. She perceived the oppression of one nation by another as a consequence of capitalism and believed that the socialist revolution would resolve it since it would end all forms of oppression. Till then fighting for national independence would harm the cause of revolution and destroy the international solidarity among the workers. She contended that national movements were always in favour of a particular class. Since no class could represent the national cause on an economic basis, the matter ended there and then. Even on this issue, she was oblivious of social realities. As a thorough doctrinaire Marxist, she accused the social democrats for the outburst of nationalism in 1914 and the resulting collapse of the International (Kolakowski 1981b: 93). She did not support the independence of Poland or, in general, the right of nations to self-determination.

Vision of a Socialist Society

In *What Does the Spartakus League Want?* Luxemburg outlined the following measures to protect the socialist revolution: (*a*) disarmament of the entire police force, and of all members; (*b*) confiscation of all weapons and munitions stock; (*c*) workers' militia; (*d*) abolition of command authority of officers and non-commissioned officers; (*e*) expulsion of officials and capitulation's from all soldier's councils; (*f*) replacement of all political organs by workers' and soldiers' councils; (*g*) establishment of a revolutionary tribunal to try the criminals responsible for starting the war; and (*h*) immediate confiscation of all food-stuffs.

The political and social measures included: (*a*) abolition of all principalities; establishment of a United German Socialist Republic; (*b*) elimination of all parliaments and municipal councils, and establishment of workers and soldiers' councils; (*c*) election of workers' councils in Germany by the entire adult population; (*d*) election of delegates of the workers' and soldiers' in the entire country to the central council of the workers' and soldiers' councils which would elect the executive council as the highest organ of legislative and executive powers; (*e*) to maintain constant control over the activity of the executive council and to create an active identification between the masses of workers' and soldiers' councils in the nation and the highest governmental organ; right of immediate recall by the local workers' and soldiers' councils and replacement of their representatives in the central council; right of the executive council to appoint and dismiss the people's commissioners as well as the central national authorities and officials; (*f*) abolition of all differences of rank, all orders and titles and complete legal and social equality of the sexes (Luxemburg 1971: 372–73).

The pyramid of councils that Luxemburg proposed in 1918 dealt with the question of direction and democracy by creating an executive council with strong legislative and executive powers representing the dictatorship of the proletariat but not amounting to it (Miliband 1977: 180–1). What would have happened to the executive council proposed by Luxemburg was difficult to judge for, unlike Lenin, his contemporaries did not succeed in making a revolution.

An examination of the aims and course of the revolutionary movement in Germany during the First World War revealed that the Spartacists exercised no influence on them. The aims of the revolutionary movement reflected peace and a bourgeois democracy, and certainly not the overthrow of the government or the proclamation of a republic, even less the establishment of a socialist society. The demands made by the striking workers of January 1918 were: (*a*) peace without annexation; (*b*) inclusion of workers' representatives in the peace negotiations; (*c*) abundant food supplies; (*d*) lifting of the state of siege; (*e*) demilitarization of industrial concerns; (*f*) immediate release of all political prisoners; and

(g) democratization of the state and electoral reform. The 1918 November resolution of the sailors of the High Sea Fleet demanded amnesty for all convicted sailors, immunity for those who had taken part in the revolutionary movement with no adverse comments on the conduct sheet, the same food for officers and men, a committee to hear complaints from the men, dispensation from having to salute officers except when on duty and from having to address them in third person.

The revolution ended on 10 November 1918. It was clear that the leaders of the social democrats lacked a constructive democratic, socialist conception of state and society which would have enabled them to utilize the revolutionary situation. Though the leaders of the SPD tried to convince the rank and file that they were trying to save Germany from Bolshevism, their assessment of the political situation was unrealistic. Those who opposed parliamentary democracy were ideologically and numerically weak and disunited even to succeed. The trade unions succeeded in getting their demands like eight hour day, unrestricted right to organize and to be recognized by the state and the employers but they lost the chance of reordering the economic structure.

Ultimately, the difference between Lenin and Luxemburg rested on their different perceptions of the organization and the role of the workers' party. While Lenin believed that the working class consciousness had to be instilled from outside, Luxemburg believed in creative spontaneous arousal of consciousness from within.

Conclusion

Luxemburg was pre-eminently a Marxist who enjoyed a position as an autonomous political thinker outside the context of the Marxist tradition. She espoused and defended a moral doctrine that viewed social revolution not only as the fulfillment of the laws of dialectical materialism but the liberation and progress of humanity. The key political idea in her theorizing and activism was participation. Her 'controlling doctrine was not democracy, individual freedom, or spontaneity, but participation-friction leading to revolutionary energy, leading in turn to the maturity of class-consciousness and revolution' (Nettl 1996: 7).

Luxemburg's political ideas and personality made her a champion of spontaneous revolution. She regarded socialism as the inevitable goal of human society and was confident that it would be able to withstand the temporary setbacks like war or imperialism. Socialism could not be manufactured or decreed for it embodied the aspirations and hopes of the proletarian masses. The political experience of the working class was the arena in which it would originate. She frequently reiterated two cherished Marxist themes: that the emancipation of the working class had to be won by the working class itself and that the proletarian revolution would be long drawn, arduous, tortuous and difficult. Her fear of a deformed rather than an unsuccessful revolution set her apart from the Bolsheviks and Lenin (Arendt 1969: xxx).

The events in the Soviet Union vindicated Luxemburg when she spoke about the moral collapse without foreseeing the open brutality and terror that would eventually undermine the revolutionary cause. She was proved right when she castigated Lenin for the means that he advocated and when she insisted that the only salvation was the 'school of public life itself, the most unlimited, the broadest democracy and public opinion'. She remained a friendly critic of Bolshevism. 'Rosa Luxemburg's Attitude towards the Revolution in 1917 was similar to many North and Latin American Fidelistas' view of the Cuban Revolution in 1961: the pluses far outweigh the minuses, but there is worry about the minuses' (Mills 1962: 150).

Luxemburg's major theoretical weakness arose from the fact that she could not comprehend, as Bernstein did, the important changes that capitalism was undergoing and the enormous potential of democracy as a weapon with the working class for advancing its cause even though she spoke of spontaneity and cherished basic civil and political liberties. She could never work out an institutional arrangement to secure them. It was the fast moving and unexpected worker's militancy in Tsarist Russia between 1905 and 1916 that gave credence to her theory of spontaneity. This was reflected by the fact that Lenin who had a pessimistic view of the workers' revolutionary consciousness in 1902 accepted more or less the position of Luxemburg and Bukharin in 1916 for he mentioned the role of the Communist Party only thrice in *The State and Revolution*. However, with the rise of Stalin and his proclamation of socialism in one country, the internationalist and libertarian aspect of Marxism got buried, of which Luxemburg was the finest exponent.

Leon Trotsky

His (Trotsky) personal fearlessness, his combination of firm political ends with tactical ingenuity, and his incomparable gifts as an orator helped to transform him, at the age of twenty six, into a leader of the first rank; he had entered upon the stage of modern history and only the axe of a murderer would remove him (Howe 1978: 25).

Nothing is more characteristic of the young Trotsky, as indeed of the familiar figure who was to emerge in later years, than his independence of mind and disdain for authority. By his own account, which is corroborated by all who know about him from other sources as well, he was by nature suspicious of all received opinion; in his autobiography he describes, not without a measure of self-delight, this ingrained scepticism, which often took the form of an almost exhibitionistic rebelliousness—against parents, teachers, schoolmates (Knei Paz 1978: 9).

It did not occur to Trotsky that a proletarian party would in the long run rule and govern an enormous country against the majority. He did not foresee that the revolution would lead to the prolonged rule of a minority. The possibility of such a rule was implicit in his theory; but its actuality would still have appeared to him, as to nearly all his contemporaries, incompatible with socialism. In fact, he did not imagine, in spite of all he had written about Lenin's "Jacobinism", that the revolution would seek to escape from its isolation and weakness into totalitarianism (Deutscher 1954b: 160).

Lev Davidovich Bronstein (1879–1940), known to the world by his pseudonym Leon Trotsky, was a brilliant orator who mesmerized the masses and leaders alike, a skillful organizer and a revolutionary. He was the creator of the Red Army. He was a Marxist theoretician of considerable repute and originality. His interests, like those of Engels, were diverse, ranging from military tactics to proletarian culture. He furnished a first-hand account of the Bolshevik Revolution. His theories were intertwined with his career as a revolutionary and could not be regarded as a system isolated from the contexts in which they grew, the events that shaped them and the debates that clarified them.

Trotsky's most significant contribution to Marxism was his analysis of 'uneven and combined' development which crystallized as the theory of permanent revolution. He was also extremely critical of the Leninist style of party organization before and after 1917 for he felt it would deteriorate into a self-serving, cruel and exploitative bureaucratic dictatorship and eventually result in the rule of one person. He lived up to see his prediction come true following the bitter power struggle that ensued after Lenin's death. His differences with Stalin were both personal and ideological. He accused Stalin of renouncing collective leadership and abandoning the ideal of world proletarian revolution. His critique of Stalin led to his exile and assassination. He died believing in the future of communism which gave him the power to resist more than any religion. Though an atheist, he remained a defiant humanist. He refused to analyze society and the national question in purely rational and scientific terms, giving concessions to non-rational factors.

Biographical Sketch

Trotsky was born in a Jewish family on 7 November (26 October old calendar) 1879 in the Ukrainian province of Kherson. His father David Leontievich Bronstein was a hardworking farmer, and regarded as 'a man of the soil'. This in itself was unusual as, for a Jew, to work on a large farm rather than trade was virtually unknown. Though not religious, David wanted his son to know the Hebrew Bible in the original language. At the age of seven Trotsky was sent to a Jewish religious school which he did not like. It did little to confirm him to his ancestral faith. Neither his religion nor his nationality deterred him from becoming a revolutionary. However, with the rise of Nazism, he was increasingly concerned about the European Jews and linked their liberation with the overthrow of the capitalist system.

In 1888 at an age of ten Trotsky went to Odessa to stay with his cousin Moissei Spentzer, a cultured person from whom he learned to speak Russian and imbibed a keen interest in books, music, conversation, oration and the arts. He discovered the pleasures of reading and listening to Italian opera. Odessa's liberal environment made Trotsky 'more than any other Russian revolutionist of his generation a man of the West' (Howe 1978: 11). He lost a year in school since at the secondary levels Jewish pupils were restricted to just 10 per cent of the total strength.

In 1896 Trotsky went to Nikolayev to finish his studies. Here he became acquainted with Populism and by the end of 1897 became a Marxist. A group of like-minded people met regularly in the home of a gardener to discuss radical ideas and soon Trotsky became a leading voice amongst them. At 18 he decided to become a professional revolutionary and never reconsidered it though few suffered the way he did in this century for being one. In 1897 his little group formed a clandestine organization, the South Russian Workers Union, with the purpose of holding political discussions and highlighting factory conditions through its leaflets. In 1898 Trotsky was arrested and sent to Siberia from where he fled in 1902. He joined Lenin and the editorial staff of *Iskra*. He also met emigrés like Plekhanov, Zasulich and Martov. He was sent to Paris for a lecture tour and became acquainted with Western art. In Paris he met Natalya Sedova who became his second wife and remained with him till the day of his death.

In 1903 Russian Socialist Democratic Labour Party (RSDLP) held its Second Congress. Initially he supported Lenin on the issue of party discipline and organization but took an independent position following the Bolshevik-Menshevik split. In 1905 he returned to Russia and became the chairman of the St. Petersburg Soviet. He was arrested in December 1905. While in prison he wrote *1905*. He also spent a great part of his time refining his theory of permanent revolution. He escaped from the prison once again in 1907 and went to Vienna.

During the First World War Trotsky organized the Zimmerwald conference. He was against the participation of the workers in the war. He edited several Russian language Marxist journals in France and left for New York in 1917. He returned to Russia in the Spring of 1917 and joined the Bolshevik party. As the Chairman of the Petrograd Soviet he directed the Fall 1917 revolution which brought the Bolsheviks to power. He became the Commissar of Foreign Affairs in the first Lenin cabinet. In 1918 spring he resigned and became the Commissar of War.

Trotsky found himself in opposition with Kamnev, Stalin and Zinoviev following the death of Lenin in 1924, which made him lose his party and state positions. He was expelled from the party in 1927 and was exiled to Soviet central Asia . He was expelled from the Soviet Union in 1929 and was deprived of his Soviet citizenship in 1932. His first wife Alexandra Sokolovskaya was also exiled. Their two children were harassed and both of them met with tragic ends. Trotsky's son from his second marriage, a scientist, was arrested in 1937 and charged with planning a 'a mass poisoning of workers'. He was sent to Vorkuta labour camp in the

Arctic and subsequently shot. Another son Leon Sedov died under mysterious circumstances in 1938.

Trotsky spent 11 years in exile, first in Turkey from 1929 to 1933, then in France from 1933 to 1935, Norway 1935–36, and finally settled down in Mexico from 1936 to 1940. He formed the Fourth International in 1938 with its base in Paris with the purpose of opposing Stalin's leadership of the world working class. He was accused and tried in absentia of directing subversive activities against the Soviet regime in a trial from 1936 to 1938. He was sentenced to death in March 1938. He was brutally assassinated by an ice-pick aimed at the back of his skull by a Soviet security agent in his own home in Coyoacan, Mexico on 20 August 1940.

During his exile he wrote his memorable books. These were political in nature addressed to the world at large and represented 'the culminating achievement of a major twentieth-century writer for whom the bitterness of defeat and the sufferings of persecution nevertheless brought an opportunity to fulfill his talent' (Howe 1978: 136). His *My Life* was not a biography nor did it chronicle the public events for it contained both. *The History of the Russian Revolution*, a three-volume book which narrated the story of the revolution as it unfolded and progressed. It lacked the dispassionateness of Thucydides for he wrote it from the 'perspective of the embroiled participant' (Ibid.: 143). *The Revolution Betrayed* analyzed Stalinist Russia.

Critique of Leninist Party

Trotsky argued that Lenin's vanguard party smacked of conspiracy and was against the Marxist premise that the workers would consciously liberate themselves by their own efforts. He accused Lenin for converting a party into a 'committee of public safety'. Trotsky was joined by Luxemburg who pointed out that the vanguard party would enslave the nascent workers' movement and eventually lead to the dominance of the central committee.[11] While Luxemburg was explicit, Trotsky was implicit, but both felt that the Bolsheviks resembled the Jacobeans who, while claiming to be spokespersons of the people, established themselves as an elite group of revolutionaries independent of the masses.

In a pamphlet *Our Political Tasks* (1904), dedicated to his teacher Axelrod, Trotsky criticized Lenin for elevating the vanguard to a higher status than the worker and anticipated its substitution. This pamphlet 'was the most strident bill of impeachment that any socialist had ever drawn up against Lenin' (Deutscher 1954b: 89). Like Luxemburg, Trotsky desired a party that would work with the 'self reliant proletariat' rather than become a self appointed caucus. He observed that the party organization would substitute at first the party as a whole, then the central committee would replace the organization and finally a single dictator would appoint himself in the place of the central committee. This, he observed was the theory of an 'orthodox theocracy' which would proxy for the workers and act in a manner without any concern for them. He felt that Lenin was combining Jacobinism with Marxism and, in the process, was renouncing socialism and becoming a leader of the revolutionary wing of bourgeois democracy. He pointed out that the idea of vanguard party was based on the assumption that the working class was homogenous in its interests and outlook when it was not the case. He concluded by pleading against uniformity.

> The tasks of the new regime will be so complex that they cannot be solved otherwise than by way of a competition between various methods of economic and political construction, by way of long "disputes", by way of a systematic struggle not only between the socialist and the capitalist worlds, but also between many trends inside socialism, trends which will inevitably emerge as soon as the proletarian dictatorship poses tens and hundreds of new . . . problems. No strong, "domineering" organization . . . will be able to suppress these trends and controversies . . . . A proletariat capable of exercising its dictatorship over society will not tolerate any dictatorship over itself . . . . The working class . . . will undoubtedly have in its ranks quite a few political invalids . . . and much ballast of obsolescent ideas, which it will have to jettison. In the epoch of its dictatorship, as now, it will have to cleanse its mind of false theories and bourgeois experience and to purge its ranks from political phrasemongers and backward looking revolutionaries . . . . But this intricate task cannot be solved by placing above the proletariat a few wicked people . . . or one invested with the power to liquidate and degrade (Trotsky 1904: 105).

In this pamphlet Trotsky was vicious and personal in his attack on Lenin with phrases like 'hideous', 'dissolute', 'demagogical', 'malicious', 'slovenly attorney' and 'morally repulsive'. These remarks were in bad taste for the Mensheviks, the group which Trotsky belonged, refrained from personal criticisms. Subsequently Trotsky aligned with Lenin.

> The oscillations, indecisions and uncertainties in Trotsky's pre-1917 views regarding party organization may profitably be seen as a reflection of an inner struggle within the entire Marxist tradition, and especially its Bolshevik wings between democratic, fraternal, even utopian impulses and what are taken to be authoritarian necessities imposed by the struggle for power (Howe 1978: 23–4).

Permanent Revolution

The idea of 'permanent revolution' formulated by Trotsky before 1917 borrowed the expression from Marx's and Engels' address to the General Council of the Communist League in 1850. It presupposed that Russian revolution would develop into a socialist one, but its success would depend on the world revolution which would be inspired by it. Most Marxists agreed that the need to overthrow the Tsarist autocracy and establish a government that would herald in democratic rights and complete the bourgeois revolution was the immediate task. The Mensheviks contended that the lead would be taken by the liberal bourgeoisie with the working class as a loyal opposition. Trotsky disagreed and instructed that the socialists maintain a distance from the bourgeois parties and not compromise with liberalism. This formed the core idea of his theory of permanent revolution.

In 1905 Trotsky pointed to the absolutist and centralized nature of Tsarist autocracy which was due to the weakness of the dominant economic classes rather than the temporary equilibrium between the opposing class as in the West. Here he picked up a stream from Marx's writings on Bonapartism[12] to explain the features of Tsarism. In the intermediate stages of the two revolutions in Russia—1905 and 1917—he developed his theory of permanent revolution setting forth a Marxist strategy for underdeveloped areas.

Trotsky considered Tsarist Russia as backward in need of a bourgeois democratic revolution for that would overthrow the autocracy, abolish feudal relations, establish the right of self-determination for oppressed national minorities, convene a constituent assembly to establish a republic and ensure civil liberties. In Russia the state was all-powerful because of Russia's backwardness, in which case even capitalism would be created and sustained by the state. Furthermore, the task of a bourgeois revolution had to be accomplished since the bourgeoisie lost its revolutionary arduor. Russia's backwardness and isolation made the bourgeois timid and indecisive. It was dependent on the autocracy for safeguarding its petty interests out of a fear of the peasantry and the working class. Hence the bourgeois revolution had to be carried out by the workers and peasants. Once this was achieved, it would automatically proceed towards a socialist one, thus becoming a *permanent* revolution. Moreover, in a country with a huge peasant majority the working class would suffer politically and economically unless it was supported by revolutions in the advanced European countries. In considering the peasantry as revolutionary he was reiterating Marx.

> Without the direct state support of the European proletariat, the working class of Russia will not be able to remain in power and transform its temporary rule into a stable and prolonged socialist dictatorship . . . . In a country where the proletariat has power . . . as the result of democratic revolution, the subsequent fate of the dictatorship and socialism is not only and so much dependent in the final analysis upon the national productive forces, as it is upon the development of the international socialist revolution (Trotsky 1919: 42, 44).

Right from the outset Trotsky established the internationalist perspective to the events in Russia. He solved the annoying problem of the relation between industrialization and backwardness. For the Mensheviks Trotsky's proposition was absurd. Lenin agreed with Trotsky about the inexperience and weakness of the Russian bourgeoisie but wondered whether they could be entrusted with such a mammoth task that Trotsky had set. In clarity of thought no other Russian Marxist could match Trotsky's calibre. But his theory proceeded from Marx's idealism rather than a correct appraisal of contemporary reality. The working classes in the advanced countries were recipients of the technological advantages and the surplus from the colonies and, therefore, uninterested in a revolution and the ones in the underdeveloped countries were unorganized and weak. Trotsky did not grasp the sea changes in the lives of the workers as Bernstein did, but he could understand that, without the help and support from the workers of the advanced industrialized countries, the revolution in Russia would get distorted and authoritarian. Paradoxically Trotsky and his followers regarded 1917 as a vindication of the theory of permanent revolution. It was precisely the same theory that warned of collapse and degeneration if the Russian revolution was not accompanied by revolutions in the West.

Proletarian Dictatorship

Trotsky replied to Kautsky's second tract criticizing the Bolshevik system. It bore the same title as the latter's *Terrorism and Communism* (1920).[13] He defended the use of terror by the Soviet government for that helped to reinforce the political supremacy of the working class, and protect socialism within Russia. Thus, at the outset he declared that means depended on the ends that were to be protected and did not see any contradiction between the two. The tract 'breathes the arrogance of the ruler lodged in power' and 'supports those who believe Leninism and Stalinism to be closely linked or to form a continuous descent' (Howe 1978: 67, 70).

Trotsky presented general principles of the dictatorship of the proletariat in the same way as Lenin did. He dismissed bourgeois democracy as a class institution and observed that important issues in a class struggle were not decided by votes, but by force. Unlike Kautsky who praised the commune for respecting human life and democracy, features that were absent in the soviets, Trotsky dismissed them as mistakes. He insisted that the soviets learnt from these mistakes and saw the need for a centralized organization, discipline, strong leadership, ruthlessness towards enemies and absolute control of the organs of government by force. In short, he dismissed those very elements of the commune as shortcomings which Kautsky regarded praiseworthy. He disregarded the possibility of sustaining a revolutionary regime through formal democracy. The concept of parliamentary majority was fetishism. It was a form of rule typical of bourgeois society in which the majority did not rule but only safeguarded their economic interests.

The dictatorship of the proletariat conversely assured true representation of the majority. It organized state power to combat reactionary forces and enabled the workers to lay the foundations for the eventual transformation of society. In a revolutionary transformation of society, political force was essential because parliamentary means with majority support could never change society. He declared that repudiation of the notion of the dictatorship of the proletariat meant renunciation of the socialist ideal.

> . . . the dictatorship of Soviets became possible only by means of the dictatorship of the party. It is thanks to the clarity of its theoretical vision and its strong revolutionary organization that the party had afforded to the Soviets the possibility of becoming transformed from shapeless parliaments of labour into the apparatus of the supremacy of labour. In this "substitution" of the power of the party for the power of the working class there is nothing accidental and in reality there is no substitution at all (Trotsky 1919: 104).

Trotsky believed that the attainment of socialism in other countries would depend on the creation of a communist party as authoritative as the one in Russia. He considered the vanguard party as representing and safeguarding the proletarian cause and interests. He wanted the government to absorb the trade unions, abandon proletarian democracy and concentrate on building producers' democracy. The party could legitimately deny the workers their political and civil rights by giving them managerial responsibility in the economic reconstruction. He proclaimed the 'historical birthright of the party' and argued at the Tenth Party Congress held in 1921:

> The party is obliged to maintain its dictatorship, regardless of temporary waverings in the spontaneous moods of the masses, regardless of the temporary vacillations even in the working class . . . . The dictatorship does not base itself at every given moment on the formal principle of a workers'

democracy, although the workers' democracy is of course, the only method by which the masses can be drawn more and more into political life (Trotsky, cited in Howe 1978: 72).

Martov could foresee, which Trotsky could not, the inherent tendency of the state towards intensified centralism with its principles of hierarchy and compulsion, and its desire to develop a specialized system of repression. He accused the Bolsheviks for wanting to repudiate parliamentary democracy but not the instruments of state power, namely, bureaucracy, police and permanent army. For the Bolsheviks:

> the dictatorship of the proletariat (was) not merely a new form of representative government, in which only the working men and women have votes . . . . They think that "proletariat" means "proletariat", but "dictatorship" does not quite mean "dictatorship". This is the opposite of the truth. When a Russian Communist speaks of dictatorship he means the word literally, but when he speaks of the proletariat he means the word in a Pickwickian sense. He means the "class conscious" part of the proletariat, i.e. the Communist Party. He includes people by no means proletarian . . . who have the right opinions, and he excludes such wage earners as have not the right opinions (Russell 1948: 22).

Stalinism and its Denunciation

'Socialism in one country' formulated towards the end of 1924 against Trotsky and his idea of 'permanent revolution' is regarded as a major contribution of Josef Stalin (1879–1953) to the Marxist theory. Its gist was that since in Russia the dictatorship of the proletariat was established through an alliance between the workers and peasants, a wide social basis existed for organizing a socialist economy without waiting for revolutions to break out elsewhere. Trotsky, in Stalin's view, had overestimated the possibility of securing aid from outside, thereby underestimating the importance of support from the peasants. Therefore, Trotsky's theory of permanent revolution was 'a variant of Menshevism', since, like Menshevism, it ignored the possibility of socialism in Russia. Nevertheless, Stalin was careful to add that complete victory of socialism still depended, on revolution in other countries. Thus, world revolution, he agreed, remained an essential objective. 'Socialism in one country' was made the official doctrine in 1926 when he published the essay *On the Problems of Leninism* (1926).

In the *Revolution Betrayed* (1936) Trotsky attributed poverty as the main reason for the bureaucratization in the former Soviet Union.

> The basis of bureaucratic rule is the poverty of society in objects of consumption with the resulting struggle of each against all. When there are enough goods in the store the purchasers can come whenever they want to. When there are little goods, the purchasers are compelled to stand in line. When the lines are very long, it is necessary to appoint a policeman to keep order. Such is the starting point of the power of Soviet bureaucracy (Trotsky 1945: 112).

Trotsky castigated Lenin for assuming that bureaucratization merely reflected the 'unfamiliarity of the masses with administration'. He did not comprehend the character of the state in conditions of economic backwardness and isolation. In Trotsky's view the problem was not political or administrative but social and historical. He confronted the bitter truth that backwardness and socialism were incompatible but refused to describe the soviet society as 'state capitalism' on the grounds that the soviet bureaucracy, though powerful and dominant, did not constitute a class. He acknowledged the existence of a privileged group which exploited the work of others but did not own the means of production nor did it amass huge wealth. Though private property existed, it was adequately socialized. There was state regulation. He admitted that the soviet bureaucracy was "the sole privileged and commanding stratum with considerable degree of independence" (Trotsky 1945: 248-9). Nevertheless, he argued, that its power was derived from the functions it performed and not from social or economic status.

Trotsky pointed to the growth and intensification of the bureaucratization of the society, the perpetuation of bourgeois norms of economic rewards and distribution. He could see that even after two decades the state was not withering away. Instead it was becoming increasingly powerful and independent of the society (Trotsky 1945: 55). Soviet society at best could be described as a 'contradictory society half-way between capitalism and socialism' (Ibid.: 254–55).

The central theme of the *Revolution Betrayed* was the parallel that Trotsky drew between the French and Russian Revolutions. Russia like France witnessed a Thermidor[14], which meant the transfer of power within a revolutionary movement from the masses to a small powerful minority. This process began from 1924 onwards. It was not a counter-revolution but a reaction against a revolution. 'Socialism in one country' was the doctrine of Thermidor and Bonapartism which led to bureaucratic consolidation and domination. In the late 1920s Trotsky identified the dangers of Thermidor as coming from Bukharin and the Right opposition since by then he interpreted the French Thermidor as being the restoration of the bourgeoisie. He regarded Stalin as the Soviet Bonaparte.

Trotsky differentiated between Soviet Bonapartism and Fascist Bonapartism. The latter arose in response to the crises, disarray and decline of capitalism, and its goal was its restoration and defence. In contrast, Soviet Bonapartism was characterized by its protection of non-capitalist property and the coming to power of a 'young' class, the workers. In an article *The Workers' State, Thermidor and Bonapartism* (1934–35) Trotsky held that the dictatorship of the proletariat was preserved, as the state owned the means of production, though political power had passed into the hands of the bureaucrats. The Soviet bureaucracy was not a new 'class' but a 'caste' which deprived the proletariat of its political rights and introduced brutal despotism. It performed a dual role: to defend the economic base of the workers' state against world imperialism and to maintain a balance of power in the international system. It was the duty of the world proletariat to defend the Soviet Union unconditionally, it being the first workers' state, while simultaneously fighting against Stalinism, though Trotsky did not explain how to actualize these two tasks in practice. By 1936 he concluded that Stalinism could not be overthrown by reforms but only by a revolution which would not be social for there was no need to alter the system of ownership. On the contrary, it would be political which would be carried out by the *avant-garde* of the proletariat, recapturing the essence of old Bolshevism destroyed by Stalin.

Trotsky's arguments of the Soviet Thermidor in 1924 was untenable for the defeat of the opposition by no means could be equated with the collapse of Jacobinism. Moreover, the French Thermidor marked the end of the revolutionary transformation of the social relations of production. This was not the case in the former Soviet Union. Stalin's rise actually witnessed the most radical and violent extension of forced collectivization of the peasantry (Deutscher 1963: 316).

Trotsky continued to see the Soviet Union as a workers' state in spite of 'socialism in one country', Stalinism and bureaucratization. It remained the only bulwark against the spread of fascism. However, the proletarian state had degenerated. Bolshevism, according to Trotsky, represented the progressive forces of Russian society but Stalinism was seen as a consequence of an heritage of oppression, misery, ignorance, backwardness, primitive technology, absence of an appropriate cultural and ideological consciousness, and lack of support from the European proletariat at large. In a 'dialectical' confrontation between the two, it was Stalinism or backwardness which triumphed.

In an Essay (1937) Trotsky rejected the notion that Stalinism was rooted in the Bolshevik tradition though he asserted that what was characterized as Stalinism — rule from above and independently of the masses — was true of Lenin and the Tsarist autocracy as well. This was due to poverty and economic backwardness which Bolshevism inherited. However, unlike Tsarism, Bolshevism was committed to the principle of popular legitimacy and revolutionary change even though these changes were introduced from above and, in certain situations, through coercive methods (Knei Paz 1978: 431). The dictatorship of the party and techniques of coercion were established during Lenin's time when Trotsky was at the helm of affairs. At that time they were regarded as temporary exigencies, a bulwark against counter-revolution. Stalin merely consolidated these tendencies. Trotsky realized the painful truth that the measures considered temporary seemed to have acquired a stamp of permanence and legitimacy with increase in social and economic problems.

In the New Course (1936) Trotsky regarded the dictatorship of the party in general and the principle of 'centralism' as an inviolable foundation of the soviet society and government. He was concerned about the internal character of the party and the dictatorship of power within it. A central demand which he made was for a policy that widened the mass basis of the party, increased workers' membership, encouraged genuine mass participation and compelled party officials to be open to the influence of the rank and file. He pleaded for freedom of expression, freedom to criticize and independence of thought.

While analyzing the Stalinist phase, Deutscher considered it as a continuation of the socialist premises articulated by Lenin and Trotsky. Though horrified by measures like forced collectivization, he regarded the communist state as progressive. In the second volume, he characterized Stalinism as 'primitive socialist accumulation', a phrase which he borrowed from Trotsky, in order to achieve a classless and stateless society. He considered the Stalinist phase as a tragic and an unavoidable episode in the building of socialism.

Analysis of Fascism

Through a series of essays written in the early thirties Trotsky attributed the rise of Nazism to the mounting crisis of capitalism and not just to its periodic disturbances. In order to maintain itself, capitalism had to abandon parliamentary democracy. Political losses were compensated by economic gains. Fascism differed from traditional dictatorships for it had mass support which enabled it to create conditions of mass terror that wiped out workers' organizations, centres of social resistance and political independence. The mass support came from the lower middle class or petty bourgeoisie who were desperate to overcome inflation, unemployment, bankruptcy and social instability. The petty bourgeoisie were hostile to capitalism but were equally hostile to proletarian revolution. Fascism became victorious because of the failure of the working class to seize power and resolve the crises of society.

Trotsky analyzed fascism with the intention of arousing the German Left towards concerted action. He was insistent that Hitler could be stopped and resisted only through an united front of the social democrats and communists. Their failure to do so signified to Trotsky the total bankruptcy of traditional reformism and Stalinism. He proposed a new Fourth International in 1938 to tackle the problem. The reason for its failure was that the European working class was not prepared to adopt Leninist strategies either because they were horrified by turn of events in the Soviet Union or they valued parliamentary democratic institutions (Howe 1978: 132).

However, the Fourth International generated world wide debate on Trotsky's doctrines and created many Trotskyist groups which rejected parliamentarism and supported pluralistic socialism, revolutionary class struggle, workers' control and proletarian dictatorship. A classless society, according to Trotsky, was possible only through a revolutionary destruction of the existing order. He looked to the totalitarian tendencies with Stalinism not as a form of government but as the socio-political dominance of class. Trotsky's criticisms of Fascism and his characterization of Western parliamentary democracies as bourgeois dictatorships protecting the interests of the propertied sections reflected his commitment to the deterministic outlook of orthodox Marxism.

Conclusion

Trotsky, reiterating Marx, argued that the independence of the bureaucracy was because it was an instrument of class interests. The Soviet bureaucracy was due to economic and social backwardness which he felt could be obviated with the introduction of socialism for the problems of economic want were solved by socializing means of production. Before 1917 he exaggerated the progress made by socialism, but subsequently, often warned of the 'vengeance' of backwardness, seeing it as the root cause of all problems.

> Trotsky's theses are now dated in some respects, but his general approach represented a phenomenal advance for classical Marxism . . . it became a reference point for all those engaged in a serious study of post revolutionary Russia. Trotsky defined Stalinist Russia as a society in transition with specific relations of production characterized by the permanent contradiction between the collective ownership of the means of production and bourgeois norms of distribution. This view was further developed by Ernest Mandel . . . (Ali 1984: 17).

For Trotsky socialism did not mean mere industrialization and higher standard of living but a society that was better than even advanced capitalist societies. This meant that the proletariat would have to be at the commanding heights of the world economy which he feared was impossible in Stalin's Russia. Proletarian democracy was secured by the soviets, socialist organization of production and consumption, workers' control and management of industry, and association of producers and consumers which would regulate distribution and pricing of consumer goods.

Trotsky was reluctant to examine the origins of totalitarianism in the former Soviet Union in general. Instead, he restricted himself to analyzing Stalinism when the latter was an offshoot of Leninism and Marxism. His own position vis-á-vis Lenin vacillated from strong condemnation of his party organization which he feared would lead to centralization and lack of democracy to one of support and defence. In his critique of Stalin he found virtues in Lenin looking upon the Leninist phase as being democratic and enlightening. He felt that if Bolshevism, instead of Stalinism, had prevailed, then totalitarianism in its excessive form would have been averted. He forgot his own prophecy that the Leninist one party system would eventually lead to personal dictatorship. In his younger days he 'grasped the causes of the decline of the Bolshevik Revolution in a way that the older Trotsky refused to acknowledge' (Howe 1978: 22). He did not want to state that the root of Stalinism was in Leninism which advocated a minority revolution through a violent seizure of power in a backward country, distorting democracy and perpetuating of tyranny.

Commenting on the distortion of history under the Stalinist regime, Trotsky remarked that 'history is becoming a clay in the hands of the potter' (cited in McLellan 1983: 87). In fact, Trotsky's own actions led to such a situation. After the collapse of the Second International and rise of Bolshevism, Marxism, instead of becoming a 'science of society' became 'the ideology of a political regime'. 'Indeed it had already begin to acquire this character in the writings of Lenin and Trotsky—both of whom were political pamphleteers and activists rather than thinkers, before the Revolution, and the transformation was finally accomplished by Stalin, who imposed by force, under the name of Marxism-Leninism, an intellectually impoverished doctrine which bolstered his own power and policies' (Bottomore 1983: 116).

Few would dispute the fact that Trotsky was an integral part of the Bolshevik leadership that created a regime which eventually developed into a personal dictatorship of Stalin. Unlike Plekhanov, he did not denounce the revolution though his analysis of its failure was brilliant and scholarly. He too was consumed by the very 'revolution' that he helped to make. Perhaps that was the fate of all minority revolutions that it betrayed not only its ideals but also its loyal supporters. It was ironic that the two most talented and outstanding Marxist theoreticians — Gramsci and Trotsky — were unseated from power, one by imprisonment and other by exile, yet they achieved fame and immortality by wielding their pens for causes they cherished. This in itself was far more spectacular than the combined strengths of all those Marxists who remained in power.

Nikolai Ivanovich Bukharin

The life and the tragic end of Nikolai Ivanonich Bukharin whom Lenin described as the favourite of the whole party is symbolic of the promise of the Soviet Revolution and its subsequent degeneration under the terror regime of Stalin. Lenin also added that Bukharin was Party's most eminent and valuable theoretician (Coates 1978: 73).

He was the most lovable of all the Bolshevik leaders, and though the youngest of all, he was recognized as the theoretical authority second only to Lenin. The latter looked upon him as his spiritual son. Although he disapproved of left communism he treated Bukharin very, very gently (Roy 1964: 498).

In his early thirties, yet an "old" Bolshevik, he (Bukharin) was the party's leading theorist, brilliant and profoundly educated. Lenin criticized his inclination to scholasticism and the doctrinaire angularity of his ideas. These ideas, however, exercised a strong influence even on Lenin who often adopted them and gave them a more realistic and supple expression Bukharin's was indeed an angular mind, fascinated more by the logical neatness of abstract propositions than by confused and confusing realities. Yet angularity of intellect was combined in him with an artistic sensitivity and impulsiveness, a delicacy of character, and a gay, at times almost schoolboyish, sense of humour. His rigidly deductive logic and his striving for abstraction and symmetry induced him to take up extreme positions: for years he had been the leader of the "left Communists" and by a process of radical reversal he was to become the leader of the party's right wing (Deutscher 1959: 82).

The belated rehabilitation of Nikolai Ivanovich Bukharin (1888–1938) after years of efforts by the Bertrand Russell Peace Foundation, A. M. Larina (widow), Yu N. Larin (Bukharin's son), Professor Eduard Goldstucker, Althusser, de Beauvoir, Galtung, Sweezy,

Howe, Chomsky, the Italian Communist Party and many other known figures from a number of countries in the centenary year of his birth along with Rykov and Tomsky was an event of great importance. It raised many questions about the nature and content of early socialist utopianism of the Bolsheviks, their later acceptance of mistake of attempting to create a socialist society too quickly, the subsequent developments within the Soviet Union and their impact on the communist movement and thinking throughout the world. Commenting on the extraordinary significance of this rehabilitation, Jonathan Steele (*Guardian Weekly* 1988) remarked that it opened a debate 'about whether there was any alternative to Stalinism. It was as though the Pope was to restore Martin Luther to membership of the Roman Catholic Church'.

Biographical Sketch

Bukharin, one of the youngest and most popular amongst the Bolshevik leaders, was born on 27 September 1888 in Moscow and was executed for treason and espionage at the third great Moscow trial (commonly known as the 'show trials') on 13 or 14 March, 1938. A son of teachers, he joined the Bolsheviks in 1906 when he was only 18-years-old. After his third arrest, he left Moscow in 1911, settled down in Vienna and made a critical study of the Austrian marginal utility school of economics. In 1914 after his deportation from Austria he went to Switzerland. He attended the Bolshevik anti-war conference in Berne in February 1915 when he picked up an argument with Lenin on the question of self determination. He reached Moscow in May 1917 after spending time in Scandinavia and the USA. In 1918 he led the 'Left Communists' to oppose the signing of the Brest-Litovsk Treaty with the Germans and called for a revolutionary war. He was elected to the party's central committee three months before the October Revolution and remained a full member till 1934. After that he was a candidate till 1937. In 1920–21 he desired the incorporation of trade unions to the state system. He argued for concessions to the peasants and favoured a balanced economy in which the peasants and the socialists had a role. He edited the party daily *Pravda* from December 1917 to April 1929. He was the editor of the *Izvestia* from 1934 to 1937. He played an instrumental role in the framing of the constitution adopted in 1936. Between 1925 to 1928 he was a co-leader, with Stalin, of the Communist Party. In 1929 he openly attacked Stalin's policies for bleeding the peasant dry in order to finance industrialization. In 1937 he was expelled from the party. A year later he was tried and sentenced to death.

Ever since 1901 like Marx himself, Bukharin combined in himself the three important aspects of a philosopher, a social scientist and a revolutionary. The German communist leader Rosa Mayer-Levine recounted her impression when she first saw him in Vienna in the winter of 1913–14. She held that he looked more like a saint than a rebel or a thinker. After Lenin he was the first of the party leader to systematically outline the general philosophy of the Party. In 1926 he published *The Theory of Historical Materialism: A Popular Manual of Marxist Sociology*.

Joseph Berger, one-time secretary of the Palestine Communist Party, described Bukharin's role in generational and intellectual terms. Lenin belonged to the first generation of the Bolsheviks, Trotsky to the second and Bukharin to the third. Taking note of the open political culture of the early Bolsheviks, as Berger pointed out, often Bukharin spoke freely and disagreed openly perhaps with the intention of making up his own mind after gauging other people's opinions. Bukharin was extremely popular among students and the younger members of the party.

Imperialism and the Question of the State

Bukharin made his first major contribution to Marxist theory in *Imperialism and World Economy* in 1915. In this work he characterized the bourgeois state in the context of the contemporary phase of imperialism as 'state capitalism'. The imperialist state had become the direct organizer of the economy. It regulated production within the nation state and competed with other capitalist states in the same way as did the individual capitalists during the days of Marx. Following the arguments advanced by Luxemburg, Bukharin argued that this led to militarization of the state and the economy with intense competition for arms. On the basis of this, he concluded that imperialism and militarism were the inevitable consequences of finance capitalism. Many of these arguments were incorporated in Lenin's *Imperialism, the Highest Stage of Capitalism*.

A more important consequence of Bukharin's finding of the linkage between capitalism and the state concerned the question of state power and its relationship to the socialist movement. The state in this changed context had become the main exploiter of the proletariat and, in this situation, the purpose of the socialist movement could not merely be the capture of state power but rather to smash the entire state machine. In this assertion Bukharin was in agreement with the overall perception of the German Left as articulated by Luxemburg and Pannekoek, and rejected the moderate position of Kautsky.

Kautsky argued that the Russian revolution of 1905 took place outside the ambit of parliamentary sphere not because the direct action of the masses supplemented parliamentary system but because the parliamentary machinery was not available and that proved that Russia was not ready for a revolution. Pannekoek questioned Kautsky's position on the relationship between the socialist movement and the state. He argued that the increasing strength of the labour movement was wrongly directed towards increased parliamentary representation as, under the prevailing conditions of imperialism, parliament was becoming less and less powerful. The German Left desired to create a proletarian alternative to the bourgeois state itself.

Bukharin disagreed with Lenin on the question of national self-determination on two grounds. First, self-determination was unrealizable in this period of imperialism and internationalization of the capitalist economy, and second, it was politically harmful as the essential plank of the socialist movement was to be a total and uncompromising opposition to state power. Lenin disagreed with Bukharin and wrote to the latter that the war made him take semi-anarchist ideas. He also rejected an essay by Bukharin on this subject in which Bukharin stated that the socialist revolution was to outgrow the framework of the state and break it from within as they organized their own state power. The other option was to get absorbed within the system of state capitalism. Lenin, while rejecting the article, commented that this total opposition to state power was 'either supremely inexact or incorrect' (Gankin and Fisher 1960: 241).

Bukharin, even after this rejection and Lenin's adverse comments, was convinced about the correctness of his line and published another version of his article in an organ of the German Left entitled *Arbeiterpolitik*. This article reaffirmed his earlier view. He described the modern state as a present day Leviathan which exploited people not indirectly like the earlier epochs but openly and directly, in which process all organizations and cooperatives integrated and transformed themselves into one organization of the rulers. This new development which became apparent during the war years clearly manifested that 'there comes into being a single, all-embracing organization, the modern imperialist private state, an omnipotent organization of bourgeois domination, with innumerable functions, with gigantic power, with spiritual (various methods of obscurantism, the Church, the press, the school, etc.,) as well material methods (police, solidity)' (Gankin and Fisher 1960: 237).

Lenin replied to this view of Bukharin in the same month in an article published in *Spornik Sotsial-Demokrata* in which he stated that the socialists favoured using the existing state and its institutions and facilitate the emancipation of the working class. He also maintained that the state had to be used for a specific form of transition from capitalism to socialism. This transitional state was the dictatorship of the proletariat. He also pointed out that the anarchists and Bukharin wanted to destroy the existing state which was not the goal of the socialists. Though he thought Bukharin's views to be mistaken yet it was closer to truth than the one articulated by Kautsky.

Bukharin, like Lenin, was critical of Kautsky and contended that the dictatorship of the proletariat was necessary as a period of transition. In 'the theory of the Dictatorship of the Proletariat' (1919) Bukharin laid utmost emphasis on the necessity of defeating the numerous forms of bourgeois opposition and for meeting this extraordinary challenge there had to be a strong, firm, comprehensive state organization of the working class. Since the bourgeoisie as a class would resist till the last even with external intervention the dictatorship of the proletariat was linked with the very survival of the socialist state. The resultant authoritarian character of the soviet state was supported by Bukharin. He could also see the pivotal importance of the question of economic development and declared that the fundamental purpose of the dictatorship of the proletariat was in the fact that it was a means of economic revolution.

Bukharin contended that in semi-capitalist countries, pure dictatorship of the proletariat was not possible and therefore pressed for 'a democratic dictatorship of the proletariat and peasantry' in which the proletariat dominated while sharing power with the non-proletarian masses. Thus he broadened the conception of the proletarian revolution to encompass various types of revolutionary movements in countries with different levels of economic and social development. More than Marx and Engels, he emphasized the role of a conscious leadership as being crucial role in the making of a revolution. Only after a period of economic development in which the socialist base of society would be broadened a true proletarian dictatorship moving towards pure socialist objectives could be realizable. He also pointed out that the bourgeois would offer resistance as long as they could and, with outside support, the dictatorship of the proletariat was linked to the survival of the socialist state. In the process, if the state became authoritarian, it was justified.

In an interesting analysis of the nature of the working class, Bukharin pointed out that the proletarian class, as a class, was not homogenous and, as a consequence, a 'proletarian vanguard' was to lead the other sections of the proletariat. He supported the role of the proletarian vanguard since the working class was not a homogenous class. This was a restatement of Lenin's position in *What is to be done*? Bukharin's views on the transitional state led to a change in Lenin's position which was articulated in *The State and Revolution*.

The year 1919 also saw the publication of the *ABC of Communism*. It was the work of two young party intellectuals Bukharin and Evgeny Alexeyevich Prebrazhensky, (1886–1937). The theoretical portions were written by Bukharin. The book was constantly reprinted and translated, and circulated widely in a number of countries as an authoritative exposition of communist theory and practice. Significantly, the book was not reprinted in the former USSR during the 1930s when both the leaders had fallen into disgrace.

> The *ABC of Communism* provides an unrivalled key to the purposes and policies of communism as they were conceived in the first years of the regime (Carr 1959: 28).

The theoretical portion dealt with the crisis, decline and fall of capitalism culminating in the communist revolution. The practical aspect dealt with the dictatorship of the proletariat and the establishment of the communist state. The October Revolution of 1917 was described in terms of the destruction of the existing Russian state and the new state apparatus as the dictatorship of the proletariat. It was conceded that the present state was also a class state, and its task was the destruction of the old state machine and the elimination of the bourgeoisie. It also dealt with the question of the withering away of the state, the 'most conspicuously utopian element in Marxist doctrine' which had to be 'seen in the light of the familiar nineteenth century dichotomy of society and state' (Carr 1959: 29).

Adam Smith conceived of a society of producers and traders in which the state would perform only a limited number of functions. Marx followed this trail and, like Smith, gave more importance to economics than politics. The realm of civil society was economics and state was the political arena which was inherently an evil. *ABC of Communism* was written when the communist Soviet Union was in existence for about two years and cautiously predicted the gradual disappearance of the state. It also dealt with the problem of equality, and here also the same caution was exercised with regard to the withering away of the state. The utopian element ended with the announcement of the NEP in 1921. Bukharin defended his utopianism as necessary to escape stagnation.

War Communism and its Aftermath

Bukharin attempted to analyze and justify the policies of an authoritarian socialist state during the period of transition making him one of the most important leaders of the left spearheading war communism. Its theoretical defence came from Bukharin's *Economics of the Transition Period* published in 1920. He developed an interesting thesis that initially, after a revolutionary transformation, there was a reduction in productive power which had to be dealt with compulsion, including compulsory labour and an all-encompassing role for the state where trade unions did not have any role. Lenin read this book carefully and made critical comments. Though he disapproved of some of the terminologies, he generally agreed with Bukharin's thesis (McLellan 1979: 117).

The war communism ended in a disaster and, with the inauguration of the new economic policy, Bukharin accepted a more gradual process of socialist transformation and moved towards a more moderate position. In his defence of NEP, Bukharin argued that the Soviet Union could mature into socialism in isolation utilizing its own resources. The state could control credit and gradually incorporate non-socialist elements, including those in agriculture. This created the theoretical basis for socialism in one country adopted by Stalin.

In the 1920s Bukharin championed the cause of peasantry. In 1925 he went to the extent of advocating the right to lease land and employ hired labour. The rich but efficient peasants, the *kulaks*, would grow into socialism through cooperatives. Stalin changed the meaning of socialism in one country to mean the creation of an industrial society at the cost of agriculture.

By 1928 Stalin returned to the original intent of war communism and ordered forcible seizure of grain when the peasants were unwilling to part with their stocks at a low price. Bukharin, Rykov and Tomsky became critical of Stalin's policy when they realized that Stalin would continue with these emergency measures. The former allies of Stalin against Trotsky now turned anti-Stalin. Bukharin criticized Stalin for becoming dictatorial and for abandoning the principle of collective action. Stalin replied by accusing Bukharin of being a right-wing deviationist. Between February and July 1929 the life and future of Bukharin, Rykov and Tomsky was at stake. In November Bukharin and Tomsky were expelled, followed by Rykov in 1930, annihilating any opposition to Stalin's policies. Bukharin lost his editorship of the *Pravda* and ceased to be the head of the Communist International which he held since 1926.

The Last Phase

Though the remarkable career of Bukharin as a Marxist revolutionary and theoretician came to an end by the late 1920s, yet some interesting developments took place before his execution. He contributed to the drafting of the constitution which was known as the Stalin Constitution. Bukharin introduced some important features like universal suffrage and establishment of equality of all citizens before the law. Generally it provided for the peaceful transition from the dictatorship of one party to genuine people's democracy for it contemplated multiple candidacy for elections, a suggestion eventually implemented by Gorbachev on a selective basis. It was

no small credit to Bukharin that the critics of the Soviet establishment in the 1950s and 1960s did not want to scrap the 1939 Constitution but wanted its enforcement.

The last great act of Bukharin took place immediately before his
execution. Since he could not rely any more on written words, he
drafted a letter 'to a future generation of communist leaders' explaining the turn of events and his role in it and told his wife Larina
to memorize it. In part, the letter said:

> . . . any member of the central committee, any member of the
> Party, can be rubbed out, turned into a traitor, terrorist,
> diversionist, spy, by these "wonder-working organs". If Stalin
> should ever get any doubts about himself, confirmation would
> instantly follow . . . . my one head, guilty of nothing, will drag
> down thousands of guiltless heads . . . . know, comrades, that
> on that banner, which you will be carrying in the victorious
> march to communism, is also my drop of blood (Bukharin,
> cited in Coates 1978: 51).

By executing Bukharin 'Stalin broke all records for political terror' and that 'the simple truth must be stated, not one of the tyrants
and despots of the past persecuted and destroyed so many of his
compatriots' (Medvedev 1971: 239). The rehabilitation confirmed
what was known for a number of years that there was no worthwhile evidence against people like Bukharin, Rykov, Syrtsov,
Lominadze, Krestlinsky and many others who were well-known
and associated with the party for a very long time. The personal
confessions came out of physical and psychological torture. One
admission of Khurshchev deserved a special mention in this context for, when he questioned Rudenko about the actual basis for
the execution of these men, Rudenko did not reply. Though
Khurshchev postponed the rehabilitation of Bukharin, Rykov and
Zinoview, he realized that it was a mistake for 'it would have been
better to tell everything. Murder will always be out. You cannot
keep things like that a secret for long' (Khurshchev, cited in
Medvedev 1971: 352–53). This confession by Khurshchev placed
the non-Russian Marxists in an embarrassing position as, without
any realistic appraisal of the serious failings of the Soviet state,
they agreed with the Stalinist version based on total fabrication
and use of terror.

Gramsci's Criticisms

Bukharin's efforts to make Marxism as the basis of scientific sociology was severely criticized by Gramsci, for the latter alleged the neglect of historical dimension and application of categories of natural to human behaviour without comprehension of the dialectical process. For Bukharin such an interpretation would be in purely scientific language.

> The world consists of forces, acting in many ways, opposing each other. These forces are balanced for a moment in exceptional cases only. We then have a state of "rest" i.e. their actual "conflict" is concealed. But if we change only one of these forces, immediately the "internal contradictions" will be revealed, equilibrium will be disturbed and if a new equilibrium is again established it will be on a new basis . . . . It follows that the "conflict"; the "contradiction", i.e. the antagonism of forces acting in various directions determines the motion of the system (Bukharin, cited in Joll 1977: 80–81).

For Gramsci such explanations did not clarify anything as the true function of the dialectic could only be grasped if the philosophy of *praxis* was conceived as an integral and original philosophy which opened up a new phase of history and a new phase in the development of world thought. It did this to the extent that it went beyond both traditional idealism and traditional materialism, philosophies which were expressions of past societies, while retaining their vital elements. If the philosophy of *praxis* was not considered except in subordination to another philosophy, then it was not possible to grasp the new dialectic through which the transcending of old philosophies was affected and expressed. Gramsci's views were much more in common with Hegel and Marx (Ibid.: 81).

Conclusion

Gramsci's criticisms brought out the serious limitations of the dogmatic exercises like Bukharin in the formative years of Bolshevik seizure of power and consolidation of its rule giving the impression that Bukharin was an eccentric Bolshevik (Lichtheim 1961: 313). But the doctrinal commitment of Bukharin continued even after the revolution and Lenin was furious to know that he was reprinting parts of the *State and Revolution* because at this time 'if he could, would have liked to forget and make others forget that he ever wrote *State and Revolution*' (Ulam 1922: 462). But the leader of the left-wing opposition Bukharin remained committed to the original plank even when the leadership was clearly moving away from it to hold on to total power. Similarly, on the Leninist theory of self determination, Bukharin had reservations since he was committed to class analysis and looked to nationalism as being of only secondary importance. Bukharin's criticisms angered Lenin who retorted 'scratch a Russian Communist and you will find a Russian Chauvinist' (Ibid.: 594). In reality it was the early communists like Bukharin and Luxemburg who remained committed to the utopianism of communism which was sacrificed by others when they captured state power and became part of the *nomenklatura* of the new class. He did not forget that the essential commitment of Lenin was that every cook would be taught to run the state.

The historic importance of Bukharin lies in the fact that his life was an example of dedication and faith in the principles of revolutionary Marxism. His contribution in explaining and elaborating Marxist theory was rich and varied, and included all the important dimensions including the role of the state. He attempted to 'sustain the character of Marxism as a science of society, engaged in scientific controversy with other sociological theories' (McLellan 1983: 116). Again in the 1920s on the dialectics of plan and the market in the post-capitalist society, the main participants were the authors of *ABC of Communism* (Mandel 1983: 219).

Bukharin's life and the tragic end vividly described the promise of the October Revolution and its subsequent degeneration reaching its peak during the show trials under Stalin's personalized ruthless dictatorship. Bukharin's position in the 1920s brought out the other possibilities that the Soviet Union had other than the forced collectivization and industrialization initiated by Stalin. In pointing out the possible alternatives Bukharin would always remain an important reference point for comprehending and dissecting the Stalinist totalitarian phase of Soviet communism.

Antonio Gramsci

... the greatest Marxist writer of the twentieth century, paradoxically, is also one of the greatest examples of the independence of the human spirit from its material limitations (Joll 1977: 117).

.... an extraordinary philosopher, perhaps a genius, probably the most original communist thinker of the twentieth century in Western Europe (Hobsbawm, cited in Davidson 1977: 1).

Gramsci is probably the most original political writer among the post-Lenin generation of Communists.... Although Gramsci's writings do not amount to a coherent theory but rather to a vague and embryonic sketch, some aspects of them are clear and original enough to justify the view that they constitute an independent attempt to formulate a Communist ideology, and not merely an adaptation of the Leninist schema (Kolakowski 1981c: 220).

It was Antonio Gramsci (1891–1937) who assumed the mantle of Marx and Engels for he strictly followed their prescriptions with the idea of its suitability in the twentieth century. Both Marx and Engels were essentially critics of nineteenth century advanced capitalism and their theory of revolution was supposed to apply to the areas of advanced civilization. They mistakenly thought that both capitalism and liberalism had exhausted themselves by the mid nineteenth century and that a socialist revolution was imminent to replace the inherently contradictory capitalist society. This optimism of Marx and Engels was never vindicated during their lifetime, and one of the shortcomings of the twentieth century Marxism was that very few Marxists attempted to give a satisfactory explanation for the resilience of capitalism.

One of the most important reasons for Gramsci's significance in spite of the fragmentary nature of his writings was that he suggested reasons for the strengths of liberalism and capitalism, and also the ways of revolutionary transformation of society. Rejecting the crude dialectical materialism propagated by theorists like Bukharin, he developed a highly sophisticated theory of historical materialism to deal mainly with the problems of class consciousness and a theory of revolution for the advanced capitalistic countries where a highly developed civil society exists. The attribution of Gramsci as a Western Marxist was perfectly justified. However, one should also remember that the very originators of Marxism, Marx and Engels, were also Western Marxists.

This assessment gets vindicated by the fact that at the trial of Gramsci in 1926 which led to his long imprisonment, Mussolini demanded, which was repeated by the prosecutor at the trial, that 'we must prevent these brains from functioning for twenty years'. The Fascists, in spite of their best efforts, failed in their objective as by any reckoning Gramsci's contribution to twentieth century Marxism was very impressive and the very fact that he is a reference point in practically every Marxist or radical debate even today reflects both his extraordinary originality in his Marxist analysis and the continued practical relevance of most of his formulations. There could not possibly be a better tribute to his memory than the recognition of the theory of *praxis*, a unity of theory and practice, which was reflected in his remarkable life itself.

Biographical Sketch

Gramsci was born in 1891 in a poor family in a small town of Ales in Sardinia. His father was a native of Naples and desired to be a lawyer which he had to abandon at the death of his father. He took up a job as a registrar in Ghilarza, a small town in Sardinia. There, he met his future wife and Gramsci's mother, a daughter of a local inspector of taxes. In 1897 Gramsci's father became jobless without pay on suspicion of embezzlement. In 1898 he was arrested, and in 1900 he was sentenced for six years in jail. The charges were never proved for many felt it was politically motivated. Moreover, corruption was endemic in Italian society. During these seven years, Gramsci's mother had to single-handedly bring up her seven children with no steady source of income other than the pittance that she earned as a seamstress and the proceeds from the sale of a small plot of land.

As a young man Gramsci did not keep good health. He had a malformation of the spine, which the doctors tried to cure in vain. Gramsci became hunch-backed and was barely five feet tall as a result of this spinal problem. He also suffered from internal disorders from which he nearly died when he was a small child and which continued to recur during his adulthood .

In 1898 Gramsci attended school in Ghilarza which had to be interrupted due to financial problems. He resumed school after the release of his father, and managed to pass the examination to enter the senior *liceo* in Cagliari. Around this time Gramsci got involved in politics influenced by his brother, a militant socialist. The brutal repression of the social protest that erupted in Sardinia also left an imprint on him. However, it was his involvement with the working class movement in Turin that led him to abandon his attachment to nationalism though he remained concerned with the problems of the peasants. From his school days Gramsci was an internationalist and anti-colonialist and a virulent critic of European imperialism. Subsequently, he discovered the class struggle between the industrial 'north' and rural 'south'. He took the cause of fellow Sardinists, their impoverishment and exploitation which was due to neglect and, to some extent, the privileges enjoyed by an expanding industry of northern Italy. At this stage Gramsci's outlook was not socialistic but more in the nature of regional and separatist aspirations.

In 1911 Gramsci won a scholarship for poor students from Sardinia to the University of Turin appearing for a examination at the same time as a future student friend and fellow communist Palmiro Togliatti. The scholarship amount was very meagre and Gramsci's heath suffered for want of proper nutrition. He remained ill during 1913–15, which forced him to abandon his studies. He also became politically more committed and took greater interest in national politics. The absence of liberal ideas created the climate for socialist ideas even among the middle class. Many professors at the university had socialist learnings. Among them were Umberto Terracini and Dante Scholar, who were good friends of Gramsci. Another important influence was Annibale Pastore whose lectures on Marxism Gramsci attended. Here, he became familiar with the Hegelian philosophy of *praxis* with which he retained an ambivalent relationship right till the end of his working life.

It was Antonio Labriola (1843–1904) who introduced the phrase 'philosophy of praxis', a term with which Gramsci remained associated. Labriola was the founder of Marxism in Italy before the First World War. He interpreted Marxism as a synthesis between theory and practice, between philosophy and history though he distinguished himself from Hegelianism by emphasizing the concrete over consciousness. Labriola's interpretation of history was extremely influential, particularly among the intellectuals though the tatter emphasized the idealistic over the materialist content. Rudolfo Mondolfo and, to some extent, Giovanni Gentile also interpreted the phrase 'philosophy of praxis' meaning anti-materialism. Mondolfo, the most influential figure in Italian socialism after Labriola, distinguished the philosophical Marx from the empirical Engels. He was largely responsible for the idealistic interpretation of Labriola. Gramsci tried to rescue the substantive portion of Labriola's Marxism from those Marxists who criticized Labriola's idealism and also those idealists who claimed Labriola as their own.

Another important influence on Gramsci was that of Benedetto Croce (1866–1952), a pupil of Labriola who professed to be a Marxist from 1895 to 1900. Croce forsake Marxism declaring it to be useful only as a 'simple canon of historical enquiry and research' and pronounced the 'death of theoretical Marxism in Italy'. Croce's secularism and opposition to positivism remained influential among the intellectuals. Politically, Croce's role remained ambivalent. He supported Mussolini in the early twenties. He was also an associate of Sorel, giving the impression that his commitment to the philosophy of the Left was intact.

Gramsci described critically his early intellectual leanings as 'Crocean' and his philosophical notebooks contained a rigorous critique of Crocean philosophy in connection to Marxism. In his prison writings Gramsci emphasized the need to counter 'Croceanism both as a diffuse ideology and as a specific philosophical system, sometimes casting Croce in the role of a Duhring, to be polemically destroyed, but more often seeing him as comparable to Hegel as a thinker whose work could be profited from in the struggle to renew Marxist thought and liberate it from positivistic accretions' (Gramsci, cited in Hoare and Nowell Smith 1971: xxiii).

In Turin Gramsci befriended Togliatti and Terracine, future leaders of the Communist Party of Italy (PCI). These three along with Angelo Tasca were responsible for the founding of L' Ordine Nuovo in 1919. Gramsci spent the war years alone in Turin. In 1915 he gave up university education, joined the staff of the Socialist Party weekly Il Grido del Popolo and became a full-time journalist. He acquired extensive knowledge of history and philosophy. He also matured as a political commentator, writing on every aspect of the social and political life of Turin. In 1916 he addressed his first public meeting speaking on Romain Rolland, on the French Revolution on the Paris Commune, on the emancipation of women. From

1917 he began to play an active role in the Turin party organization. From August 1917 he assumed an important post within the
Turin party when he was elected to the 'Provisional Committee'.
He became the editor of *Il Grido del Popolo* at a time when, except
for the press, the party activity had no legal standing. Gramsci attended the 1917 October conference as a delegate from Turin. The
conference issued a declaration of support for the Zimmerwald
and Kienthal congresses of anti-war socialists, and a formal condemnation of the reformists, Turati and his compatriots. Here he
also met Amadeo Bordiga. He slowly emerged as a spokesman
and the main theorist of the factory council movement which highlighted the struggles of the most advanced segment of the Italian
working class in Turin. This shot him to national prominence.

From 1913 Gramsci emerged as a professional politician. He
became the editor from 1914 of the Italian socialist press and from
1916 the co-editor of the Piedmont edition of *Avanti* for which he
made political observations, reviewed books and plays, and began
educating the workers of Turin. He played a leading role during
the revolutionary riots in Turin in 1917. During this year he also
wrote an article entitled 'The Revolution against *Das Kapital*' in
which he observed that the Bolsheviks won in spite of Marx's prediction that a country would have go through a phase of advanced
industrial capitalism. In 1918 the First World War ended. Following the success of the October Revolution in the erstwhile Soviet
Union there was intense speculation on the possibility of class struggle in Italy. It was Bordiga who realized the importance of the need
for a highly disciplined, organized revolutionary party and hence
explained his total dominance within the PCI in its initial stages.

In April 1919 Gramsci, Tasca, Togliatti and Terracine decided
to start a weekly 'review of socialist culture'. They called it the
Ordine Nuovo. The journal was different from other similar publications in three ways. First and most importance, it linked its theories directly to the practice of the Turin working class. It had a
programme for realizing the soviet system and towards this end
established councils in all the main factories of the city by 1920.
Secondly, these new institutions were made completely independent of the traditional working class organizations, making them
institutions of the whole proletariat including the non-organized
sectors, the anarchists. Gramsci looked upon these councils as
organs through which the controversial but ambiguous Marxist

concept of dictatorship of the proletariat would be exercised. Thirdly, the factory councils were seen as the nascent form of the future socialist state.

In 1919 at the Socialist Party Congress held at Bologna to decide whether to join the Third International, Bordinga expressed the view that too much parliamentary activity dampened the spirit of the workers and hence there must be more revolutionary activity. Gramsci and others articulated the importance of worker's councils, making it the most dominant idea of the movement. Though Gramsci considered these councils to be akin to the soviets but, like Sorel, he thought that the task of the real producers was not merely to produce but to organize the whole of social life. Gramsci's arguments were unacceptable to all groups. The Left believed that a socialist revolution must destroy all the institutions of political power through force and set up organs of the proletariat. The Right looked to the rule by the proletariat to imply the domination of the socialist party. The reformists desired representative democracy with socialist majority while the Left wanted the dictatorship of the proletariat.

There were a series of strikes accompanied by the establishment of factory councils but that did not develop into a nation wide struggle. Gramsci remained the lone voice in support of the workers' council as an instrument for the liberation of the proletariat. L'Ordine Nuovo decried reformism. Meanwhile in August-September 1920 there was another attempt by the Turin workers to occupy factories but that too failed, and, as a result, the Communist group in accordance with the wishes of Lenin transformed itself into a separate party. In November a separate manifesto was issued, and in January 1921 the split was formalized. A serious issue confronting the party was whether to seek an alliance with other socialist parties in view of the increasing popularity of Fascism. Gramsci favoured a broad alliance. In 1922 he went to Moscow as the party representative on the Executive Committee of the Comintern. He remained in Moscow for a-year-and-a-half taking part in the Fourth Comintern Congress in November 1923.

Meanwhile, Mussolini captured power. The Comintern withdrew support to Bordiga for his failure to distinguish between bourgeois democracy and Fascism. The Fascist government arrested many communists. Gramsci left for Vienna from Moscow at the end of 1923 and returned to Italy in May 1924. He was elected a member of parliament, which gave him personal immunity. The party was in disarray. It took a long time for Gramsci to defeat Bordiga's faction. Though Bordiga was in prison, he was still able to control the local groups. It was only in January 1926 at a congress held in Lyons that Gramsci was able to muster up support for his policy for forging an united front to re-establish democracy in Italy. Along with other anti-Fascist groups the communists had seceded from parliament in June 1924, only to return to some form of parliamentarism. In November 1926 Gramsci was arrested and sentenced to imprisonment for 21 years and 4 months. He spent the rest of his life in prison. He continued to write and read in spite of his frail health and the prison conditions. He remained a lone critic of Moscow and Stalin. In 1933 his health failed and he died on 27 April 1937.

Gramsci remained a prolific writer. He wrote nearly 3,000 pages in prison. Most of his writings were published after the Second World War. Like Marx himself, Gramsci looked to industrialization as a precondition for human liberation and his cherished dream was the rapid transformation of a backward Italy to a progressive society of the twentieth century by technological progress. The proletarian revolution would follow industrialization. His observations to Agnelli, the founder of the famous automobile industry in Turin, and other industrialists of Turin would have gladdened Marx.

I have a profound admiration for these men. They are the dominating rulers of our time, the kings much stronger and more useful than the kings of other times as well as of our own. They are the people who uproot the ignorant, surly masses of the countryside from their quiet passive insolence and throw them into the glowing crucible of our civilization . . . Agnelli founds factories, and of necessity the workers becomes socialists (Gramsci, cited in Joll 1977: 20).

Croce's Influence

As Hegel dominated the German intellectual scene in the early nineteenth century the decisive influence in Italy in the early twentieth century was that of Croce. The latter attacked the positivist doctrine of advocating the methods of natural sciences to those of social sciences and emphasized the subjective and intuitive factors in moulding historical change and artistic creation. Croce was well-versed with the writings of both Hegel and Marx, he had learned a lot from them but was also critical of them. He viewed the entire process of history as a record encompassing human activity, art, economics, philosophy, and emphasized, like Hegel, the supreme importance of human spirit. 'To the young Italian intellectuals before 1914 Croce's philosophy gave a sense of meaning and of moral purpose to the study of history and an awareness of the continuous relevance of the past the present' (Gramsci, cited in Joll 1977: 21).

Gramsci was no exception and even when he became a committed Marxist, the influence of Croce and other non-Marxist thinkers remained with him. Throughout his life he conducted a dialogue with Croce and the *Prison Notebooks* was full of reference to him. He appreciated Croce's thought ' . . . as a valuable instrument, and so it can be said that he directed attention energetically to the facts of culture and thought in the development of history, to the function of the great intellectuals in the organic life of civil society and the state' (Ibid.: 24).

A series of essays written by Croce in the early 1920s attracted a great deal of Gramsci's attention. In these essays Croce endorsed Machiavellian approach to the study of politics popularized by the Italian elitist thinkers Pareto and Gaetano Mosca (1858–1941). Gramsci was pleased with this approach which shared with Marxism a distrust for traditional political categories.

Both Croce and Gramsci believed in a close relationship between consensus and force, and liberty and authority. In one crucial area of Gramsci's thought, Croce exerted an extraordinary influence, namely, the concept of civil and political societies. In using these terms Gramsci used the language of Hegel and Marx but gave them novel meanings. For Hegel and Marx, civil society was to be discovered not in the structure but in the superstructure of society, not in commerce and industry but in ideology and cultural organizations. For both Croce and Gramsci, it was in the sphere of Church or civil society that the intellectuals operate and 'for both men, whatever "ethical" content a state may have is to be found in this sphere, not within the state proper' (Bates 1975: 157). Gramsci acknowledged the instrumental value of Croce to Italian Marxism as highlighting ' . . . the importance of cultural and intellectual factors in historical development, to the function of great intellectuals in the organic life of civil society or of the state, to the moment of hegemony and consensus and the necessary form of the concrete historical bloc' (Bates 1975: 356).

Gramsci praised Croce's scale and depth which he described as Gothean aspect of Croce's thought. Other than Croce, Gramsci borrowed from Gentile's thesis of self constitution through the unity of theory and practice. Though Gramsci acknowledged his intellectual debt to Croce in understanding history as an intellectual activity and limitation of positivism, yet he was also critical of Croce for a number of reasons. He believed Croce to be a spokesman of European liberalism mainly because of his criticism of Marxism. He was also critical of Croce's speculative philosophy as Gramsci believed in a theory of *praxis*, combining theory with practice. Though their philosophical motives were similar, their political motives differed totally for 'if Croce's aim was to create an alternative to Marxism, Gramsci's was to offer Italians a Marxist alternative to Croce' (Ibid.: 356).

Factory Councils

The end of the First World War plunged Italy into a prolonged crisis which ultimately led to the fascist victory under Mussolini's leadership in 1922. But before this turn of events, many thought that a successful socialist revolution was imminent in Italy. In fact, it was the alarm of such a prospect in the background of a faltering liberal parliamentary system that led the industrialists and the middle class to support Mussolini whose strength grew dramatically in 1921 and 1922.

The years 1919–20 saw a vast expansion in socialist activity, and the trade union membership increased from a quarter million in 1918 to two million in 1920. In the November 1919 parliamentary election, the Socialist Party gained significantly. It was in this period of crisis and socialist consolidation that Gramsci's transformation from a little-known journalist to one of the founders and leaders of the Italian Communist Party took place.

The most important development in the early years of Gramsci's political life was his enthusiastic support for the movement for Factory Councils in Turin during the years 1919–20. Immediately after the First World War, Italy was amidst an acute economic crisis which led to large-scale militancy of the workers as they were looked to as very mild and ineffective organizations without any link with the grassroots. The movement for the Factory Councils was an off-shoot of this crisis and, for Gramsci, the Councils were to be the key organizations, like the soviets in the former USSR, for the revolutionary transformation of the Italian system. Their origin could be traced back to the 'internal commissions' elected by trade union leaders to deal with minor matters of arbitration and discipline. They were seen as expressing and defending the interests of the workers. Contrasted to political parties and the trade unions, Gramsci wanted these internal commissions to be converted into Factory Councils for they 'limit the power of the capitalist in the factory and perform functions of arbitration and discipline. Tomorrow, developed and enriched, they must be organs of proletarian power, replacing the capitalist in all his useful functions of management and administration' (Gramsci, cited in Joll 1977: 66). Their true representative had to be maintained by elected representatives and division of labour as existing within the factory.

> Every factory is subdivided into workshops and every workshop into crews with different skills; each crew carries out a particular part of the work process. The workers in each crew elect one of their number as delegate, giving him an authoritative and revocable mandate. The assembly of delegates from the entire factory makes up a Council, and this Council elects an executive committee from its own ranks. The assembly of political secretaries of the various executive committees forms in turn a central committee of the Councils, and this central committee selects from its own number an education committee for the whole city with the task of organizing propaganda, drawing up work plans, approving projects and proposals from individual factories and even individual workers, and finally giving general leadership to the whole movement (Ibid.: 317).

Gramsci categorically differentiated Factory Councils from trade unions and political parties.

> The actual process of the proletarian revolution cannot be identified with the development and activity of revolutionary

organizations of a voluntary and contractual nature, such as political parties and trade unions. These organizations arise in the sphere of bourgeois democracy and political liberty, as affirmations and developments of this political liberty. . . . The revolutionary process takes place in the sphere of production, in the factory, where the relations are those of oppressor to oppressed, exploiter to exploited, where freedom for the worker does not exist, and democracy does not exist (Gramsci, cited in Joll 1977: 317).

A significant aspect of this proposal was an emphasis on the improvement of technology and productivity within the factory because it allowed the workers to move towards building a socialist process of production rather than merely compete with the capitalists for cornering greater share of profit. In revolutionary transformation these Councils would play an important role for they would instill self confidence in the working class. By administration and acquisition of technical skills the Factory Councils would show 'the socialist state already exists potentially in the institutions of social life characteristic of the exploited working class. To link these institutions, coordinating and ordering them into a highly centralized hierarchy of competencies and power, while respecting the necessary autonomy and articulation of each, is to create a genuine workers' democracy here and now — a worker's democracy in effective and active opposition to the bourgeois state, and prepared to replace it here and now in all its essential functions of administering and controlling the national heritage' (Ibid.: 65).

The Factory Councils was a solution to the endemic problems of all revolutionary movements, the need to reconcile liberty and authority, and spontaneity and discipline. This system of workers' democracy 'would give shape and permanent discipline to the masses, it would be a magnificent school of political and administrative experience, it would involve the masses to the last man, accustoming them to tenacious perseverance, accustoming them to consider themselves as an army in the field, which needs cohesion if it is not to be destroyed and reduced to slavery' (Ibid.: 39).

The idea of Factory Councils was very similar to the position of Council Communists like Luk'acs, Korsch and Pannekoek who propounded the thesis that the proletariat as a class would be the first to achieve self-emancipation. Some important similarities could be found between the Factory Councils and the Guild Socialist plank in England on workers' participation and industrial democracy. The influence of Syndicalism and Sorel was also clearly discernible. Though the Factory Council movement failed, its essential principles continued to inspire Gramsci throughout his life. Out of the failure of the Council movement Gramsci also realized the cardinal importance of the Communist Party in the revolutionary transformation of society. But what was striking was that though he recognized the importance of the Party he did not substitute it for Industrial democracy. Instead he attempted to make them complementary.

Conception of the Party

One of Gramsci's major efforts when he led the Communist Party was to broaden its support base. Along with this he wanted to maintain unity in the party. In this context, his position at an Italian Communist Party Congress in January 1926 at Lyons in France deserved special mention for he defended the thesis that the party had to be a part of the working class itself and not separate as contended by Bordiga. He wanted a united front against Fascism. Another significant point that he made was that since Italy's economic development was uneven compared with other industrial countries of Western Europe, the structure of capitalism was more vulnerable and, consequently, more easily to be overthrown here. This shift in Gramsci from orthodox Marxism which always propagated the thesis that the socialist revolution would first take in an area of advanced capitalism was of crucial significance and had to be understood in terms of his more voluntaristic interpretation of Marx's theory of revolution. This led him to characterize the Russian Revolution of 1917 as a revolt against Marx's Capital. Explaining this he commented that Marxist 'thought considers not economic facts the main force in history, but man, the society of men who are close to each other and this collective wish dominates the economic facts and becomes the motor of the economy' (McLellan 1979: 178).

The Southern Question

Another important dimension to Gramsci's evolution in this period was his preoccupation with the 'southern question', the question relating to the role of the peasantry in the political process of Italy. He could easily grasp the fact that though Marx himself had a very poor opinion of the peasantry and the proletariat, which in practice meant a close coordination between the industrialized north and the backward agricultural south. A new national unity would emerge out of this alliance. He realized that the successful completion of this mission was an extremely difficult task. Looking to the organization and success of the Roman Catholic Church, Gramsci envisaged that an intellectual led movement would be able to establish the necessary rapport with the peasantry. In understanding this important role of the peasantry he was a precursor of Mao.

Hegemony and the Role of Intellectuals

Hegemony was a key and unifying concept in the *Prison Notebooks* and of his entire theoretical edifice. Its basic idea was that people were not ruled by force alone but by ideas. A hegemonic crises arose when the rule was by force and not primarily of the ideological apparatus of civil society. Gramsci made an important distinction between civil and political society. Civil society consisted of private institutions like schools, churches, clubs, journals and parties which were instrumental in crystallizing social and political consciousness, and political society consisted of public institutions like the government, courts, police and the army, the instruments of direct domination. It was in the civil society that the intellectuals played an important role by creating hegemony. If the hegemony was successfully created by the intellectuals then the ruling class ruled by controlling the apparatus of civil society, and if they failed then the rule was through coercion.

Gramsci distinguished between traditional and organic intellectuals. The traditional intellectuals thought themselves as one and performed the functions in that role independently. The organic ones were closely linked to the class to which they belonged. An example of traditional intellectuals was the clergy and their relation with the feudal ruling class in the Middle Ages, which was organic but subsequently became autonomous. Another example of traditional intellectual was Croce. Gramsci argued that the idea of independence was an illusion as the intellectuals were linked to the class structure in which they lived. An independent class of intellectuals did not exist, but rather every social group had its own intellectuals.

> However, the intellectuals of the historically progressive class . . . exercise such a power of attraction that they end . . . by subordinating the intellectual of other social groups and thus create a system of solidarity among intellectuals, with links of a psychological (vanity) or caste nature. This fact is realized spontaneously in historical periods in which the given social group is truly progressive (Bates 1975: 353).

The shift from traditional to organic intellectualism took place when the revolutionary class itself produced its intellectuals. The role of the intellectuals was a practical one. 'The mode of being of the new intellectuals can no longer consist in eloquence, which is an exterior and momentary mover of feelings and passions, but in active participation in practical life, as constructor, organizer, "permanent persuader" and not just a simple orator' (Gramsci 1971: 10).

Again, emphasizing on the need for a linkage between the intellectuals and the masses, Gramsci stated:

> The position of the philosophy of *praxis* is the antithesis of that of Catholicism. It does not tend to leave the "simple" in their primitive philosophy of common sense, but rather lead them to a higher conception of life. If it affirms the need for contact between intellectuals and "simple" it is not in order to restrict scientific activity and preserve unity at the low level of the masses, but precisely in order to construct an intellectual-moral bloc which can make politically possible the intellectual progress of the mass and not only of small intellectual groups (Ibid.: 332–33).

Gramsci rejected the Leninist conception of the 'party' and its principle of democratic centralism. He contended that such a party would be more a policing organ than a deliberative body. He believed that a cultural consensus around a shared moral vision would render a coercive state redundant under communism. He argued that factory system was self-regulating and what was required was to ensure that production was related to needs of the producers, to raise workers' consciousness of their role within the productive process and their relationship with the rest of the global economy. In course of time a collective will would emerge.

Analysis of a Fascism

A significant contribution of Gramsci was his analysis of fascism. In his paradigm, Italy, like Spain, Portugal, Poland and the Balkans, occupied a mere peripheral status in the capitalist world. The other two kinds of European nations were characterized as *advanced* and *transitional*. This peripherally created some problems for Italy; for instance, the political connotations of different classes continued to remain confusing and vexed. The primary reason for this weakness stemmed from the fact that Italy, like Germany, entered the capitalist phase not by either class conflict or a bourgeois revolution but by the impact of a foreign war. Its inevitable consequence was that Italy reflected a very imperfect capitalistic order. In such an order, the hegemony of the dominant class remained only partially successful leading to a perpetual hegemonic crises.

The phenomenon of fascism had to be understood as a device that could contain the capitalist crisis, but only with machine guns and revolvers. As such, the hegemonic crisis continued. Gramsci characterized fascism as a passive revolution which was congenial to the situation of Italy as it enabled it to modernize and restructure its economy within capitalism with massive state support, which created a situation that was just the opposite of the modernization process initiated in the Soviet Union after the proletarian revolution. Fascism as such was not mere Bonapartism, as Trotsky thought it to be, but rather it was a new kind of organization with mass support from the petty bourgeoisie. Gramsci contended that this happened for the first time in history.

Fascism could contain, but not solve, the Italian crisis and the consequent static equilibrium could usher in true hegemony. Gramsci predicted a 'long life' for the fascist regime but denied that it constituted an epoch. His analysis was vindicated by subsequent history when, within eight years of his death, fascism was wiped out not only from Italy but also from entire Europe.

In the process of analyzing fascism, Gramsci developed three general concepts, *caesarism, war of attrition* and *passive revolution*.

Caesarism referred to a situation when some previously dormant or unknown forces capable of asserting domination intervened politically and restored a static equilibrium in a hegemonic crisis situation. There may be variants in this intervention, progressive (Caesar and Napoleon I) and reactionary (Napoleon III and Bismarck. 'Caesarism always involves a perpetual struggle for the hearts and minds of the population beyond that usually associated with processes of legitimization in normal politics' (Adamson 1980: 629).

Such a struggle for Gramsci represented a *war of attrition*. Fascism was an example of this. He contrasted this with a *war of movement* which meant seizure of power through military confrontation. The example for this was the Bolshevik coup of November 1917. The rise of fascism demonstrated that such methods were outmoded and the *war of position* whether won by incumbents or insurgents became decisive. Discussing the process of the war of movement becoming a war of position, Gramsci stressed their differences and, on this basis, criticized Trotsky's theory of permanent revolution. 'The formula (of permanent revolution) is appropriate to a historical period in which the large mass of political parties and the large economic unions did not exist and when society was so to speak still in a state of fluidity' (Ibid.: 243).

The third concept was passive revolution which did not launch frontal attacks 'because they possess either substantial hegemonies force without a capability for domination or, like Caesarism, a capability for domination without substantial hegemonic force' (Adamson 1980: 629). Under the Roman Empire the passive revolution of the Christians was an example of the first type and the Italian Risorgimento was an example of the second.

Relative Autonomy of Politics

A pertinent question remained about the causes that led to the survival of fascism in spite of the its inability to solve basic contradictions of the Italian society. For seeking an answer to this question, Gramsci dissected the vital relationship between economics and politics, and also dealt with the nature of the state. In dealing with these important issues, he discovered that the art of politics had a dynamics and autonomy of its own which could be clearly distinguished from the realms of economics, morality and religion. For him, as it was for Machiavelli, political activity was the human activity par excellence. One of his major unfulfilled ambitions was to deal specifically with this political aspect in a book significantly titled *The Modern Prince*.

Apart from Gramsci's interest in the period of Italian unity, Risorgimento, he put a lot of efforts in comprehending the political theory of the Italian Renaissance in general and of Machiavelli in particular. Following Croce's description of Marx as the 'Machiavelli of the proletariat' Gramsci tried to analyze the contemporary situation. Many pages of the *Prison Notebooks* were devoted to notes on Machiavelli, and Gramsci thought that Machiavelli's greatness consisted in his distinction of politics from ethics. The 'modern prince' for him had to be the 'party'.

> The Modern Prince, the Prince-myth, cannot be a real person, a concrete individual: it can only be an organism, a complex element of society, in which a collective will . . . begins to take concrete form. Such an organism had already been provided by historical development and it is the political party, the first cell in which germs of a collective will come together and tend to become universal and total (Gramsci 1971: 129).

Gramsci accepted the fact that the economic and the political factors were interlinked and that the politicians could be relatively autonomous. But he also asserted that the political developments had their own independent characteristics. The degree and extent of this autonomy depended on a number of variables. In the case of Italian fascism, Gramsci perceived that it enjoyed a great deal of autonomy both internally and externally and, as such, its immediate collapse could not be expected. However, he was also confident that, because of its own internal contradictions, fascism would not continue indefinitely. It was no small credit for Gramsci that his formulation of relative autonomy of politics was reaffirmed by Poulantzas four decades later.

Theory of the State

Gramsci's theory of the state developed out of his notion of the proper relationship between the state and the civil society. Whereas

Marx's emphasis was on the totality of all the economic relations, in Gramsci there was an enormous emphasis on the superstructure. The hegemony of the dominant class was exercised through the civil society, culturally, and not through coercion. But this hegemony of the civil society did not exist equally in all societies. For instance, making a categorical distinction between Russia and the West European countries he asserted that in:

> Russia the state was everything, civil society was primordial and galantines; in the West, there was a proper relationship between state and civil society, and when the state trembled a sturdy structure of civil society was at once revealed. The state was only an outer ditch, behind which there stood a powerful system of fortresses and earth works (Gramsci, cited in McLellan 1979: 189).

This marked difference between two different kinds of states called for revolutionary strategies in the East and the West. In simple terms, it meant that the Leninist model which was successfully applied in the Russian situation was inapplicable in the more sophisticated political orders of the West. A frontal attack could only be launched in states which were less developed. But in the more developed ones the attack could not possibly be directed exclusively against the state. It had to be primarily directed against the civil society. Using military vocabulary, the frontal attack was characterized by Gramsci as 'a war of movement or maneouver' and the other a 'war of position'. For a wel-developed capitalist state, the second course was the correct one. Gramsci believed that Lenin before his death had accepted this fact whereas it was Trotsky who continued to be 'the political theorist of frontal attack in a period in which it only leads to defeats' (Kiernan 1972: 25). This Gramscian position had a lot of similarity with the position that Kautsky took up in his polemics against Lenin, which proved that such a position had lot of support among the Marxist theoreticians at that time. Moreover, in the significant recent developments in Western Marxism that ultimately led to the emergence of Eurocommunism, the most important inspirer was undoubtedly Gramsci (McLellan 1979: 181).

On Gandhi

Though Gramsci's primary concern was with the dissection of advanced capitalism, he also dealt with some other important contemporary developments and drew inspiration from them. For instance, he mentioned the phenomenon of Gandhi. With his utmost concern of evolving strategies to counter fascism, he accepted the fact that the 'war of position' had to be followed which in practice meant complex political struggles, much more difficult than the one that was needed in the 'war of movement' in the early days of the former Soviet Union. The most important guideline in developing this strategy was that the political element would always prevail over the military apparatus. It was in this context that Gramsci gave the example of the anti-colonial struggles led by Gandhi. He referred to the boycott movement as a preparatory stage for further advanced action. The Gandhian movements reflected 'forms of mixed struggles, fundamentally of a military character, but mainly fought on the political plain' (Gramsci 1971: 107). Complimenting Gandhi, he further asserted that:

> this type of struggle is suitable for a country that is technically disarmed and militarily inferior being dominated by technically developed and superior countries . . . . Gandhi's passive resistance is a war of position (boycott) which at certain moments becomes a war of movement (strikes), . . . the secret preparation of Weapons of combat troops belongs to underground warfare (Ibid.: 229).

The striking thing in Gramscian perspective on Gandhi was that, writing in virtual seclusion in a fascist prison, he could grasp the revolutionary potentialities of the Gandhian movements.

Conclusion

In both his earlier writings when Gramsci was a journalist and a political activist as well as in his more mature writings, there were remarkable insights into crucial issues related to Marxism. The first important thing that strikes us is the remarkable unity of themes in his activism and theory. He criticized the crude empiricism of certain positivist Marxists on the grounds that facts do not speak for themselves but only make sense within a theory that explains and analyzes. Second, he correctly grasped that Marxism had to be analyzed and studied as a development from Hegelianism and also that it would be a mistake to identify the ideas of Engels with that of Marx. Third, mainly because of the influence of the Hegelian philosopher Croce, 'he absorbed more history than any other Marxist since Marx' (McLellan 1979: 176). This exceptional knowledge enabled him to acquire remarkable insights into the forces that moulded politics. Fourth, he was very critical of Marxists like Bukharin, who mistakenly attempted to reduce everything to a single ultimate or final cause and dismissed all other philosophies except Marxism as nonsense and, because he had a more realistic and also a wider perspective, he did not fall into the trap of either Stalinism or crude Marxist determinism'. While in Russia success hardened Bolshevik thinking into dogma, failure taught Gramsci to question, doubt, analyze over and over again (Kiernan 1972: 4). Fifth, he admired not only Lenin but also Luxemburg and Pannekoek. The Lenin he admired was the Lenin of *The State and Revolution* in which the Communist Party played an insignificant role and was mentioned only in the passing. This fact assumed great importance because, unlike Lenin for whom the professional revolutionaries played the most crucial role, for Gramsci it was the intellectuals who fulfilled that purpose. However, the intellectuals, unlike the professional revolutionaries who remained a distinct category, became part and parcel of the struggle and life of the peasantry and the workers. This fact enables us to comprehend Gramsci's most important contribution to Marxism, a total commitment to a majoritarian revolution led by the party and its collective leadership. Any deviation, either in the name of strategy or success, was not acceptable. In spite of innumerable hardships and sacrifices, Gramsci remained committed till the last to the advancement of human freedom, dignity and genuine democracy.

Herbert Marcuse

The book (*One Dimensional Man*) is brilliant, it contains a series of minute and honest observations. But when the substance is examined it is easy to see that it is not an indictment of capital but of technology (Colletti 1969: 138).

... the whole of Marcuse's critique of positivism, and most of his interpretation of Hegel and Marx, are a farrago of arbitrary statements, both logical and historical. These statements, moreover, are integrally bound up with his positive views on the global liberation of mankind and his ideas on happiness, freedom and revolution (Kolakowski 1981c: 402).

One Dimensional Man marks a sharp break in Marcuse's thought, even though the substance of his thesis about Western industrial society is already found in *Eros and civilization,* and that about Soviet society in *Soviet Marxism.* What is new is twofold: his virtual relinquishing of any distinctively Marxist—as against Hegelian—categories, and his pessimism.... For Marcuse's thesis is that "technical progress, extended to a whole system of domination and coordination, creates forms of life (and of power) which appear to reconcile the forces opposing the system and to defeat or refute all protest in the name of historical prospects of freedom from toil and domination" (MacIntyre 1970: 69–70).

The most popular defence of advanced capitalism as a viable and relatively just system was provided by the democratic pluralist view. Its major emphasis was that within advanced capitalism there was equality of opportunity, for most, if not all the people, and because of this crucial factor, the concepts of a ruling class, power elite and class politics were largely irrelevant. In these systems 'all the active and legitimate groups in the population can make themselves heard at some crucial stage in the process of decision' (Dahl 1965: 137–38) and 'the fundamental political problems of the industrial and political citizenship have been solved, conservatives have accepted the welfare state; and the democratic left has recognized that an increase in overall state power carries with it more dangers to freedom than solution to economic problems' (Lipset 1963b: 443).

This theory of classlessness of advanced capitalism had obvious limitations. Though it was generally conceded that the welfare state lessened inequalities to a considerable degree by improving living standards of the poorer sections, it was acknowledged that far from any indication of withering away of classes, they continued with in-built cleavages. In other words, the Marxist analysis of these societies still retained validity to a very considerable degree.

In recent times, one of the most penetrating class analysis of the welfare state emerged from Ralph Miliband who, in his *The State* in Capitalist Society (1969), made a detailed critique of the pluralist view and asserted the superiority of the Marxist analysis. He began by examining the concepts of ruling class or the power elite which the pluralists totally ignored. In most of the advanced capitalist countries there were two features, (1) they were highly industrialized and (2) the largest portion of their economic activity was under private ownership and control. Miliband also pointed out that there was state intervention, of varying degrees, in the economic life in all the countries of advanced capitalism. Their economic base was identical, resulting in notable similarities within their social structure and class distribution. There, continues to exist a relatively small number of people who owned a very large and disproportionate share of wealth, deriving their incomes from ownership. This class could be described as the ruling class in the Marxist sense and despite 'all the instances of growing or achieved "classlessness"... the proletarian condition remains a hard and basic fact in these societies, in the work process, in the levels of income, in opportunities or the lack of them, in the whole social definition of existence' (Miliband 1969: 16).

These affluent societies also carried with them large sections of people who lived in misery. Managerial capitalism was not a selfless neutral institution but maintained definite class interests. They appeared social in character but were largely for private purposes. The social origins of this managerial class was similar to people with large incomes and ownership of property. The elite recruitment was mostly hereditary. Education was very important to rise in the ladder, though the elite institutions were usually accessible to upper and middle classes. The working class students did not get better jobs. The differences among the dominant classes were confined within a given ideological framework. The property owners controlled the state system. For instance, a very small percentage of the American army officers came from the working class background. It was the same in Sweden and Japan. The main purpose of the government was to further the interests of capitalism for it 'genuinely believed in the virtues of capitalism, and ... have accepted it as far superior to any possible alternative economic and social system' (Ibid.: 170). Contrary to the general belief, the higher civil service was not neutral. The military maintained close relationships with large-scale business houses. The judges were appointed by the government, who in turn appointed conservative judges. All these factors combined to create an imperfect competition. In different ways this process was legitimized, for instance, the bourgeois political parties were in a position to spend more money than the working class ones.

Miliband also pointed out that the most significant political fact of advanced capitalism 'is the continued existence . . . of private and ever more concentrated economic power. As a result of that power, the owners and controllers in whose hands it lies, enjoy a massive preponderance in society, in the political system, and in the determination of the state's policies and actions' (Miliband 1969: 265). The basic fact in these societies was that unequal economic power produced unequal political power.

> . . . it is the capitalist context of generalized inequality in which the state operates which basically determines its policies and actions. The prevalent view is that the state in these societies can be and indeed mostly is the agent of a "democratic" social order, with no inherent bias towards any class or group; and that its occasional lapse from "impartiality" must be ascribed to some accidental factor external to its "real" nature. But this too is a fundamental misconception; the state in these class societies is primarily and inevitably the guardian and protector of the economic interests which are dominant in them. Its "real" purpose and mission is to ensure their continued predominance, not to prevent it (Ibid.: 265–66).

Miliband's views were known as instrumentalist because he argued that capitalism used 'the state as its instrument for the domination of society' (Ibid.: 23).

The Structuralists, beginning with Louis Althusser (1918–85) challenged this contention. He began with Gramsci's assertion of the relative autonomy of the state which explored not only the economic dimension but also the various other components — political, legal and ideological segments — of society. The repressive apparatus of the state worked out the mechanism of domination of the working class by the ruling class with its apparatuses like the bureaucracy, police, courts, prisons and the army. Besides these, there were the ideological and structural dimensions like the church, schools, family, political parties, trade unions, communications and cultural organizations. Althusser argued that in advanced capitalism the ruling class maintained itself in power by using both the repressive and the ideological apparatuses. In mature capitalism education was a mechanism of ideological domination and was similar to the role performed by the church in the pre-capitalist phase. It was the real mechanism of control behind the formal parliamentary setup with universal suffrage and competing party system.

Nicos Poulantzas elaborated on Althusser's basic formulations and related them to the major function of capitalism, namely, the reproduction of the capitalist society in its totality. The state along with maintaining the political interest of the ruling class also performed the functions of ensuring cohesion and equilibrium in society in a manner that blurred class divisions. As a result, social relations appeared competitive and individual-based. Any notion of class and class struggle disappeared in that situation. The competitive party system concealed the contradictions, factions and disunity. It did not allow hegemony of any particular class, including the bourgeoisie. Since the state was not the instrument, as Miliband assumed, of a dominant class, the state was relatively autonomous and a stabilizing factor. The structuralist view, like the instrumentalist one, did not deal with the mechanism of change or the essential reasons for the continuance of the capitalist state.

The refreshing originality of Herbert Marcuse (1898–1979) was in the fact that though he accepted the fact of inequalities in advanced capitalism and its irrationalities yet he concluded that there was no probable escape from it because there was some rationalities in these irrationalities which were cherished and valued by all, irrespective of class and status. One of these was the prevailing false consciousness in an overwhelming number which allowed disguised violence of the state to continue making the state look legitimate to the majority of people. His uniqueness was in the fact that he was a first-rate critic of this system as well as one of its best defenders.

Criticizing empirical research, Marcuse argued that political terms like *freedom*, *equality* or *democracy* denoted a specific set of attributes; 'the ritualized concept is made immune against contradiction' (Marcuse 1964: 79–80). Similarly, he observed in *Soviet Marxism* (1958) that Marxism had become a ritualized medium in the former Soviet Union obliterating reality and illusion.

Biographical Sketch

Marcuse was born on 19 July 1898 in Berlin. During the First World War he completed his military service and became involved in the politics of a soldier's council. Between 1917 and 1918 he was a member of the SPD which he left following the murder of Liebknecht and Luxemburg. After that he remained unaffiliated and did not join any party.

Marcuse studied in Berlin and Freiburg. His doctoral dissertation was on Hegel which he completed under the supervision of Heidegger. He was also a student of Husserl. In 1931 his *Hegel's Ontologie had Grundziige einer Theorie der geschicht Lichkeit* was published. He joined the Institute of Social Research in 1933 with the purpose of exploring the relationship between philosophy and politics. He was forced to leave Germany in the same year. He wrote a number of articles on Marx and was the first to highlight the importance of Marx's *Paris Manuscripts*. He spent a year in Switzerland and then moved on a permanent basis to the United States. During the Second World War he served in the Office of Strategic Services. He taught at various American Universities—Columbia, Harvard, Brandies and San Diego. He retired from teaching in 1970.

In 1941 Marcuse published *Reason and Revolution*, an interpretation of Hegel and Marx with particular reference to a critique of positivism. In 1955 he published *Eros and Civilization* with the purpose of setting a new utopia on the basis of Freud's theory of civilization. In 1958 he published *Soviet Marxism* and in 1964 his famous book *One Dimensional Man* which provided a critique of technological civilization. Marcuse was a spokesman and theorist of the New Left in the 1960s and early 1970s. He was the most well known of the Frankfurt School theorists. He was also the only one member of the original group who never renounced his revolutionary commitment. He died on 30 July 1979.

The Frankfurt School and Marcuse

The Frankfurt School emerged in Germany in the 1920s and attracted some of the best minds of social sciences. Its origin could be traced back to the debate about the nature of Marxism that followed the defeat of the left wing workers' movement in West

Europe after the First World War, the collapse of the mass left wing political parties in Germany, the rise of Stalinism and, with its institutionalization, the total degeneration of the Soviet revolution, and the meteoric rise of Fascism and Nazism in Europe eclipsing Marxism. These bitter experiences shattered the School's faith in the inevitability of the historical march towards socialism.

'The Frankfurt School can be associated directly with an anti-Bolshevik radicalism and an open ended or critical Marxism' (Held 1983: 182). It was a 'para Marxist movement' (Kolakowski 1981c: 341). It rejected both capitalism and Soviet socialism and, like the Eurocommunists, tried to project a third alternative. But a great deal of pessimism and anti-utopianism prevented them, as with Marx, from projecting a bright future. With an emphasis on totality and rejection of crude determinism, they produced a large number of scholarly works in empirical sociology, humanistic science, law, philosophy, political theory, psychoanalysis and theory of literature. Their works assumed the term *critical theory* but there was no attempt to form a core unity. They differed widely in their approaches and emphasis. Their commitment ended with a general agreement of a need to provide a critical theory of Marxism. They were opposed to all forms of positivism for they doubted the possibility of a value-free social science. They rejected Marxist interpretations based on crude materialism or dogma.

The Frankfurt School was open-ended and self-critical. It was one of the first groups of intellectuals to draw attention to the early writings of Marx seeing it as an important component of Marxism. As such, Marx's early writings became available only in the 1930s. Like Lukacs, it pointed out its debt to Hegel and Marx. The first generation within the school included philosopher, sociologist and social psychologist Horkheimer, economist Pollock, philosopher, sociologist, musicologist Adorno, social psychologist Fromm, philosopher Marcuse, political scientists Neumann and Kirchheimer, literary and popular culture specialist Lowenthal, economist and sociologist Gurland, and essayist and literary critic Benjamin. The second generation included philosopher and sociologist Habermas, philosopher Wellmer, political scientist Offe and anthropologist Eder.

The basic characteristics of the school was classified under six categories (Kolakowski 1981c: 341–42). First, it did not treat Marxism as sacrosanct but as a starting point and a helpful tool in analyzing and criticizing existing culture. It had many other non-Marxist sources of influence like Kant, Hegel, Nietzsche and Freud. Second, its programme was strictly non-party in orientation. It never identified itself with any political movement, either of communism or of social democracy. It remained hostile towards both these groups. Third, it was profoundly influenced by the interpretation of Marxism developed by Lukacs and Korsch[15] in the 1920s. Fourth, though they were influenced by the concept of reification developed by Lukacs, they were opposed to the concept of *praxis* for they wished to emphasize the independence and autonomy of theory. This was in spite of the fact that they were critics of society and desired to transform it. Fifth, in spite of their divergences with Lukacs, they accepted the Marxist position on exploitation and alienation of the proletariat. This, they did, without identifying themselves with the proletariat or the communist party. Moreover, the school doubted the potential of the proletariat as a revolutionary force and hence dropped this aspect of Marxist thought altogether. Sixth, the school was a revisionist one revising orthodox Marxism but remained a revolutionary intellectual movement. It rejected reformism and advocated a complete break with the present. Critical theory of society was still alive in the works of Habermas (Held 1983: 187).

Marcuse's starting point, like the other leading figures in the Frankfurt School, was provided by two decisive moves made by Lukacs in *History and Class Consciousness* (1923). First Lukacs developed the general theory of commodity fetishism in Marx into a theory of reification. He claimed that capitalist society to its participants was a collection of fragments; while individuals might adopt the instrumentally rational means to achieve their particular ends, they lacked a coherent understanding of the social whole. Second, he identified an unique vantage point from which an understanding could be gained, that of the proletariat, whose reduction to that of a commodity gave it power to grasp the meaning of the social whole and aspire for the revolutionary overthrow of capitalism. The Frankfurt School was influenced by the theory of reification but found the idea of the proletariat, equated with the Hegelian Absolute, as unacceptable. As a result, Horkheimer and Adorno's *Dialectic of Enlightenment* (1947) depicted liberal capitalism as implicitly totalitarian in the same sense as the explicit fascist and Stalinist systems. The critical theorists looked upon their task to expose the unjust and irreconcilable nature of contemporary society rather than attempt a social transformation. Marcuse continued with his task though he was independent of it.

Marcuse accepted the irrationality of advanced capitalism. He pointed out that, as in the early stages, even in advanced capitalism the bourgeois and proletariat remained the basic classes with a crucial difference that the technological developments had significantly altered their structure and function to such an extent that they did not any longer appear as agents of historical transformation. This was because of an 'overriding interest in the preservation and improvement of the institutional status quo which unites the former antagonists in the most advanced areas of contemporary society' (Marcuse 1964: x). Such a phenomenon was further strengthened by the technological progress in the communist societies which guaranteed their cohesion and growth. As a result 'the very idea of qualitative change recedes before the realistic notions of a non-explosive evolution' (Ibid.: xx). Furthermore, the national communist parties within advanced capitalist countries ceased to be radical and acted merely as a legal opposition. Since there was virtually no revolutionary situation and consciousness, there could be no prospect for a revolutionary transformation either.

The highly organized and efficient capitalist system of the contemporary world carried with it the social need for private gain With synthesis between the welfare state and warfare state, life became easier for most and particular interests assumed the form of interests of all sensible persons. The irrational character of advanced capitalism was successfully concealed by ideological mystifications.

We are again confronted with one of the most vexing aspects of advanced industrial civilization: the rational character of its irrationality. Its productivity and efficiency, its capacity to increase and spread comforts, to turn waste into need, and destruction into construction, the extent to which this civilization transforms the object world into an extension of man's mind and body makes the very notion of alienation questionable. The people recognize themselves in their commodities, they find their soul in their automobile, hi-fi set, split level home, kitchen equipment. The very mechanism which ties the individual to his society has changed, and racial control is anchored in the new needs which it has produced (Marcuse 1964: 9).

There were new methods of persuasion and domination which appeared to be rational but in reality created a situation where mystification and alienation pervaded ah aspects of human life and activity. Domination was perpetuated by false needs which hampered self-realization. The dominating class continued to be in power not only by its control of the means of production but by creating a whole range of social consciousness. Criticizing the democratic pluralist view, Marcuse argued that in reality pluralism became ideological and deceptive because the prevalent system rather than reducing, extended 'manipulation and coordination, to promote rather than counteract the fateful integration' (making) 'democracy the most efficient system of domination' (Ibid.: 1). All these led to a paradox of a one dimensional society and thought process which was labeled as 'democratic unfroze form' (Ibid.). In an interesting manner Marcuse argued:

> . . . the classical Marxian theory envisages the transition from capitalism to socialism as a political revolution: the proletariat destroys the political apparatus of capitalism but retains the technological apparatus, subjecting it to socialization. There is continuity in the revolution: technological rationality, freed from irrational restrictions and destructions, sustains and consummates itself in the new society (Ibid.: 22).

This point was made on the basis that Marx looked to this continuity for 'the satisfaction of freely developing individual needs (Ibid.: 23). But the basic transformation that took place was in the fact that the promise of an increasingly a more comfortable life which was realizable because 'over powering productivity' had created a situation where people 'cannot imagine a qualitatively different universe of discourse and action' (Ibid.: 23).

Marcuse dissected the problem of alienation and found that the concept had become questionable for the individuals identified 'themselves with the existence which is imposed upon them and have in it their own development and satisfaction' making 'false consciousness into true consciousness' (Ibid.: 11). He also introduced a new dimension to it, namely, artistic alienation. He rejected the Marxian identification of alienation with the self and work, and looked to artistic alienation as being more individualized and minority in character. It involved 'conscious transcendence of the alienated existence — a higher level of mediated alienation' (Marcuse 1964: 60). For Marcuse, freedom and happiness were intimately linked for one needed the other for fulfillment and happiness. The bourgeois society — exploitative, competitive and divisive — was unable to realize happiness for it could never reconcile a particular happiness with general happiness.

Marcuse, like C. Wright Mills, complained about the existence of a power elite without using the phrase and or invoking the idea of a mass society. He lamented the loss of individual's control within the advanced capitalist system which included even 'decisions over life and death, over personal and national security' (Ibid.: 32). This concern for free individuality was in consonance with that articulated by Locke and Jefferson, and which, as Talcott Parsons (1957) pointed out in the context of Mills, reflected essentially the inability to come to terms with the altered reality of the American system after the Second World War.

In the 1960 *Preface to Reason and Revolution* Marcuse spoke of the obliteration of mental faculty, namely, the power of negative thinking. Since it was the source of creative social criticism, he feared obliteration of creativity in social life. This fear became the theme of *One Dimension Man*. Its fundamental thesis was that the elimination of conflict in the advanced countries was due to technology which created affluence. Abundance led to a creation of 'false needs' rather than liberation, for its satisfaction led to euphoria, preventing individuals from making autonomous decisions. Once individuals' needs were satisfied, they lost their reasons for dissent and protest, and become passive instruments of the dominating system. In an affluent society the forms of consumption had twofold effect: they satisfied material needs which might otherwise lead to protest and they fostered identification with the established order.

If the worker and his boss enjoy the same television program and visit the same resort places, if the typist is as attractively made as the daughter of her employer, if the Negro owns a Cadillac, if they all read the same newspaper, then this assimilation indicates not the disappearance of classes but the

extent to which the needs and satisfactions that serve the preservation of the Establishment are shared by the underlying
population (Marcuse 1964: 8).

Moreover, these consumption patterns conditioned the population which in turn was reinforced and created by the mass media.
The conditions of work also rendered the worker passive, destroying any consciousness of being in opposition with the work system.
The distinction between white and blue collared workers was
blurred. However, this was not true happiness.

Marcuse argued that the three negative elements of critique,
contradiction and transcendence were the elements which could
not be assimilated with the positive. He incorporated ideas from
Freud to explain why people accept and internalize repression in
these societies and pointed as to how technology 'de-eroticized'
the world in which humans derived sensual pleasure. Behind the
facade of a liberal society was fear, frustration and tension which
stifled individuals' creative and libidinal energies. Since 'irrational
is reason' by the sheer force of the 'overwhelming, anonymous
power and efficiency of the technological society general consciousness and consciousness of the critic became one, and the positive
absorbed the negative' (Ibid.: 225–26). He gave some interesting
examples to explain this process of harmonization.

(1) I ride in a new automobile. I experience its beauty, shini-
ness, power, convenience — but then I become aware of the
fact that in a relatively short time it will deteriorate and need
repair; that its beauty and surface are cheap, its power unnecessary, its size idiotic; and that I will not find a parking
place. I come to think of *my* car as a product of one of the Big
Three automobile corporations. The latter determine the appearance of my car and make its beauty as well as its cheap-
ness, its power as well as its shakiness, its working as well as
its obsolescence. In a way, I feel cheated. I believe that the car
is not what it could be, that better cars could be made for less
money. But the other guy has to live, too. Wages and taxes
are too high; turnover is necessary; we have it much better
than before. The tension between appearance and reality melts
away and both merge in one rather pleasant feeling.

(2) I take a walk in the country. Everything is as it should be; Nature at its best. Birds, sun, soft grass, a view through the trees of the mountain, nobody around, no radio, no smell of gasoline. Then the path turns and ends on the highway. I am back among the billboards, service stations, motels and road-houses. I was in a National Park, and I now know that this was not reality. It was a "reservation", something that is being preserved like a species dying out. If it were not for the government, the billboards, hot dog stands, and motels would long since have invaded that piece of Nature. I am grateful to the government; we have it much better than before . . .

(3) The subway during evening rush hour. What I see of the people are tired faces and limbs, hatred and anger. I feel someone might at any moment draw a knife — just so. They read, or rather they are soaked in their newspaper or magazine or paperback. And yet, a couple of hours later, the same people, deodorized, washed, dressed-up or down, may be happy and tender, really smile, and forget (or remember). But most of them will probably have some awful togetherness or aloneness at home (Marcuse 1964: 226–27).

Marcuse declared that 'the standard of living attained in the most advanced industrial areas is not a suitable model of development if the aim is pacification' (Ibid.: 242). In a critique of the 'affluent society' he said that these societies were permanently mobilized against the risk of annihilation. His prescription for an alternative was not going back to a 'earthy and robust poverty' but 'elimination of profitable waste' for that would 'increase the social wealth available for distribution, and the end of permanent mobilization would reduce the social need for the denial of satisfactions that are the individual's own denials which would now find their compensation in the cult of fitness, strength and regularity' (Ibid.: 242).

Since the advanced societies were fundamentally alike, Marcuse noticed trends in the former Soviet Union which were identical with those in the West. He made little reference to particular national traditions or cultures exerting influence on social development. Like Bell and Lipset, he pointed out that changes in consumption, the structure of the labour force and the institutions of the welfare state had domesticated the working class and the labour movement rendering Marxist notion of class conflict obsolete. Marcuse implicitly accepted the end of ideology doctrine meaning an end of ideological conflict.

The one-dimensional society with totalitarian tendencies had rendered 'the traditional ways and means of protest ineffective — perhaps even dangerous because they preserve the illusion of popular sovereignty' (Marcuse 1964: 256). Since the majority was cooped leading to social cohesion, the protest of the 'great refusal' had to be carried on by 'the substratum of the outcasts and outsiders, the exploited, persecuted of other races and other colors, the unemployed and unemployable'. Pointing out that they lived outside the democratic apparatus he adds 'their life is the most immediate and the most real need for ending intolerable conditions and institutions. Thus their opposition is revolutionary even if their consciousness is not' (Ibid.: 256). It was their refusal that could mark the beginning of an end to this one dimensionality and with their refusal they kept alive their critical dimension. However, true to the critical theory tradition, he refused to predict whether the end would be good for the affluent societies had enough capacity of either to absorb these underdogs or to terrify them into submission. It would by mere chance that 'the historical extremes may meet again: the most advanced consciousness of humanity and its most exploited force' (Ibid.: 257).

In his essay on 'Repressive Tolerance' (1967) Marcuse argued that the tolerance within these societies was one of deceit. Minority view was allowed expression because it was ineffective. The majority was effectively controlled and moulded by the system so that it could not hear or comprehend radical criticism. It meant that people had no voice and had to choose between the repressive elite of the present and the liberating elite of the Marcusean future. Truth was with the revolutionary minority and its intellectual spokesmen like Marcuse and the majority had to be liberated by being re-educated into the truth by this minority.

Marcuse dealt with the possibility of backward countries like India and Egypt emerging as 'relatively independent powers', as a third force (Ibid.: 45). These countries were entering the phase of industrialization with an untrained population 'in the values of self-propelling productivity, efficiency and technological rationality' (Ibid.). They had yet to witness a transformation of separating the labour force from the means of production. Their conditions did not provide the possibility of a synthesis between industrialization and liberation and would very likely 'succumb either to one of the various forms of neo-colonialism, or to a more or less terroristic system of primary accumulation' (Marcuse 1964: 47).

Critical Appraisals

Colletti criticized Marcuse's concept of the 'great refusal' as being ahistorical. It negated everything. Alienation and fetishism did not originate with wage labour and the 'evil for him is not a determinate organization of society, a certain system of social relation but rather industry, technology and science' (Colletti 1969: 131). Marcuse did not separate machinery from capitalism and his critique of technology under both socialism and capitalism was anti-modern. Colletti observed that Marcuse, in his attempt to show that to surpass and reject Marx, borrowed ideas from Bernstein and Kautsky (Ibid.: 140).

The major shortcoming of Colletti's criticism was in the fact that he did not refute the core of Marcuse's arguments. Instead he merely proved that these were similar to the post-Second-World-War liberal social democratic consensus. He used old Marxist rhetoric rather than come to terms with the issues raised by Marcuse, namely, that in today's world there could be no proletarian class consciousness nor any prospect of a revolution. Colletti was also guilty of misrepresentation for, contrary to his allegation, Marcuse never abandoned the modern industrial civilization. In fact, in pointing out the colossal waste that modern industrialization brought about, he only pleaded for rationalization and in this sense he could be seen as one of the forerunners of modern ecologists.

Kolakowski pointed out that Marcuse's philosophy was popular 'among those who have never had anything to do with material and economic production. His contempt for technique and organization goes hand in hand with a distaste for all forms of learning that are subject to regular rules of operation or that require rigorous effort, intellectual discipline and a humble attitude towards facts and the rules of logic'. Kolakowski made a good point that the problems of science could be tackled only by science itself and, for a rational society, the pre-requisites were tolerance, democracy and freedom of speech. But Marcuse's views were just the opposite of this and for this reason he was labelled as 'the ideologist of obscurantin' (Kolakowski 1981c: 420).

Conclusion

Marcuse claimed till the very end of his life that he was a Marxist and even an orthodox one. But in spite of this claim he rejected some of the important concepts of Marx and the subsequent Marxists. His basic thrust was that the modern blue-collar worker had nothing in common with the nineteenth century proletariat and lacked the class consciousness which was of pivotal importance in Marx's theory of revolution. In developing his theory of the one-dimensional society, he borrowed heavily from non-revolutionary traditions of negation primarily from Hegel. The influence of psychoanalysis and liberal humanism was also discernible in Marcuse's thought (Katz 1982). He also incorporated the Sorelian myth in his projection when he revolted against the 'streamlined domination' and 'triumphant violence' of the one dimensional modern technological society.

For Marcuse, Marxism was not a body of empirical tools or a method, but a philosophy of genuine humanism which negatively dealt with exploitation, surplus value, profit and the fragmented nature of capitalist society. He looked to Marx's reasoning as important but not the conclusion. He was confident that there would be a revolution in the twenty-first century since no irrational society would last for ever. The task for the present, within the prevailing order of repressive tolerance, was to keep alive the protest against the violence of the establishment by the feminist movement, philosophical works and the struggle of students and lumper proletariat. 'Historically it is again a period of enlightenment prior to material change, a period of education but education which turns into praxis' (Marcuse 1967: 53).

Marcuse's claim that he was a Marxist is hard to accept not because of his rejection of Marxist categories but because of his belief that the minority rather than the majority would keep alive the critical dimension. Marx was himself totally committed to a majoritarian revolution and in disregarding this, Marcuse negated Marx's view of liberation. In this negation of Marx's Marxism he was closer to Lenin than to Marx for, like Lenin, he thought of an elite to keep alive revolutionary consciousness. Another serious shortcoming of Marcuse's theory was the glorification of violence. Apart from the question of inhumaneness involved in such a position, there was also a philosophical error in it. Since the twentieth century has amply demonstrated that it was a world of relative and not absolute truth, a non-violent revolution was more satisfying than a violent one for that would offer sufficient scope for rectifying one's mistakes which were bound to happen. In not accepting this essential framework of the contemporary world Marcuse, in spite of his theory of one dimensionality, remained a prisoner of nineteenth century dogmatism and positivism. However, in accepting the liberating role of contemporary technology which had transformed work into play, since manual work had become unnecessary in most parts of the world, he kept alive the utopian and humanistic dream of nineteenth century socialism in the twentieth century, an age of pessimism and pragmatism. This was evident in his *Eros and Civilization* (1969). His original insights made him a legend during his lifetime and, even after his death, he would remain a reference point for understanding the complexities of advanced capitalism and its staying power.

Endnotes

1. See the sections on Marx and Lenin in this book.
2. Counter-revolution meant any force that did not accept the Bolshevik rule which was projected as expressing the will of the proletariat. Struggle against counter-revolution meant directing energies against the non-Bolsheviks without the restraint of law.
3. Mehring held that morality was not neutral but in fact conditioned by the social environment, especially in the interests of the ruling class. As a Marxist intellectual, Mehring dealt with the general principles of historical materialism and rigidly interpreted and applied Marxism. This led Engels to caution him against reductionism. Mehring asserted that classical German literature of Klopstock, Lessing, Goethe and Schiller represented nothing more than the fight of the bourgeois for emancipation. Artistic values were relative and, in that sense, Mehring was a precursor of Mannheim's theory of sociology of knowledge. Mehring pointed out that the greatness of a writer depended primarily on a successful depiction of the hopes and aspirations of the class to which he belonged. In the closing years of the nineteenth century there was a popular theory that Marxism did not have any philosophical content. The Austro-Marxists argued that, to fill this void, Kant's moral philosophy

could be incorporated in the socialist paradigm. But Mehring along with Kautsky and Plekhanov rejected such a notion and argued that this absence was not an omission but in fact a quality.

4. See the section on Trotsky in this book.

5. Manabendra Nath Roy disagreed with Lenin on two points. First he argued that a stage was reached where the breaking up of the capitalist system of Europe was not possible without breaking up of the link between the European powers and the colonies. Consequently, the liberation of colonies was of crucial importance as the entire revolutionary process depended on their liberation struggles. Because of this, the Comintern would have to widen the sphere of its activities and establish relations with those revolutionary forces that were working for the overthrow of imperialism in colonies. Second, Lenin, in spite of this emphasis of colonial revolution, could not agree with this extreme statement of Roy and modified it to include the role of the proletarian revolution in the European countries themselves and emphasized the coordination between these two movements which could guarantee the success of the world revolution. As a result of Roy's views, Lenin acknowledged the different forms of bourgeois democratic movements in the colonies. Both Roy and Lenin agreed that in most of the colonies the communist organizations were too weak to lead an independent struggle. In this context Lenin considered Gandhi as a revolutionary leader, anti-imperialist in aim, whereas Roy thought Gandhi was reactionary providing leadership to the bourgeois.

6. See the sections on Kautsky and Luxemburg (in this book) for their individual views.

7. When Kropotkin fell ill in January 1921 Lenin sent a special train with doctors and medical supplies. Kropotkin died finally on 8 February 1921. A state funeral was offered but his family refused. After his death the anarchist movement was crushed in the former Soviet Union. His house, which became a museum, was closed in 1938.

8. See the section on Kautsky in this book.

9. On hearing the brutal and tragic death of Luxemburg and Liebkhecht, an ailing Mehring lost the will to live. He too died on 28 January 1919. Mehring's famous biography of Marx, its English edition, was dedicated to Luxemburg and Zetkin, the two women whose friendship he regarded as a source of tremendous inspiration and consolation because of their steadfast commitment to socialism.

10. Antonie Pannekoek (1873–1960) studied mathematics at the University of Leyden and received a doctorate in astronomy. He was a leading member of the left-wing of the SPD. He clarified the relationship between science and Marxism and, in particular, Darwinism. He supported the revolutionary self-organization of the workers through workers' councils and, after making a break with the Third International in 1920, became a leading figure in the Council Communist movement along with Korsch.

11. See the section on Luxemburg in this book.

12. See the section on Marx in this book.

13. See the section on Kautsky in this book.

14. In case of France, Thermidor signalled the collapse of Jacobinism and the rise of Bonapartism.

15. Karl Korsch's (1886–1961) original contribution was *Marxism and Philosophy* (1923) written with the purpose of understanding every change, development and revision of Marxist theory since its inception. He pointed out that the members of the Second International paid little attention to philosophical issues within the doctrine. He stressed the activist and subjective element in Marxism as opposed to the determinism of the orthodox school. His *Karl Marx* (1938) restated the most important principles and contents of Marx's social science and focused on its materialistic content which had three principles: historical context, critical dimension and practical application.

7

❖ Unconventional Marxists

William Morris

Morris will always occupy a position of unique importance in the British revolutionary tradition. Some part of his work remains of international significance: *News from Nowhere* has crossed many national boundaries: and the significance of his utopian realism is gaining increasing international recognition. But Morris's strength, no less than the strength of Gramsci, draws deeply upon the strengths of a more local intellectual tradition. The Romantic critique of industrial capitalism, the work of Ruskin and of Carlyle, assumes a new kind of significance in the light of Morris's transformation of the tradition (Thompson 1977: 728).

It serves little purpose to insist that Morris belonged more to one branch of Socialism, or Communism, or anarchism, than to another. He obviously borrowed fragments of his working Socialism from several sources, and different points of view predominated in his thinking at different times . . . . Morris's socialism might best be described as catholic, borrowing from the Middle Ages and from Russian nihilism as well as from Mill and from Marx (Hulse 1970: 109–110).

Morris's socialist writings are not simplistically didactic, and they seldom employ the detailed characterization of realistic fiction, but they do explore recurrent psychological and historical cycles of utopian and tragic experience. Their primary aim is usually not detailed analysis of an unjust system or advocacy of revolutionary doctrine, but re-creation of the underlying motives of communist belief and endeavour (Boos and Silver 1990: 166).

William Morris (1834–96) was an artist, a craftsman and a socialist. He was known for his poetry and as an advocate of craftsmanship which included printing, dyeing, making wall papers and furniture.

The utopian tradition that began with Plato ended with Morris. Unlike Plato's ideal, Morris' was libertarian. His greatest contribution to political theory was his elaborate and detailed literary pictures that he drew of the future society. Morris had an Anarchist and a Marxist phase. He was seen as a guide and mentor of British socialism in the 1890s. A common and predominant perception in his multi-faceted personality was his rejection of the commercial, industrial and scientific society of his times which he described as 'this accursed age' and the 'squalor of civilization' for it spelt misery and was wasteful and vulgar. As a socialist he rejected industrialization and capitalism for it degraded human beings and undervalued craftsmanship. He preached joy and fellowship, and desired that everyone share in the beauty that was available. He admired the medieval society of Chaucer for its purity and fellowship, and used it to improve the contemporary class ridden Victorian society. He was rightly described as a socialist with a vision of the future but with a heart in the past. Morris, more than Marx, supplied the moral dimension to socialism (Thompson 1977). The Marxists regarded him as one of their apostles who provided a healthy antidote to Fabianism within the British socialist tradition.

As a poet Morris wrote about violence, willful destruction and envy, and how these could destroy the good things that life had to offer. Many of these themes continued even in his socialist tracts. He regarded grinding poverty more than inequality as the worst social evil. He rejected competitive economic system by alleging that the system did not create wealth but instead created differences between the rich and poor, thereby destroying wealth – the product of artistic work. He envisioned an alternative in which all enjoyed equal opportunities for education. Division of labour would be restricted so that the works of artists and craftsmen would be admired, respected and cherished. He did not advocate class struggle nor revolutionary violence. He offered a model of 'reconstructive socialism' with the hope of preventing disorder and destruction. He was critical of British colonial policies for he looked to imperialism and international war as a result of capitalist competition.

Morris was a conservationist for he believed in the preservation of ancient buildings and the natural world. He founded the Society for the Protection of Ancient Buildings in 1877–88 with the hope of sharing art with all. His interest in typography led him to establish the Kelmscott Press which produced many beautiful books, including some of his own. Hailing from a wealthy and luxurious background, he was a socialist who believed that only by sharing the fruits of one's labour one could give back one's heritage of beauty.

Biographical Sketch

Morris was born on 24 March 1834 at Elm House, Clay Hill Walthamstow. As a child he remained quite sick with digestive problems. He was the third child in a family of four boys and four girls. He was a voracious reader. By the age of seven he had read all the novels of Sir Walter Scott. He went to Marlborough School and Exeter College, Oxford. Morris married Jane Burden on 26 April 1859 at St. Michael's, Oxford. By the middle of 1868 their marriage ran into problems for Jane was involved with one of Morris' friends, Rossetti. Morris himself fell in love with Geogiana Burene-Jones, the wife of his best friend. He built the Red House with his architect friend Philip Webb. He designed its wall papers, textiles of all kinds, rugs, carpets and furniture. Forced to leave the Red House he founded the Kelmscott Manor on the upper Thames in the southwestern corner of Oxfordshire in May 1871. He went to Iceland for two years from 1871 to 1872.

In 1883 Morris joined the Social Democratic Federation and became close to Henry Mayers Hyndman (1842–1921). During this time he became acquainted with Marxism. In 1884 along with Ernest Belfort Bax (1854–1926) and Avelings he founded the Socialist League after breaking away from Hyndman. At this time his theories were anarchistic in temper. Though he maintained extensive contacts with leading revolutionaries in London, including Kropotkin, his revolutionary philosophy was undogmatic and less rigid. He started a newspaper *Commonweal* in 1885 and was its editor and financier till 1890. This coincided with his exit from the League as well. He remained active within the socialist movement till 1890s, after which he withdrew and became a moderate. 'Like the pilgrims in his romances, Morris wandered from one camp to another, searching for the answer — or perhaps the magic — that would satisfy his quest' (Hulse 1970: 78). He lectured and wrote extensively. His range was diverse and included poetry, prose, romance, art and socialism. His participation in the socialist movement in the last years became ceremonial. In late 1895 he appeared in the inauguration of the Oxford Socialist Union and his last speech was given at the Waterloo station on the funeral day of Sergei Mikhailovich Kravchinskii (Stepnaik). In 1890 he founded the Hammersmith Socialist Society. His activities decreased because of ill health. He was plagued by itching or burning feet, growing weakness, periodic faintness and insomnia. He found solace in writing romances and production of beautiful books. He was an atheist who rejected God as the proprietor of all things and persons.

Morris died in London on 3 October 1896, after being in coma for three days. He suffered from diabetes. The cause of death was attributed to overexposure to the heart-breaking ugliness of the workers' hovels and to the vagaries of the British weather. He was buried in the Churchyard at Kelmscott.

The Socialist Phase

In January 1883 Morris joined the Social Democratic Federation. He did not have any specific political theory and was, by and large, discontented with the state of art and politics in Britain. He acknowledged the influence of Mill in his conversion to socialism. Marx's works were unknown in England. Therefore, like many other socialists, he too read the latter's works in French. When he became a socialist he was ignorant of economics.

> I had never so much as opened Adam Smith, or heard of Ricardo, or of Karl Marx . . . Well, having joined a Socialist body (for the Federation soon became definitely Socialist), I put some conscience into trying to learn the economical side of Socialism, and even tackled Marx, though I must confess that, whereas I thoroughly enjoyed the historical part of "*Capital*", I suffered agonies of confusion of the brain over reading the pure economics of that great work (Morris, cited in Husle 1970: 79).

Morris depended on Bax, Hyndman and Andreas Scheu for understanding the technical part of socialism. He visited the home of Engels and read Shaw's works to get better acquainted with socialist ideas. He was also influenced by John Ruskin's (1819–1900) perception of work as redeeming moral power and art as an expression of one's pleasure in work, and Thomas Carlyle's (1795–

1881) acknowledgment of the worker's contribution to human progress.[1] Interestingly, instead of the technical side, it was the hopes and aspirations of socialism that converted him as is evident from a letter that he wrote to a friend in 1883.

> Also of course, I do not believe in the world being saved by any system—I only assert the necessity of attacking systems grown corrupt, and no longer leading any whither: that to my mind is the case with the present system of capital and labour: as all my lectures assert, I have personally been gradually driven to the conclusion that art has been handcuffed by it, and will die out of civilization if the system lasts. That of itself does to me carry with it the condemnation of the whole system, and I admit has been the thing which has drawn my attention to the subject in general (Morris, cited in Husle 1970: 80).

Morris decided to address himself to the mitigation of the conditions that created this detestable situation. He observed in the same letter, 'Now it seems to me that, feeling this, I am bound to act for the destruction of the system which seems to me mere oppression and obstruction . . . such a system can only be destroyed, it seems to by me, by the united discontent of numbers' (Ibid.).

Keeping this discontent in mind, he wrote several pamphlets and delivered hundreds of lectures. During 1883–84 his lectures focused on the state of art as evident from the following themes that he covered: *Art and the People* (1883), *Art, Wealth and Riches* (1883), *Art Under Plutocracy* (1883), *Art and Socialism* (1884), and *Art and Labour* (1884). He argued for socialism and against the competitive economic system by alleging that the system had not created wealth but instead riches on one hand, and poverty on the other hand, destroying wealth—the product of artistic work. He demanded a utopia in which all would have equal opportunities in education, in which the wealthy would not enjoy privileged positions for advancement, in which division of labour would be restricted and the work of the artists and craftsmen would be admired, respected and cherished. In these lectures he did not advocate class struggle and, in fact, desired to forestall the destructive power of revolutionary violence by 'trying to fill up the gap that separates class from class' (Ibid.: 81).

Morris gradually and partially integrated the Marxian idea of class struggle with his philosophy. He did not believe that the proletariat as a class had a special historical destiny though he did see the growing friction between the capitalist property-owners and the poor. He accepted the Marxist theory of inevitability of change but rejected change through violence and instead offered his model of 'reconstructive socialism' with the hope to prevent disorder and destruction.

In his subsequent lectures Morris tended to rely heavily on the Marxist idea of class struggle but he still appealed to his middle-class comrades to change sides for failing to do would make them collaborators of oppressors and thieves. His tone and ideas became more radical as his knowledge about socialism increased. In an essay *Useful Work versus Useless Toil* that Morris wrote in early 1884 and published as *The Socialist Platform in* 1885 one could discern the additions that he had made from scientific socialism. He described class struggle at length and incorporated surplus value in some detail. In his *Misery and the Way Out and How We Live and How We Might Live* the basic economic arguments highlighting imperialism and international war as a result of capitalist competition was enunciated.

By mid-1880s Morris was convinced that Hyndman's parliamentarism would not advance the 'cause' and would only deceive the poor and drag the process of complete transformation of society. He was disgusted with 'theatrical boasts and warnings about immediate violent revolution' for that would frighten or dissuade those who would have otherwise joined the movement. He dismissed Hyndman's brand of socialism as Bismarckian state socialism. Writing to a friend he observed:

> I cannot stand all this, it is not what I mean by Socialism either in aim or in means: I want a real revolution, a real change in Society: Society a great organized mass of well-regulated forces used for the bringing about a happy life for all. And means for attaining it are simple enough, education in Socialism and organization for the time when the crisis shall force action upon us: nothing else will do us any good at present: the revolution cannot be a mechanical one, though the last act of it may be civil war, or it will end in reaction after all (Morris, cited in Husle 1970: 85).

Morris wrote the manifesto of the Socialist League which contained a gist of his theoretical position. He dismissed Hyndman as too authoritarian, too wild, too militant, too opportunistic and too Marxist. He wanted some of the Marxist ideas without their hatred and their flexible political techniques.

The Socialist League's *Commonweal* claimed to represent the genuine Marxist tradition. Engels contributed an article on 'England in 1885 in contrast to 1845'. In a letter to Bernstein he referred to Morris, Aveling and Bax as 'the only honest men among the Intellectuals — but men as unpracticed as you could possibly find'. Interestingly, after that Engels never took interest in the English socialist movement. With the help of Bax and Aveling, Morris continued to carry on the Marxist heritage. He accepted their understanding of the technical questions. By the middle of 1885 he became sympathetic to the anarchists within and outside the Socialist League.

The Anarchist Phase

Morris associated with the anarchists on the question of strategy within the League and continued till 1888 when many prominent leaders, including Bax and Avelings, withdrew from it. In 1886 Morris met Kropotkin when the latter visited England for the commemoration of the Paris Commune. Engels too noted the anarchist affiliations of the League and regarded it as 'children's ailment' of the nascent English socialist movement. But Morris vehemently protested against being labelled as an anarchist. He proclaimed himself to be a Marxist and a Communist.

Physical confrontation with the police and courts, with the workers in 1880s became evident, which made him realize that freedom of expression and public assembly was in jeopardy. This became evident in the Dod-Street affair of October 1885 and the Trafalgar Square demonstration of February 1886. Government became the identifiable enemy. He commented on the futility of a policy of conventional political activity.

Will you think the example of America too trite? Anyhow, consider it! A country with universal suffrage, no king, no House of Lords, no privilege as you fondly think; only a little standing army, chiefly used for the murder of red-skins; a

democracy after your model; and with all that, a society corrupt to the core, and at this moment engaged in suppressing
freedom with just the same reckless brutality and blind ignorance as the Czar of all the Russias uses (Morris, cited in Husle
1970: 92–3).

This readiness to equate the events in England and America with
those of Russia and his willingness to risk physical injury for free
speech made Morris participate in other demonstrations, including
the famous 'Bloody Sunday' affair in Trafalgar Square on 13
November 1887. This experience reaffirmed his opposition to
government but also convinced him of mass action against well
organized police violence. After the squashing of the demonstration
Morris was reticent about parliamentarism and was also equally
cautious regarding use of violence. He rejected the tactics of the
anarchists, particularly their advocacy of violence. He tried to
balance the two and steer clear of extremes.

The League's anarchism became more pronounced once the
parliamentary faction left the organization in 1888. Morris got increasingly entangled in controversies relating to education and
agitational methods. On 10 April 1888, he wrote:

But to return to our "government" of the future, which would
be rather an administration of *things* than a government of
persons. Without dogmatizing on the matter I will venture to
give you my own views on the subject, as I know that they
are those held by many Socialists. Nations, as political entities, would cease to exist; civilization would mean the feder-
alization of a variety of communities great and small, at one
end of which would be the township and the local guild, in
which administration would be carried on perhaps in direct
assemblies "in more majorum", and at the other some central
body whose function would be almost entirely the guardian-
ship of the *principles* of society, and would when necessary
enforce their practice; e.g. it would not allow slavery in any
form to be practiced in any community. But even this shadow
of centralization would disappear at least when men gained
the habit of looking reasonable at these matters. It would in
fact be chiefly needed as a safeguard against the heredity of
bad habits, and the atavism which would give us bad

specimens now and again. Between these two poles there would be various federations which would grow together or dissolve as convenience of place, climate, language, dictated, and would dissolve peaceably when occasion prompted. Of course public intercourse between the members of the federation would have to be carried on by means of delegation, but the delegates would not pretend to represent any one or anything but the business with which they are delegated; ex. we are a shoemaking community chiefly you cotton spinners, are we making too many shoes? Shall we turn some of us to gardening for a month or two, or shall we go on? – and so forth (Morris, cited in Husle 1970: 93–4).

Marx and Engels borrowed from Morris the idea that the future society would be one where the 'government of persons would be replaced by administration of things'. Morris, like Kropotkin, did not worry about the transitional state but was concerned with the coming social order. He spoke of class struggle but it did not receive the importance that the Marxists attached to it. He felt the need to keep anti-parliamentary, anti-political movement alive and expressed the wish to be identified with it. He differed with Kropotkin about the speed with which the existing society could be abolished. He was more than willing to accept gradual transition. He also wanted the preservation of handicrafts in an era of modern machine technology. He differed from the anarchists on the question of authority. He saw the need for an authority if freedom of all individuals had to be ensured and none could coerce the other. Furthermore, in an equal society it would not be possible to satisfy everyone's desires and sometimes the satisfaction of individual interests would clash with that of common good making the need for an authority all the most necessary. By authority he meant public conscience. Of course he was opposed to the tyranny of the collective in the same way that he opposed the tyranny of capitalism. His version of socialism was more libertarian than authoritarian.

The Poetic Phase

The 1880s was a period when Morris' poetry did not flourish much. Most of his socialist poems and prose pieces he wrote during his anarchist phase. In *The Pilgrims of Hope* (1886) and *A Dream of John*

Ball (1886–87) he wrote about the importance of fellowship and voluntary community of individuals based on tranquillity, social cooperation and communal instincts. In *News from Nowhere or an Epoch of Rest* (1889–90) Morris rejected Edward Bellamy's (1850–98) view of a centralized authority, large and tightly-organized communities based on a machine economy as depicted in *Looking Backward, 2000–1887* (1887).[2] Instead he advocated the need for:

> the unit of administration to be small enough for every citizen to feel himself responsible for its details, and be interested in them; that individual men cannot shuffle off the business of life on to the shoulders of an abstraction called the State, but must deal with it in conscious association with each other. That variety of life is as much an aim of true Communism as equality of condition, and that nothing but a union of these two will bring about real freedom. That modern nationalities are mere artificial devices for the commercial war that seek to put an end to, and will disappear with it. And, finally, that art, using that word in its widest and due signification, is not a mere adjunct of life which free and happy men can do without, but the necessary expression and indispensable instrument of human happiness (Morris, cited in Husle 1970: 98).

Kropotkin regarded *News from Nowhere* as embodying in a thorough and deep sense the principles of anarchist society. It was a story of a narrator, Dick, who returned home from the meeting of the League and fell asleep. In course of a dream he imagined that he was in London about two centuries after the Victorian era and discovered that human beings had become instinctively cooperative and happy because the exploitative nature of capitalism and private property had gone. The manufacturing cities of the nineteenth century had disappeared. Instead there were mills that were small, tastefully designed and run by volunteers. Machinery was used only for tasks that were unpleasant. None drew salaries and there were no monetary transactions. Good life was ensured for those who enjoyed working. Following Fourier, he looked upon work as a human occupation and was indignant that it had become toilsome without a sense of fraternity in contemporary society. His aim was not to reduce labour but to minimize its pain and drudgery, 'so small that it will cease to be a pain . . . the true incentive to useful and happy labour is and must be pleasure in the work itself' (Morris, cited in Sargent 1990: 68). Art would integrate leisure and work. Work had to be creative and pleasurable leading to fulfillment in the worker. There would be material abundance and individual well-being.

Morris was critical of the capitalist system for separating mental and manual work and reducing the worker to a mere cog in the machinery. He rejected capitalism for it viewed society as a product of a contract composed of classes pursuing a hedonistic policy of self-aggrandizement. It entailed mass production and mechanization eliminating creativity and individuality. In its place he proposed voluntary work and appropriate technology. In many respects Morris' portrayal of the future was similar to that of Kropotkin except that the former desired minimum of industrialization. There would be no government and no politics. He advocated decentralization of social decision-making so that individuals could control their lives collectively. He also stressed on variety or diversity as an essential subset to equality for together they would ensure freedom.

In matters which are merely personal which do not affect the welfare of the community — how a man shall dress, what he shall eat and drink, what he shall write and read, and so forth — there can be no difference of opinion and everybody does as he pleases. But when the matter is of common interest of the whole community, and the doing or not doing something affects everybody, the majority must have their way; unless the minority were to take up arms and show by force that they were the effective or real majority; which, however, in a society of men who are free and equal is little likely to happen; because in such a community the apparent majority is the real majority, and the others know that too well to obstruct from mere pigheadedness; especially as they have had plenty of opportunity of putting forward their side of the question (Ibid.: 69).

Morris advocated majority rule as the last resort. He was, like Fourier, equally against waste and desired that the basic wants of life had be secured. There would be no law courts, or police, no criminal class and crime would be punished by relying on the conscience of the offender. There would be no central authority.

Nor were children required to undergo formal schooling for they would be educated in fields and shops which would be leisurely, practical and voluntary. They would know swimming, reading, writing and foreign languages. This would be the case with higher education also. Formal education would be provided only if there was a motivation for it. Like Fourier, he recommended abolition of legal marriages and advocated various kinds of free love. Women and men would enjoy equal status and women would no longer be domestic slaves. Human relationships would be honest with no room for false niceties and bitter enmities that prevailed in the nineteenth century.

Morris also wrote about the way the revolution would be staged to get rid of commercial slavery and patriarchy. There would be a general strike which would paralyze the London economy affecting the rich and the middle classes. The spontaneity of the poor with their instinct to cooperate would humble the old regime to surrender. There would be a committee of public safety that would ensure the supplies of essential items to everyone in need. He did not provide much details about the revolution for he felt that, when the hour of action would arrive, the socialists would know what action was necessary to translate their principles into practice.

During the period that Morris wrote *News from Nowhere* he also became engrossed in movements for arts and crafts. His social commentary was minimum in the typical Gothic style. Through the Kelmscott Press he hoped to revive the art of fine printing that had disappeared from Europe. For the next five years he remained busy with publication of Kelmscott books. Gradually he moved from non-political writings and applied his new-found art to his political activities. He also wrote the *House of the Wolfings* in which he suggested the inter-relationship between the individual and society on an artistic and moral plane.

After 1889 Morris wrote a number of romances like *The Roots of the Mountains, The Story of the Glittering Plain, The Wood Beyond the World, Child Christopher, The Well at the World's End, The Water of the Wondrous Isles, The Well at the World's End* and *The Sundering Flood.*

The Last Phase

In the 1890s Morris collaborated with Bax in republishing some of their essays and also wrote articles for Hyndman's *Justice*. In many of his views he sounded like a Fabian giving the Fabians the belief that he was one among them. He participated in election campaigning. His views had become moderate and he was regarded as the guide and mentor of British Socialism after 1890.

In his last major socialist lecture entitled *Communism* delivered in February 1893 Morris expressed his worries about the future of the movement. He was sceptical about the labour-oriented political parties. He feared that the emphasis on gradual gains on the political front by the Fabians and the social democrats may distract the working classes from their ultimate goals. He stressed that immediate material gains should not be mistaken for the final objective, namely the creation of a 'new society of equals'. These immediate political gains would serve the end of socialism only if they formed a part of the education of the masses for communism.

Morris reiterated his critique of the waste and idleness, the results of inequality under capitalism, but the general tone of the essay was one of uncertainty and indecisiveness which was not there in his earlier essays. He was also doubtful about the readiness of·the working class to learn about the progress of communism or whether the poor were so hopelessly oppressed as he had imagined and felt that they did not seem so enthusiastic or willing about their own emancipation. In his essay on *Freedom* delivered on March 10, 1893 he defended a limited concept of property and indicated the need for some kind of authority to ensure that all individuals would perform their share of the necessary labour in the new society. This suggestion annoyed the anarchists. He also defended the need for a policy of non-violence as a part of socialist philosophy.

I confess I am no great lover of political tactics; the sordid squabble of an election is unpleasant enough for a straight forward man to deal in: yet I cannot fail to see that it is necessary somehow to get hold of the machine which has at its back the executive power of the country, however that may be done, and that the organization and labour which will be necessary to effect that by means of the ballot-box will, to say the least of it, be little indeed compared with what would be necessary to effect it by open revolt; besides that the change effected by peaceable means would be done more completely and with less chance, indeed with no chance of counter-revolution. On the other hand I feel sure that some action is even now demanded by the growth of Socialism, and will be more and more imperatively demanded as time goes on. In short I do not believe in the possible success of revolt until the Socialist party has grown so powerful in numbers that it can gain its end by peaceful means, and that therefore what is called violence will never be needed; unless indeed that reactionists were to refuse the decision of the ballot-box and try the matter by arms; which after all I am pretty sure they could not attempt by the time things had gone so far as that. As to the attempt of a small minority to terrify a vast majority into accepting something which they do not understand, by spasmodic acts of violence, mostly involving the death or mutilation of non-combatants, I can call that nothing else than sheer madness. And here I will say once for all, what I have often wanted to say of late, to wit that the idea of taking any human life for any reason whatsoever it horrible and abhorrent to me (Morris, cited in Hulse 1970: 108–9).

From 1894 onwards till his death Morris played very little part in socialist activities. His participation was more ceremonial as one of its leaders but did very little by way of adding to the socialist message.

Conclusion

Morris' socialism steered clear of both parliamentarism and anarchism. He desired the establishment of socialism through constitutional means which would prepare the individuals for a revolution and, in that sense, he rejected the senseless destruction of revolutionary violence. He was willing to use trade unions, even if they used parliamentary methods, for that would help in the education of the workers towards the real tasks of the revolution. But he outrightly rejected reformistic socialism. His vision of the future was similar to that of the anarchists but he was not prepared to destroy the state unless the individuals were ready for a way of life in which it would become redundant. He wanted the state to naturally wither away. He, like the anarchists, disliked the centralized state system.

Morris' socialism arose out of his discontent with the state of arts under capitalism. It was also sustained by his intense desire for fellowship and social equality. Like Owen and Fourier, he desired a society free of poverty, hunger and ignorance. He conceived of true pleasure as being derived from performance of daily work. Industrialization degraded human labour and he sought to restore its dignity and wholesomeness. He disliked machines that depersonalized product and was against the system of mass production. He would remain important 'in the history of decorative arts and in the narrative history of British Socialism . . . . he is a pioneer of responsible "ecological" consciousness and . . . had definite and uncomfortable views on the question of work . . . was a major intellectual figure. As such he may be seen as our greatest diagnostician of alienation, in terms of the concrete perception of the moralist and within the context of a particular English cultural tradition' (Thompson 1977: 801). Morris desired to create beautiful things in the same way as he wished to create a beautiful society by weeding out ugliness in all its aspects. To him nothing was more ugly and miserable than the life of a worker under capitalism. Shaw attributed Morris' greatness to his versatility and multi-faceted approach to realize socialism.

Morris has been claimed by the environmentalists as their founding father. The socialists in general and the British Labour Party in particular in the 1990s made him the starting point in the hope of making socialism relevant in the post-industrial and post-cold-war society. For the common man he was remembered as the 'wallpaper man'. As a craftsman his range was varied for it included painting, stained glass designing, book printing and binding, dyeing and making of period furniture. He influenced Antonio Gaudi (1852–1926) who was one of the most influential exponents of the Gothic style in architecture. Morris believed that a 'good decoration was the impress of imagination strong on it and is something which can be done by a great many people and without too much difficulty and with pleasure'. It was this idea that inspired both his art and socialism. Like Fourier, he wrote about the future with an eye on the past. He favoured restoration of rural values and relieving the workers of the health and safety hazards in Victorian factories, attempted to dismantle the centralized and oversized bureaucracy and unwieldy educational system and establish communes without private property that created happy, healthy and productive workers. In this he sought to integrate the general values of Ruskin's medievalism with socialism, the ideology of the growing social force, the organized working class (Williams 1961: 153).

Georges Sorel

Georges Sorel is one of the most provocative and baffling figures of modern thought . . . . To the world he is known as the author of one book the *Reflections on Violence* and, more vaguely, as a man who influenced the ideologies of fascism and communism (Humphrey 1951: 1).

Sorel and Marx are the only truly original thinkers socialism has had (Croce 1926: vi).

From the viewpoint of Marxism he (Sorel) may be considered an accidental oddity: at the outset of his literary career he had nothing in common with it, and his name hardly figure in the later development of the doctrine . . . . At the time of his main writings, however, Sorel not only considered himself a Marxist but believed that he could extract the core of Marx's philosophy — the class war and the independence of the proletariat — and oppose Marx himself to the whole body of contemporary orthodoxy, whether reformist or revolutionary (Kolakowski 1981b: 149).

Towards the closing years of the nineteenth century both in industrial development and labour movements the situation in France was markedly different from Britain and Germany. The French industries were medium-sized and its working class was heterogeneous and plural. French socialism was largely inspired by Proudhon's emphasis on decentralization, small units and respect for the individual worker and these 'genuinely corresponded to the structure of the French economy in a way that Marx's teachings did not' (Joll 1977: 63). Initially the repression that followed the failure of the Paris Commune delayed the crystallization of a powerful labour movement in France. But an amnesty in 1879 and permission for trade unions in 1884 altered the situation drastically with regard to universal male suffrage under the Third Republic, facilitating open socialist activity in the parliamentary setup demanding reform. The French political and economic structure was distinctive in character, and that led to an independent socialist thought between 1880–1900. There were three different streams.

A united party came into existence in 1905. For understanding these different groups an important event in France was the Drefuys case.[3]

Broadly the three streams of French socialism was represented by Guesde, the Marxist variant which ultimately led to the formation of the French Communist Party. The second was the more moderate version, akin to social democracy, led by an able theoretician and orator Jaurez.[4] The third was the anarcho-syndicalists who were influenced by Blanqui, Proudhon and Marx. They functioned outside the parliamentary system. Its most important theoretician was Georges Sorel (1847–1922) who made the most original, profound and exhaustive contribution to socialist theory and practice in France during the period of the Second International. He was the first French Marxist to react strongly against mechanical determinism which was both the cause and result of dry and unimaginative socialist *praxis*. In the process he explored the philosophical basis of Marx's thought and explained how Hegel's influence made it different from the superficial determinism of French socialism. He also incorporated the ideas of Bergson and Nietzsche.

Sorel became the leader of the French revolutionary syndicalist movement of the 1890s. He was not keen on organizing it nor in taking charge of its administrative aspects. His role was one of a true revolutionary intellectual, applying his powers of analysis to facilitate the revolution without any thought of personal gain. Many of the issues that he grappled with regard to revolutionary analysis and strategy remain unresolved even today.

Anachro-syndicalism crystallized in France in the 1890s and later spread to Italy, Spain and the United States as espoused by Daniel de Leon (1852–1914).[5] Though it incorporated within itself many radical traditions, the most important of them all was the Proudhonist perception which led to a rejection of any kind of political mobilization, activity and participation within the parliamentary system. Trade unions provided its support basis. The whole thrust was on the imminent proletarian revolution which would create a society of independent producers. By propounding a philosophy of exclusiveness it wanted a total rupture from the contemporary bourgeois morality and ideas. It looked to party politics with suspicion nor did it believe in a conception of a vanguard party modelled on the Leninist principles. It also excluded the middle class and intellectuals. However, in spite of militant trade unionism before 1914 the number of trade unions remained numerically small. This did not deter them from securing concessions for the workers though they failed in their ambition to create an alternative culture as the basis of capturing state power.

Sorel was not an orthodox Marxist. He did not belong to any political movement that claimed to be spiritual followers of Marxism but he participated actively in most of the polemics of his day. He desired to be the Luther of the Marxist movement (Kolakowski 1981b: 149). Interestingly, it was not politics but ethics that interested him. He searched for a new moral principle that would rejuvenate modern society though he never attempted to define what he meant by morality. At best he understood it as an outcome of action, an expression of will. He distrusted and feared nature for being arbitrary and non-discriminating for it thwarted the small measure of liberty that the individual had won in an effort to become civilized and human. His mission in life was to strive for deliverance. His conception of proletarian socialism was based on the idea of syndicates of 'social authorities' that would assume the functions of an aristocracy.

Sorel was less concerned with the question of proletarian consciousness for he knew that no political organization would lead to a revolution if the proletariat was not psychologically and ideologically prepared and ready for change. He was mainly concerned with the development of proletarian consciousness, and revolutionary strategy and tactics. Anything short of it would only lead to reformism, which would eventually stabilize capitalism. Being a revolutionary gadfly, he attacked the organized French socialist movement from the outside criticizing it for its simplistic thinking and opportunism. Though he claimed to be a Marxist, he never discussed the practicability of his thesis nor did he submit it to a dialectical critique.

Biographical Sketch

Sorel was born in Cherbourg in Normandy 1847 at a time when the French society was becoming modern, getting transformed into a capitalist economy with a democratic polity. His family was certainly bourgeois, considering that his father was a director of a business concern and his mother was the daughter of an army officer. He obtained a diploma from the Ecole Polytechnique, the state technical school, and secured a position with the Department of Roads and Bridges at the age of twenty. Till 1871 he worked in Corsica and was then transferred to a southern village of Albi, to Gap, and to Algeria for three years. His last transfer was to Perpignan where he worked from 1879 till he retired in 1892. During this time he did not produce any social theory, did not analyze capitalism or the nature of the proletarian revolution.

Sorel never married though he had a lifelong companion in Marie David, a chamber-maid who was his inspiration. From her he learnt to fight against social injustice without becoming interested in politics. After retiring from the civil service he refused pension for he felt he did not want to be compromised in any way. He embarked upon an intensive study of social dynamics and gradually his vision of the proletarian movement crystallized.

Sorel's literary and political writings began in the mid-1880s. He wrote two books before his retirement. One was an analysis of the *Bible* and the other was the trial of Socrates. The book on the *Bible* detailed heroic tales emphasizing their educative values against utilitarianism and various revolutionary ideologies. In the second book he criticized Socrates for his abstract ideas which undermined instinctive realities, the value of tradition and the tested institutions of the state.

In 1892 Sorel moved to Paris and spent a lot of time studying the various developments in social theory, whether of Marxist or strictly academic nature. He frequented the Sorbonne and became familiar with the emerging new discipline — sociology. He became acquainted with the works of Durkheim and attended the latter's doctoral defence. From 1893 Sorel became involved with Marxism by publishing articles on the importance of Marx's work. In 1894 he contributed extensively to *L'Ere Nouvelle*, the first French journal devoted to Marxist philosophy and analysis. In 1894 along with Paul Lafargue, Paul Bonnet and Georges Deville he founded a new journal *Le Devenir Social* ('The Social Process'). In the latter he published a long review article '*Superstition Socialiste?*' wherein he stated his philosophical positions which he retained for the rest of his life.

In 1898 his work dealing with the Roman Empire was published. He analyzed its strength, values and institutions but also looked to its weaknesses like spread of oriental influence and introspective outlook which led to the path of despair, preferring personal salvation to the country, family and social ties, respect for law, poverty to productive efforts, renunciation of responsibility, contemplation of virile struggle and the city of God to the city of man. These themes identified earlier were developed in the later writings.

From the mid 1890s until his death in 1922, Sorel applied the Marxist analysis to questions like role of education in French social and political life, the foundations of economic value from a Marxist perspective and changes within the political life. He stressed on the ideological dynamic of the revolutionary process, both within the proletariat and the bourgeoisie, distinguishing his Marxism sharply from the reigning economic determinism.

Revulsion to Politics

By 1893–94 Sorel became a Marxist.

> I hold the theory of Marx for the greatest innovation introduced into philosophy for centuries . . . All our ideas are bound today to congregate around the new principles posed by scientific socialism . . . The human spirit refuses to be content with the old economic scepticism . . . with registering of facts, with reasoning about the balance of profits, with comparing the increase of prosperity in the various countries (Sorel, cited in Talmon 1940: 49).

Sorel was not interested in listing and analyzing the shortcomings of capitalism or with the problem of eradicating poverty. He was critical of objective certainty and impersonal needs and preferred subjective personal experience as the basis of philosophy. The most important point in the Marxist philosophy was the inseparable link between the producer and his tools with which he earned his living in contrast with the abstract and vague ideas of the intellectuals. Since socialist parties were corrupt like the bourgeois ones, an authentic voice had to be found in those who were outside the democratic process. Sorel was confident that a new morality and a new civilization would emerge out of militant trade unionism.

Sorel's essential mission was not the elimination of the Church, the army or militant nationalism but to innovate a philosophy of

abstract justice and undefined truth to fight the political apparatus. It was a reversal of his earlier position when he criticized
Socrates. The lesson that he learnt from the Dreyfus affair was that
accidents and unexpected turns of events were common which
could not be explained by long methodological study. Rather they
proved the gross inefficiency of contemporary socialist theory. Anti-
clericalism was used by the bourgeois, radical and socialist politicians to gain power for themselves. In this process all principles
of class war were forgotten 'in the democratic ocean of the unity
of the people' (Sorel, cited in Talmon 50). Its end result was the
loss of prestige for the parliamentary socialist and 'men of violence covered themselves with glory'. This experience brought to
the surface the great significance of uninterrupted direct action
based not on sporadic act of violence but with 'very frequent
accompaniment of acts of violence'.

The Sorelian revision of Marxism was caused by the Dreyfus
affair and Bernstein's revisionism. He rejected Luxemburg's radical critique of Bernstein. In general he endorsed the economic but
not the political doctrines of revisionism. He agreed with Bernstein
that most of Marx's predictions did not materialize for developments within capitalism and the consolidation of trade unions had
raised the standard of living of the workers and consequently
blunted class war. Collective bargaining enabled the workers to
participate in management. Compared to the early years after the
Industrial Revolution, the trained workers handled technology
skillfully and efficiently. Marx's prediction that capitalism would
not be able to overcome its own crises was also negated, thereby
proving that, on grounds of technology and socio-economic factors,
capitalism could not be faulted. The salaries of the workers and
their working conditions had improved considerably and seemed
just. In view of these changes, the original Marxist critique of capitalism and the clarion call for its revolutionary overthrow was
invalid. Beyond this remarkable similarity, Bernstein and Sorel
differed. The former denounced violent revolution in an age of
democracy whereas Sorel endorsed it as the surest way to recapture
the essence of Marxism. Its guiding force was the dream of a new
civilization and heroic morality which would replace the decadent
bourgeois one. This decadence was brought about by the deliberate
actions of professional politicians, intellectuals and the inevitable
corruption that parliamentary party politics entailed. Sorel looked

to Marx as the prophet of the proletariat as a class and a virulent critic of party politics and quoted from Marx's *The Poverty of Philosophy* to support his observation.

> The antagonism between the proletariat and the bourgeoisie is a struggle of a class against class, a struggle which carried to its highest expression is a total revolution . . . the clash of body with body, as its final denouement . . . combat or death: bloody struggle or extinction . . . It is in this form that the question is inexorably put (Sorel, cited in Talmon 1940).

Within a brief period Sorel established himself as a reputed Marxist and popularized Marx's teachings in France, who until then, was virtually unknown. For Sorel, Marxism was not a scientific doctrine but a moral doctrine, a 'social poetry'.

Sorel's *Reflections on Violence* originated in a series of articles published in the first half of 1906 in *Le Mouvement Socialiste*, and after considerable persuasion published it as book in 1908 with an additional sub-title *Letter to Daniel Halevy*, his principal inspiration. During Sorel's lifetime four editions were published with three appendixes, the most important of which was *In Defence of Lenin* written in 1919, two years after the Bolshevik Revolution. He admitted that writing a book was not his primary interest for he was essentially self-taught. He was also against a well-argued and logically coherent text for 'philosophy is after all perhaps only the recognition of the abysses which lie on each side of the footpath that the vulgar follow with the serenity of somnambulists' (Sorel, cited in Jennings 1996: 39). Sorel did not wish to contribute to human knowledge nor refute the arguments of important thinkers. Instead he desired to provide a guide to action and, in that sense, the *Reflections* compared favourably with Lenin's *What is to be done?*, for these were written as manuals for capturing state power. Both felt that Marx's optimism about a majoritarian proletarian revolution was impractical. The *Reflections* began with an eulogy of the conception of 'wandering Jew, a symbol of the highest aspirations of mankind, condemned as it is to march for ever without knowing rest' (Ibid.: 37). This designation of the true purpose of life at the very beginning of the book clarified Sorel's conviction that moral salvation had to be selfless, beyond the calculations of personal gain or glory.

Optimism vs Pessimism

Sorel conceived of political projects as being either optimistic or pessimistic, rejecting the first and endorsing the second. Optimistic politics was pursued by dangerous men as they were oblivious of the great hurdles that confronted their projects. The optimists mistakenly thought that minor reforms within the constitution and change in office-bearers would mitigate the evils of contemporary world. They moved easily from a commitment to revolution to social pacifism. An optimist, with absolute power, led the country to disaster for he assumed social transformation to be easy and simple. If he failed, he would blame his compatriots and, instead of searching for an explanation for failure, would try to eliminate whom he thought resisted or criticized.

> During the Terror, the men who split most blood were precisely those who had the greatest desire to let their equals enjoy the golden age they had dreamt of, and who had the most sympathy with human wretchedness: optimists, idealists, and sensible men, the greater desire they had for universal happiness the more inexorable they showed themselves (Curtis 1962b: 270).

The optimists included Socrates, Jesuits, the *philosophers,* ideologues of the French Revolution the utopians, believers in progress and socialist politicians. They believed that the evils could be eliminated through proper and good legislations, spread of knowledge, creating awareness and inculcating fellow feeling. But their greatest failure was their colossal ignorance of social reality which led to the failure of their policies giving rise to terror, as it happened during the French Revolution. Their approach was simplistic and abstract ignoring the fact that the world was complex and importance had to be given to historical antecedents, religious beliefs, local customs and individual's psychological and physical characteristics. Engels fell in this category as he overlooked the many differences between human beings. It was equally true of the utopian projects beginning with Plato. The conception of an ideal state, and stress on charity and education would only weaken the proletariat. Sorel found Marxism to be a break from traditional socialist utopianism because of its insistence on the inevitability of class conflict and the fact that it did not make any predictions about an ideal society. It was clear that he tailored his own version of Marxism to suit his purpose.

Pessimism, in sharp contrast to optimism 'is a philosophy of conduct rather than a theory of the world' (Curtis 1962b: 270). It was based on two assumptions: (a) social determinism and (b) acceptance of natural weakness of human beings. These two were inter-linked and were inseparable. Pessimism's basic premise was that a 'march towards deliverance is narrowly conditioned'. A pessimist undertook a heroic act only when was convinced that total salvation was possible when helped by his companions. Unlike an optimist, he was certain that human actions were possible only on small scale for the actions determined by factors like trade, limitations of one's knowledge, shortcomings in human beings, and that change could only come 'in a catastrophe which involves the whole' for society was holistic (Ibid.).

For Sorel, the early Christian communities were pessimists as they were convinced that it was impossible for any human effort to reform the world and if it was possible, it would only happen with the second coming of Christ. Protestantism revived at first the early Christian pessimism but got swayed with the optimistic projections of Renaissance humanism. True Marxism was based on pessimism as it discounted any automatic law of progress, rejected the possibility of gradual reforms and had no plans of imposing from above any measures for comprehensive happiness. It did not have any utopian schemes and actually relied on a myth of human liberation. By deducing this inner essence of Marxism, Sorel convinced himself that such a gigantic task could be undertaken by the French working class. He was not sure if salvation or moral progress would emerge out of such actions. But since the action was more important than its consequences, his entire emphasis was on a heroic action without any thought of victory or personal consideration of power.

It was ironic that Sorel, like Bernstein, insisted that there was no final goal of socialism for the movement was everything and yet rejected the latter's stress on gradual non-violent and democratic social transformation. This was because he did not believe in human rationality and idea of progress, and reposed faith in a myth that negated intellectualism. He also defended the use of violence as morally elevating for it helped overcome complacency, indifference and inactivity.

Myth and Moral Revolution

People joined a struggle on the basis of some convictions. An action assumed the form of a battle where triumph was certain and defeat inconceivable. This illusory construction which was extremely important for the historians was termed as a 'myth'. The Syndicalist notions of a general strike and Marx's conception of an apocalyptical revolution were also myths. Other examples of myths were cited from primitive Christianity, Reformation and Mazzini's followers.

The perceptions of such groups had to be understood in their entirety as a historical force. A myth established a corelation between an actual fact and the images that the participants conceived of. In this context Sorel cited the example of the Catholics who unflinchingly believed that the history of the Church was primarily a series of battle between the force of Satan and that of Christ. Any obstacle was purely transitory in a war as the final victory of Christ was certain. This belief of a long story of revolutionary persecution was revived at the beginning of the nineteenth century by Joseph Marie Comte de Maistre (1754–1821), and the religious Renaissance at that time was largely due to an articulation of a myth. Sorel added that the contemporary danger to Catholicism arose because of a lack of such militancy.

Sorel looked to intellectual perceptions of societal evolution as grossly faulty and of little help to a historian in understanding people's real motivations and actions. To explain this point, he cited the examples of Napoleon' soldiers who sacrificed for the glory of France knowing fully well that their own poverty would continue, or the case of Romans who came from a highly unequal order and suffered considerably for conquering the world. Similarly, there was no intellectual explanation for the behaviour of devout Catholics since their religious beliefs were inexplicable in scientific and rational terms. Analogically, the philosophical arguments against revolutionary myths were applicable to only those who were looking for an escape route from the revolutionary path.

Without a myth the masses would never revolt. The idea of a general strike was the motive force behind the myth in contemporary times. The intellectuals projected the myth as utopian and their task was made easier by the fact that there was hardly any myth which did not have an utopian element in it. However, Sorel also asserted that the contemporary myths were free from utopianism. A myth was the motivation for getting into a decisive struggle. It was a force that inspired militant consciousness within a group. It enabled the workers to maintain solidarity, heroism and a spirit of self-sacrifice. It was a state of mind that prepared them to get ready for a violent destruction of the existing order with one single blow but without a ready-made blueprint of the alternative which they would be establishing. It perceived the need to weed out the existing state totally and was essentially a creative act. The crucial thing was that they believed in its efficacy. A myth, in contrast to a utopia, was negative for the latter was an intellectual product aiming at reform which ultimately absorbed the utopia within the system without any hope or scheme of transcendence.

The positive advantage of a myth was that it could not be refuted, whereas a utopian scheme could be debated like any other societal or constitutional arrangement. The socialist doctrines for a long time had a high degree of utopian components but Marxism changed that to myths of a future society. The revolutionary myths were like religious myths, and Sorel cited Bergson who offered the conceptual means to contrast scientific determinism with its belief in predictable social processes as against the notion of unforeseen spontaneous action. The myth of the Syndicalist movement was the general strike, the supreme and final aim, subordinating all other actions. It was an original creation of the movement itself which was clear about its purpose. The parliamentary socialists, on the other hand, were a confused lot for they could not afford to be consistent since they had to please different segments of a society. They disliked the idea of general strike. Under their leadership the real meaning of all socialist programmes were lost because they subordinated class war to national solidarity, and patriotism to internationalism. Though they espoused that the workers' emancipation would be achieved by the workers themselves, their mission ended by voting for a professional politician and making him supreme. They in turn postponed the socialist ideal of a withering away of the state to a distant future and helped in strengthening governmental machinery. Sorel rejected political parties for, normally, they subordinated the proletariat to professional politicians who frustrated their aspirations for liberation and established their tyranny. The hope of the proletariat was not with the parties or trade unions but with revolutionary non-political syndicates which would devote its time and energies to building and sustaining consciousness and solidarity among the workers. Revolutionary Syndicalism was clear and decisive, for it expressed the holistic sentiment of a declaration of war against modern society by using the concept of the general strike. This mechanism ensured that there was only one interpretation of socialism which even the intellectuals could not alter.

The Syndicalist movement undermined bourgeois morality and modes of thought. It rejected parliamentarism. It insisted on preserving the proletarian character of the workers by deliberately keeping the intellectuals out of the movement. The new proletarian culture was based on labour. The future society would have the technology of capitalism but not its culture. Sorel also dismissed any scheme that delineated the nature of the future struggles as utopian. He followed David Hume (1711–76) by arguing that none could predict the future scientifically. But, in spite of such uncertainties, a guide to action could be found in a myth, provided it articulated the feelings of the people belonging to a party or a class with the hope of immediate action. There was no need for any details since a myth would never materialize. It was judged not for its correct projections but for the intensity of its appeal to arouse the people for immediate action. It was irrelevant whether it reflected reality, for the only important point was that it ought to contain 'everything that the socialist doctrine expects of the revolutionary proletariat' (Curtis 1962: 277). Sorel felt that the general strike united all socialists, strengthening their determination to fight against the modern society.

From Proudhon, Sorel learnt that socialism was a moral issue which meant justice and dignity rather than welfare. The idea behind a socialist revolution was the moral transformation of the proletariat and restoring its dignity, pride, independence, and a sense of purpose and exclusiveness. Sorel regarded the use of violence as appropriate if it brought about moral education of its users. He had in mind military, rather than political, violence for it would be free of cruelty since it refrained from the wealth of the proprietied classes. The revolution would try and do away with government altogether. Its aim was not to make life easy or ensure abundance of material goods, but to entrust the organization of production to the workers. Like Marx, he looked to socialism as a complete transformation of every aspect of human existence and endeavour and just not a better social organization.

Syndicalism was opposed to democracy for it was demoralizing, corrupt and damaging to class solidarity. The general strike was different from a political revolution. It was not economic in nature as it did not try to improve the position of the working class within capitalism. Its aim was not to attain political power but to destroy the existing order without setting up a new authority or a master. It was not conspiratorial in nature either, for it did not rely on force or repression.

The parliamentarians opposed the idea of general strike for it negated the present privileges of its office-holders who would lose their power, patronage and authority if the workers succeeded in making their revolution. The general strike was similar to a warlike situation for it believed that it was a great motive power of history overriding all other considerations. It was glorious and heroic. Since no conquest was planned, there was no need for future plans except the certainty of expulsion of the capitalists from the domain of production. The material benefits were of no consideration and the general end was the abolition of the state.

Support for Violence

A core aspect of Sorel's theory was his support and endorsement of violence.[6] He took note of the spurt of violent activities and strikes in France and argued that any important work of socialism had to find out the causes and functions of violence. He was aware of the revulsion the middle class had towards violence, equating it with barbarism and hoping that it would disappear with the dawn of reason and enlightenment. He regarded such a perception as erroneous, for revolutionary and direct methods would continue to be important components of socialist strategy. Strikes were like military battles and prepared the ground for the ultimate general strike that would sound a death-blow to capitalism.

Proletarian violence carried on as a pure and simple manifestation of the sentiment of class war, appears thus a very fine and very heroic thing; it is at the service of the immemorial

interests of civilization. It is not perhaps the most appropriate method of obtaining immediate material advantages but
it may save the world from barbarism (Sorel, cited in Jennings
1996: 43).

Sorel described it as 'manchestarianism' since it combined the principles of classical liberal economic theory with the idea of self-
development of the revolutionary proletariat.

According to Sorel, economic decadence was because of a major difference between contemporary and classical capitalism which
led to doctrines like democracy and social peace. It was for this
reason that the middle class abhorred violence seeing it as a 'clear
and brutal expression of class war'(Ibid.: 44). Violence compelled
capitalists to restrict their activities as producers and separated
classes, and if both flourished, their historic destiny would be fulfilled. Sorel rejected any comparison between the violence that followed the French Revolution, especially the Jacobin violence under
Robespierre espoused by the Syndicalists. The former was perpetrated by the middle class. The Dreyfus case demonstrated that a
very large number of people, and that included parliamentary socialists as well, were prepared to protect the interests of the state
and repeat the old blunders.

In contrast, the proletarian violence both in nature and content
was totally different, for it was a war without hatred or revenge.
Its purpose was not to reform or preserve the state, which was the
aim of the middle class, but its destruction. War had a noble and
glorious purpose and was best exemplified in the myth of the general strike. Sorel distinguished between force and violence with
the former attempting to impose an order whereas the latter destroyed an order. Force had a statist and a class connotation whereas
violence was the means for the workers' liberation. He conceded
that violence might impede economic progress and too much of it
would be dangerous to morality, and even a threat to civilization
itself. But this would not be the case with proletarian violence for it
would be regenerative and cite the sacrifice of Christian martyrs
for proving righteousness and truth of their religion. It would involve minimum gallant exercises with minimum brutality. Sorel
was contemptuous of the democratic politics, the most democratic
in contemporary Europe, of the Third Republic for that meant an
association between politician and criminals. He referred to

Nietzsche's praise for 'Homer's Archean type, the indomitable hero' and cited it as an example for the future. The difference between the present and the future was in the change in the workers' status from consumers to producers. While the former symbolized immorality and decadence, the latter would be ethical without any master.

Sorel's glorification of violence and the myth of the general strike was borrowed by the Fascists. Mussolini expressed his indebtedness to Sorel. 'Sorel's appeals were well adapted to the spiritual conditions out of which Fascism was bred. He did not set up to be the planner of a new order, but the herald of catastrophe' (Kolakowski 1981b: 172).

As early as 1906 Sorel predicted that a foreign war could reinvigorate the waning energies of the bourgeoisie. He did not regard Mussolini as an ordinary socialist but an 'Italian of the fifteenth century, a condottiere'. The world did not know him yet, but he was the only energetic man capable of redressing the feebleness of the parliamentary government. He admired the Russian Revolution as a dramatic apocalypse, a death-blow to intellectualism, a triumph of human will and an assertion of indigenous Muscovite traditions over Western ones. He admired Lenin as the prophet of the Apocalypse, as the new Messiah, as the greatest socialist theorist since Marx. However, he did not approve of the repressive and terrorist methods that marked the Bolshevik Revolution though he regarded these as necessary in view of the foreign intervention and civil war conditions in Russia. He felt that Lenin had to be judged in the light of Russian history, by the standards set up the Tsars. He hoped that the Bolshevik revolution would renew and revitalize civilization. However, Lenin never took Sorel's theory seriously. He dismissed Sorel as a muddle-head and a mischief-maker.

Conclusion

Like the movement that Sorel represented, he was outside the major schools of socialist theorizing. He relied on the myth which by his own admission could not be rationally explained or systematically and logically analyzed except that it could be grasped intuitively. It was his irrationalism that made him welcome Mussolini and the

Fascists even though he claimed to be a Marxist. He admitted that he had nothing to do with the scientific claim of socialism. Like Marx, he did not delineate the future society except that it would represent a decisive break from the past and a new dawn. His ideal was self-sufficiency and workers' independent production units with direct democracy. He was against commercial exchange and had a low opinion of merchants. He idolized the independent and self-sufficient producer along the lines of the Jeffersonian individual. The libertarian aspect of early liberalism was manifest in Sorel's scheme.

Gramsci described Sorel as the French Plekhanov or Labroila for being the single-most important individual for popularizing Marxism in his home country, Sorel's Marxism was a departure from the Marxism of Marx or his followers. It was ironic that from Marx's own scheme so many varieties arose within a few decades of his death. Sorel's Marxism not only differed sharply from the other French variants but also from the other schools of European Socialism.

Sorel, like the contemporary post-Modernists, challenged the idea of uninterrupted progress and faith in human rationality. The First World War vindicated his point. 'What Sorel realized—and as the twentieth century has confirmed—was that a radical transformation of society directed by intellectuals and politicians and achieved largely through the mechanisms of the state would only serve to produce a new tyranny and oppression' (Jennings 1996: 55). Sorel, like Gandhi, bestowed faith in moral transformation which he knew was extremely difficult to achieve. It is a strange coincidence that, with regard to the ultimate faith in human morality, the spokesman of violence shared the same concern as the greatest apostle of non-violence in the twentieth century.

Mao Zedong

Mao Tse Tung's great accomplishment has been to change Marxism from an European to an Asiatic form (Strong 1947: 161).

Lacking any native Marxist ancestry, Chinese Communism descends straight from Bolshevism. Mao stands on Lenin's shoulders (Deutscher 1954a: 12).

Maoism in its final shape is a radical peasant utopia in which Marxist phraseology is much in evidence but whose dominant values seem completely alien to Marxism (Kolakowski 1981c: 495).

Mao Zedong (1893–1976), next to Lenin, is rightly credited with the establishment of a new state with a new regime. Among the architects and makers of the twentieth century, he deserves a rightful place. He was an immensely popular leader and a revolutionary and his theoretical writings were incidental to this primary role. Mao's Marxism was pragmatic which could be because it had its roots in Chinese history and philosophy. He also adapted Marxism to the Asian context. Initially a radical, he became a Marxist in 1918. As in many parts of the Third World, Marxism in China was integrally related to its nationalistic spirit and aspirations.

Mao's image underwent changes resulting in varying assessments. In the 1940s, he was perceived as a talented guerrilla leader whose Marxists credentials were undecidely true. In the 1950s, he was seen as the leader of a totalitarian party state under the control of Moscow. During the Cultural Revolution, for many student leaders in the West and for the Chinese people, he was a visionary whose plan of realizing socialism was far more humane, purer and radical than the one in the former Soviet Union. In the last years of his life, he was seen as a dictator in the mould of the traditional Chinese ones. Mao encompassed all these images in his personality. 'It is often been said that Mao Zedong was both China's Lenin and her Stalin . . . . it would be appropriate to say that Mao Zedong was China's Lenin, Stalin and Peter the Great' (Schram 1981: 22).

Like Lenin, Mao did not create the Chinese Communist Party but framed its strategies which enabled the Party to achieve victory and acquire power. Like Stalin, he laid the foundations of a socialist economy, achieved collectivization of agriculture and came close to vanquishing his rivals. Like Peter the Great, he was the creator of the Modern Chinese nation whose beginning was made by Sun Yat-Sen.

Mao's most original contribution to Marxism lay in recognizing and accepting the revolutionary role of the peasantry whom he looked upon as the vanguard of the revolution. In his anti-urban bias and pro-countryside sentiments, he echoed the writings of the early socialists and Russian radicals. He also emphasized on man's activity in production as the most fundamental practical activity which determined all his other activities. Interestingly, he realized and emphasized the importance of the human mind over matter, of overcoming material want and technological backwardness by superior will, and mass support and organization.

Unlike Bolshevism, which as Lenin asserted, stood on the shoulders of many generations of Russian revolutionaries who had breathed the air of European philosophy and socialist ideas, Chinese communism had no such ancestry. China was a hermit kingdom totally isolated from Western and European influences. Marxism penetrated into China through the Soviet Union, so Chinese communism descended straight from Bolshevism and Maoism was the application of Leninism. Though Mao's importance as an original political thinker is a matter of considerable debate, yet his historical and political significance is beyond doubt, for Maoism was a logical extension of Marxism-Leninism.

Biographical Sketch

Mao was born on 26 December 1893 in Shaoshan in the Hunan province of South Central China. His father was a poor peasant who became fairly well-off by trading in grain. Mao joined his father at work after leaving school at the age of thirteen. In 1909 he enrolled himself in a nearby secondary school, and in 1911 he moved to Changsha to continue his studies.

Mao joined the Republican army in 1911 after the proclamation of the Republic. He served in the army for six months. His formal education made him a radical nationalist. He encountered Marxism while working as an assistant librarian in Beijing in 1918. Though Marxism or Leninism was relatively unknown in China, it was the success of the Bolsheviks in Russia that influenced many Chinese intellectuals, as it was the case in India.

In 1919 nationalism became a real force with the May Fourth Movement in which there were widespread demonstrations and rioting against corrupt officials. The government decided to hand over the important province of Shantung, previously held by the Germans, to the Japanese against the Western promise that it would revert back to China. The general disillusionment with the West diverted the Chinese intellectuals towards Marxism.

In 1921 the Chinese Communist Party was (CCP) formed in Shanghai with 13 members, and amongst them was Mao. From the start, the CCP had to decide on the nature of the policies it would adopt in view of the nationalist republican bourgeois-democratic revolution that was brewing. In early 1920 the revolutionary nationalist forces supported the Koumintang (KMT) of Dr. Sun Yat-Sen. Lenin sent Michael Borodin to coordinate the Comintern efforts in China. He favoured an alliance between the CCP and KMT. Stalin also supported the alliance after Lenin became ill in 1923. Since the West refused support, Sun Yat-Sen turned to the Soviet Union agreeing to the first KMT-CCP alliance. The purpose of the alliance was to eliminate the reactionary warlords who controlled the far-flung areas of China. The alliance ran into problems with Sun Yat-Sen's death. The latter was succeeded by Chiang ke-Shek in 1926. Under his leadership, the KMT started the Northern Expedition to drive out the warlords and the Western imperialists who aided them. In 1927 Chiang also attacked the communists.

In that context, the CCP adopted an attitude of distrust of bourgeois parties and decided to rely on the revolutionary potential of the working class. Mao returned to Hunan in 1925 and began to explore the possibilities of the peasants as a revolutionary class. From 1927 onwards, a distinct brand of Chinese Communism began to develop. In 1934 when the Koumintang army gained decisive military advantage, they overwhelmed the communists and threatened their destruction. To avoid annihilation, the communists fled to Northern China. The epic retreat called the *Long March* was a journey by 100,000 people covering 6000 miles. Only 35,000 survived. Within the CCP, there was a leadership struggle and Mao gained the top position, one of total dominance which he enjoyed till his death.

Meanwhile in view of the Japanese attack, there was a temporary truce between the KMT and CCP. Stalin also encouraged the truce. However, after the defeat of Japan in 1945 the China question assumed importance. The United States supported the KMT and tried to negotiate a coalition government between Mao and Chiang. Stalin supported this move. Eventually Chiang lost because he could not control the warlords and because his government was corrupt and coercive. Mao, on the contrary, was popular. With the capture of power by the CCP of mainland China, Chiang fled to Formosa (Taiwan) in 1949. Inheriting a bankrupt economy the CCP initiated a series of measures to set the economy in order. Large capitalist enterprises were nationalized. The Land Law of

June 1950 was adopted guaranteeing each individual at the age of sixteen a minimum land-holding such that a family of five would have about one hectare. Fearing that the peasants would oppose sudden collectivization and, after the Soviet experience, social reforms were gradually enforced. The land of absentee landlords were redistributed to begin with and subsequently economic differences were narrowed down through fiscal measures, Through the First Five Year Plan (1953–57) attempts to socialize the economy were initiated beginning with heavy industries and then moving on to light industries and retail enterprises, and finally collectivize farms. The last two measures were stiffly opposed by the majority of the peasantry and the small producers.

Stalin died in 1955. The de-Stalinization campaign and reforms initiated by Khurshchev made Mao announce surprise initiatives in political liberalization. He welcomed criticisms of the government and its policies with the view to improve the system. This was called 'let a hundred flowers bloom, let a hundred schools contend' which was abruptly terminated following the virulent criticisms that poured in from all quarters. Needless to say, Mao was not prepared for such a shock. He reversed his stance and stifled all further criticisms. He launched the Great Leap Forward and the Great Cultural Proletarian Revolution as a part of the image-building exercise.

Mao was not happy with Khurshchev's policy of peaceful coexistence. China tried to project itself as the third world power and that it would lead the developing countries to prosperity. The break with the former Soviet Union came in 1957. Besides ideological differences, there were territorial disputes between the USSR and China. Meanwhile, the US initiated its policy of détente with China officially recognizing it. Deng Xiapong who was purged during the Cultural Revolution was rehabilitated and made successor to Chouen-lai who died in 1976. In the same year Chairman Mao also died.

Historical Background

China in the 1920s was an economically backward country which meant that the Communist Party had to rely on the peasantry as the single powerful section in society for advancing the cause of the revolution. China was not, as Trotsky described it, capitalist in character, nor was it feudal or semi-feudal in nature. The Chinese society was complex and intricate with myriad social relations and classes existing from different historical epochs, each finding sustenance from domestic and foreign influences. The society consisting of a limited but rapidly growing urban working class, national bourgeoisie, a small but powerful land owning class, peasants, rich and poor, landed and landless, artisans, bureaucrats, militarists, monks, bandits, rural vagabonds and 'compradors' in the service of foreign capitalists. Mao captured this situation in his concept of 'principal contradiction' and the 'principal aspect of the principal contradiction' in his interpretation of the dialectics.

The Chinese Communist Party was founded by Li Dazhao (1888–1927) and Chen Duxiu (1879–1942). Li was the chief librarian at Beijing University and the first communist to join the Guomindang. Chen, the editor of the influential journal *New Youth* advocated guild socialism under the influence of John Dewey (1859–1932). Li felt that Marxism lacked ethical perspective for Marx did not stress the fact that good persons emerge as they learn through mutual aid. The early Chinese Marxists entertained the idea of a glorious future for China but were anxious about the long time it would take to reach socialism if the full path of capitalist development was allowed. In order to find a solution, they turned to other theories, selecting those that would help them realize their goals within a reasonable period of time.

One such selective borrowing was from German Marxism. Li played down the base-superstructure determinism and its concomitant idea, inevitable sequence of events. They left out the materialist conception of history, the idea of historical stages and definition of classes in economic terms. Instead they contended that human consciousness or right-minded and strong-willed persons could shape the future. This was described as voluntarism, the ability of the conscious will to change the material world. In framing this perspective, Li and others were helped by non-Marxist ideas.

On the Peasants

Prior to 1925 Mao adopted the 'orthodox' Marxist position. In his article entitled *Analysis of Classes in Chinese Society*, he did not display any enthusiasm for the peasantry as a revolutionary class.

To sum up, it can be seen that our enemies are all those in league with imperialism—the warlords, the bureaucrats, the comprador class, the big landlord class, and the reactionary section of the intelligentsia attached to them. The leading force in our revolution is the industrial proletariat. Our closest friends are the entire semi-proletariat and petty-bourgeoisie. As for the vacillating middle bourgeoisie, their right wing may become our enemy and their left wing our friend—but we must be constantly on our guard and not let them create confusion within our ranks. (Mao 1954: 19).

In 1925 in his *Report on the Hunan Peasant Movement* Mao instructed the Communists to return to the countryside for the peasantry was the revolutionary class in China. They were described as the 'vanguard of the revolution'. This report formed the basis of Maoism and, coupled with the betrayal by Chiang and the failure of the communists to arouse the proletariat in the cities, led to the emergence of a distinct brand of Chinese communism. He defended the anti-landlord measures initiated by the Hunan Peasant Association. As early as 1926 the Comintern stressed on the urban proletariat though Mao saw the potential of peasant organizations believing that peasants could successfully help in ushering in communism. Peasants have working class ideas, and a class could be defined partly in economic terms and partly in terms of consciousness.

The present upsurge of the peasant movement is a colossal event. In a very short time, in China's central, southern and northern provinces, several hundred million peasants will arrive like a mighty storm, like a hurricane, a force so swift and violent that no power, however great, will be able to hold it back. They will smash all the trammels that bind them and rush forward along the road to liberation. They will sweep all the imperialists, warlords, corrupt officials, local tyrants and evil gentry into their graves. Every revolutionary party and every revolutionary comrade will be put to the test, to be accepted or rejected as they decide (Ibid.: 23).

Mao argued that since the forces of imperialism and its allies had entrenched themselves and built their base strongly in the cities, and since the revolutionary forces did not seek any compromises, it became imperative to look for alternatives. In that context, he looked to the villages with the hope that they could be turned 'into, advanced, consolidated base areas, into great military, political, economic and cultural revolutionary bastions, so that they can fight the fierce enemy who utilizes the cities to attack rural districts and, through a protracted struggle, gradually win an over-all victory for the revolution' (Mao 1954: 85).

Mao's idea ultimately triumphed for the communist movement moved to rural areas. His 'ruralism' emphasized the need for socio-economic development of the countryside for it was here that the true source of socialist reconstruction was possible. He instructed the urban city-dweller to go to the villages, to live and work among the peasants by doing hard manual work. Neither the peasants nor the city dweller liked this idea. Mao defended his actions by insisting that ideological purity was more important than economic experience and that a proletarian mentality could be developed through educational as well as economic simulation.

While Lenin recognized the significance of the peasantry in societies not highly industrialized, it was Mao who moved them to a central place in revolutionary strategy. Whether Mao's stress on the peasantry was a heresy or the enlightened application of Marxist-Leninist thought was another matter, but it certainly had its roots in the Chinese situation. Much of his inspiration grew from Chinese history.

Mao distrusted the bourgeoisie in general. He distinguished between a reactionary comprador bourgeoisie and a progressive national bourgeoisie. He viewed Chinese capitalism in general as potentially reactionary and alien. In 1939 he wrote:

National capitalism has developed to a certain extent and played a considerable part in China's political and cultural life, but it has not become the principal socio-economic form in China; quite feeble in strength, it is mostly tied in varying degrees to both foreign imperialism and domestic feudalism (Ibid.: 22).

Mao observed that China had a rich revolutionary tradition and a splendid historical heritage but was sluggish in its economic, political and cultural development once it transited from a slave society to feudalism. Feudalism in China lasted for about 300 years. It was because of foreign intervention that the Chinese economy witnessed internal changes and rudiments of national capitalism. The national bourgeoisie remained loyal to the external force that gave birth to it.

In Maoist theory, the basic contradiction within Chinese feudalism was not between the bourgeoisie and the feudal classes but between the peasants and landlords. Mao asserted that the class struggles of the peasantry 'alone formed the real motive force of historical development in China's feudal society' (Mao 1954: 11). He also pointed out that while capitalism was historically natural in the West, that was not the case in China. Therefore, while in the West one could use 'capitalism' and 'proletariat' as the appropriate categories for analyzing the prospects of socialist revolutions, in China one would have to talk of 'imperialism' and the 'Chinese people'.

> From the beginning Maoism looked not to the Marxist-defined socialist potentials of capitalist forces of production, but rather to "the Chinese people" for the sources of a socialist future. And "the people" of course, are basically the vast peasant masses, the overwhelming majority of that organic entity of 395 million identified in 1926 as the true friends of revolution (Meisner 1982: 58).

In 1960 Mao contended that it was easier for socialism to take roots in China than in the advanced West for the former was not corrupted by modern capitalism. He rejected the fundamental Marxist premise that socialism presupposed capitalism. Though he made a formal distinction between the bourgeois-democratic and socialist stages of revolution this distinction vanished in his redefinition of a 'bourgeois-democratic revolution'. The aim of the latter would be to steer clear of a capitalist system and head towards socialism.

On Contradiction

In his essay '*On Contradiction*' (1937) Mao contended that the universality or absoluteness of contradictions had a two-fold meaning: (1) that contradiction existed in the process of development of all things, and (2) that in the process of development of each thing, a movement of opposites existed from the beginning to its end. He believed that there was nothing that did not contain contradictions, for without contradictions, nothing would exist. He differentiated between antagonistic and non-antagonistic contradictions. The former was between the revolutionaries representing the people and the enemies of the people while the latter may exist among the people themselves. Contradictions among people differed. He identified these as contradictions within the working class, within the peasantry, within the intelligentsia, contradictions between the workers and peasants on the one hand and intellectuals on the other, between the working class and other sections of the working class on the one hand and the national bourgeoisie on the other, and contradictions within the national bourgeoisie itself. These contradictions for Mao were not antagonistic for, if handled properly, they could be transformed into non-antagonistic ones.

Mao was critical of Stalin's view that contradictions had gradually ceased to exist during the course of the socialist phase of development in the Soviet Union. He held that the socialist society also developed through contradictions between the productive forces and the productive relations. Since individuals live in society they reflected, in different circumstances and to varying degrees, the contradictions that existed in each form of society. Therefore, not everybody would be perfected even when a Communist society was established. His conviction that contradictions existed even within a socialist society and not merely between the individual and nature set him apart from the Russian Communists.

Mao argued that even after all class conflicts have been eliminated, contradictions would continue to arise between the forces of production and relations of production because of the continuous development of the former which would endanger contradictions between the members of society. These contradictions would be resolved by an endless series of 'qualitative changes' baptized as 'revolutions'. As a result there would be an infinite number of revolutions of the old type even after communism was fully established. For the present moment revolutions of the old type endangered by antagonistic contradictions between the classes and revolutions of the new type caused by the non-antagonistic contradictions within a socialist society would continue to coexist, but ultimately the development of the productive forces and the efforts of the individuals to adapt to them would replace the class struggle and the process of endless revolutions would stop.

Permanent Revolution

The theory of 'permanent revolution' was first enunciated by Marx and Engels. It contended that the proletariat would have to effect a permanence of revolution after the bourgeois-democratic revolution with the purpose of overthrowing the bourgeoisie and establishing their transitional state — the dictatorship of the proletariat — to create the material basis of true communism. It was restated by Plekhanov and Trotsky.

For Mao, revolution was the modicum through which people achieved their goals. The road to socialism would be a violent one for conflict was the essence of dialectics. It was out of social disruptions and turmoil that great progress could be achieved. Mao was categorical that there could be no compromises with the bourgeoisie and that a violent struggle between the two systems was unavoidable. Peaceful coexistence was a myth that could be pursued at the risk of betraying the revolution itself.

For Mao the agent which precipitated class struggle in historical materialism had changed. This agent was no longer the tension between technology and class structure but the ideas in the minds either of a few elites who teach the masses. Armed with these ideas elites could telescope the course of history and shorten the normal duration of a historical course. They could take charge of historical periods which would otherwise normally be led by the capitalists. Mao held that China did not have to wait for capitalism to develop. The elite could acquire right ideas rapidly and then lead the class struggle, assume the leadership of the revolution and introduce socialism. This revolution was permanent in then sense that the attainment of one stage (bourgeois democracy) need not be followed by a long period of gradual growth into the next.

By 1960s Mao's idea of permanent revolution crystallized and though it seemed similar to that of Trotsky it differed for it gave importance to the peasantry. For Mao, proletarian meant a set of moral qualities symbolizing collectivism and these values could be inculcated in the peasants also.

Mao rejected the elitism and bureaucratization of Leninism. He insisted that revolutionary goals could be attained through mass mobilization and, with this in mind, he launched his various movements like the anti-landlord campaign (1949–52), First Five Year Plan (1953–57), Hundred Flowers Bloom campaign (1957), the Great Leap Forward (1958–60) and the Great Cultural Proletarian Revolution (1966–76). Other smaller campaigns like the anti-insect and rodent campaign, anti-corruption movement, sanitary campaigns and tree planting campaigns were started with the same aim that people could be entrusted with revolutionary aims. Besides mass support Mao was also ready to use guerrilla warfare tactics for he felt these were necessary in less developed areas.

Mao stated his views on the future of the revolution and the transitional society in his *New Democracy* (1940). He spoke of a revolution by stages – a bourgeois democratic revolution preceding the socialist revolution. He pointed out that China was still a colonial and a semi-feudal country and it was after its elimination that new politics, a new economy and a new culture could be built. Writing about this new culture Mao observed,

> In the historical course of the Chinese revolution two steps must be taken: (*a*) the democratic revolution, and (*b*) socialist revolution; these two revolutionary processes are different in character. The democracy in question no longer belongs to the old category – it is not old democracy; it belongs to the new category – it is New Democracy (Mao 1954: 109).

For Mao the Chinese revolution could be conducted under the hegemony of the proletariat. It could establish a socialist society.

> Although in its social character the first stage of, or the first step taken in this revolution in a colonial and semi-colonial country is still fundamentally bourgeois democratic and although its objective demand is to clear the path for the development of capitalism, yet it no longer belongs to the old type of revolution led with the aim of establishing a capitalist society and a state under bourgeois dictatorship but belongs to the new type of revolution which, led by the proletariat, aims at establishing a new democratic society, a state under the joint dictatorship of all the revolutionary classes. Thus, this

revolution exactly serves to clear a path even wider for the development of socialism (Mao 1954: 111–2).

Dictatorship of the Proletariat

Mao contended that the Soviet model of the dictatorship of the proletariat was appropriate for advanced countries but unsuitable for colonial and semi-colonial countries. He argued that democratic republic would be the most appropriate form for though it would be transitional in nature, it would be unalterable and necessary. Mao identified the revolutionary classes that would manage the dictatorship of the proletariat. He called it the United Front consisting of the Chinese working class, peasantry, petty-bourgeoisie, national bourgeoisie and other patriotic democratic elements based on an alliance between the industrial proletariat and the peasants but led by the former. Thus he went beyond Lenin in stating that the dictatorship of the proletariat would be one of several revolutionary classes (McLellan 1979: 208).

The theory of the new democratic revolution was an application of the Marxist theory of bourgeois-democratic revolution to colonial situations. The Russian Marxists also recognized the need for such an alliance between the peasants and the proletariat with the latter at the helm of affairs. Of course, Marx dismissed the peasantry as reactionary for they were used to the 'idiocy of village life'. The later Marxists, including Mao, however, followed the prescriptions of Bakunin in regarding the peasantry rather than the industrial proletariat as the revolutionary class. The anti-urban bias that Mao articulated was found in the writings of the early socialists like Buonarroti and the Russian radicals.

Mao insisted that a transition to socialism could be accomplished under the continued existence of the national bourgeoisie whereas the Russian Marxists following Marx insisted that the dictatorship. of the proletariat would have to crush the resistance offered by the bourgeoisie and build the basis for a socialist society. Mao did not insist on smashing of the state machinery regarded as an essential prerequisite by Lenin and Marx. The Chinese 'new democratic revolution' was visualized as having a dual nature. In its minimum programme the revolution would seek a united front to overthrow 'feudal landlord elements', bureaucratic-capitalists and foreign imperialists and consolidate the new democratic revolution. In its minimum programme the non-proletarian classes in the united front would gradually be transformed and the new democratic revolution would inevitably lead to a socialist and eventually a communist society. Mao was vague as to how long this entire process would take.

For Mao the proletarian dictatorship was not exercised by the proletariat as a class but by those who possessed a 'proletarian consciousness'. The rural people's communes were the main institutional basis for revolutionary social and economic transformation. He was generally vague about the post-revolutionary future and very rarely used the terms socialism and communism. He regarded communism as the most progressive and the most rational system that human history had ever known.

As far as the organization of the party was concerned Mao adopted the Leninist concept of democratic centralism right at the outset which meant freedom to discuss issues before a decision was taken, but once a decision was taken it had to be obeyed implicitly. All party members would be consulted but the subordination of the lower to the higher was clear and rigid. In reality within the communist parties of both the Soviet Union and China there was greater reliance on centralism than democracy. Mao tried to temper it with his idea of mass line.

Mao understood democracy to mean allowing the ordinary people to speak their minds on topics of which they had direct knowledge. This would enable officials to make good policies and promote unity and solidarity between the people and party. During the guerrilla period the term 'mass line' was introduced referring to consultation with local people. In general, Mao followed the Leninist line that the elite know better, that leaders were teachers who could transform the knowledge of the ordinary people into higher rational knowledge. Maoism intertwined centralism and democracy with a theory of knowledge.

It was during the Great Leap Forward campaign that Mao gave full expression to his vision of the socialist future. He promised good material life for that would abolish the distinction between the town and the country, between mental and physical labour and between workers, peasants and the intellectuals. This would quicken the dissolution of the state. True communism could be built through basic industries and a modern economy. The Great

Leap Forward was proclaimed to be a period of transition from socialism to communism. While speculating about the future Mao relied on classical Marxist-Leninist writings. The communes were envisioned as instruments of 'the dictatorship of the proletariat' for these would usher in a classless-stateless society. He firmly believed that the human spirit was a decisive factor in bringing about the new society. By applying superior will power and by organizing people he believed one could overcome both material want and poor technology.

The Great Leap Forward tried to reverse the process of centralized heavy industrialization that was started during the First Five Year Plan period by encouraging enterprenuership among the people. Every household unit was encouraged to produce or manufacture something with the state providing capital and resources. The family as a social unit was attacked by extending communalism beyond work and ownership. The idea of communal living was propagated.

All these were abandoned for there was a steep fall in production and the threat of a famine loomed large. By the mid-1960s backyard industries were abandoned and barrack communes disappeared. The Great Leap Forward also led to a reassertion of the power of the state and party bureaucracies which were targeted during the Cultural Revolution. In the summer of 1959 Mao abandoned the talk of imminence of the transition to communism. He realized that the modern economic and social transformation in China would be an arduous process. He also abandoned the talk of overtaking the advanced West in 15 years time. In this admission he showed more maturity than Khurshchev who made an elaborate plan of overtaking the USA in production and reaching full communism by the 1980s.

Post-Mao Developments

The post-Mao developments were titled 'Humanism'. First and foremost the Maoist view that class struggle was the principal agent of historical change creating the basis of a modern society in China was repudiated. Class struggle suggested the presence of different and distinctive classes, and that led to class hatred and class war. Mao looked to class antagonisms as inevitable. Within a class there are uniformities in natures but different classes would have different natures. The humanists reiterated the Confucian belief in universal human nature. After Mao's death many Marxists supported the idea of free development of the individual which they saw as a humanistic goal. But they deflected its content from Confucian focus on humaneness to mean absence of alienation, a dominant theme in early Marxism. In this context the dictatorship of the party was criticized for it contributed to alienation among the Chinese people for the bureaucrats constantly interfered, allowing very little freedom. Alienation could not exist in a socialist society.

Conclusion

Maoism rejected the Marxist premise that socialism could develop only within the context of modern industrial capitalism. As a corollary to this belief, it rejected the idea that the industrial proletariat would be the bearers of socialism. Instead it placed more importance on the peasants seeing them infused with pure revolutionary ardour. The highlight of Maoism was its anti-urban bias. Perhaps Maoism was akin to the views of the early Socialists, who preceded Marx, and the Russian radicals. Moreover Maoism placed more importance on the voluntaristic side of human action rather than on objective laws of history. It looked to consciousness and moral potentialities within human beings as being decisive in bringing about socio-historical development and the transition to communism.

Mao's positive contributions included his notion of mass line which meant democratic participation from below but under the strict guidance of the party, a feature that distinguished itself from Leninism and the Soviet culture. He emphasized certain puritanical values like thrift and common good for he was sanguine that change in human nature had to precede technological and economic development and not remain merely its byproduct. He was able to integrate non-proletarian elements in the revolutionary struggle. He brought the peasantry to the centre stage and ensured that they did not become victims of development. His conception of guerrilla warfare inspired others like Frantz Fanon (1925–61), 'Che' Ernesto Guevara (1928–67)[7] and Regis Debray (1940).[8] Mao believed that the proletariat in Europe, Russia and Eastern Europe had betrayed its revolutionary mission. He was confident, like Fanon, that the peoples of Asia, Africa and Latin America were truly revolutionary and their struggles would redeem both themselves and the decadent Europe. In this struggle Mao perceived himself as representing these dynamic and progressive forces.

It is generally recognized that Mao's revolution succeeded at a terrible human cost. During the Cultural Revolution more than three million people died. The death of millions in a famine in Mao's China was, as Sen pointed out, due to the lack of democracy. But paradoxically, compared to other countries, China's spectacular record in basic indicators like literacy, nutrition and rural development is largely due to Mao's policies. The impressive economic performance which began 3 years after Mao's death largely succeeded because of his policies. Liquidation of feudal landowning class and ruthless rationalization of agricultural production enabled Deng to transform China into a highly efficient country of productive small-scale farmers and rural entrepreneurs. Similarly, Mao's destruction of the corrupt business class enabled Deng to attract foreign and overseas Chinese investors. If China is today a near literate, adequately nourished strong rural economy with a productive agricultural base, a functioning national infrastructure and a booming economy, it is largely a consequence of Mao's policies, though today's China is a negation of Mao's ideals. It is an irony of history that Mao remains seminally important to understand modern China though the course of developments after his death hardly resembles his dreams and vision.

Endnotes

1. Ruskin violently attacked capitalism for it distorted affections and responsibility in social relationships. He did not think socialism would remedy these evils for it too would be contaminated by capitalist values. Only through education and precept could values be changed and without it political action and democracy would be ineffective. He reposed faith in enlightened leaders to act responsibly and thereby subscribed to the notion of moral paternalism. He argued that the character of a society was revealed in its architecture and concluded that a corrupt society and inhuman work would not produce art of any value. He was convinced that Victorian capitalism would destroy civilization, art, society and traditional values. He castigated modern economists for confusing value with wealth. Ruskin influenced Morris and Gandhi, elaborated and extended a radical tradition different from Marxism and helped in the formation of the idea of the welfare state. Carlyle was equally suspicious of *laissez-faire* economics, democracy and liberal legal philosophy which rejected

man's social existence in favour of a more individualistic ethic. He desired a society that would be organic and guaranteed the spirit of community.

2. Bellamy's good society was free of greed and competitiveness. Its inhabitants cherished centralized community, solidarity and reciprocity, and were free of deceptiveness and manipulation that characterized the market society. Bellamy's aim was good life and was influenced by Plato's *Republic*. His *Equality* (1897) which was a sequel to *Looking Backward* tried to develop some of the socialist proposals and refute the misreadings of the first novel. Bellamy reposed faith in the managerial elite to be able to satisfy all citizens by assuring material comfort and avoiding overproduction. This exerted considerable influence on Morris.

3. In 1894 Captain Alfred Dreyfus, a French Jewish general staff officer was condemned to life imprisonment for betraying secrets to Germany. The charges were flimsy and there was a demand for a re-trial. Fearing that he might be acquitted, senior army officers forged evidence and secured a re-trial in 1899. The case divided France and dominated French politics. Guesde saw it as a quarrel between two groups of the ruling classes. Juarez saw Drefuys' condemnation as unjust and had to be reversed if France had to move towards a just society.

4. Juarez was a convinced republican and democrat, and campaigned for the separation of the state and church. He was the earliest to study the social bases of the French Revolution. He projected socialism as the logical and inevitable aim of the proletarian revolution. Though he spoke of class struggle, he stressed more on the worker as an emancipated individual than a unit in a mass. He was also a passionate spokesman for internationalism and peace.

5. de Leon's writings influenced Sorel. He envisaged a socialist republic that would be administered by government-supported economic syndicates. The government would be composed of representatives from trade unions. The future socialist society would be a cooperative commonwealth consisting of diverse industrial units.

6. Sorel's theory of violence influenced Fanon's creation of the white man who identified totally with the Black resurgence and negritude as manifest in *Black Skin, White Mask* (1967). His *The Wretched of the Earth* (1961) offered a solution to Third World problems. He observed that, unlike European bourgeoisie which was both productive and parasitic, the colonial bourgeoisie was just parasitic and without any skill of enterpreneurship this class merely acted as the agent of Western capitalism. In the process, it was part of an exploitative colonial system which ruthlessly exploited the native proletariat and peasantry. The native proletariat was not revolutionary and it was the peasants and the lumpenproletariat who were the genuine revolutionary class. This class would unite with the urban intellectuals. Unlike Mao, who forged a link between the peasants and the proletariat, for Fanon in a colonial situation, the peasantry with the urban underclass would foment a revolution. Like Debray, he believed, that revolutionary struggles would create a political party. The reliance on lumpenproletariat was contrary to Marxism, for Marx dismissed them as bohemian. In the Marx-Bakunin debate, the latter felt that the proletariat was bureaucratized and non-revolutionary and felt that the underclass would be the liberating agent. Fanon advocated a massive violent upheaval

and rejected guerrilla warfare and two-staged revolution. Violence was a cleansing agent. Unlike the brutality of colonialism, he favoured that the liberation had to be clean and without barbarity.

7. Guevara's strategy along with the theoretical formulations by Debray have made the Cuban experience a model for revolutionaries in the rest of Latin America. Guevara emphasized the moral dimension of communism and pointed out that, in order to build communism, a new man had to be simultaneously created along with the material base. Hence it was important to chose correctly the instrument of mass mobilization, which would be moral without forgetting the correct use of material incentives, especially those social in nature.

8. Debray's views were in sharp contrast with the orthodox communists for whom Latin America was experiencing a democratic revolution led by the progressive bourgeoisie against feudal landowners and US imperialism. The socialist revolution would follow once the national democratic revolution succeeded. The duty of the communists was to help in the success of the first revolution by participating in the parliamentary and electoral process in order to establish popular front governments led by middle class parties. This attitude was based on the erroneous assumption that there was a fundamental clash of interests between the urban capitalists, on the one hand, and either the feudal landowners or American capitalists, on the other. The unsatisfactory nature of this strategy led Debray to evolve a distinct Latin American Marxism in the shape of *foco* theory which rejected the Moscow scheme, Trotsky's concept of permanent revolution and Mao's four-group united front strategy. For Debray, the capitalist state could be destroyed from centres of guerrilla operations with three cardinal rules — constant vigilance, constant mistrust and constant mobility. This meant cutting off the guerrillas from the rest of the population and elevating the military above the political, which was uncharacteristic of Marxism.

❖ *References*

Adamson, W.L. 1980. 'Gramsci's Interpretation of Fascism', *Journal of the History of Ideas*, XLI, pp. 615–34.

Ali, T. (ed.). 1984. *The Stalinist Legacy: Its Impact on Twentieth Century World Politics.* Harmondsworth: Penguin.

Althusser, L. 1969. *For Marx.* London: Allen Lane.

Arendt, H. 1969. 'Rosa Luxemburg', in *Man in Dark Times.* New York: Harcourt Brace and World.

Ash, T.G. 1990. 'Eastern Europe: The Year of Truth', *New York Review of Books*, 10 February, pp. 17–22.

Avineri, S. 1969. *Karl Marx on Colonialism and Modernization: His Despatches and Other Writings on China, India, Mexico, the Middle East and North Africa.* New York: Cambridge University Press.

———. 1976. *The Social and Political Thought of Karl Marx.* New Delhi: S. Chand.

Bahro, R. 1978. *The Alternative in Eastern Europe.* London: New Left.

Barker, R. 1978. *Political Ideas in Modern Britain.* London: Methuen.

Baron, S. 1963. *Plekhanov: The Father of Russian Marxism.* London: Routledge and Kegan Paul.

Bates, T.R. 1975. 'Gramsci and the Theory of Hegemony', *Journal of the History of Ideas*, XXXVI, pp. 351–66.

Bebel, A. 1988. *Woman in the Past, Present and Future,* edited with an Introduction by M. Donald. London: Zwan Publications.

Bell, D. 1966. *The End of Ideology: On the Exhaustion of Political Ideas in the Fifties.* New York: Collier Books.

———. 1968. 'Socialism', in *Encyclopaedia of Social Sciences.* London: Macmillan.

———. 1974. *The Coming of Post Industrial Society.* New York: Penguin.

Berki, R.N. 1975. *Socialism.* London: John Dent & Sons.

Berlin, Sir I. 1939. *Karl Marx.* New York: Time Books.

———. 1979. *Russian Thinkers.* Harmondsworth: Penguin.

Bernstein, E. 1961. *Evolutionary Socialism.* New York: Schoken Books.

Blackburn, R. (eds.). 1970. *Revolution and Class Struggle: A Reader in Marxist Politics.* Glasgow: Fontana.

———. (ed.). 1991. *After the Fall: The Failure of Communism and Future of Socialism.* London: Verso.

Bodenheimer, S. 1974. 'Dependency and Imperialism: The Roots of Latin American Underdevelopment', in *Readings in US Imperialism* edited by Fann and Hodge. Boston: Beacon.

Boos, F.S. and **C.G. Silver,** 1990. *Socialism and the Literary Artistry of William Morris.* Columbia: Columbia University Press.

Bottomore, T. 1983. 'Sociology', in *Marx: The First Hundred Years,* edited by D. McLellan. Glasgow: Fontana.

Bowle, J. 1954. *Politics and Opinion in the Nineteenth Century.* London: Jonathan Cape.

Brezezinski, Z. 1979. *Between Two Ages: America's Role in the Technocratic Era.* New York.

Burnham, J. 1948. *The Managerial Revolution: What is Happening in the World.* New York: John Day.

Cabral, A. 1983. *Revolutionary Leadership and People's War.* Cambridge: Cambridge University Press.

Carnoy, M. 1984. *The State and Political Theory.* Princeton, NJ: Princeton University Press.

Carpenter, L.P. 1973. *G.D.H. Cole: An Intellectual Biography.* Cambridge: Cambridge University Press.

Carr, E.H. (ed.). 1959. *Introduction to ABC of Communism,* Harmondsworth, Penguin.

————. 1979. *The Russian Revolution: Lenin to Stalin.* London: Penguin.

Carver, T. 1981. *Engels.* Oxford: Oxford University Press.

Caute, D. 1966. *The Left in Europe since 1789.* London: Weidenfeld & Nicolson.

————. 1967. *Essential Writings of Marx.* New York: Collier.

Chang, S. 1965. *Marxian Theory of the State.* New York.

Charvet, J. 1982. *Feminism.* London: John Dent & Sons.

Coates, K. 1978. *The Case of Nikolai Bukharin.* Nottingham: Spokesman.

Cole, G.D.H. 1917. *Self-Government in Industry.* London: G. Bell & Sons.

————. 1918a. *Labour in Commonwealth: A Book for the Younger Generation.* London: Headley Bros.

————. 1918b. *An Introduction to Trade Unionism.* London: Allen & Unwin.

————. 1920a. *Guild Socialism Restated.* London: Leonard Parsons.

————. 1920b. *Social Theory.* London: Methuen.

————. (ed.). 1934. *William Morris: Prose, Verse, Lectures and Essays.* London: Nonesuch Press.

————. 1953. *A History of Socialist Thought I: The Forerunners 1789–1850.* London: Macmillan.

————. 1954. *A History of Socialist Thought II: Marxism and Anarchism 1850–1890.* London: Macmillan.

————. 1956a. *A History of Socialist Thought III: The Second International 1889–1914* (2 parts). London: Macmillan.

————. 1956b. 'World Socialism Restated'. London: *New Statesman* Pamphlet.

————. 1958. *A History of Socialist Thought IV: Communism and Social Democracy 1914–1931.* London: Macmillan.

————. 1960. *A History of Socialist Thought V: Socialism and Fascism 1931–1939.* London: Macmillan.

Colletti, L. 1969. *From Rousseau to Lenin.* New Delhi: Oxford University Press.

Conqest, R. 1972. *Lenin.* London: Fontana.

Cornforth, M. 1968. *The Open Philosophy and the Open Society: A Reply to Sir Karl Popper's Refutation of Marxism.* London: Lawrence and Wishart.

Crick, B. 1998. *Socialism.* New Delhi: World View Publications.

Croce, B. 1926. *Sorel's Reflections on Violence*. Bari: Laterza.

Crosland, A. 1956. *The Future of Socialism*. London: Cape.

Curtis, M. 1962. *The Great Political Theories*, 2 Vols. New York: Avon.

Dahl, R.A. 1965. *A Preface to Democratic Theory*. Chicago: University of Chicago Press.

————. 1986. *Democracy, Liberty and Equality*. Oslo: Norwegian University Press.

Dahrendorf, R. 1959. *Class and Class Conflict in an Industrial Society*. London: Routledge and Kegan Paul.

Davidson, A. 1977. *Antonio Gramsci: Towards an Intellectual Biography*. London: Merlin.

Deutsher, I. 1954a. 'Maoism: Its Origins, Background and Outlook', *Socialist Register*.

————. 1954b. *The Prophet Armed Trotsky: 1897–1921*. Oxford: Oxford University Press.

————. 1959. *The Prophet Unarmed Trotsky: 1921–1929*. Oxford: Oxford University Press.

————. 1963. *The Prophet Outcast Trotsky: 1929–1940*. Oxford: Oxford University Press.

Djilas, M. 1990. 'Social Democracy is a Worldwide Movement'. *Moscow News Weekly*, 12 March.

Dolgoff, S. 1973. *Bakunin on Anarchy*, edited, translated and introduced. New York: Vintage.

Donald, M. (ed.). 1988. *Bebel's Woman and Socialism*. London: Zwan Publications.

Draper, H. 1977. *Karl Marx's Theory of Revolution: State and Bureaucracy*. New York: Monthly Review Press.

Drucker, P. 1989. 'The Coming of the Post Industrial Society', *New Perspective Quartely*, 6, 1, pp. 44–46.

Dunn, J. 1988. *Modern Revolutions*. London: Clarendon Press.

Eliot, T.S. 1975. 'The Hollowman', *T.S. Eliot Selected Poems*. London: Faber.

Elliot, C. 1967. 'Problems of Marxist Revisionism', *Journal of the History of Ideas*, Vol. 28, pp. 71–89.

Elliott, L. 1991. 'The Rolling Economic Disaster'. *Guardian*, August 20.

Elster, J. 1986. *Making Sense of Marx*. Cambridge: Cambridge University Press.

Engels, F. 1952. 'Democratic Panslavism' in *The Russian Menance to Europe*, edited by P.W. Blackstone and B.F. Hoselitz. Glencoe: Free Press.

Engels, F. 1977. *Selected Writings*. Moscow: Progress Publishers.

Engeman, D.S. 1982. 'Hythloday's Utopia and More's England: An Interpretation of Thomas More's *Utopia*', *Journal of Politics*, 44, pp. 131–49.

Fanon, F. 1965. *The Wretched of the Earth*. Harmondsworth: Penguin.

Fischman, D. 1991. *Political Discourse in Exile: Karl Marx and the Jewish Question*. Amherst: University of Massachussetts Press.

Fletcher, R.A. 1983. 'Cobden as Educator: The Free Trade Internationalism of Eduard Bernstein, 1888–1915'. *American Historical Review*.

————. (ed.). 1987. *Bernstein to Brandt: A Short History of German Social Democracy*, London.

Fourier, F.M.C. 1901. 'Design for Utopia', in *Selected Writings of Charles Fourier*, edited by Frank E. Manuel, translated by Julia Frankin. New York: Schoken Books.

Fried, A. and R. Sanders (eds.). 1964. *Socialist Thought: A Documentary History*. New York: Vintage.

Fukuyama, F. 1992. *The End of History and the Last Man*. Harmondsworth: Penguin.

Gankin, O. and H. Fisher, 1960. *The Bolsheviks and the World War*. Stanford: University of California Press.

Gay, P. 1979. *The Dilemma of Democratic Socialism: Eduard Bernstein's Challenge to Marx*. New York: Columbia University Press.

Geras, N. 1976. *Legacy of Rosa Luxemburg*. London: New Left.

Giddens, A. 1974. *The Class Structure of the Advanced Societies*. London: Hutchinson.
————. 1995. *A Contemporary Critique of Historical Materialism*. London: Macmillan.

Goodwin, B. 1992. *Using Political Ideas*. Chilchester: Wiley and Sons.

Gramsci, A. 1971. *Selections from Prison Notebooks*, edited and translated by Quintin Hoare and Geoffery Nowell-Smith. London: Lawrence and Wishart.

Gray, A. 1946. *The Socialist Tradition: From Moses to Lenin*. London: Longsman Green.

Greanleaf, W.I. 1973. *British Political Tradition*. 2 vols. London: Methuen.

Grebing, H. 1969. *The History of the German Labour Movement: A Survey*, translated by Edith Korner. London.

Grenville, J.A.S. 1980. *A World History of the Twentieth Century, 1900–45*, Vol. I. London: Fontana.

Gouldner, A.W. 1980. *The Two Marxisms: Contradictions and Anomalies in the Development of Theory*. New York: Oxford University Press.

Guy, J.A. 1980. *The Public Career of Sir Thomas More*. New Haven: Yale University Press.

Habermas, J. 1991. 'What Does Socialism Mean Today? The Revolutions of Recuperation and the Need for New Thinking', in *After the Fall: The Failure of Communism and Future of Socialism*, edited by R. Blackburn. London: Verso.

Hague, R., M. Harrop and S. Breslin, 1992. *Comparative Government and Politics: An Introduction*. London: Macmillan.

Harding, N. 1981. *Lenin's Political Thought*, 2 vols. New York: St. Martin's Press.

Harrington, M. 1989. 'No Alternative to Capitalism' by R.L. Heilbroner, *New Perspective Quartely*, 6, pp. 4–10.

Harris, N. 1986. *The End of the Third World: Newly Industrialized Countries and the Decline of an Ideology*. Harmondsworth: Penguin.

Hearnshaw, F.J.C. 1952. *The Social and Political Ideas of Some Great Thinkers in the Seventeenth Century*. London: George Harrap and Co.

Heilbroner, R.L. 1989. 'No Alternative to Capitalism', *New Perspective Quarterly*, 6, pp. 4–10.

Held, D. 1983. 'The Frankfurt School', in *A Dictionary of Marxist Thought*, edited Tom Bottomore. Oxford: Blackwell.

Hill, C. 1975. *Puritanism and Revolution*. London: Fontana.

Hindess, B. 1983. *Parliamentary Democracy and Socialist Politics*. London: Routledge and Kegan Paul.

Hobsbawn, E. 1991. 'Goodbye to All That', in *After the Fall: The Failure of Communism and the Future of Socialism*, edited by Robin Blackburn. London: Verso.

Hook, S. 1933. *Towards an Understanding of Karl Marx*. New York: John Day.
————. 1961. *Bernstein's Evolutionary Socialism*, edited with an Introduction. New York: Schoken Books.

Howe, I. (ed.). 1972. *A Handbook of Socialist Thought*. New York: Pantheon.
————. 1978. *Trotsky*. Glasgow: Fontana.
Howe, I. 1990a. 'Soviet Transformation', in *Dissent*. Spring, pp. 133–34.
————. 1990b. 'From the Dustbin of History', in *Dissent*. Spring, pp. 184–86.
Hulse, J.W. 1970. *Revolutionists in London: A Study of Five Unorthodox Socialists*. Oxford: Oxford University Press.
Humphrey, R. 1951. *Georges Sorel: Prophet Without Home*. Cambridge, Mass.: Harvard University Press.
Hunley, J.D. 1991. *The Life and Thought of Friedrich Engels*. New Haven: Yale University Press.
Hunt, R.N. 1975. *The Political Ideas of Marx and Engels*. London: Macmillan.
Ionescu, G. 1976. *The Political Thought of Saint Simon*. Oxford: Oxford University Press.
Jennings, J. 1996. 'Georges Sorel: Reflections on Violence', in *The Political Classics: Green to Dworkin*, edited by Murray Forsyth and Maurice Keens-Soper. Oxford: Oxford University Press.
Johnson, P. 1988. *Intellectuals*. London: Orion.
Joll, J. 1977. *Gramsci*. Glasgow: Fontana.
Katz, B. 1982. *Herbert Marcuse: Art Liberation*. Boston.
Kautsky, K.J. 1964. *Dictatorship of the Proletariat*, edited with an Introduction by J.H. Kautsky. Ann Arbor: University of Michigan Press.
————. 1971. *The Class Struggle*. Chicago: C.H. Kerr.
Kautsky, J.H. 1961. 'J.A. Schumpeter and Karl Kautsky', *Midwest Journal of Political Science*, 5, pp. 101–128.
Keane, J. (ed.). 1988. *Civil Society and the State*. New York: Verso.
Keep, J.L.H. 1963. *The Rise of Social Democracy in Russia*. Oxford: Oxford University Press.
Kiernan, V. 1972. 'Gramsci and Marxism', *The Socialist Register*, London: The Merlin Press, pp. 1–33.
Knei-Paz, B. 1978. *The Social and Political Thought of Leon Trotsky*. Oxford: Oxford University Press.
Kolakowski, L. 1981a. *Main Currents of Marxism: The Founders*. Oxford: Oxford University Press.
————. 1981b. *Main Currents of Marxism: The Golden Age*. Oxford: Oxford University Press.
————. 1981c. *Main Currents of Marxism: The Breakdown*. Oxford: Oxford University Press.
Kolmerton, C.B. 1990. *Women in Utopia: The Ideology of Gender in American Owenite Communities*. Bloomington: Indiana University Press.
Kowalik, T. 1968. 'Rosa Luxemburg', in *Encyclopaedia of Social Sciences*. London: Macmillan.
Laidler, H.W. 1927. *A History of Socialist Thought*. New York.
Laski, H. 1925. *Socialism and Freedom*. London: Unwin.
Lasky, M.J. 1976. *Utopia and Revolution*. London: Macmillan.
Lassalle, F. 1920. *Reden and Schriften*, edited by Hans Feigl. Berlin: Universities Press.
Lee, Kuan Yew. 1998. *The Singapore Story*. Singapore: Prentice Hall.
Lehning, A. 1973. *Michael Bakunin: Selected Writings*. London: Jonathan Cape.

Lenin, V.I. 1977. *The State and Revolution and Proletarian Revolution and Renegade Kautsky*. Moscow: Progress Publishers.

Lichtheim, G. 1961. *Marxism: A Historical and Critical Study*. London: Routledge.

————. 1963. *The New Europe: Today and Tomorrow*. New York: Frederick A. Praeger.

————. 1969. *The Origins of Socialism*. New York: Frederick A. Praeger.

————. 1975. *A Short History of Socialism*. Glasgow: Fontana.

Lipset, S.M. 1963a. 'The Sociology of Marxism', *Dissent*, X, 1.

————. 1963b. *Political Man*. New York: Doubleday.

————. (ed.). 1979. *The Third Century: America as a Post Industrial Society*. Stanford: Hoover Institute Press.

Lively, J. 1980. *Democracy*. Oxford: Blackwell.

Lowy, M. 1976. *The Politics of Combined and Uneven Development*. London: New Left.

Luxemburg, R. 1961. *Russian Revolution: Leninism or Marxism*, Introduction by B.R. Wolfe. Ann Arbor: University of Michigan Press.

————. 1971. *Selected Writings*, edited by Dick Howard. London: Monthly Review Press.

MacIntyre, A. 1970. *Herbert Marcuse*. Glasgow: Fontana.

MacRae. 1974. *Weber*. Oxford: Oxford University Press.

Magee, B. 1984. *Popper*. Oxford: Oxford University Press.

Maitland, F.W. 1911. *Complete Works of James Harrington*. London.

Manual E, M. and **P.F. Manual,** 1979. *Utopian Thought in Western World*. Oxford: Basil Blackwell.

Manuel, F.E. 1997. 'Comte de Saint-Simon: The Pear is Ripe', in *The Classical Tradition in Sociology: The European Tradition*, edited by Raymond Boudon, Mohammed Cherraoin and Jeffrey Alexander. London: Sage Publications.

Mao, Z. 1954. *Selected Works*, 3 Vols. Peking: Foreign Languages Press.

Mandel, E. 1983. 'Economics', in *Marx: The First Hundred Years*, edited by David McLellan. Glasgow: Fontana.

Marcuse, H. 1964. *One Dimensional Man*. Boston: Beacon.

————. 1967. *An Essay on Liberation*. Boston: Beacon.

————. 1969. *Eros and Civilization*. Boston: Beacon.

Marquand, D. 1997. 'Reaching for Levers', *Times Literary Supplement*. April, p. 3–4.

Martel, M.U. 1968. 'Saint Simon', in *International Encyclopaedia of Social Sciences*. London: Macmillan.

Marx, K.H. 1975. *The Communist Manifesto*. Moscow: Progress Publishers.

Marx, K.H. and **F. Engels,** 1977. *Selected Works*, 3 Vols. Moscow: Progress Publishers.

McLellan, D. 1971. *The Thought of Karl Marx*. London: Macmillan.

————. 1977. *Engels*. London: Macmillan.

————. 1979. *Marxism after Marx*. London: Macmillan.

————. (ed.). 1983. *Marx: The First Hundred Years*. Glasgow: Fontana.

————. 1995. *Ideology*. Buckingham: Open University Press.

Medvedev, R. 1971. *Let History Judge: The Origins and Consequences of Stalinism*. New York: Alfred A. Knopf.

Mehring, F. 1936. *Karl Marx*. London: John Lane.

Meyer, A.H. 1977. 'Marxism and the Women Movement', in *Women in Russia*, edited by D. Atkinson. Stanford: University of California Press.

Meyerson, A. 1989. 'Adam Smith's Welfare State', *Policy Review*, 50, Fall, pp. 66–67.

Meisner, M. 1982. '*Marxism, Maoism and Utopianism*'. *The Socialist Register*, London: The Merlin Press, pp. 309–19.

Miliband, R. 1965. 'Marx and the State', *The Socialist Register*, pp. 309–19.

——— . 1969. *The State in the Capitalist Society*. London: Weidenfeld & Nicholson.

——— . 1977. *Marxism and Politics*. Oxford: Oxford University Press.

Miller, S. and **H. Potthoff**, 1986. *A History of German Social Democracy: From 1848 to the Present*, translated J.A. Underwood. New York: Praeger.

Mills, C.W. 1962. *The Marxists*. New York: Dell.

Moses, C.G. 1982. 'Saint-Simonian Men/Saint-Simonian Women: The Transformation of Feminist Thought in 1830s' France', *Journal of Modern History*, 82, pp. 240–67.

Mukherjee, S. 1992. 'Dependency Theory Revisited: South Korea's March Towards an Independent Development', *Korea Observer*, 23, pp. 19–43.

Nettl, J.P. 1966. *Rosa Luxemburg*, 2 Vols. New York: Oxford University Press.

Nisbet, R. 1969. *History of the Idea of Progress*. New York: Basic Books.

Nove, A. 1983. *The Economics of Feasible Socialism*. London: George Allen and Unwin.

Parekh, B. 1982. *Marx's Theory of Ideology*. London: Croom & Helm.

Plamentaz, J. 1969. *German Marxism and Soviet Communism*. London: Longman.

Pocock, J.G.A. 1992. *James Harrington's The Commonwealth of Oceana and A System of Politics*. Cambridge: Cambridge University Press.

Popper, K. 1945. *The Open Society and its Enemies*, 2 Vols. London: Routledge.

——— . 1996. *The Lessons of the Century: Talks on Freedom and the Democratic State*. London: Routledge.

Poulantaz, N. 1973. *Political Power and Social Classes*. London: New Left.

Prebisch, R. 1950. *The Economic Development of Latin America and its Principal Problems*. New York: United Nations.

Rappaport, A. 1924. *A Dictionary of Socialism*. Paris: L' Emancipatrice.

Ray, S. 1962. 'India: Urban Intellectuals and Rural Problems', in *Revisionism* edited by Leopold Labedz. New York: Frederick A. Prager.

Reckitt, Maurice B. 1919. *The Guildsman*, No. 31. June.

Remnick, D. 1998. 'Vladimir Ilyich Lenin'. *Time*, April 13, 151, pp. 42–44.

Roos, L. 1990. 'Two Fundamental Mistakes that Doomed the Centrally Planned Economy'. *The German Tribune*, 14 February, 1408, p. 6.

Roth, G. 1963. *The Social Democrats in Imperial Germany*. Princeton, NJ: Princeton University Press.

Roy, M.N. 1964. *Memoirs*. Calcutta: Renaissance.

Russell, B. 1916. *Principles of Social Reconstruction*. London: Unwin.

——— . 1918. *Roads to Freedom, Socialism, Anarchism and Syndicalism*. London: Unwin.

——— . 1948. *Bolshevism: Practice and Theory*. London: Unwin.

——— . 1950. *Unpopular Essays*. London: Unwin.

Russell-Smith, H.F. 1914. *Harrington and His Oceana*. Cambridge: Cambridge University Press.

Sabine, G.H. 1939. 'What is Political Theory?', *Journal of Politics*, 1, pp. 1–16.

——— . 1973. *A History of Political Theory*, IVth edition. New Delhi: IBH and Oxford.

Satvadori, M. 1979. *Karl Kautsky and the Socialist Revolution 1880–1938,* translated by J. Rothchild. London: New Left.

Sargent, L.T. 1990. 'William Morris and the Anarchist Tradition', in Boos and Silver, *Socialism and the Literary Artistry of William Morris.* Columbia· Columbia University Press.

Sartori, G. 1995. 'How Far can Free Governments Travel', *Journal of Democracy,* 6, pp. 100–117.

Sawer, M. 1977. 'Genesis of State and Revolution', *Socialist Register,* pp. 209–27.

Schram, S.R. 1981. 'Makers of the 20th Century: Mao Zedong', *History Today,* April. pp. 22–29.

Shaw, George Bernard. 1889. *Fabian Essays.* London: Fabian Society Tract.

Shklar, J.N. 1959. 'Ideology Hunting: The Case of James Harrington', *American Political Science Review,* 53, pp. 662–92.

Singer, P. 1980. *Marx.* Oxford: Oxford University Press.

Steele, J. 1988. 'Bukharin Rehabilitated', *Guardian Weekly,* 17 July.

Strong, A.L. 1947. 'The Thought of Mao Tse Tung', *Amerasia,* XI, 3, pp. 160–82.

Tagore, R. 1960. *Letters from Russia.* Calcutta: Visva Bharathi.

Talmon, J.L. 1940. 'The Legacy of Georges Sorel: Marxism, Violence and Fascism', *Encounter,* pp. 47–62.

Tawney, R.H. 1941. 'The Rise of the Gentry', *Economic History Review,* 11, pp. 15–35.

Thompson, E.P. 1977. *William Morris: Romantic to Revolutionary.* London: Lawrence and Wishart.

Thonnessen, 1969. *The Emancipation of Women: The Rise and Decline of the Women's Movement in German Social Democracy 1863–1933 Trans. Joris de Bres.* Frankfurt.

Tofler, A. 1979. *Future Shock: A Study of Mass Bewilderment in the Face of Accelerating Change.* New York: Random House.

Toynbee, A. 1934. *A Study of History,* 12 Vols. Oxford: Oxford University Press.

Trotsky, L. 1904. *Our Political Tasks.* London: New Park.

———. 1919. *The Permanent Revolution and Results and Prospects.* New York: Pioneer.

———. 1945. *The Revolution Betrayed: What is the Soviet Union and Where is it Going?.* London: New Park.

Tucker, R. 1987. *Political Culture in the Soviet Union.* New York: W.W. Norton & Co.

Tudor, H. 1988. *Marxism and Social Democracy.* New York.

Turner, B.S. 1986. *Equality.* Chichester: Ellis Horwood Ltd.

Ulam, A.B. 1922. *Lenin and the Bolsheviks.* Glasgow: Fontana.

Watkins, F.M. 1976. *The Age of Ideology: Political Thought 1750 to the Present.* New Delhi: Prentice Hall.

Webb, S. 1919. *A Stratified Democracy.* London: Longman.

———. 1920. *History of Trade Unionism.* London: Longman.

Williams, R. 1961. *Culture and Society.* Harmondworth: Penguin.

Wilson, E. 1941. *To the Finland Station.* Glasgow: Fontana.

Wolfe, B. 1969. *Marxism: One Hundred Years in the Life of a Doctrine.* New York: Doubleday.

Wolin, S. 1960. *Politics and Vision: Continuity and Innovation in Western Political Thought.* Boston: Little Brown.

Wolin, S. 1987. 'Democracy and the Welfare State', *Political Theory*, 15, pp. 467–500.

Woodcock, G. 1944. *Anarchy and Chaos*. Glasgow: Fontana.

Wright, A.W. 1979. *G.D.H. Cole and the Socialist Democracy*. London: Clarendon Press.

❖ *Index*

❖ About the Authors

Subrata Mukherjee is Professor of Political Science, at the University of Delhi, South Campus. He obtained his Ph.D. under a Fulbright grant from Indiana University, Bloomington, USA. He is a member of the editorial board of *Korea Observer*, Seoul, South Korea. Professor Mukherjee has previously published *Gandhian Thought: Marxist Interpretation*, *Essays in Marxist Theory and Practice* and *A History of Political Thought: Plato to Marx* (co-author). He specialises in political theory, comparative politics and Gandhian studies.

Sushila Ramaswamy is Reader in Political Science at Jesus and Mary College, New Delhi. She obtained her Ph.D. from the University of Delhi. Dr. Ramaswamy has been a recipient of the Fulbright postdoctoral grant and the British Council grant and has been a Visiting Fellow at the National University of Singapore. She is the author of *Liberty, Equality and Social Justice: Rawls' Political Theory* and *Marxist Theory of the State: Dictatorship of the Proletariat* and the co-author of *A History of Political Thought: Plato to Marx*. Dr Ramaswamy specialises in political theory and gender studies.

Of Related Interest

Justice, Equality and Community

An Essay in Marxist Political Theory

Vidhu Verma

While considerable debate on justice has taken place within liberal political theory, the concept of distributive justice in Marx's writings has received very little attention. This book provides a careful and wide-ranging assessment of the notion of justice in the Marxist tradition. Vidhu Verma argues that Marx's analysis of exploitation provides a fruitful starting point for analyzing current social conflicts, especially since he highlighted specific non-distributive issues which form part of the agenda of on-going struggles for democratization.

Dr Verma reflects on Marx's ideas on formal justice, equality, community, distributive (material) and non-distributive (e.g., health and education) issues, and oppression and exploitation of social structures. She discusses three main themes: Marx's theory of justice; disagreements about what justice is as reflected in the different politics of social change; and the relevance of Marx's theory in the contemporary world in which new social movements—such as the peace, ecological, women's and ethnic-based movements—have looked to forge new conceptions of justice.

Overall, this significant theoretical treatise substantively demonstrates how a reinterpretation of Marx's theory is relevant for understanding the multiple forms of oppression confronted by contemporary social groups. It will interest scholars in political science, social and political theory, social movements, sociology and economics.

220mm x 140mm/218 pages/Hb/Pb

Sage Publications
New Delhi/Thousand Oaks/London